LIBERALIZATION OF TRADE IN BANKING SERVICES

The financial crisis struck with full force in autumn 2008. Very soon after the start of the crisis, culprits were sought. An important recurring argument was that liberalization of trade in banking services, as pursued at the European (within the European Union) and international level (in the World Trade Organization), had seriously reduced the possibilities for governments to regulate and supervise the banking sector. This book examines the validity of this claim and considers how EU law and WTO law deal with the trade-off any policy-maker must make between stability and efficiency in the market for banking services. The book considers specifically the interaction between EU and WTO law because the EU is itself a member of the WTO, in addition to its own member states. This implies that the EU must respect the obligations it undertook within the framework of the WTO when the EU determines its policy towards third-country banks.

BART DE MEESTER is a member of the Legal Service of the European Commission. He previously worked as an associate at the Geneva office of Sidley Austin LLP and, prior to that, as a legal affairs officer at the Trade in Services Division of the World Trade Organization. He is also Associate Fellow of the Leuven Centre for Global Governance Studies at the University of Leuven.

LIBERALIZATION OF TRADE IN BANKING SERVICES

An International and European Perspective

BART DE MEESTER

CAMBRIDGE
UNIVERSITY PRESS

CAMBRIDGE
UNIVERSITY PRESS

University Printing House, Cambridge CB2 8BS, United Kingdom

Cambridge University Press is part of the University of Cambridge.

It furthers the University's mission by disseminating knowledge in the pursuit of education, learning and research at the highest international levels of excellence.

www.cambridge.org
Information on this title: www.cambridge.org/9781107038493

First published 2014

Printed in the United Kingdom by Clays, St Ives plc

A catalogue record for this publication is available from the British Library

Library of Congress Cataloguing in Publication data
De Meester, Bart.
Liberalization of trade in banking services : an international and European perspective / Bart De Meester.
pages cm
ISBN 978-1-107-03849-3 (hardback)
1. Banks and banking, International. 2. Banks and banking, International – Europe. 3. Banks and banking, International – Law and legislation. 4. Banks and banking, International – Law and legislation – Europe. 5. Banks and banking – State supervision. 6. Banks and banking – State supervision – Europe. 7. Banking law. 8. Banking law – Europe. I. Title.
HG3881.D3413425 2014
332.1′5–dc23
2014004718

ISBN 978-1-107-03849-3 Hardback

CONTENTS

ACKNOWLEDGEMENTS

Upon his arrival in Ithaca, Odysseus concluded that it was not so much his arrival home that filled him with joy, but, rather, the adventures he experienced on his journey home. The journey towards a finalized PhD thesis and eventually a published book can only be undertaken thanks to a group of people who support the author and share his adventures. I therefore would like to thank a number of people.

Professor Dr Jan Wouters hired me in October 2003 as a scientific collaborator at the Institute for International Law and later the Leuven Centre for Global Governance Studies. He encouraged me in every step taken and managed to gather together a group of exceptional people over the years. Professor Dr Koen Lenaerts was always ready to share his immense knowledge and experience in European law. Professor Dr Petros Mavroidis critically reviewed the first drafts of this book. Professor Dr Geert Van Calster entered my office at the right moments to answer my questions on methodology. Professor Dr Dirk Heremans discussed with me the economic aspects of my research. Professor Dr Geert De Baere stood ready to review the European law aspects. Professor Dr Bart Kerremans supported me in my first steps as researcher and in submitting my application as an FWO Aspirant.

The research would never have been possible without the support of the Fund for Scientific Research Flanders (FWO Vlaanderen).

Exchanges at international conferences with Professor Dr Mads Andenas, Professor Dr Piet Eeckhout, Professor Dr Markus Krajewski, Professor Dr Joost Pauwelyn and Professor Dr Emilios Avgouleas helped me to refine further the conclusions of my book. At Oxford, Professor Stefan Talmon introduced me to the law of the external relations of the EU. Professor Stephen Weatherill as well as Professor Derrick Wyatt laid the foundations of my knowledge of the law of the internal market of the EU.

My former colleagues at the institutes of international and European law at the KU Leuven not only provided a stimulating working environment, but also formed a great group of friends. Friends in Bruges, Leuven and

Oxford guarded over the necessary relaxation. Dr Dominic Coppens was my fellow World Trade Organization (WTO) student, researcher and friend. Mathias Hansebout and Koen Verstraete forced me to get away from my books from time to time to play squash or tennis. Tommaso Canepa and Dr Thomas Papadopoulos made my year in Oxford an unforgettable experience. Viviane Verbist provided the administrative support and had her door always open for a friendly talk.

The research for this book took its final form during my internship at the Trade in Services Division of the World Trade Organization in Geneva in spring 2010. The exchanges with the people at the division gave me the confidence to finalize my research and put forward my views on a number of questions relating to trade in services. More particularly, I would like to thank the director of the division, Abdel-Hamid Mamdouh, as well as Hoe Lim, Markus Jelitto, Rudolf Adlung, Peter Morrison and Juan Marchetti for their support. I am also grateful for the encouragement I received in Geneva from my colleagues at Sidley Austin LLP and from Weiwei Zhang. However, I should stress that all the views expressed in the book are my own.

Finally, I would like to thank my family. My parents supported me from the very beginning until today. Without the unconditional love of my wife Annelies, this research would never have been accomplished. She was the first to hear about exotic legal reasoning and stood ready to help me through the inevitable weak moments in the research. I am forever grateful to her for this and I dedicate this book to her.

Leuven – Geneva – Brussels, 1 March 2014

TABLE OF GATT PANEL REPORTS

Working Party Report on Border Tax Adjustments, 2 December 1970, BISD 18S/97.

Canada – Administration of the Foreign Investment Review Act (*Canada – FIRA*), L/5504, adopted 7 February 1984, BISD 30S/140.

United States – Taxes on Petroleum and Certain Imported Substances (*US – Superfund*), adopted 17 June 1987, BISD 34S/136.

European Economic Community – Restrictions on Imports of Dessert Apples – Complaint by Chile (*EEC – Dessert Apples*), adopted 22 June 1989, BISD 36S/93.

United States – Restrictions on Imports of Tuna (*US – Tuna (Mexico)*), DS21/R, 3 September 1991, unadopted, BISD 39S/155.

United States – Measures Affecting Alcoholic and Malt Beverages, DS23/R, adopted on 19 June 1992, BISD 39S/206.

United States – Restrictions on Imports of Tuna (*US – Tuna (EEC)*), DS29/R, 16 June 1994, unadopted.

United States – Taxes on Automobiles, DS31/R, 29 September 1994, unadopted.

United States – Measures Affecting the Importation, Internal Sale and Use of Tobacco (*United States – Tobacco*), BISD 41S/131, adopted on 4 October 1994.

TABLE OF WTO PANEL REPORTS

Japan – Taxes on Alcoholic Beverages (*Japan – Alcoholic Beverages II*), WT/DS8/R, WT/DS10/R, WT/DS11/R, adopted 1 November 1996, as modified by Appellate Body Report WT/DS8/AB/R, WT/DS10/AB/R, WT/DS11/AB/R.

Canada – Certain Measures Concerning Periodicals (*Canada – Periodicals*), WT/DS31/R and Corr.1, adopted 30 July 1997.

European Communities – Regime for the Importation, Sale and Distribution of Bananas (*EC – Bananas III*), WT/DS27/R/ECU (Ecuador), WT/DS27/R/GTM, WT/DS27/R/HND (Guatemala and Honduras), WT/DS27/R/MEX (Mexico), and WT/DS27/R/USA (United States), adopted 25 September 1997, as modified by Appellate Body Report WT/DS27/AB/R.

Japan – Measures Affecting Photographic Film and Paper (*Japan – Film*), WT/DS44/R, adopted on 22 April 1998.

Canada – Measures Affecting the Export of Civilian Aircraft (*Canada – Aircraft*), WT/DS70/R, adopted 20 August 1999, upheld by Appellate Body Report, WT/DS70/AB/R.

United States – Sections 301–310 of the Trade Act of 1974 (*US – Section 301 Trade Act*), WT/DS152/R, adopted 27 January 2000.

Australia – Subsidies Provided to Producers and Exporters of Automotive Leather, Recourse to Article 21.5 of the DSU by the United States (*Australia – Automotive Leather II*), WT/DS126/RW and Corr.1, adopted 11 February 2000.

Canada – Patent Protection of Pharmaceutical Products, WT/DS114/R, adopted 7 April 2000.

Canada – Certain Measures Affecting the Automotive Industry (*Canada – Autos*), WT/DS139/R, WT/DS142/R, adopted 19 June 2000, as modified by Appellate Body Report WT/DS139/AB/R, WT/DS142/AB/R.

Argentina – Measures Affecting the Export of Bovine Hides and Import of Finished Leather (*Argentina – Hides and Leather*), WT/DS155/R and Corr.1, adopted 16 February 2001.

European Communities – Measures Affecting Asbestos and Asbestos-Containing Products (EC – Asbestos), adopted 5 April 2001, as modified by Appellate Body Report WT/DS135/AB/R.

United States – Anti-dumping Measures on Certain Hot-Rolled Steel Products from Japan (*US – Hot-Rolled Steel*), WT/DS184/R, adopted 23 August 2001, as modified by Appellate Body Report WT/DS184/AB/R.

Canada – Export Credits and Loan Guarantees for Regional Aircraft, WT/DS222/R and Corr.1, adopted 19 February 2002.

United States – Sunset Review of Anti-Dumping Duties on Corrosion-Resistant Carbon Steel Flat Products from Japan (*US – Corrosion-Resistant Steel Sunset Review*), WT/DS244/R, adopted 9 January 2004, as modified by Appellate Body Report WT/DS244/AB/R.

United States – Measures Affecting the Cross-Border Supply of Gambling and Betting Services (*US – Gambling*), WT/DS285/R, adopted 20 April 2005, as modified by Appellate Body Report WT/DS285/AB/R.

Dominican Republic – Measures Affecting the Importation and Internal Sale of Cigarettes (*Dominican Republic – Import and Sale of Cigarettes*), WT/DS302/R, adopted 19 May 2005, as modified by Appellate Body Report WT/DS302/AB/R.

Mexico – Tax Measures on Soft Drinks and Other Beverages (*Mexico – Taxes Soft Drinks*), WT/DS308/R, adopted 24 March 2006, as modified by Appellate Body Report WT/DS308/AB/R.

United States – Laws, Regulations and Methodology for Calculating Dumping Margins (Zeroing) (*US – Zeroing (EC)*), WT/DS294/R, adopted 9 May 2006, as modified by Appellate Body Report WT/DS294/AB/R.

European Communities – Measures Affecting the Approval and Marketing of Biotech Products (*EC – Approval and Marketing of Biotech Products*), WT/DS291/R, WT/DS292/R, WT/DS293/R, Corr.1 and Add.1, 2, 3, 4, 5, 6, 7, 8 and 9, adopted 21 November 2006.

European Communities – Selected Customs Matters (*EC – Selected Customs Matters*), WT/DS315/R, adopted 11 December 2006, as modified by Appellate Body Report WT/DS315/AB/R.

Turkey – Measures Affecting the Importation of Rice (*Turkey – Rice*), WT/DS334/R, adopted 22 October 2007.

Brazil – Measures Affecting Imports of Retreaded Tyres (*Brazil – Retreaded Tyres*), WT/DS332/R, adopted 17 December 2007, as modified by Appellate Body Report WT/DS332/AB/R.

United States – Subsidies on Upland Cotton, Recourse to Article 21.5 of the DSU by Brazil, WT/DS267/RW and Corr.1, adopted 20 June 2009, as modified by Appellate Body Report WT/DS267/AB/RW.

China – Measures Affecting Trading Rights and Distribution Services for Certain Publications and Audiovisual Entertainment Products (China – Publications and Audiovisual Products), WT/DS363/R, adopted 19 January 2010, as modified by Appellate Body Report WT/DS363/AB/R.

China – Measures Affecting Electronic Payment Services (*China – Electronic Payment Services*), WT/DS413/R, adopted 31 August 2012.

TABLE OF WTO APPELLATE BODY REPORTS

United States – Standards for Reformulated and Conventional Gasoline (*US – Gasoline*), WT/DS2/AB/R, adopted 20 May 1996.

Japan – Taxes on Alcoholic Beverages (*Japan – Alcoholic Beverages II*), WT/DS8/AB/R, WT/DS10/AB/R, WT/DS11/AB/R, adopted 1 November 1996.

Canada – Certain Measures Concerning Periodicals (*Canada – Periodicals*), WT/DS31/AB/R, adopted 30 July 1997.

European Communities – Regime for the Importation, Sale and Distribution of Bananas (*EC – Bananas III*), WT/DS27/AB/R, adopted 25 September 1997.

United States – Import Prohibition of Certain Shrimp and Shrimp Products (*US – Shrimp*), WT/DS58/AB/R, adopted 6 November 1998.

Korea – Taxes on Alcoholic Beverages (*Korea – Alcoholic Beverages*), WT/DS75/AB/R, WT/DS84/AB/R, adopted 17 February 1999.

Turkey – Restrictions on Imports of Textile and Clothing Products (*Turkey – Textiles*), WT/DS34/AB/R, adopted 19 November 1999.

Chile – Taxes on Alcoholic Beverages (*Chile – Alcoholic Beverages*), WT/DS87 and 110/AB/R, adopted 12 January 2000.

Canada – Certain Measures Affecting the Automotive Industry (*Canada – Autos*), WT/DS139/AB/R, WT/DS142/AB/R, adopted 19 June 2000.

Korea – Measures Affecting Imports of Fresh, Chilled and Frozen Beef (*Korea – Beef*), WT/DS161/AB/R, WT/DS169/AB/R, adopted 10 January 2001.

European Communities – Measures Affecting Asbestos and Asbestos-Containing Products (*EC – Asbestos*), WT/DS135/AB/R, adopted 5 April 2001.

Thailand – Anti-Dumping Duties on Angles, Shapes and Sections of Iron or Non-Alloy Steel and H-Beams from Poland (*Thailand – H-Beams*), WT/DS122/AB/R, adopted 5 April 2001.

United States – Transitional Safeguard Measure on Combed Cotton Yarn from Pakistan (*US – Cotton Yarn*), WT/DS192/AB/R, adopted 5 November 2001.

United States – Sunset Review of Anti-Dumping Duties on Corrosion-Resistant Carbon Steel Flat Products from Japan (*US – Corrosion-Resistant Steel Sunset Review*), WT/DS244/AB/R, adopted 9 January 2004.

United States – Sunset Reviews of Anti-Dumping Measures on Oil Country Tubular Goods from Argentina (*US – Oil Country Tubular Goods Sunset Reviews*), WT/DS268/AB/R, adopted 17 December 2004.

United States – Measures Affecting the Cross-Border Supply of Gambling and Betting Services (*US – Gambling*), WT/DS285/AB/R, adopted 20 April 2005.

Dominican Republic – Measures Affecting the Importation and Internal Sale of Cigarettes (*Dominican Republic – Import and Sale of Cigarettes*), WT/DS302/AB/R, adopted 19 May 2005.

United States – Laws, Regulations and Methodology for Calculating Dumping Margins (Zeroing) (*US – Zeroing (EC)*), WT/DS294/AB/R, adopted 9 May 2006.

European Communities – Selected Customs Matters (*EC – Selected Customs Matters*), WT/DS315/AB/R, adopted 11 December 2006.

Brazil – Measures Affecting Imports of Retreaded Tyres (*Brazil – Retreaded Tyres*), WT/DS332/AB/R, adopted 17 December 2007.

China – Measures Affecting Trading Rights and Distribution Services for Certain Publications and Audiovisual Entertainment Products (*China – Publications and Audiovisual Products*), WT/DS363/AB/R, adopted 19 January 2010.

China – Measures Relating to the Exportation of Various Raw Materials (China – Raw Materials), WT/DS394/AB/R, WT/DS395/AB/R, and WT/DS398/AB/R, adopted 22 February 2012.

United States – Measures Affecting the Production and Sale of Clove Cigarettes (United States – Clove Cigarettes), WT/DS406/AB/R, adopted 24 April 2012.

TABLE OF CASES OF THE COURT OF JUSTICE OF THE EUROPEAN UNION

Case 22/70, Commission *v.* Council (ERTA), [1971] ECR, 263.

Case 2–74, Reyners *v.* Belgian State, [1974] ECR 631.

Case 5/77, Tedeschi, [1977] ECR 1555.

Case 98/78, Firma A. Racke *v.* Hauptzollamt Mainz [1979] ECR 69.

Case 120/78, Rewe-Zentral AG *v.* Bundesmonopolverwaltung für Branntwein, [1979] ECR 649.

Case 148/78, Ratti, [1979] ECR 1629.

Case 270/83, Commission *v.* France, [1986] ECR 273.

Case 79/85, Segers, [1986] ECR 2375.

Case 60/86, Commission *v.* United Kingdom (Dim-Dip), [1988] ECR 3921.

Case 382/87, Buet *v.* Ministère Public, [1989] ECR 1235.

Case C-76/90, Säger/Dennemeyer, [1991] ECR I-4221.

Case C-286/90, Poulsen and Diva Navigation, [1992] ECR I-6019.

Case C-369/90, Micheletti and others, [1992] ECR I-4239.

Cases C-267 and C-268/91, Keck and Mithouard, [1993] ECR I-6097.

Case C-330/91, Commerzbank, [1993] ECR I-4017.

Case C-70/94, Fritz Werner Industrie-Ausrüstungen GmbH *v.* Federal Republic of Germany, [1995] ECR I-3189.

Case C-55/94, Gebhard/Consiglio dell'Ordine degli Avvocati e Procuratori di Milano, [1995] ECR I-4165.

Case C-53/96, Hermès International *v.* FHT Marketing Choice, [1998] ECR I-3603.

Case C-162/96, Racke *v.* Hauptzollamt Mainz, [1998] ECR I-3655.

Case C-212/97, Centros, [1999] ECR I-1459.

Case C-255/97, Pfeiffer Großhandel, [1997] ECR I-2835.

Case C-251/98, C. Baars *v.* Inspecteur der Belastingen/Ondernemingen Gorinchem, [2000] ECR I-2787.

Case C-376/98, Germany *v.* European Parliament and Council, [2000] ECR I-8419.

Case C-208/00, Überseering BV *v.* Nordic Construction Company Baumanagement GmbH (NCC), [2002] ECR I-9919.

Case C-167/01, Inspire Art, [2003] ECR I-10155.

Case C-442/02, Caixabank France, [2004] ECR I-8961.

Joined Cases C-281/03 and C-282/03, Cindu Chemicals BV and Others, [2005] ECR I-8069.

Joined Cases C-402/05 P and 415/05 P, Kadi and Al Barakaat *v.* Council and Commission, [2008] ECR I-6351.

Case C-478/07, Budějovický Budvar *v.* Rudolf Ammersin GmbH, [2009] ECR I-7721.

Case C-414/11, Daiichi and Sanofi-Aventis/DEMO, not yet reported.

TABLE OF OPINIONS OF THE COURT OF JUSTICE OF THE EUROPEAN UNION

Opinion 1/75, Understanding on a Local Cost Standard, [1975] ECR 1355.

Opinion 1/78, International Agreement on Natural Rubber, [1979] ECR 2871.

Opinion 1/94, Competence of the Community to conclude international agreements concerning services and the protection of intellectual property (WTO), [1994] ECR I-5267.

Opinion 1/08, Conclusion of agreements on the grant of compensation for modification and withdrawal of certain GATS commitments following the accession of new Member States to the EU, [2009] ECR I-11129.

General introduction

> Although Europe was not at the root of the current financial crisis, it has nevertheless both contributed to it and been hit severely by it. Global economic and financial integration has by now reached a level where no country or region can any longer insulate itself from developments elsewhere in the world.
>
> Report by the High-Level Group on Financial Supervision in the EU Chaired by Jacques de Larosière, Brussels, 25 February 2009, para. 219

1. The global financial crisis started in 2007 and struck with full force in autumn 2008. At the time of concluding this book, the world is still suffering from its consequences. The crisis has shown that the interconnectedness of the global economy implies that problems that occur in banks in one state may quickly spill over to banks in other states and eventually to the real economy worldwide. While in the last decade of the twentieth century many governments gradually removed regulatory restrictions on banking activities and thus increased competition in their markets for banking services, the global financial crisis made policymakers again realize that opening up the market for banking services to foreign competition implies also serious risks for financial stability. Nonetheless, policymakers, academics and commentators disagree on how much and what type of regulation is appropriate in the banking sector. It seems that much depends on personal beliefs in the ability of regulation to modify behaviour of market participants. Still, except for some more radical voices, there appears to exist also a general recognition that competition in the banking sector has also brought benefits in the form of increased efficiency in the channelling of funds from savers to investors.

2. At the level of the European Union (EU) as well as at the international level (more particularly, within the World Trade Organization (WTO)), states have accepted that competition between banks from different countries will improve efficiency and thus lead to a higher degree of welfare for society. They have developed legal rules to remove barriers to trade in banking services. Nonetheless, such legal obligations also affect the possible ways in which states can regulate and supervise the access of foreign banks to the domestic market and the way in which they can carry out activities. Hence they limit the extent to which countries can pursue domestic policy goals.

The interaction of EU and WTO law

3. The system of legal rules developed within the EU and the WTO both address the same question: how to intensify cross-border competition in the market for goods and services while at the same time taking into account the domestic policy concerns that underlie regulation of these markets. It is therefore no surprise that comparative studies of the systems of the EU and the WTO are quite common.[1] In November 2009, the former Director-General of the WTO, Pascal Lamy, called for the drawing of lessons for global governance from European integration.[2] As a political statement, this certainly has merit. However, a comparative legal analysis of these two projects of trade liberalization should be approached carefully. Although many questions with regard to identifying protectionist measures are the same for both the EU and the WTO, and it is thus interesting to compare the different approaches taken in answering these questions, the political, economic and legal contexts of the EU and the WTO are very different. The

[1] See for instance K. Byttebier and S. Fares, 'The EU Liberalisation of Financial Services: The EC Obligations in Comparison to the GATS Commitments', in K. Byttebier and K. Van der Borght (eds.) *WTO Obligations and Opportunities: Challenges of Implementation* (London: Cameron May, 2007) 85–119; F. Ortino, *Basic Legal Instruments for the Liberalization of Trade: A Comparative Analysis of EC and WTO Law* (Oxford: Hart, 2004); L. Panourgias, *Banking Regulation and World Trade Law* (Oxford: Hart, 2006); M. Pallemaerts, *EU and WTO Law: How Tight is the Legal Straitjacket for Environmental Product Regulation?* (Brussels: VUB Press, 2006); G. Van Calster, *International and EU Trade Law: The Environmental Challenge* (London: Cameron May, 2000); A. Von Bogdandy, P. Mavroidis and Y. Mény (eds.), *European Integration and International Co-ordination. Studies in Transnational Economic Law in Honour of Claus-Dieter Ehlermann* (The Hague: Kluwer Law International, 2002); J. Weiler (ed.), *The EU, the WTO and the NAFTA: Towards a Common Law of International Trade?* (Oxford University Press, 2001); and J. Wiers, *Trade and Environment in the EC and the WTO: A Legal Analysis* (Groningen: Europa Law Publishing, 2002).

[2] P. Lamy, 'Global Governance – Lessons from Europe', speech made at Bocconi University, Milan, 9 November 2009, available at www.wto.org/english/news_e/sppl_e/sppl142_e.htm.

international process for intensifying competition in banking can never go as far as the European project. In a regional process like the European Union, transaction costs linked to cooperation are lower than in an international process like the WTO. Since the Treaty of Rome of 1957 (Treaty establishing the European Economic Community – EEC Treaty), the EU has combined liberalization (negative integration) with re-regulation of the banking sector by means of the approximation of laws (positive integration). At the international level, liberalization and possible regulatory convergence are spread over different international bodies. The WTO has, as at the time of writing, never engaged in regulatory convergence for trade in services and it is unlikely that this will happen soon. However, some non-binding convergence of banking regulations has been produced by the Basel Committee on Banking Supervision.

4. The situation of the EU and its member states in the WTO merits specific attention. The EU promotes a preferential trade integration project, while at the same time being a fully fledged WTO member, along with its own member states. Like any other WTO member, the EU has to comply with the obligations it has assumed on the basis of the General Agreement on Trade in Services (GATS). When regulating and supervising their market for banking services with regard to activities used by third-country banks, EU member states have to comply with their obligations under EU law as well as those under the GATS. Moreover, the EU aims at progressively abolishing restrictions on international trade and foreign direct investment.[3] When exercising its competences in respect of banking services provided by banks from third countries in the EU, the EU has to respect its obligations under the GATS. In *Poulsen*, the Court of Justice of the European Union (CJEU) famously stated that 'the European Community must respect international law in the exercise of its powers'.[4] This is certainly the case when the EU is itself party to an international agreement such as the GATS. This creates a specific legal reality that has not been fully examined.

[3] Art. 206 of the Treaty on the Functioning of the European Union (TFEU) provides that the EU 'shall contribute, in the common interest, to the harmonious development of world trade, the progressive abolition of restrictions on international trade and on foreign direct investment, and the lowering of customs and other barriers'.

[4] CJEU, Case C-286/90 *Poulsen and Diva Navigation*, [1992] ECR I-6019, para. 9. See also CJEU, Case C-53/96 *Hermès International* v. *FHT Marketing Choice*, [1998] ECR I-3603, para. 28; CJEU, Case C-162/96 *Racke* v. *Hauptzollamt Mainz*, [1998] ECR I-3655, para. 45; and CJEU, Joined Cases C-402/05 P and 415/05 P, *Kadi and Al Barakaat* v. *Council and Commission*, [2008] ECR I-6351, para. 223.

5. Some authors have paid attention to these issues in the past. In a 1994 study, Eeckhout carried out a legal analysis of the European internal market and international trade. He included the competence of the European Communities to regulate trade in services with third countries in his analysis, and devoted a chapter to financial services. In several instances, the study also refers to the GATS. However, because the study was published shortly before the conclusion of the Uruguay Round and thus before the entry into force of the WTO Agreements, the focus is mainly on the EU law aspects of the external dimension of the internal market in services. Eeckhout notes, however, that 'this draft GATS will often be referred to, because if it enters into force, *it will play an important role in defining the external dimension of the internal market in services*'.[5] Further, in a book chapter published in 2002, Cremona noted,

> The challenge for the unified Community market, and the Community's own external economic policy, is in presenting and justifying to its trading partners its own regulatory policy choices, whether these are development-based preferences or environmental or public health priorities.[footnote omitted] *The additional element, which we are not specifically addressing here, is that this process is carried out against a background, not only of existing bilateral and regional treaty obligations, but also in the context of a developing world trading system which is itself exploring methods for reconciling these potentially conflicting goals.*[6]

6. Still, this does not mean that there are no other elements in primary and secondary EU law that affect third-country banks. For instance, the implications of the obligation imposed on national supervisors to evaluate the *equivalence* of consolidated supervision by third-country supervisors is one of the many issues that persist. Further, the entry into force of the Lisbon Treaty on 1 December 2009 implied important modifications to the competence of the EU in the field of the common commercial policy. What is more, in 2013, significant steps were taken towards the creation of a 'banking union'. Questions arise with regard to the implications for the competence of the EU to regulate activities of third-country banks in the EU. Further, the case law with regard to the WTO Agreements in general, and the GATS in particular, has developed through reports by the WTO panels and the Appellate Body and now

[5] P. Eeckhout, *The European Internal Market and International Trade: A Legal Analysis* (Oxford: Clarendon Press, 1994) 13 (emphasis added).

[6] M. Cremona, 'The External Dimension of the Single Market: Building (on) the Foundations', in C. Barnard and J. Scott (eds.), *The Law of the Single EU Market. Unpacking the Premises* (Oxford University Press, 2002) 351–93, at 389 (emphasis added).

provides some clearer insights into the implications of the GATS obligations for the competence of WTO members to regulate and supervise their market in banking services. This merits a fresh analysis.

7. The present book addresses the following central question: to what extent does the combined application of the EU law and the GATS restrict the leeway the EU and its member states have with regard to the regulation and supervision of their market for banking services?

The balance between efficiency through competition and stability through regulation

8. Policymakers at the national or regional level that want to define their approach to the liberalization of trade in banking services have to balance two objectives. On the one hand, they consider the objective of achieving more *efficiency* through *competition* between foreign and domestic banks. On the other hand, they consider the objective of ensuring financial *stability* by means of the *regulation and supervision* of their market for banking services. The international and European projects for liberalizing trade in banking services determine the leeway policymakers have to do so. Depending on the extent to which the obligations in WTO law and EU law restrict the possibility of regulating banks and making supervisory assessments, the balance may tilt more towards efficiency or more towards stability. The experience of the global crisis shows what dramatic consequences may follow if policymakers get the balance wrong. It is thus important to know to what degree the interaction between WTO law and EU law influences the possibility of performing this balancing exercise.

9. To the extent the GATS or EU law limit the leeway of policymakers in national governments in designing their regulatory approaches and making the supervisory decisions they consider appropriate, financial stability may be threatened, unless measures for ensuring financial stability are adopted at a higher (European or international) level. At the same time, if the GATS or EU law do not limit the possibility for WTO members or EU member states to create barriers to trade in banking services at all, the objective of increased efficiency in the banking sector may be threatened.

The structure of this book

10. The book consists of three parts. In Part I, the policy concerns underlying the regulation and liberalization of the market for banking services are examined. We examine why regulation is required to address market failures in the market for banking services. Next, we consider the economic arguments that support the case for competition in the market for banking services.

11. In Part II, we examine the *international approach to the liberalization of trade in banking services.* The focus is mainly on the legally binding obligations contained in the GATS, but, where it is useful, we pay attention to the Basel standards and principles. We draw conclusions with regard to the limitations imposed by the GATS on the right of WTO members to regulate and supervise their markets for banking services. One cannot fully understand how foreign banks can carry out activities in a host market when considering only the *general rules* that apply to these banks. These rules often leave a margin of appreciation to the competent authorities in these host territories to apply these rules and make *supervisory assessments.* Therefore the analysis in Part II is broadly divided into the right to regulate and the right to supervise the banking sector.

12. This distinction between regulation and supervision reappears in Part III of the book. In it, we examine the *European approach to the liberalization of international trade in banking services and its interaction with the GATS.* We make an analysis of the right of the member states and the EU to regulate and supervise the provision of banking services by third-country banks in the EU. This analysis focuses on one specific form in which third-country banks can operate in the EU: through the establishment of credit institutions in the EU that are subsidiaries of the third-country bank.

13. The banking sector is, certainly after the global financial crisis, subject to a body of legal rules that undergoes constant modifications. The state of the law as described here is up to date as at 1 March 2014.

PART I

Policy concerns underlying the regulation and liberalization of banking

1

Introduction to Part I

It was the best of times, it was the worst of times, it was the age of wisdom, it was the age of foolishness, it was the epoch of belief, it was the epoch of incredulity.

Charles Dickens, *A Tale of Two Cities*, 1859

It's human nature, unless somebody can find a way to change human nature, we will have more crises and none of them will look like this because no two crises have anything in common, except human nature.

Alan Greenspan, interviewed as part of BBC2, *Love of Money* series, broadcast on 10, 17 and 24 September 2009

Economics teaches us that when there is huge uncertainty about catastrophic risks, it is dangerous to rely too much on the price mechanism to get incentives right. Unfortunately, economists know much less about how to adapt regulation over time to complex systems with constantly evolving risks, much less how to design regulatory resilient institutions. Until these problems are better understood, we may be doomed to a world of regulation that perpetually overshoots or undershoots its goals.

Kenneth Rogoff, 'The BP Oil Spill's Lessons for Regulation', 1 June 2010, www.project-syndicate.org

14. In Part I we examine the policy concerns underlying the regulation and liberalization of banking. Several studies have tried to identify the degree of competition that is desirable without compromising stability. However, authors disagree greatly on this question. It appears that, to a considerable extent, the trade-off between efficiency and stability is a matter of belief and even ideology.

15. Part I consists of five chapters. Following this introductory chapter, Chapter 2 discusses the role of banks as intermediaries and thus the reasons why banks have been created. In the next two chapters, the economic theory underpinning the regulation and supervision of banking services, on the one hand, and the liberalization of trade in banking services, on the other hand, are discussed.

16. We explain in Chapter 3 that the specific nature of the banking services market gives rise to specific *market failures*. It is far from clear what types of regulation are appropriate to remedy such market failures. Economists have paid much attention to *market-based regulation*, whereby many of them argue that regulation should attempt to encourage the exercise of market discipline on banks. However, the global financial crisis has caused this market-based approach to be much questioned.

17. In Chapter 4, we explain that the liberalization of trade in banking services takes place over different stages. First, liberalization may mean that policymakers decide to deregulate the market for banking services. This implies that national regulatory restrictions on permitted banking activities are reduced. Second, liberalization may also involve the opening up of the national market to foreign banking, either in the form of cross-border banking or through commercial presence. In this book, we focus on this second stage of liberalization: the 'internationalization' of the market for banking services. Economic studies that consider whether the liberalization of trade in banking services increases welfare often arrive at different conclusions. However, these studies do agree that international liberalization of trade in banking services has benefits, provided that it is accompanied by adequate prudential regulation. Chapter 5 concludes Part I.

2

The role of banks as intermediaries

2.1 Financial intermediaries as a response to market failures

18. Banking services are sometimes referred to as the 'central nervous system of the body economic'.[7] The financial system reallocates resources from entities with surplus funds to entities with funding needs.[8] This 'channelling of funds' may take place directly through financial markets where savers and borrowers meet, or may happen indirectly through financial intermediaries.[9]

19. Because of a number of market failures, financial markets are often not able to allocate financial resources optimally. In financial markets, savers buy stocks or bonds and thereby provide funds to the borrowers. Such a transaction supposes a face-to-face relation where the saver knows the person to whom he or she lends the money and the borrower knows from whom he or she is borrowing. The market failures are linked

[7] P. Sauvé, *Trade Rules behind Borders: Essays on Services, Investments and the New Trade Agenda* (London: Cameron May, 2003) 131. Among the first authors to have linked financial intermediation to economic development are Gurley and Shaw. See J. Gurley and E. Shaw, 'Financial Aspects of Economic Development', (1955) 45 *American Economic Review* 515.

[8] See F. Allen and A. Santomero, 'What Do Financial Intermediaries Do?', (2001) 25 *Journal of Banking and Finance* 271, at 273; Gurley and Shaw, above n. 7, at 519; and R. Schmidt, A. Hackethal and M. Tyrell, 'Disintermediation and the Role of Banks in Europe: An International Comparison', (1999) 8 *Journal of Financial Intermediation* 36, at 39.

[9] Channelling funds directly through financial markets and indirectly through financial intermediaries are two extremes. However, in practice, a combination of both ways of channelling funds is present. Countries may differ in this respect. The United States is said to be more capital-market driven, whereas the European Union is arguably more bank driven. See K. Alexander, R. Dhumale and J. Eatwell, *Global Governance of Financial Systems* (Oxford University Press, 2006) 19. These two alternatives have different implications. Financing through banking institutions may alleviate moral hazard through monitoring. However, it will create less public information. In contrast, market-based finance will reduce monitoring, but may enhance public information (S. Das and A. Nanda, 'A Theory of Banking Structure', (1999) 23 *Journal of Banking and Finance* 863, at 865).

to information asymmetries.[10] When savers want to invest their surplus resources and borrowers want to obtain financing, information asymmetries can impede the conclusion of contracts. For instance, the saver cannot know exactly the reputation of the borrower, or will find it difficult to assess the quality of the investment project the borrower proposes. Because of this uncertainty, the saver is likely to lend less money than would otherwise be the case.

20. What is more, once the loan is granted, it is often difficult for the individual lenders to monitor the activities of the borrower. The borrower may engage in risky activities, threatening the repayment of the loan to the lender ('moral hazard'). Even if the lender were to know exactly what the borrower was doing once the loan was granted, the lender might find it too burdensome to restrict the borrower in his actions.[11]

21. If lending takes place through the financial market, the fact that a lender decides to grant a loan to a borrower or decides not to grant a loan on the basis of an assessment of the quality of the borrower is immediately visible to other players in the market. The other players can thus 'free ride' on the efforts of the lender to determine the quality of the borrower. Because of this free-rider problem, no one will be willing to make the effort to collect the information.

22. Finally, once a saver has lent money to a borrower, the saver cannot get hold of the borrowed money within a short period of time; the saver has to respect the time period for which the money is lent. Savers normally prefer committing money for a short period, whereas borrowers prefer having to repay the loan with a long-term horizon. Because of this 'maturity mismatch', it may be difficult for loans to be agreed between individual consumers and borrowers.

23. Financial intermediaries are therefore necessary to soften the mentioned market failures.[12] *Banks* are the traditional intermediaries to channel funds from savers to borrowers.

[10] F. Mishkin, 'Prudential Supervision: Why is it Important and What Are the Issues?', *NBER Working Paper* 7926, September 2000, available at www.nber.org/papers/w7926, at 2; also published in F. Mishkin (ed.), *Prudential Supervision: What Works and What Doesn't?* (University of Chicago Press, 2001) 1–29, at 2.

[11] Mishkin, above n. 10, at 2.

[12] See D. Heremans, 'Regulation of Banking and Financial Markets', in B. Bouckaert and G. De Geest (eds.), *Encyclopedia of Law and Economics. Volume III. The Regulation of Contracts* (Cheltenham: Edward Elgar, 2000) 950–86, at 953.

2.2 The role of banks

24. The traditional role of banks is to collect deposits from individuals and to use these deposits to lend money to borrowers. Repayments by borrowers are retransferred as returns to the savers.[13] Because of their experience and because of economies of scale, banks are better at selecting and monitoring borrowers and thereby reducing information asymmetries (without eliminating them completely). Financial intermediaries thus have a natural monopoly in the provision of information about borrowers. If each individual has to monitor the borrower to whom he or she lends, there is wasteful duplication.[14]

25. Thus financial intermediaries have emerged to reduce the transaction costs that normally impede private bargaining. Thanks to financial intermediaries, savers are able to negotiate more efficiently with borrowers.[15] As explained, information asymmetries form an aspect of the transaction costs that may impede effective bargaining between savers and borrowers. Efficiency in bargaining increases, since bargaining through financial intermediaries creates economies of scale. Further, by making private loans, banks avoid free-riding on their monitoring efforts. Other investors have no access to the information collected by banks about their borrowers. Banks engage in so-called 'relationship lending' with the borrower. Over time, banks build up a relationship with their clients which provides them with valuable information about the client (punctuality in payments, income evolution, etc.). It is therefore essential for banks that other market participants do not free-ride on the information collected by the bank. They may want to start lending to a client of another bank that has turned out to be very reliable and creditworthy, thus free-riding on the efforts of the first lender. Therefore it was said that loans must be private, in the sense that they

[13] CPB Netherlands Bureau for Economic Policy Analysis, 'Competition and Stability in Banking', December 2001, available at www.cpb.nl/eng/pub/cpbreeksen/document/15/, at 15.

[14] See D. Diamond, 'Financial Intermediation and Delegated Monitoring', (1984) 51 *Review of Economic Studies* 393, at 399, 409; see also G. Gorton and A. Winton, 'Financial Intermediation', Wharton Financial Institutions Center Working Paper 02–28, March 2002, 10; also published in G. Constantinides (ed.), *Handbook on the Economics of Finance* (Amsterdam: Elsevier, 2003) 431–530.

[15] B. Scholtens and D. van Wensveen, 'The Theory of Financial Intermediation: An Essay on What It Does (Not) Explain', *SUERF Studies* Vienna 2003/1, available at www.suerf.org/download/studies/study20031.pdf, at 17.

must not be traded.[16] This was at least the case initially. As will be explained further (below, paras. 40–49), loans have been 'securitized' and traded. However, the information about the quality of the borrowers remains the private information of the banks. The difficulty of knowing the exact quality of the traded loans (especially when a number of loans are packaged together) is in fact one of the reasons why securitization became problematic and contributed to the global financial crisis.

26. Another specific aspect of banks as financial intermediaries is their ability to transfer short-term deposits made by consumers into loans that are mostly granted with a long-term perspective. Thus they engage in 'term transformation': short-term deposits are transformed into long-term loans.[17] Banks 'borrow short and lend long' and thereby ensure *liquidity* to savers.[18] However, because of the short time-horizon of the deposit, the savers obtain a relatively low return on their investments. When financial markets become more developed, savers see more attractive ways of investing surplus resources. Indeed, it was traditionally thought that when markets develop further (become more 'complete'), information asymmetries will decrease and therefore financial intermediaries will become less important and eventually disappear.[19] However, the global financial crisis has shown that liquidity in financial markets is far from evident. As will be explained, if all market players adopt the same conduct at the same time, liquidity in the market disappears.

27. Finally, banks have always had a role of *risk management*.[20] They already reduce risk by monitoring the behaviour of lenders and thus reduce information asymmetries. However, banks also manage risks that cannot be reduced merely by addressing information asymmetries (e.g. general market shocks). They do so by sharing the risk over different actors (cross-sectional risk-sharing) and over time (inter-temporal risk-smoothing). Cross-sectional risk-sharing takes place when actors having a low risk appetite are able to sell their risk to those with a higher risk

[16] Mishkin, above n. 10, at 4. If loans were to be traded, buyers would not be willing to pay a price that compensates the expensive monitoring efforts made by banks. This would lead banks to stop monitoring effectively.

[17] M. Dewatripont and J. Tirole, *The Prudential Regulation of Banks* (Cambridge, MA: MIT Press, 1994) 104.

[18] D. Diamond and P. Dybvig, 'Bank Runs, Deposit Insurance, and Liquidity', (1983) 91 *Journal of Political Economy* 401, at 402, 405.

[19] Allen and Santomero, above n. 8, at 272.

[20] B. Scholtens and D. van Wensveen, 'A Critique on the Theory of Financial Intermediation', (2000) 24 *Journal of Banking and Finance* 1243, at 1247.

appetite. Inter-temporal risk-smoothing is achieved by spreading the risk over different generations (intergenerational risk-sharing) or by means of asset accumulation. This second type of risk-spreading is useful when it is not feasible to spread risk over different actors, for instance when all market participants behave in the same manner in the case of a macroeconomic shock.[21]

28. The activities performed by banks are traditionally financed by deposits. As investors delegate the monitoring, term transformation and risk management function to banks, they deposit funds with this bank. Banks therefore rely much less on equity financing than other companies.[22] Therefore it is said that they have a 'high gearing' (i.e. a high debt-to-equity ratio).

[21] It was Allen and Gale who distinguished between these two forms of risk spreading. F. Allen and D. Gale, 'Financial Markets, Intermediaries and Intertemporal Smoothing', (1997) 105 *Journal of Political Economy* 523, at 525.

[22] Studies found that capital-to-asset ratios lay between 4 and 8 per cent in the banking sector, whereas this ratio is between 30 and 40 per cent in industry and commerce. CPB Netherlands Bureau for Economic Policy Analysis, above n. 13, at 47.

3

The regulation of the banking sector

29. Reasons for regulating the banking sector are diverse. The different approaches are linked to the question whether the banking sector is so different from other services sectors. There is wide recognition of the existence of a number of market failures with regard to banking services. However, authors disagree on whether these market failures are specific to banking services or occur equally in other sectors; on whether these market failures are sufficiently serious to warrant regulation; and on the types of regulation to address market failures. With respect to the specificity of banking services, the nature of traditional banking activity (collecting short-term deposits and providing long-term loans) indeed leads to important market failures. Surely, similar market failures also occur for non-banking services. However, the consequences of market failures in the banking sector are different from other sectors, providing a very strong argument for regulation.

3.1 Market failures

30. Financial intermediaries, such as banks, emerge because of the need to reduce transaction costs and to resolve information asymmetries and other sources of market failures in the capital market (above, paras. 18–28). Because savers and lenders are unable to contract efficiently, monitoring, liquidity provision and risk management are delegated to intermediaries. However, new market failures may occur at the moment one makes use of financial intermediaries.[23] The fact that contractual relationships between banks and clients are based on confidence and trust, combined with the inter-linkages among banks and between banks and the economy as a whole, makes certain banks of 'systemic importance'. Problems experienced

[23] Diamond, above n. 14, at 399.

by one bank may easily spill over to other banks and eventually to the entire economy.

31. Essentially, there is a market failure when the market fails to reach an equilibrium whereby goods or services in the market are efficiently allocated.[24] An efficient allocation of credit by banks is achieved when all costs that would emerge in the case where a loan is not repaid are taken into account when banks put a price on credit. This price should then include not only the private costs to the individual bank, the shareholders of this bank and the depositors of this bank, but also the costs society as a whole will have to bear ('social costs').[25] The specific characteristics of the banking sector imply that individual bank failures may spill over to other banks in the market and even affect the real economy. These costs are external to the bank that has initially granted risky credit. Since the bank does not bear this cost, it does not take this cost into account in determining its level of output of credit.[26] As some of these costs are not included in the price a bank sets for credit, more credit will be offered than is efficient and thus total welfare in society will be below what could be achieved.

3.1.1 Market failures in services markets

32. Before turning specifically to banking services, we briefly consider the nature of trade in services and the specificities of such trade. In general, trade in services is clearly different from trade in goods. In contrast to goods, services are not tangible, and service provision often requires interaction between a service provider and the service consumer.[27] At a time when no effective telecommunication infrastructure existed, services trade necessarily required the physical proximity of the provider and the receiver and thus physical movement of at least one of them in order to meet in person. Services trade would thus primarily be a matter of migration. However, the

[24] A situation is 'Pareto-inefficient' if it is possible to increase the welfare of one individual in society without making any other individual in society worse off. See R. Cooter and T. Ulen, *Law & Economics*, 5th edn (Boston, MA: Addison-Wesley, 2008) 17.

[25] D. Llewellyn, 'The Economic Rationale for Financial Regulation', FSA Occasional Paper Series No. 1, April 1999, available at www.fsa.gov.uk/pubs/occpapers/OP01.pdf, at 13.

[26] Cooter and Ulen, above n. 24, at 44–5.

[27] J. Bhagwati, 'Economic Perspectives on Trade in Professional Services', (1986) 2 *University of Chicago Legal Forum* 45, at 46–8. It is sometimes said that the production and consumption of a service happen simultaneously (see, e.g., T. Hill, 'On Goods and Services', (1977) 23 *Review of Income & Wealth* 315, at 329).

technological developments that took place in the twentieth century, especially with regard to telecommunication technologies, have created huge opportunities for services trade. When services can be 'transported' by means of the telephone or the Internet, the transaction becomes much more like trade in goods.

33. Still, because the principal characteristic of services trade concerns the interaction between suppliers and consumers, the characteristics of a service are essentially linked to the characteristics of the provider of the service. In other words, it is difficult to separate the production process from the product itself. This fact often makes it very hard for consumers to assess the quality of a service before it is consumed.

34. Severe information asymmetries exist in services sectors. Services are generally 'experience goods', meaning that their quality can be assessed only *after* purchase and consumption.[28] The problem is exacerbated when the period required for determining the quality of the service is longer and the costs for assessing the quality are higher. This characteristic may induce service suppliers to provide low-quality services, and, indeed, provides a justification for regulatory intervention.

35. A further reason why regulatory intervention is prevalent in services sectors is the consideration that certain services (energy, water, etc.) should be available to every citizen at an affordable price. Certain services would not be provided to all citizens if their allocation were left entirely to the market. For instance, postal services would not reach citizens who live in remote areas of the country unless a very high price were paid for these services.[29] Further, the government might also consider that credit is insufficiently targeted at socially desirable projects.[30]

36. In the next section, the market failures in the banking sector will be examined more in detail.

[28] It is Nelson who has developed the concept of 'experience goods'. See P. Nelson, 'Information and Consumer Behavior', (1970) 78 *Journal of Political Economy* 311, at 312. On financial services in general see Llewellyn, above n. 25, at 34. On automobile insurance see M. Israel, 'Services as Experience Goods: An Empirical Examination of Consumer Learning in Automobile Insurance', (2005) 95 *American Economic Review* 1444, at 1444–63.

[29] S. Claessens, 'Access to Financial Services: A Review of the Issues and Public Policy Objectives', World Bank Policy Research Working Paper No. 3589, May 2005, at 13–14.

[30] J. Barth, G. Caprio and R. Levine, *Rethinking Bank Regulation. Till Angels Govern* (Cambridge University Press, 2006) 61.

3.1.2 Information asymmetries between depositors and banks

3.1.2.1 Principal–agent problems between depositors and banks

37. When savers delegate the monitoring of borrowers to financial intermediaries, they place their savings with an intermediary (e.g. a bank). The bank then makes use of the funds to lend money to borrowers. The returns from this activity are again channelled back to the depositors. However, these bank clients want to be reassured that banks perform their task in the interests of the clients. While clients rely on intermediaries because it is difficult for the individual savers to assess the quality of the borrowers, these clients may also wonder whether the bank is in fact performing its role in an optimal way. Depositors have an important sanctioning mechanism in this respect: they can withdraw their deposits at short notice.[31] Benston has concluded on this basis that banks will ensure high-quality services and avoid engaging in overly risky activities. If there is sufficient competition in the financial market and thus alternative repositories for depositors to invest their funds when they encounter problematic bank activity, no further regulation would be necessary.[32]

38. However, it is very difficult for consumers to assess in advance (i.e. at the time of purchase) the quality of the service they receive ('experience goods'). The time required for a consumer to assess the quality of the service provided by the bank may be very long. Depositors may only find out about problematic bank activity after several years have passed. What is more, the complicated nature of the service provided by banks (risk management and monitoring borrowers) requires advanced skills. The fact that depositors lack these skills is exactly the reason why they make use of intermediaries. Banking services can therefore be called 'credence goods' – that is, the quality can be assessed only at serious cost after a long period of time.[33] Confidence in the bank's activities is thus essential.

[31] X. Freixas and J. Rochet, *Microeconomics of Banking* (Cambridge, MA: MIT Press, 1997) 17. An additional device to ensure that banks perform their monitoring activity optimally when providing loans is to require banks to participate in the projects they finance.

[32] G. Benston, *Regulating Financial Markets: A Critique and some Proposals* (London: Institute of Economic Affairs, 1998) 38. See also K. Bowd, 'The Case for Financial Laissez-Faire', (1996) 106 *Economic Journal* 679, at 681; and C. Calomiris and C. Kahn, 'The Role of Demandable Debt in Structuring Optimal Banking Arrangements', (1991) 81 *American Economic Review* 497, at 509–10.

[33] Llewellyn, above n. 25, at 34.

39. As depositors find it difficult to assess the quality of the services provided by the bank, banks may engage in risky activity that is not sufficiently penalized by the depositors. Delegation thus creates a 'principal–agent' problem. The principal (depositor) finds it difficult to control the agent (bank). A saver has in fact limited incentives to monitor the bank, since other depositors will free-ride on any monitoring effort undertaken by the individual saver.[34] For these reasons, banks may decide to engage in behaviour that is not in the depositors' interests. This is exacerbated if banks feel that they should engage in risky, short-term profit-making behaviour because all other banks are doing the same and they fear that they will miss out on the gains that can be made.

3.1.2.2 Increased information asymmetries resulting from new financial instruments to transfer risk

40. Competition from non-bank financial intermediaries and the financial market in general has pushed banks towards risky behaviour to the detriment of consumers and shareholders. The increased sophistication of financial markets made it difficult for banks to raise sufficient deposits to fund their lending activity.

41. New forms of non-bank intermediaries have grown. Many of these intermediaries are collective investment schemes, bringing different individual investors together to engage in investments that are not feasible on an individual basis, in the form of, for example, pension funds, insurance companies, private equity funds and hedge funds. These non-bank financial intermediaries seemed better at raising money from savers because of the higher returns savers received. Since holding deposits is expensive for banks, they were unable to provide high returns to depositors and thus deposits were no longer sufficiently attractive to savers. Therefore banks decided to rely on alternative sources of funding, and engaged in activities which went beyond traditional banking activity.[35]

42. Moreover, by engaging in 'securitization', banks developed an innovative tool to supplement deposit funding. They were able to convert

[34] Dewatripont and Tirole, above n. 17, at 31–2; Heremans, above n. 12, at 956.

[35] P. Lescrauwaet, 'Links between Institutional Investors and Banks', background paper prepared for the Working Group on institutional investors, global savings and asset location of the Committee on the Global Financial System, December 2006, available at www.bis.org/publ/wgpapers/cgfs27lescrauwaet.pdf, at 4.

non-marketable assets into marketable assets represented by securities.[36] As financial markets became more efficient, savers sought investments that provided higher returns than deposits. When banks moved loans to separate companies, they were able to tap this investment potential. They were no longer required to rely solely on expensive deposit financing for lending activities.[37] Moreover, these instruments made it possible to reduce the risks incurred by the banks.

43. Traditionally, loans could not be traded. They stayed on the balance sheet of the bank and were funded by the deposits. However, once a loan can be sold to investors, the credit risk linked to the loan is moved from the bank to the investor. The bank sells its claim on the borrower to another entity that from then on will carry the credit risk.[38] The 'selling' of credit risk (separate from the loan itself) was made possible by means of 'credit derivatives'. These derivatives are financial contracts for which the value is derived from the underlying asset (here, the loan).[39] By means of these financial instruments, banks 'insured' themselves against credit risk.

44. However, the entities that bought this risk tried to fund their operations by borrowing on the market. Banks have, for instance, set up structured investment vehicles that buy long-term loans and fund them by short-term debt. These vehicles can make a profit because the interest to be paid on short-term debt is generally lower than the return obtained from long-term loans. Other entities may buy credit risk and fund it by selling bonds to

[36] The marketable assets are secured on the non-marketable assets (namely the receivables, such as, e.g., interest payments for a loan). See P. Wood, *Project Finance, Securitisations, Subordinated Debt, Vol. 5, The Law and Practice of International Finance Series* (London: Sweet & Maxwell, 2007) 112.

[37] K. Alexander, J. Eatwell, A. Persaud and R. Reoch, 'Financial Supervision and Crisis Management in the EU', Study for the Policy Department on Economic and Scientific Policy of the European Parliament, IP/A/ECON/IC/2007-069, December 2007, available at www.europarl.europa.eu/activities/committees/studies/download.do?file=19191#search=%20Financial%20supervision%20, 8.

[38] Wood, above n. 36, at 134.

[39] The best-known example of a credit derivative is a credit default swap. This is a contract in which the buyer of the credit default swap pays a periodic fee to the protection seller. If the underlying asset (e.g. a loan) is defaulted on, the protection seller will pay an agreed amount to the buyer. It is not even necessary for the buyer of the credit default swap actually to own the underlying asset (e.g. the loan); the buyer can merely speculate on the default of the underlying asset. This is an important difference from an insurance contract. (See F. Schwartz, 'Risk Distribution in the Capital Markets: Credit Default Swaps, Insurance and a Theory of Demarcation', (2007) 12 *Fordham Journal of Corporate and Financial Law* 167, at 174–6.)

investors. To this end, pools of risk are bundled into a 'collateralized debt obligation'.[40] The collateralized debt obligation allows the bank to sell a pool of assets (loans or merely the risk linked to the loan[41]) to a special purpose vehicle. This vehicle then divides the pool into different parts (tranches), corresponding to different levels of risk, which are sold to investors with a different risk appetite. The so-called 'junior' tranche will first experience possible losses in the underlying assets. Next, possible losses will be allocated to 'mezzanine' tranches and finally to the 'senior' tranche.[42]

45. By engaging in securitization, banks can to an important extent reduce the credit risk. By means of collateralized debt obligations, a diversified risk portfolio would be traded. Given the large number of risks being pooled, the chance that one of the underlying assets defaults becomes lower and thus aggregate risk is reduced. The securitization of loans by means of collateral debt obligations thus leads to increased efficiency: more credit is available to borrowers and risk is managed more efficiently. However, it is difficult for investors to assess the quality of the investment packages that are offered.

46. As a consequence of these financial techniques, the incentives for banks to engage in adequate monitoring of borrowers are reduced. When banks are able to move loans off their balance sheets and transfer risk to separate entities, they have no real restraint against making loans to bad borrowers. If a borrower defaults, the consequences will be borne by the investors in the securities that are backed by the loan and not by the bank that has originated the loan. This is exacerbated by the fact that loans are pooled into collateralized debt obligations. Indeed, while an investor may be hesitant to invest in securities that have bad underlying assets (e.g. bad loans), the determination of whether the underlying assets are effectively of low quality becomes very difficult in cases where different credit risks are pooled. The necessary market discipline to avoid banks engaging in overly risky lending becomes thus flawed.[43]

47. Therefore, when buying packages, investors relied on ratings by credit rating agencies. These rating agencies assess the quality of the

[40] G. Fuller and F. Ranero, 'Collateralised Debt Obligations', (2005) 20 *Butterworths Journal of International Banking and Financial Law* 343, at 343–51.

[41] This can be done by means of credit default swaps (above n. 39).

[42] M. Hellwig, 'Systemic Risk in the Financial Sector: An Analysis of the Subprime-Mortgage Financial Crisis', Preprints of the Max Planck Institute for Research on Collective Goods, Bonn 2008/43, November 2008, 10–11.

[43] For a detailed account, see ibid., at 14–35.

diversification in the packages and also consider other economic and systemic factors. Hence the monitoring of the quality of the risk packages is 'delegated' to the credit rating agencies. In theory, independent ratings by these agencies should ensure that the process of diversifying and relocating risk indeed leads to a reduction of risk. Nevertheless, several authors have argued that the wide availability of the methodology of credit rating agencies reduced the independence between the packaging of risk by banks and the rating of the package by rating agencies.[44] Banks could make use of the available methodology to build the packages so that they would obtain a favourable rating. It has also been suggested that credit rating agencies have underestimated the credit risk of collateralized debt obligations and that conflicts of interest come into play with regard to credit rating agencies (the agencies are paid by the companies whose financial instruments they rate).[45]

48. Because of the information asymmetries mentioned, the lack of incentives for banks to perform optimal monitoring when granting loans may lead to bank failures. The individual depositors of a failing bank will be the ones bearing the cost of such failure.[46] However, when loans are 'securitized', and credit risk is thus transferred, it would be, rather, the investors in the credit derivatives that feel the consequences of imprudent lending. Still, as the global financial crisis has shown, depositors may still become affected as the insurers of the debt are overstretched and eventually fail. The banks would thus not receive the agreed insurance payments when the borrowers default. What is more, bank lending activity became much more difficult as investors lost faith in the credit derivatives and stopped buying them. Risk could no longer be transferred by the banks. They had to cut back their extensive lending, reducing an important source of income. Finally, the vehicles for securitizing loans were set up by the banks themselves. As these vehicles faced difficulties they had to turn to the banks that had created them. Hence, even if banks had transferred credit risk to other market players, it was clear that the banks still underwent the consequences of defaulting loans. The depositors of the banks were thus nevertheless affected.

[44] See, e.g., Alexander, Eatwell, Persaud and Reoch, above n. 37, at 18.

[45] The United States has since 2007 had legislation on credit rating agencies; see the US Credit Rating Agency Reform Act of 2006, S.3850. The EU has had a regulation since September 2009; see Regulation 1060/2009 of the European Parliament and of the Council on Credit Rating Agencies, OJ 2009 L 302/1.

[46] Llewellyn, above n. 25, at 38.

49. The private costs of bank failures provide a first reason for regulating banking services. These costs are not, however, specific to banking services, but also figure in other services markets. What makes banking activity of such importance to public policy is that individual bank failures create costs that go beyond these private costs.

3.1.3 Contagion and systemic risk: the social costs of bank failures

50. Besides the private costs linked to banking services, there are also important social costs (or 'externalities'). When a bank fails, the impact is not limited to the clients of this bank or to its managers and shareholders. Other banks and financial institutions will be affected and, eventually, consequences will be felt in the real economy. This is caused by the close interconnection between banks as well as by the important role played by banks in the real economy.

51. Contagion can be defined as a situation where problems with one financial institution affect the rest of the financial system. Moreover, problems with one bank may spill over to the real economy. We discuss the channels through which such contagion takes place and which make the financial sector special as compared with other services sectors or manufacturing industries. Moreover, contagion may not be limited to the *national* financial sector, but may also spread *across borders*. We discuss international contagion when concerns with regard to the internationalization of the banking services market are addressed (below, paras. 115–117).

3.1.3.1 Contagion in the financial sector

52. When a bank fails and the depositors with this bank withdraw their deposits, depositors with other banks may also have worries on the soundness of the activities of their banks. As a consequence, savers may also start to withdraw their deposits from their bank, even when the latter bank may be perfectly solvent. Problems will thus spread to other banks. The information asymmetries that are so widespread in the market for banking services cause this reaction.

53. It is very difficult for banks to sell their assets. Their main assets are loans granted on a long term, which are difficult to market.[47] Potential

[47] Diamond and Dybvig, above n. 18, at 403. They note that '[i]lliquidity of assets provides the rationale both for the existence of banks and for their vulnerability to runs'.

buyers of these loans will not have sufficient information on the quality of the borrowers with whom the bank has built up a long-term relationship. Selling these assets, especially when a bank has run into trouble, will be very difficult. This is why the failure of a bank cannot easily be remedied by a takeover by another financial institution. Banks will have to rely mainly on the funds they have in cash to repay deposits that are called. If the bank does not have sufficient liquid assets to repay deposits, a liquidity problem quickly becomes a solvency problem. Since a bank rarely has sufficient liquid assets to repay all deposits, depositors want to be the first to withdraw their deposits. Payments are indeed made on a first-come-first-served basis. This also implies that, even if an individual depositor thinks his bank is solvent, the fear that other depositors will think that the bank is not and therefore will run to the bank, will make this individual depositor decide also to withdraw his deposits. This eventually gives rise to the so-called 'run on banks'.[48]

54. A further reason why risky activity by banks may lead to costs that surpass the private costs to the bank and its clients is linked to the important role of banks in the payment system. Through banks, clients can make payments effectively. The payer and the payee do not need to meet in person to exchange the money, but can rely on their banks to settle payments.[49] The failure to settle one payment due to this bank failure will have as a chain reaction that the other payments cannot be settled. This is especially important in today's international financial markets, since there may be a time lag between the moment of payment by one party to the bank and the moment counterparties are able to collect their payments and there are time differences between countries.[50]

55. Next, costs spread beyond the individual failing bank because there are many direct linkages between banks. Importantly, banks lend to each other to meet liquidity demands another bank may be facing. Banks may also be linked because they finance operations between companies.[51]

48 See for an analysis of the evidence that bank runs do occur G. Kaufman, 'Bank Contagion: A Review of the Theory and Evidence', (1994) 8 *Journal of Financial Services Research* 123, at 123–50.

49 This can either happen in real time for each individual payment (real-time gross settlement), or payment orders can be collected (after some minimum requirements are checked by a clearing house) and are executed at the end of the day by a settlement agent, leading only to net payments (multilateral netting system). If a bank fails at a certain moment, the settlement of payments may become problematic.

50 Alexander, Dhumale and Eatwell, above n. 9, at 188 and 254.

51 Dewatripont and Tirole, above n. 17, at 15 (footnote 2).

When certain banks suffer the consequences of their imprudent lending, confidence may be lost in interbank lending markets. Banks lose confidence in each other because of information asymmetries with regard to the quality of the assets they hold and may therefore stop lending to each other.[52] Moreover, banks are often part of a larger group, and the failure of a bank that is a subsidiary of a parent company may have consequences for other subsidiary banks, possibly in other countries. Since financial groups have been created that are composed of bank and non-bank financial intermediaries (such as pension funds or insurance companies) ('financial conglomerates'), the failure of a bank may spill over to the non-bank financial intermediaries in the group.

56. Individual bank failures may thus have an impact on the financial system as a whole ('systemic risk'). When banks make decisions, these social costs of their activities are not internalized. They can exploit information asymmetries and engage in risky activity that would be penalized in the market if it were transparent. Therefore the risk of banking activity is underpriced in relation to its total (private plus social) cost.[53] It is not reflected in the cost of individual banking services and, as a consequence, too much risk is produced. Adequate pricing of risk does not take place if this is merely left to the market mechanism. If risk is not priced effectively, excessive movements in the market will take place (runs on banks, failure of otherwise perfectly solvent banks, etc.). Financial instability is the consequence.[54]

3.1.3.2 Spillover to the real economy

57. The effects of bank failures are not limited to the financial sector, but are also felt in the real economy.

[52] B. Lyons, 'Competition Policy, Bailouts and the Economic Crisis', CCP Working Paper 09-4, March 2009, available at http://papers.ssrn.com/sol3/papers.cfm?abstract_id=1367688, at 4–5, arguing that this loss of confidence in the interbank market is much more important than loss of confidence with depositors.

[53] Alexander, Dhumale and Eatwell, above n. 9, at 24.

[54] C. Wyplosz, 'International Financial Instability', in I. Kaul, I. Grunberg and M. A. Stern (eds.), *Global Public Goods. International Cooperation in the 21st Century* (Oxford University Press, 1999) 152–189, at 157. Wyplosz notes that financial instability is a 'natural by-product of the business of dealing with risk'. Instability is normal in financial markets, since they deal with risks caused by uncertainty about future events. However, if banks are performing their monitoring tasks inadequately, uncertainty exceeds the normal levels (e.g. bank runs occur) and excessive financial instability is the result.

58. First, authors like Bernanke and Gertler have argued that a negative shock affects the income of non-financial actors as well as the value of the collateral they can offer to banks when they want to obtain a loan. Banks will therefore only be willing to extend credit at a higher price. In turn, this will worsen the financial position of non-financial actors even further, which makes credit for these actors again more expensive. Therefore, even when the first negative shock is over, the consequences will continue to be felt in the real economy long thereafter.[55]

59. Second, other authors, like Peek and Rosengren, have stressed that when the value of the assets of a bank suddenly drops sharply (e.g. the value of the asset-backed securities they hold), the bank risks not complying any more with the solvency ratio imposed by the applicable banking regulation (see below, paras. 74–77). In order to ensure compliance with the binding requirements, the bank can either seek additional capital, which is very difficult in crisis circumstances, or limit its lending activity. In turn, this reduces the availability of credit, slowing down economic activity.[56]

60. Blot, Le Bayon, Lemoine and Levasseur refer to two further channels for spillover to the real economy. When the value of stocks drops dramatically in a financial crisis, the wealth of private individuals and companies is also reduced. In view of these developments, these actors will reduce their consumption.[57] Finally, a financial crisis will also affect the confidence of individuals and companies. As they become uncertain about the future, they delay their important consumption and investment decisions.[58] This further slows the real economy. It may also finally be added that bank failures interrupt the payments system on which companies and individuals now rely heavily.[59]

[55] See, on this 'financial accelerator' model, B. Bernanke and M. Gertler, 'Inside the Black Box: The Credit Channel of Monetary Policy Transmission', (1995) 9 *Journal of Economic Perspectives* 27; and B. Bernanke, M. Gertler and S. Gilchrist, 'The Financial Accelerator in a Quantitative Business Cycle Framework', in J. Taylor and M. Woodford (eds.), *Handbook of Macroeconomics* (Amsterdam: Elsevier, 1999) Vol. 15, 1341–93.

[56] J. Peek and E. Rosengren, 'The Capital Crunch: Neither a Borrower Nor a Lender Be', (1995) 27 *Journal of Money, Credit and Banking* 625, at 626.

[57] C. Blot, S. Le Bayon, M. Lemoine and S. Levasseur, 'De la crise financière à la crise économique: une analyse comparative France–Etats-Unis', (2009) *Revue de l'OFCE* 255, at 259, noting that this effect is more pronounced in Anglo-Saxon countries than in continental Europe, since individuals in continental Europe invest much less of their wealth in financial markets.

[58] N. Bloom, 'The Impact of Uncertainty Shocks', (2009) 77 *Econometrica* 623.

[59] Kaufman, above n. 48, at 139–40.

3.1.4 Systemic risk caused by homogeneous reaction to macroeconomic events

61. The global financial crisis showed that systemic crises occur not only when individual banks take too much risk and the failure of one bank triggers problems in other banks. A systemic crisis can also occur when banks are all exposed to the same problems such that they all react in the same manner. These risks are linked to general macroeconomic events. The focus on macroeconomic developments is thus also an essential component of stability in banking markets. Commentators now agree that the lack of a combined macro- and micro-prudential understanding of the financial markets was an important cause of the global financial crisis. What is more, banking regulation that is based on internationally harmonized capital adequacy standards reinforces the homogeneity in the reactions of market players to such macroeconomic events. Since it is banking regulation, in combination with macroeconomic events, that causes such systemic consequences, this further source of systemic risk will be discussed more in detail in the next section, on banking regulation.

3.2 Regulation and market discipline

62. Because of information asymmetries, banks may engage in excessively risky activities and eventually go bankrupt. The costs of bank failures are not felt solely by the deposit-holders, shareholders or managers of the bank in question; bank failures can also provoke social costs. Difficulties with one bank may spill over to other banks and the entire financial system. Eventually, the effects may spill over to the real economy. As the global financial crisis has shown, the social costs of bank failures are far from negligible.

63. There is thus a clear case for government intervention in the banking sector to correct market failures and to avoid the incurring of these private and social costs. This government intervention takes different forms. It can be broadly subdivided into banking *regulation* (generally applicable rules that apply to banking services and to credit institutions), on the one hand, and banking *supervision* (the application of banking regulation in specific cases), on the other hand.[60]

[60] E. Wymeersch, 'The Future of Financial Regulation and Supervision in Europe', (2005) 42 *Common Market Law Review* 987, at 988; see also High Level Group on Financial Supervision in the EU, Chaired by Jacques de Larosière, 'Report', 25 February 2009, para. 38.

3.2.1 *Prudential regulation versus other types of banking regulation*

64. There exists a broad range of regulations that affect banking services. The characteristics of banking services are determined by the contract law that is applicable to it, as well as by the rules of consumer protection law. Furthermore, the characteristics of credit institutions are determined by corporate law and tax law. Competition law applies both to the banking services and to the structure of credit institutions. These different types of regulation pursue diverse objectives.[61]

65. The regulation that specifically aims at avoiding banks going bankrupt is called 'prudential regulation'. Such regulation wants to ensure that banks engage in 'prudent' conduct so that they lower the risk of bank insolvency and further contagion to the entire financial sector and the real economy. Prudential regulation thus focuses on the microeconomic level – the characteristics and activities of an individual credit institution – but has macroeconomic consequences: avoiding the spillover of negative events to the financial sector and real economy.

66. Because of the linkages between the information asymmetries in banking services markets already mentioned, the risk-taking by banks, the potential for bank failures, the contagion to other banks and financial institutions, and the systemic risk and general loss of confidence in financial markets, it can be argued that 'prudential' regulation and supervision have as their ultimate objective maintaining the stability of the financial system.[62]

[61] Dalhuisen identifies nine objectives of modern financial regulation: (a) protection of clients from bankruptcy, bad selling or advisory practices, or risky products; (b) creating a simplified enforcement regime; (c) creating a proper legal framework for financial products or services; (d) minimalization of contagion or systemic risk; (e) the integrity and smooth operation of markets; (f) addressing asymmetric markets; (g) creating a level playing field between commercial banks; (h) preventing monopolies; (i) maintaining the reputation and soundness of the financial services industry. J. Dalhuisen, *Dalhuisen on Transnational and Comparative Commercial, Financial and Trade Law* (Oxford: Hart, 2007) 1106–11. See for another overview of the reasons for bank regulation, R. Cranston, *Principles of Banking Law*, 2nd edn (Oxford University Press, 2002) 65–81. Cranston refers to (a) systemic risk; (b) prevention of fraud, money-laundering and terrorism; (c) consumer protection and deposit insurance; and (d) competition policy.

[62] Certain authors make a distinction between *prudential* regulation and *systemic* regulation. In their view, systemic regulation is about 'the safety and soundness of financial institutions for purely systemic reasons'. In contrast, prudential regulation is then 'about the safety and soundness of financial institutions vis-à-vis consumer protection, in that the consumer loses when an institution fails, even if there are no systemic reasons.'

3.2.2 Regulation based on market discipline

67. There has been an important tendency in economic literature to argue that *market discipline* is essential for 'appropriate' prudential regulation. In order to avoid bank failures, government regulation may try to ensure that market discipline functions to its fullest extent. However, the global financial crisis showed the limits of this type of prudential regulation.[63] Market players do not always react as rationally as expected to the incentives given by regulation.

68. Indeed, questions may arise as to whether governments are actually *able* to design regulation that addresses market failures effectively. Further, one may wonder which *actors* could ensure discipline in the market. Finally, it should be clarified under what *conditions* market discipline might be effective.

3.2.2.1 The role of government in solving market failures

69. The question of what constitutes 'appropriate' prudential regulation is in fact preceded by the question whether the government is able to address market failures. Even if there is recognition that serious market failures exist, it has been disputed whether the government has the capacity to remedy these failures.

70. As Barth, Caprio and Levine have discussed, there exist in fact two views on this role of the government: the public interest approach and the private interest approach. The *public interest* approach argues that the government is able to act efficiently to correct market failures and has the correct incentives to intervene.[64]

C. Goodhart, P. Hartmann, D. Llewellyn, L. Rojas-Suárez and S. Weisbrod, *Financial Regulation. Why, How and Where Now?* (London: Routledge, 1998) 5–6. However, the linkages between the objectives of different types of banking regulation mean that prudential regulation has consequences for both the safety and the soundness of an individual institution, as well as for systemic stability in general. See also Panourgias, above n. 1, at 13, who argues that 'it is difficult to see how a clear distinction between individual and systemic financial stability considerations can be maintained, both conceptually and in practice'.

[63] Financial Services Authority, 'The Turner Review. A Regulatory Response to the Global Banking Crisis', March 2009, available at www.fsa.gov.uk/pubs/other/turner_review.pdf, at 45.

[64] Barth, Caprio and Levine, above n. 30, at 22. Pigou argued in the early twentieth century (1938) that governments are able to correct market failures by means of taxes and subsidies. A. Pigou, *The Economics of Welfare*, repr. (London: Macmillan, 1950).

71. In contrast, the *private interest* (or 'public choice') approach considers that regulation might merely be a response to demands by private interest groups.[65] It furthers not necessarily the public interest, but often merely the private interest of specific groups in society that are able to 'capture' the regulation.[66] These private interests may, among others, be those of the politicians themselves,[67] those of some parts of the industry (e.g. large banks) or certain consumer groups.[68]

3.2.2.2 Private actors

72. If market discipline of banks is to work, there need to be actors that monitor the activities of the bank. Traditionally, it is said that there are two types of private actor that monitor the bank: the depositors and the investors.

73. The fact that deposits can be withdrawn within a short period provides an important tool to *depositors* for penalizing imprudent bank activity. As depositors are concerned that the money they have deposited with the bank needs to be repaid on request, they have an important stake in monitoring the bank.

74. However, besides the depositors, *investors* that have provided capital to the bank will also want to make sure that their investment is used wisely. The more they have invested, the more they have to lose when a bank goes bankrupt.[69] If a bank is required to maintain a high amount of capital, shareholders will need to invest more in the bank and therefore have much more to lose when the bank's risky loans are defaulted on.

[65] Stigler was the first to approach government regulation as a process of supply and demand. R. Stigler, 'The Theory of Economic Regulation', (1971) 2 *Bell Journal of Economics and Management Science* 3, at 3–21; and see R. Posner, 'Theories of Economic Regulation', (1974) 5 *Bell Journal of Economics and Management Science* 335, at 336.

[66] For a sceptical account of the capability of financial regulation to address financial risk-taking, see K. Dowd, 'Moral Hazard and the Financial Crisis', (2009) 29 *Cato Journal* 141, at 160–3.

[67] Several authors have described historical examples of how sovereigns were using banks to finance their operations. Furthermore, regulation may be used by politicians in power to further the narrow interests of those groups in society who ensure that they could remain in power. Barth, Caprio and Levine, above n. 30, at 37–41.

[68] Kroszner and Strahan argue that, as the power between different interest groups changes, different regulatory priorities will prevail (regulation or deregulation). If there is intensive competition between rival groups, the chance of beneficial reform increases. R. Kroszner and P. Strahan, 'Obstacles to Optimal Policy: The Interplay of Politics and Economics in Shaping Bank Supervision and Regulation Reforms', in Mishkin, above n. 10, 233–71, at 261.

[69] CPB Netherlands Bureau for Economic Policy Analysis, above n. 13, at 15.

The regulatory requirement that banks maintain minimum capital and guard their capital ratios is meant to ensure this monitoring by the investors in the bank. Capital requirements are thus regulatory techniques to give incentives to banks to take less risk.[70]

75. Governments nowadays require a bank to adhere to a minimum ratio, defined as the amount of capital divided by the risk-weighted assets of the bank. The Basel Committee on Banking Supervision has developed international standards setting out minimum capital requirements. Shortly before and during the global financial crisis, countries were implementing the so-called 'Basel II' capital accord (see below, para. 189).

76. The ability of minimum capital requirements to provide the necessary incentives to banks to discipline risky behaviour had already been criticized before the global financial crisis. Hellman, Murdock and Stiglitz argued in 2000 that when banks are required to comply with higher capital ratios, they may in fact try to offset the costs of maintaining higher capital by taking more risk.[71]

77. Furthermore, Blum and Hellwig had already warned in 1995 that capital adequacy regulation is procyclical. If a macroeconomic downturn occurs, borrowers will find it more difficult to meet the repayment demands made by their banks. This affects the returns obtained by banks from their loans. As already explained, in order not to fail to comply with the regulatory capital requirements, these banks will reduce lending. This further exacerbates the macroeconomic downturn.[72] Given the fact that the majority of banks in the world complied with requirements that were based on

[70] Alexander, Eatwell, Persaud and Reoch, above n. 37, at 53. Hellwig referred to this 'paradox of banking regulation': 'Any position in the bank's balance sheet that serves as a buffer against unforeseen contingencies ceases to serve this buffer function when a regulator imposes a rule stipulating a minimum amount for this position.' Hellwig, above n. 42, at 46.

[71] T. Hellman, K. Murdock and J. Stiglitz, 'Liberalization, Moral Hazard in Banking and Prudential Regulation: Are Capital Requirements Enough?', (2000) 90 *American Economic Review* 147, at 149–50; see also Alexander, Dhumale and Eatwell, above n. 9, at 224. Barth, Caprio and Levine demonstrated, based on empirical studies, the 'absence of a robust statistical relationship between the stringency of capital regulations and the performance of national banking systems.' Barth, Caprio and Levine, above n. 30, at 311.

[72] J. Blum and M. Hellwig, 'The Macroeconomic Implications of the Capital Adequacy Requirements for Banks', (1995) 39 *European Economic Review* 739, at 741–2. See also M. Gordy and B. Howells, 'Procyclicality in Basel II: Can We Treat the Disease without Killing the Patient?', (2006) 15 *Journal of Financial Intermediation* 395, at 395–6. See also Hellwig, above n. 42, at 46–7.

Basel II, this procyclicality manifested itself worldwide. It clearly contributed to the homogenization of all reactions by market participants.[73]

3.2.2.3 Conditions for and limits of effective private monitoring

78. Effective private monitoring requires (i) a supply of accurate information to the private actors that enables them to monitor the bank, and (ii) a mechanism for ensuring that the use of the information by the private monitors promotes prudent bank behaviour.

79. Nonetheless, even if these conditions are fulfilled, this does not necessarily mean that the private actors will react to the incentives that are provided in a way that is desirable and predicted by the regulators. This contradicts the premise of a market-based approach to law, namely that individuals pursue their private interests and aim to maximize utility when making choices between different options for behaviour ('rational choice').[74] As behavioural economics has shown, the behaviour of private monitors may be influenced by other factors besides rational choice between alternatives in order to maximize utility.[75] This is a first essential problem with banking regulation that focuses on market discipline.[76]

80. A second limit of regulation based on market discipline is its interaction with *herding* by market players. In 2000, Persaud stressed that efforts towards the international harmonization of capital rules lead to homogeneous reactions to macroeconomic events. He explained that

[73] Alexander, Eatwell, Persaud and Reoch, above n. 37, at 5–6.

[74] T. Ulen, 'Rational Choice Theory in Law and Economics', in B. Bouckaert and G. De Geest (eds.), *Encyclopedia of Law and Economics. Volume 0. General Works, History and Methodology* (Cheltenham: Edward Elgar, 2000) 790–818.

[75] R. Korobkin and T. Ulen, 'Law and Behavioral Science: Removing the Rationality Assumption from Law and Economics', (2000) 88 *California Law Review* 1051. See also the book by Akerlof and Kranton, who argue that economic studies on utility maximization have ignored that a person's preferences depends on his or her identity. G. Akerlof and R. Kranton, *Identity Economics. How Our Identities Shape Our Work, Wages, and Well-Being* (Princeton University Press, 2010) 10.

[76] Economic analysis supposes that decisions by individuals are made on a rational basis (rational choice theory). However, behavioural economics argues that in practice human behaviour is not always based on rational decisions. When faced with uncertainty and risk, people tend to give greater weight to losses than to gains (loss aversion). Hence, even if the probability of obtaining gains when putting your money with a bank that engages in very risky strategies were very low, it may be preferred over withdrawing deposits with certain, but small, loss. See A. Tversky and D. Kahneman, 'Rational Choice and the Framing of Decisions', (1986) 59 *Journal of Business* 251, at 258.

market-sensitive risk management practices and increased transparency, as introduced by regulations that are based on the work by the Basel Committee, may in fact lead to more volatility in markets and trigger contagion.[77] He argued that markets are only liquid if they are characterized by a large number of participants with different goals and expectations. However, banks and investors have the tendency to copy each other's behaviour ('herding')[78] or at least determine their actions on the basis of what the other market players are expected to do ('strategic behaviour').[79]

81. As long as banks and investors have different approaches to risk and do not have exactly the same information, some of them will be willing to sell (e.g. sell securitized loans) at the same time as others will be willing to buy. This ensures market liquidity. However, if all market participants have the same measurement of risk (based on methods that look at the past occurrence of problems) and have exactly the same information about each other's activities (because of the introduction of international standards of the measurement of risk-based capital ratios and because of standardized reporting standards), markets become illiquid. Similar arguments were made by Goodhart in the context of the global financial crisis.[80]

3.3 Conclusions on regulation of the banking sector

82. In this chapter, the first part of the balance between the goals of stability and efficiency was introduced. Failures in the market for banking services may result in a situation where banks engage in excessively risky activities. This may lead to bank failures, which imposes costs on the deposit-holders, shareholders, creditors and management of the

[77] A. Persaud, 'Sending the Herd off the Cliff Edge: The Disturbing Interaction between Herding and Market-Sensitive Risk Management Practices', Erisk, December 2000, available at www.erisk.com/ResourceCenter/ERM/persaud.pdf, at 2.

[78] Ibid., at 3; and see J. Keynes, *The General Theory of Employment, Interest and Money*, repr. (London: Macmillan, 1957) 156–8.

[79] See Alexander, Dhumale and Eatwell, above n. 9, at 255–259.

[80] Goodhart has argued (referring also to Persaud) that there should be a requirement for banks to hold in good times more capital and liquidity to be able to tackle times of trouble. In his view, the requirement should be based on the growth rate of the bank: if it is growing quickly, more capital would be required. This would ensure that capital requirements are *counter*-cyclical. See C. Goodhart, 'The Regulatory Response to the Financial Crisis', CESifo Working Paper No. 2257, March 2008, 14.

bank. Moreover, because of the specific features of banking activities, the problems of individual banks may spill over to the entire financial sector and possibly to the real economy. These features clearly support government intervention in the market for banking services. Regulation of the banking sector should thus seek to achieve financial stability.

83. Nevertheless, even if there may be a clear need for market corrections, it is far from undisputed whether government intervention is able to produce the necessary corrections. Opposing views (public interest/private interest) have been expressed with regard to the ability of regulators to address market failures. In the end, as the former US Federal Reserve chairman Alan Greenspan has admitted when replying to his critics, the trust or distrust one places in the government to regulate financial markets is a matter of 'ideology'.[81] If one believes in the role of the government to correct market failures, the question becomes what constitutes 'appropriate' regulatory intervention.

84. For a long time many economists shared the view that banking regulation that is based on market discipline produces the best results when trying to achieve financial stability. Nonetheless, the global financial crisis created a 'shock' that pointed to the deficiencies of this type of regulation. The internationally harmonized capital requirements had procyclical effects and lead to homogenization of the behaviour of market participants. Furthermore, behavioural finance suggests the need of rethinking the 'efficient market hypothesis': market players do not always react as expected to incentives.

[81] See A. Greenspan, 'A Response to My Critics', *Financial Times* Economists Forum, 6 April 2008, available at http://blogs.ft.com/economistsforum/2008/04/alan-greenspan-a-response-to-my-critics/.

4

Liberalization in the banking sector

85. In this chapter we address the second element in the balance between stability and efficiency. From the 1990s, governments gradually allowed more competition in banking services markets.[82] National competition policy is applied to banks, and restrictions on bank activities have been removed (e.g. restrictions on branching and the prohibition from combining banking and securities activities in one company). While competition policy addresses restrictions of competition created by private undertakings, liberalization takes place through the process of removing barriers imposed by governments. Efforts were also undertaken at the European and international levels to enhance *cross-border* competition between banks from different countries. These projects promote competition between banks from different countries. In the following sections we discuss the alleged benefits and concerns of competition in the banking sector.

4.1 Competition in the banking sector

4.1.1 Financial development and economic growth

86. In economic literature, much attention is paid to the link between financial development and economic growth. Already in 1911, Schumpeter had argued that financial development contributes to the growth of a country's economy.[83] On the other hand, other economists, such as Robinson, did not consider that financial development creates economic growth.[84]

[82] E. Carletti, *Background Note to OECD, Competition and Financial Markets* (Paris: OECD, 2009) 17.

[83] J. Schumpeter, *The Theory of Economic Development* (Cambridge, MA: Harvard University Press, 1968 [1934, first published in German, 1911]) 95–127.

[84] J. Robinson, *The Rate of Interest and Other Essays* (London: Macmillan, 1952) 86. Robinson famously stated that 'where enterprise leads finance follows'. For an overview see R. Levine, 'Finance and Growth: Theory, Evidence and Mechanisms', in P. Aghion

87. In their much-cited paper, Rajan and Zingales defined financial development as 'the ease with which borrowers and savers can be brought together, and once together, the confidence they have in one another'.[85] Financial development is 'related to the variety of intermediaries and markets available, the efficiency with which they perform the evaluation, monitoring, certification, communication and distribution functions, and the legal and regulatory framework assuring performance'.[86] Levine has identified five functions of financial systems: 'financial development involves improvements in the (i) production of ex ante information about possible investments, (ii) monitoring of investments and implementation of corporate governance, (iii) trading, diversification, and management of risk, (iv) mobilization and pooling of savings, and (v) exchange of goods and services'. He argues that '[f]inancial development occurs when financial instruments, markets, and intermediaries ameliorate – though do not necessarily eliminate – the effects of information, enforcement, and transactions costs and therefore do a corresponding better job at providing the five functions.'[87] If a financial system were better at channelling funds from agents with excess funds to agents with funding needs, greater economic growth would follow.

88. Much research has been devoted to establishing a causal link between the level of a country's financial development and the growth of the country's economy. The first empirical study dates from 1969. Goldsmith found a link between financial development and growth, but carefully stressed that this link did not necessarily involve causality.[88] The most cited empirical study is that by Rajan and Zingales. These authors were able to show that in countries with higher financial development, firms that are typically dependent on external finance grow faster.[89] Several other empirical studies examined the relationship between financial development and growth, and showed that better functioning financial intermediaries and financial markets influence economic growth.[90]

and S. Durlauf (eds.), *Handbook of Economic Growth* (Amsterdam: North-Holland, 2005) 865–934, at 867.

[85] R. Rajan and L. Zingales, 'Financial Dependence and Growth', (1998) 88 *American Economic Review* 559, at 569.

[86] Ibid. [87] Levine, above n. 84, at 870.

[88] R. Goldsmith, *Financial Structure and Development* (New Haven: Yale University Press, 1969) 408.

[89] Rajan and Zingales, above n. 85, at 560.

[90] See inter alia R. La Porta, F. Lopez-de-Silanes and A. Schleifer, 'Government Ownership of Banks', (2002) 57 *Journal of Finance* 265, at 267; R. Levine, N. Loayza and T. Beck, 'Financial Intermediation and Growth: Causality and Causes', (2000) 46 *Journal of*

Nonetheless, a number of studies have criticized this conclusion. One study by Ram found that there is only a weak association between the proxies used for measuring financial development and economic growth.[91] Also, Manning has criticized studies that found a causal link between financial development and economic growth.[92]

4.1.2 Competition and efficiency

4.1.2.1 The traditional paradigm of competition

89. Traditional industrial organization theory argues that competition between firms leads to the most efficient allocation of resources in the market. Competition between large numbers of companies implies that products are offered at the best quality and the lowest prices. As Mason famously argued, based on an assessment of the structure of the market, predictions can be made with regard to the conduct of companies and thus on the performance of the industry.[93] When the structure of the market is such that there is a large number of companies, the companies are price-takers. They will produce as long as their marginal profits cover the marginal costs of production. Consumers will also purchase the product as long as the marginal utility they obtain from an additional unit of the product is larger than the price they have to pay for the product. The optimal price and quantity of production is situated where offer and demand meet. However, in more concentrated industries, a small number of companies would be able to cut back production and increase prices above the competitive level. Hence, products will be sold at a price that is higher than what would be the case under conditions of perfect competition, and fewer products will be offered on the market than would be efficient.

Monetary Economics 31, at 63; R. Levine and S. Zervos, 'Stock Markets, Banks, and Economic Growth', (1998) 88 *American Economic Review* 537, at 538; P. Rousseau and P. Wachtel, 'Equity Markets and Growth: Cross-Country Evidence on Timing and Outcomes 1980–95', (2000) 24 *Journal of Banking and Finance* 1933, at 1955–6.

91 R. Ram, 'Financial Development and Economic Growth: Additional Evidence', (1999) 35 *Journal of Development Studies* 164, at 166. Ram states, 'The preponderance of evidence thus suggests a negligible or weakly negative association between economic growth and a prime proxy for financial development [namely, the size of financial intermediaries, expressed by the ration of liquid liabilities to GDP].'

92 M. Manning, 'Finance Causes Growth: Can We Be So Sure?', (2003) 3 *Contributions to Macroeconomics* Art. 12, at 16–17.

93 The so-called S-C-P paradigm was developed by Mason: E. Mason, 'Price and Production Policies in Large-Scale Enterprises', (1939) 29 *American Economic Review* 61.

90. Besanko and Thakor as well as Guzman have translated this paradigm of competition to the banking industry. In a market that is characterized by a large number of banks, banks will offer credit at the lowest price (interest rate). Moreover, since banks compete for deposits, they will offer the highest deposit interest rate that is competitively possible (provided that no interest rate ceilings are imposed by the government). In this manner, competition among banks will contribute to economic growth: banks fulfil their intermediation function and channel funds from economic agents with excess resources (e.g. households) to agents with financing needs (e.g. companies). A more competitive banking market enables companies to have easier access to external financing. In contrast, in a market that is characterized by a small number of banks, these banks could exploit their market power and set prices for credit at levels above the competitive level. Hence less credit will be offered than is optimal. Banks in concentrated industries will also offer lower interest rates on deposits.[94]

4.1.2.2 Market power in markets for banking services

91. Nevertheless, some authors pointed to the specific character of banking activity to show that limiting the number of banks in a market and thus restricting competition may be desirable in order to increase the quality of lending.

92. *Allocative efficiency* would require restriction of bank entry so that banks would have some power in the market. This is related to the specific problem of banks knowing the risk attached to potential borrowers (see above, para. 19). The screening of potential borrowers is costly. However, once one bank has screened the borrower, competing banks will free-ride on the screening efforts. Banks particularly face uncertainty with regard to the quality of new borrowers. A bank may then decide to raise the interest rate to compensate for uncertainty and to cover the costs of screening the potential borrower. However, this leads to sub-optimal allocation of credit in the market.

93. Petersen and Rajan have explained that banks may nevertheless be willing to grant a loan to the young borrower at lower rates, provided that

[94] D. Besanko and A. Thakor, 'Banking Deregulation: Allocational Consequences of Relaxing Entry Barriers', (1992) 16 *Journal of Banking and Finance* 909, at 911, and A. Guzman, 'Bank Structure, Capital Accumulation, and Growth: A Simple Macroeconomic Model', (2000) 16 *Economic Theory* 421, at 450–1.

the banks can share in the future profits of the firm. Banks thus try to build up a long-term relationship with the firm. Nonetheless, such 'relationship lending' only works if the bank has sufficient market power. As soon as one bank has granted a loan to the young borrower, this is a signal to other market players that screening by the bank showed that the quality of the borrower is sufficiently high. In competitive markets, other banks will take advantage of this information and will be prepared to offer these borrowers loans on later occasions at lower rates. This 'business stealing' effect will lead banks to refrain from engaging in relationship lending and rather focus on transactional lending, to the disadvantage of young borrowers. Only when banks have some market power will they be able to recover the costs that the bank had run up to screen the borrower the first time.[95]

94. Market power may be desirable not only for allocative efficiency, but also for *productive efficiency*. Hughes, Mester and Moon have argued that banks with market power and thus of a significant size would be able to provide credit at a minimum cost, since they would realize economies of scale.[96] Nevertheless, there is no clear evidence that productive efficiency can be better achieved by large banks with market power or, rather, by banks in competitive markets.[97] Rather, productive efficiency, realized by economies of scale, may decline once a certain bank size has been reached.[98]

95. Boot and Thakor have challenged the theory that banks need market power before they are prepared to engage in relationship lending and efficient allocation of credit. They argue that competition between banks in fact encourages banks to build long-term, high-quality service relationships with their clients to make them stand out from competing banks. Banks can thus avoid pure price competition to some extent.[99]

[95] M. Petersen and R. Rajan, 'The Effect of Credit Market Competition on Lending Relationships', (1995) 110 *Quarterly Journal of Economics* 407, at 440. Petersen and Rajan show empirically that 'young firms in concentrated markets receive more institutional finance than do similar firms in competitive markets' (ibid., at 439).

[96] J. Hughes, L. Mester and C. Moon, 'Are Scale Economies in Banking Elusive or Illusive? Evidence Obtained by Incorporating Capital Structure and Risk-Taking into Models of Bank Production', (2001) 25 *Journal of Banking and Finance* 2169, at 2200.

[97] C. Northcott, 'Competition in Banking: A Review of the Literature', Bank of Canada Working Paper 2004–24, June 2004, available at www.bankofcanada.ca/en/res/wp/2004/wp04–24.pdf, at 10.

[98] CPB Netherlands Bureau for Economic Policy Analysis, above n. 13, at 26–8.

[99] A. Boot and A. Thakor, 'Can Relationship Banking Survive Competition?', (2000) 55 *Journal of Finance* 679, at 681, 696. See also R. Hauswald and R. Marquez, 'Relationship

Empirical research by Degryse and Ongena suggests that interbank competition and relationship lending are not necessarily in conflict and thus confirms the predictions by Boot and Thakor. They find that 'Fiercer interbank competition results in more relationship banking (in most observed cases).'[100]

96. The studies that examine the link between bank concentration and economic growth do this on the basis of data relating to the market structure. Claessens and Laeven have pointed out that the market structure is not necessarily a good measure for competition.[101] Even in a market with a small number of banks, competition may be fierce.[102] Governments should thus create *contestable* markets (i.e. markets where the position of incumbent banks can be challenged by competitors, even if only a small number of banks are present in the market) rather than restrict competition to enable banks to maintain their market power.

97. In sum, there is evidence that competition in the banking sector leads to higher quantity of credit at a lower price. Better functioning financial intermediation will lead to more economic growth. The studies that found that more concentrated markets lead to better access to capital for young industries (because only banks with market power would be willing to engage in relationship lending) seem now contradicted by other studies that show that market structure is not a good predictor for competition.

98. Nonetheless, the banking sector has as a specific characteristic that individual bank failures (caused by excessively risky bank activities) can spill over to other banks, to the entire financial sector and, eventually, even to the real economy (above paras. 52–61). Therefore it is also necessary to consider the impact of competition on financial stability. Claessens and Laeven have noted in their study: 'It could be that some market power increases financial stability and thereby influences industrial growth positively over long periods.'[103]

Banking, Loan Specialization and Competition', Wharton Paper, February 2000, available at http://fic.wharton.upenn.edu/fic/papers/00/0013.pdf, at 16.

[100] See the empirical research by H. Degryse and S. Ongena, 'The Impact of Competition on Bank Orientation', (2007) 16 *Journal of Financial Intermediation* 399, at 421.

[101] S. Claessens and L. Laeven, 'Financial Dependence, Bank Sector Competition, and Economic Growth', (2005) 3 *Journal of the European Economic Association* 179, at 180–1, 183. See also Northcott, above n. 97, at 23.

[102] Claessens and Laeven, above n. 101, at 192.

[103] Ibid., at 182.

4.1.3 Competition and financial stability

99. Many authors have argued that competition in the banking sector should be restricted for reasons of *financial stability*. As discussed above, only banks with market power may be willing to bear the costs of screening borrowers. In markets with a large number of competing banks, banks will be eager to be the first to lend to a high-quality borrower. However, because of the pressures of competition, banks will have fewer incentives to monitor well and thus may in fact select risky borrowers to which to lend.[104]

100. Keeley has explained that large banks with market power have a high 'charter value' (i.e. the present value of future profits of their banking activities). Bank managers would make a trade-off when considering risky behaviour and balance the benefits of such behaviour against the losses of the charter value if the bank should fail. Competition reduces the charter value of banks, and thus more risk-taking behaviour would be the result.[105]

101. Allen and Gale have added that in a perfectly competitive market, interbank lending will not provide the necessary liquidity to banks to avoid the failure of an individual bank spilling over to other banks. They note that in the case of perfect competition, 'each bank is small, acts as a price taker and assumes its actions have no effect on the equilibrium, [hence] no bank has an incentive to provide liquidity to the troubled bank'.[106] Therefore, they conclude, 'A model of an imperfectly competitive interbank market may . . . be more stable than the case where there is perfect competition.'[107]

102. The theories mentioned suggest that governments must make a *trade-off* between competition and financial stability. Achieving more financial stability would be achieved by restricting competition in the bank sector.

103. Northcott concluded that optimal market structures for banking involve a limited number of banks. However, this would not necessarily

[104] S. Shaffer, 'The Winner's Curse in Banking', (1998) 7 *Journal of Financial Intermediation* 359, at 360. See also M. Lehner and M. Schnitzer, 'Entry of Foreign Banks and Their Impact on Host Countries', (2008) 36 *Journal of Comparative Economics* 430, at 432.

[105] M. Keeley, 'Deposit Insurance, Risk, and Market Power in Banking', (1990) 80 *American Economic Review* 1183, at 1185–6.

[106] F. Allen and D. Gale, 'Competition and Financial Stability', 36 *Journal of Money*, (2004) *Credit and Banking* 453, at 477.

[107] Ibid., at 478. They refer to a model by Saez and Shi that argues that a small number of banks may be better at coordinating their actions and thus provide liquidity to the bank in trouble. L. Saez and X. Shi, 'Liquidity Pools, Risk Sharing and Financial Contagion', (2004) 25 *Journal of Financial Services Research* 5.

imply restricted competition. In her view, markets should be contestable: entry barriers and activity restrictions should be reduced.[108] At the same time, she recognizes that market power provides incentives for banks to behave prudently. Nonetheless, 'regulation can help ensure that banks behave prudently even in a competitive market'.[109] Hence there is a role for regulation to increase the banks' opportunity costs for failing (in line with the charter value argument). In her view, this would be realized through capital requirements, disclosure rules and risk-based deposit insurance.[110]

104. If there is a trade-off between competition (contestability) and stability, the question is *how regulation can influence this trade-off*. The European and international processes determine to what extent the member states of the European Union and the WTO members still can make this trade-off between competition and stability.

4.2 Internationalization

105. The European and international liberalization projects aim to achieve the benefits of competition in the market for banking services on a supranational scale. They seek to open up the market of a country to banks from other countries. Liberalization of banking services markets thus involves enhanced competition between domestic banks, on the one hand, and openness to *foreign* banking services, on the other hand. The benefits of enhancing competition between domestic and foreign banks are generally the same as for enhancing domestic competition. However, internationalization of banking leads also to some specific benefits. At the same time, opening up domestic markets to the activities of foreign banks also gives rise to specific concerns with regard to financial stability. Regulation and supervision by national authorities need to take these concerns into account.

4.2.1 Specific benefits of cross-border banking

4.2.1.1 Efficiency

106. Competition in the market for banking services may lead to better financial intermediation and thus to a higher quantity of credit offered at

[108] She argues that 'the goal may be not to eliminate market power, but to facilitate an environment that promotes competitive behaviour (contestability)', and concludes that 'an assessment of contestability in the banking sector can be very difficult and is likely to be specific to a particular country at a particular time.' Northcott, above n. 97, at 30.

[109] Ibid., at 18. [110] Ibid., at 30.

a lower price. Hence, if competition is further intensified due to foreign bank entry this should have further positive effects on the efficiency of the financial system of the host country. Levine has argued that foreign bank entry 'will indirectly force improvements in the domestic financial system by pressuring existing institutions to improve'.[111]

107. Because domestic banks are required to become more productive and reduce their overhead expenses in order to face foreign competition, and because the presence of foreign banks in the market leads to technology transfer ('spillovers') to domestic banks, domestic banks would also become more efficient.[112] Furthermore, foreign bank entry would also lead to a higher quality and greater availability of banking services. Foreign banks could introduce new financial instruments in the host market.[113]

108. Further, when foreign banks enter a market, companies and individuals may get easier access to capital.[114] Some authors have indeed argued that foreign bank entry provides access to foreign capital for investors in the host market.[115] However, it is unclear to what extent such foreign capital provision is a stable factor, especially in the face of a crisis.

4.2.1.2 Financial stability

109. Some authors argued that foreign bank entry also contributes to financial stability in the market. Foreign banks have sometimes entered new countries as the domestic banks in these countries were about to fail,

[111] R. Levine, 'Foreign Banks, Financial Development, and Economic Growth', in C. Barfield (ed.), *International Financial Markets: Harmonization versus Competition* (Washington, DC: AEI Press, 1996) 224–55, at 238. See also A. Demirgüç-Kunt, R. Levine and H. Min, 'Opening to Foreign Banks: Issues of Stability, Efficiency, and Growth', in S. Lee (ed.), *The Implications of Globalization of World Financial Markets* (Seoul: Bank of Korea, 1998) 83–105, at 91.

[112] It is disputed to what extent the increased efficiency is the result of intensified competition or of spillovers between foreign entrants and domestic banks. See L. Goldberg, 'Financial Sector FDI and Host Countries: New and Old Lessons', (March 2007) *Federal Reserve Bank of New York Economic Policy Review* 1, at 5; and Lehner and Schnitzer, above n. 104, at 442 and 444.

[113] Levine, above n. 111, at 240; and Demirgüç-Kunt, Levine and Min, above n. 111, at 91.

[114] Committee on the Global Financial System, 'Foreign Direct Investment in the Financial Sector. Experiences in Asia, Central and Eastern Europe and Latin America', Bank for International Settlements, Basel, June 2005, 1.

[115] See, e.g., S. Claessens, 'Competitive Implications of Cross-Border Banking', World Bank Policy Research Working Paper No. 3854, February 2006, 8.

and the foreign banks were willing to recapitalize them.[116] A foreign bank that enters a market could also lead to more risk diversification. The risk an international bank runs is spread out over different countries.

110. Goldberg argued that foreign banks would engage less in procyclical finance, as they rely less on domestic deposits for their funding than do domestic banks. In good times, loan demand increases rapidly and domestic banks will respond by offering more loans. Many deposits are available to fund the loans. In times of crisis, domestic banks will be reluctant to lend, leading to greater difficulties for companies and individuals in obtaining financing. This in turn exacerbates the local crisis. However, the presence of foreign banks may help to 'smooth' these cycles, since they are not dependent on local deposits.

111. Finally, Levine argued that foreign bank entry provides incentives to the host country authorities to develop their own supervisory and legal framework.[117] Both domestic and foreign banks may push for such regulatory reform. Domestic banks will only be able to compete with the foreign banks if they are able to monitor their clients better, hence they may request better accounting standards and disclosure requirements. Foreign banks will also support these reforms because they will want to have access to the same information as the domestic banks.[118]

112. Besides providing evidence with regard to the efficiency-related benefits of foreign entry, some empirical studies have shown a positive correlation between foreign bank entry and stability. On the basis of a cross-country study, Demirgüç-Kunt, Levine and Min concluded in 1998 that 'the data suggest that foreign banks tend to lower the probability of a banking crisis'.[119] In their above-mentioned study, however, Barth, Caprio and Levine stated firmly that limitations on foreign entry and ownership are, on the contrary, associated with *more* banking system fragility.[120]

113. There is thus some limited empirical evidence that foreign bank entry is positively correlated with more financial stability. Nonetheless,

[116] This was, for instance, the case in Argentina, where participation was liberalized but foreign entry restricted. Committee on the Global Financial System, above n. 114, at 13.

[117] Levine, above n. 111, at 236 and see also Demirgüç-Kunt, Levine and Min, above n. 111, at 86.

[118] Goldberg, above n. 112, at 10–11.

[119] Demirgüç-Kunt, Levine and Min, above n. 111, at 90. See also Claessens, above n. 115, at 161, stating that the effects are 'generally found to be positive'.

[120] Barth, Caprio and Levine, above n. 30, at 223.

many of the authors referred to stress that foreign bank entry should be accompanied by appropriate regulation and supervisory capacities in the host country.[121] This is an important element to be taken into account when European and international processes seek to intensify international competition between banks. There are indeed specific concerns with regard to international banking that go beyond the already mentioned concerns with regard to intensified competition in banking services markets.

4.2.2 *Specific concerns relating to international banking*

4.2.2.1 Cherry-picking

114. A number of specific concerns arise when foreign banks enter host markets. One such concern is that foreign-owned banks will pick out the best companies in the host country to lend to, leaving the weaker ones to the domestic banks. This 'cherry-picking' or 'cream-skimming' by foreign banks implies that, even if some borrowers have improved access to international financing, smaller entrepreneurs have in fact less access to finance than before the market was opened up.[122] In contrast, Clarke, Cull and Martínez Pería have argued, on the basis of an empirical study, that because of the intensified competition in the market for large corporations, banks will turn to the market for lending to small and medium-size enterprises and retail banking, thus leading more borrowers to have access to capital.[123]

4.2.2.2 Financial instability

115. Most of the concerns with regard to foreign entry relate to the threat to financial stability. It is feared that financial instability will increase, especially in countries where prudential regulation and supervision is

[121] Levine, above n. 111, at 248; Demirgüç-Kunt, Levine and Min, above n. 111, at 90; and S. Claessens, A. Demirgüç-Kunt and H. Huizinga, 'How Does Foreign Entry Affect Domestic Banking Markets?', (2001) 25 *Journal of Banking and Finance* 891, at 909.

[122] E. Detragiache, T. Tressel and P. Gupta, 'Foreign Banks in Poor Countries: Theory and Evidence', (2008) 63 *Journal of Finance* 2123, at 2151.

[123] G. Clarke, R. Cull and M. Martínez Pería, 'Foreign Bank Participation and Access to Credit Across Firms in Developing Countries', (2006) 34 *Journal of Comparative Economics* 774, at 790. Not only will domestic banks lend more to small and medium-size companies, but foreign banks also will move to these markets. R. De Haas and I. Naaborg, 'Foreign Banks in Transition Countries: To Whom Do They Lend and How Are They Financed?', (2006) 15 *Financial Markets, Institutions and Instruments* 159, at 174–5.

not well established.[124] The presence of foreign-owned banks in a host country creates links with other countries. Hence, if one of the countries where the international bank is active suffers from a crisis, shocks may spill over to other countries where the parent bank also has activities.

116. Foreign entry also involves the risk that new financial technologies (e.g. securitization) are introduced prematurely, as domestic banks do not have the required skills to use them in a prudent manner.[125]

117. Addressing these concerns requires careful monitoring by the supervisory authorities in the host country and the home country of an international bank. As will be discussed hereinafter, such activity is indeed complicated because the bank operates in different jurisdictions.

4.2.2.3 Homogenization of financial markets

118. Finally, cross-border banking may also lead to the homogenization of financial markets. Markets are only liquid if they are characterized by a large number of participants with different goals and expectations (above para. 80). Herding creates systemic instability.[126] The fact that market players all have the same information, disclosed on the basis of international financial reporting standards and have the same approach to risk, guided by international standards on capital ratios, reduces heterogeneous behaviour in the market and thus makes the market less liquid.

119. The internationalization of banking markets further contributes to homogeneity in financial markets, as banks are no longer locked into separate geographical markets (comparable to the reduction in segmented services markets when banks were allowed to engage in investment activities at the same time as commercial banking activity). In order to be able to address the risk of all banks reacting in the same manner at the moment problems occur with one bank in one country, banking supervisors need to have a good understanding of the market and the behaviour of banks in other countries where their own banks also have operations. The dependence of supervisors on cooperation with supervisors in other countries makes very acute the risk of liquidity drying up when all reactions in the market are homogeneous.

[124] A. Demirgüç-Kunt and E. Detragiache, 'Financial Liberalization and Financial Fragility', World Bank Policy Research Working Paper No. 1917, May 1998, 10.

[125] Claessens, above n. 115, at 8.

[126] See Persaud, above n. 77 and accompanying text.

4.2.2.4 Prudential supervision

120. Addressing these concerns requires appropriate prudential supervision. However, this becomes more difficult when banks operate in different countries. Home and host supervisors may not have the correct incentives to ensure that cross-border systemic risk is prevented. Also, when a bank faces difficulties and there is danger that these problems will spill over to other banks, effective intervention is complicated by the fact that protective competences are spread over different national supervisors.

121. With regard to the supervisory competences, when a bank operates across borders, different banking supervisors will have an interest in the soundness and prudence of the bank's activities. The supervisor of the country where the bank has been authorized (home country) will be concerned about the soundness of the parent bank, since a failure of the parent will affect the economy in the country of the supervisor. Nevertheless, the activities of the branches and subsidiaries of the parent in other countries are of relevance for the home supervisor. It is then important that the supervisors of the host countries where the foreign bank has its branches or subsidiaries provide the necessary information on these activities to the home country supervisor. If these activities are not very significant from the perspective of the host supervisor, its incentives to monitor carefully and provide information to the home supervisor may be limited.[127]

122. However, it is also possible that the host countries have a strong interest in the soundness of the local branches or subsidiaries of this foreign bank as well as in the parent, since the parent may need to provide the necessary support to the local branches (and sometimes also subsidiaries) in the host country. If the parent engages in risky activities in its home country or in the other countries where it is active, this may affect the situation of the local branches and subsidiaries in the host country. The activities of the parent in the home country may be negligible when compared with its foreign activities in the host country. Furthermore, a local branch or subsidiary may be of systemic importance in the host country, whereas it represents only a very small share in the entire banking group.[128] The

[127] D. Mayes and Y. Vesala, 'On the Problems of Home Country Control', Bank of Finland Discussion Papers 20/98, 23 September 1998, 18–19.

[128] P. Bednarski and G. Bielicki, 'Home and Host Supervisors' Relations from a Host Supervisor's Perspective', in G. Caprio, D. Evanoff and G. Kaufman (eds.), *Cross-Border Banking. Regulatory Challenges* (New Jersey: World Scientific, 2006) 211–29, at 213.

host country may then have a greater interest in supervising the bank than the home country.

123. The critical issue is thus whether the supervisors in the host and home countries will be able and willing to supervise sufficiently the entire activity of the bank and thus take into account the cross-border impact of problems. Both practical limitations (limited resources and legal constraints on obtaining information from other supervisors abroad) and incentive problems may complicate the supervision of cross-border banking.

124. The distinction between cross-border banking by means of branches (and mere cross-border supply), on the one hand, and by means of subsidiaries, on the other hand is relevant in this respect. A host supervisor may feel that it has less impact on a local branch of a foreign bank (without separate legal personality or capitalization) than on a local subsidiary (with separate legal personality, management and capital). The distinction between branches and subsidiaries creates problems, because the law draws such a distinction and may attach specific consequences to it.[129] However, the practical business organization of a banking group may in fact make this legal distinction largely irrelevant.[130] Moreover, it is always possible that applicable laws require that branches comply with very similar requirements to those of subsidiaries (e.g. separate capital), making the distinction additionally irrelevant.[131]

125. Even if foreign *branches* are part of a single legal entity with the parent, the home supervisor of the parent bank (which has licensed the bank) may not be sufficiently interested in the soundness of the foreign

[129] This is for instance the case in EU law, where CRD IV extends the 'single passport' only to cross-border operations by means of cross-border supply or by means of branches. See below para. 634.

[130] It has therefore been argued that the distinction made in EU law between subsidiaries and branches is an 'artificial divide', except for the fact that it is easier in case of difficulties to let a subsidiary fail and let the other parts of the group exist. In contrast, this is not possible when the group operates through branches. D. Mayes and P. Granlund, 'Polar Approaches to Regulating Cross-Border Banking: Nordic and Antipodean Routes to Financial Stability', (2008) 9 *European Business Organization Law Review* 63, at 75.

[131] Goldberg, Sweeney and Wihlborg refer to the case of the United States, where branches are subject to the rules for deposit insurance and the assets are ring-fenced to cover claims in the United States. L. Goldberg, R. Sweeney and C. Wihlborg, 'From Subsidiary to Branch Organization of International Banks: New Challenges and Opportunities for Regulators', LEFIC Working Paper, 14 November 2005, available at http://research.cbs.dk/research/from_subsidiary_to_branch_organization_of_international_banks(12824)/, 10.

activities and foreign branches of the bank it is supervising. If a foreign branch were to experience difficulties, the home supervisor may feel that the adverse consequences of the home market will not be sufficiently serious to merit intervention.[132] Still, the host supervisor may be concerned about the negative impact of the problems experienced by the local branch. The host supervisor may also be concerned that it cannot obtain the necessary information from the home supervisor about the soundness of the parent in the home country. Branches indeed have no separate legal personality and are not incorporated in the host country. The information they maintain on their activities may in fact be located mainly with the parent. Nevertheless, the host supervisor has no jurisdiction in the home country of the bank for obtaining information or carrying out acts of investigation. Similarly, when problems emerge with the branches in the host country, the host country supervisor may inform the home country authority insufficiently because the host country has limited responsibilities with regard to the branches.[133]

126. In contrast, when a bank undertakes cross-border operations by means of *subsidiaries*, these subsidiaries will need to be incorporated and authorized in the host country. The host country has thus in principle more impact on the activities of the subsidiary. However, the activities of the parent company as well as those of the other subsidiaries of the parent (possibly in other countries) may pose a threat to the local subsidiary. Problems with the parent in the home country may lead the parent to withdraw support for the foreign subsidiaries. Moreover, it is also possible that home supervisors may not consider the bank to be of systemic importance from their home country perspective, whereas the subsidiary is of systemic importance in the host country.[134] Still, to protect its reputation, the parent of the bank may indeed decide to support the local subsidiary. However, the parent may also decide that the costs of

[132] Schüler has examined the incentive problems of home and host supervisors in the EU market for banking services in a principal–agent framework. M. Schüler, 'Incentive Problems in Banking Supervision – The European Case', Zentrum für Europäische Wirtschaftsforschung Discussion Paper No. 03–62, November 2003, available at http://opus.zbw-kiel.de/volltexte/2004/1492/pdf/dp0362.pdf, at 16. See also E. Kane, 'Confronting Divergent Interests in Cross-Country Regulatory Arrangements', in G. Caprio, D. Evanoff and G. Kaufman (eds.), *Cross-Border Banking. Regulatory Challenges* (New Jersey: World Scientific, 2006) 265–85, at 267.

[133] Schüler, above n. 132, at 16.

[134] Bednarski and Bielicki, above n. 128, at 216, referring to the failure of a healthy Hong Kong subsidiary of BCCI because of the problems of the parent bank (ibid., at 216, n. 2).

support are much higher than the reputational costs.[135] Therefore the host country supervisor may want to obtain information on the activities of the parent and the other subsidiaries. There is a further reason why a foreign bank presence by means of subsidiaries (instead of branches) may not always be of comfort to host country supervisors, even if the separate legal status of such subsidiaries may so suggest. The distinction between branches and subsidiaries is in fact becoming blurred. Since banking groups increasingly concentrate functions such as risk management at the parent level, a dichotomy is created between the legal and economic status of a subsidiary. The host supervisor may thus find it difficult to interact effectively with the subsidiary to ensure local financial stability.

4.3 Conclusions on the liberalization of banking services

127. In this chapter we have examined the economic theory and evidence relating to the second part of the balance between stability and efficiency.

128. We considered the competitive paradigm in the market for banking services. Economic literature argues that there exists a trade-off between, on the one hand, intensifying competition to increase the quantity of credit in the market and, on the other hand, allowing banks to obtain sufficient market power to make it profitable to screen borrowers and allocate credit in an efficient way such that the quality of credit improves. Some authors conclude from this that the competitive paradigm does not fit with the characteristics of the banking services market and thus that governments should limit competition in this market.

129. We then turned to the link between competition and financial instability. There is indeed a trade-off to be made between competition and stability. Several authors have argued that markets where banks operate with a certain degree of market power are desirable. However, since competition also produces beneficial effects, one should not restrict competition, but rather, through regulation and supervision, seek to

[135] J. Dermine, 'European Banking Integration and the Societas Europaea: From Host-Country to Home-Country Control', in G. Caprio, D. Evanoff and G. Kaufman (eds.), *Cross-Border Banking. Regulatory Challenges* (New Jersey: World Scientific, 2006) 49–63, at 58.

avoid its negative effects. Hence there is a role for regulation to make the banks' opportunity costs for failing higher.

130. The important trade-off between efficiency and stability is influenced by European and international processes that seek to intensify *international* competition between banks. In the final part of the current chapter we considered whether the goal of these processes – improving efficiency by means of intensifying international banking competition – also fits with economic theory and evidence. Evidence exists that foreign bank entry leads to a more efficient domestic banking industry in the host country. Nonetheless, many of the cited studies stress that liberalization should proceed in step with appropriate regulation and supervision in the host country.

5

Conclusion to Part I

131. In this first part, the nature of banking, regulation and liberalization was discussed. Banks offer a solution for the market failures that exist when entities with excess savings try to reach an agreement with entities with funding needs. Because of information asymmetries between lenders and borrowers, it is difficult to reach an agreement, and capital could be allocated in a sub-optimal way. Banks monitor the borrowers to which funds are lent, create liquidity in markets by channelling the funds between savers and borrowers, and ensure risk management.

132. Next, we turned to the economic literature that clarifies the balance between stability and efficiency in the market for banking services. Information asymmetries between banks and clients can give rise to bank failures and thus impose costs on clients and investors. However, a bank failure will often also create social costs: because of contagion, bank failures may spill over to the entire financial sector and even the real economy. A financial crisis could thus be the consequence of an individual bank failure. This distinguishes banking from other services sectors, and hence a strong case can be made in favour of regulating the market for banking services.

133. Nonetheless, much disagreement exists on what form regulation should take in order to correct the mentioned market failures. Regulators should be especially careful to avoid bank regulation distorting market discipline. At the same time, regulation that is based on market discipline has its limits and would not always be sufficient to ensure stability.

134. The European and international projects with regard to liberalizing trade in banking services seek to intensify international competition in the banking services market. The traditional competitive paradigm suggests that competition improves efficiency, since it would lead to increased efficiency in channelling funds from savers to investors, and eventually to economic growth. However, a number of studies suggest that some market power is required to achieve efficiency.

135. The impact of intensified competition on financial stability was also considered. Economic models and empirical evidence on the relationship between competition and stability are far from unambiguous; it seems that a trade-off must be made between efficiency and stability. Regulation may influence this trade-off: if regulation can raise the opportunity cost for banks engaging in risky activities, the benefits of competition can be achieved while at the same time ensuring financial stability. Many questions exist with regard to the appropriate set-up of regulation to ensure financial stability. Therefore governments need to define a balance between the regulation and liberalization of their market for banking services.

136. The global financial crisis has shown that the failure of governments to get the regulatory set-up correct, and thus to correct the negative consequences of competition, can lead to enormous costs. On the other hand, restricting competition also leads to efficiency losses. The European and international processes we discuss hereafter aim at removing barriers to trade in banking services and thus intensifying international competition. Hence they seek to identify protectionist measures. Moreover, to a certain degree (the European project more than the international), they also seek to reduce regulatory diversity and divergent supervisory assessments insofar as this hampers international competition. Thus the European and international projects limit the possibility of states determining with total freedom their regulatory and supervisory approaches in the banking services market.

PART II

The international approach to liberalization of trade in banking services

6

Introduction to Part II

> While the global economic crisis led to the sharpest decline of trade in more than seventy years, G20 countries chose to keep markets open to the opportunities that trade and investment offer. It was the right choice.
>
> G20 Toronto Summit Declaration, 26–27 June 2010, para. 35

> Trade, or more specifically financial services liberalization, was neither a villain nor a cause of this crisis but a casualty. As you all know, in the world of the GATS, 'liberalization' is essentially about opening specified sectors to competition on a non-discriminatory basis. It does not mean deregulation.
>
> Pascal Lamy, speech to the Global Services Summit, Washington DC, 14 October 2009

137. The central question of this book is as follows: to what extent do the international and EU projects limit WTO members or EU member states in determining the balance between stability and efficiency in their domestic market for banking services? On the basis of the discussion of the economic literature on banking regulation and liberalization in Part I, we concluded that governments need to make a trade-off between efficiency and stability. If governments want to ensure financial stability in their markets, but at the same time do not want to lose the efficiency gains of international competition in banking, they must adopt banking regulation and supervisory practices that address the possible negative consequences of competition. One can only blame European and international processes for contributing to financial instability if they actually restrict the right of the EU member states or WTO members to define this balance between regulation and liberalization and, if they do indeed restrict this right, fail to put alternative regulation and supervision in place that compensates for this loss of regulatory and supervisory capacity. At the same time, the benefits of international competition can only be achieved if the ability of the EU member states or WTO members to adopt measures that are protectionist is restricted.

138. In Part II we examine the extent to which international law, and especially the GATS, restrict the national authorities in applying their own banking regulations, on the one hand, and making their own supervisory assessments, on the other hand. In Part III, we turn to EU law. Two questions will be addressed. First, with regard to regulation: can individual WTO members apply their own regulations that are possibly stricter than the regulations of other members to banks and banking services from other members? Second, with regard to supervision: can members freely decide whether a bank or banking service complies with the applicable rules and can they intervene in case of non-compliance?

139. The GATS is the only international agreement containing legally binding obligations to liberalize trade in services. However, the GATS only determines what WTO members *cannot* do. It does not involve the re-regulation of markets. Such elements are developed in the form of international standards or principles by the Basel Committee on Banking Supervision. These standards or principles are merely recommendations and are not legally binding. Therefore, in examining the extent to which governments are restricted by the international project to determine the trade-off between competition and stability in the market for banking services, the focus is mainly on the obligations and exceptions in the GATS. However, the standards and principles of the Basel Committee can play a role in the application and interpretation of the GATS.

140. The GATS was concluded on 15 April 1994 as part of the broader 'Uruguay Package' that established the WTO and entered into force on 1 January 1995. The GATS is an ambitious multilateral endeavour to liberalize trade in services. It has a very broad scope of application and clearly applies also to financial services. The eagerness to secure significant liberalization of financial services is apparent from the fact that the negotiators agreed to negotiate further after the end of the Uruguay Round. A specific deal on liberalization commitments for financial services was only reached in 1997.

141. Unlike trade in goods, trade in services is not affected by border tariffs but is restricted by the web of regulations adopted by WTO members. These regulations not only concern the service itself, but most often focus on the supplier of the service. Therefore disciplines on the domestic regulation of services are today a major point of discussion within the WTO. However, the GATS has the objective of expanding trade in services only through progressive liberalization. Because there are no negotiations on tariff reductions for services and the regulation of services and service suppliers (especially in the field of banking) is so sensitive, it was impossible to eliminate outright barriers to trade in services. The most that could be achieved were provisions that can be used as a tool to determine whether regulation constitutes an unacceptable barrier to trade in services. Each individual WTO member can define the extent to which these provisions apply to its services sectors. Some of these provisions are based on discrimination, as a proxy to determine protectionism. Other provisions go beyond discrimination and impose a more intrusive test on regulation.

142. The GATS thus contains separate provisions with different techniques for liberalizing trade in services. The delineation of the scope and content of the different provisions in the GATS is far from clear. In trying to define the precise normative scope and content of the different provisions, one should take into account the structure of the GATS, with its different levels (intensity) of scrutiny and specific exceptions. The discussion that follows will show that the GATS strongly adheres to the starting point that the host country has the right to regulate and supervise banking activity in its market, even if this involves banking activity by foreign banks. At present, the GATS only prohibits WTO members from taking a series of specific market access restrictions, prohibits WTO members from discriminating when adopting measures and requires them to adhere to due process requirements. The GATS encourages mutual recognition, but contains no obligation for WTO members to recognize the equivalence of each other's banking regulation or supervision.

143. Liberalization by means of *prohibitions* for host countries from applying certain measures with regard to trade in banking services ('negative integration') quickly faces its limits. Many regulatory measures pursue perfectly acceptable objectives and, provided that they comply with the obligations in the GATS, can be maintained. This is especially the case for financial services. We shall examine the broad exception for prudential regulation that exists in the GATS. Still, even if a measure complies with the obligations of the GATS, or is exempted on the basis of one of the exceptions, this may still constitute a barrier to trade. The mere existence of regulatory diversity makes it more difficult for foreign service suppliers to provide their services in another market than for domestic suppliers in this market. *Recognition* of the financial service regulation and supervisory assessments of other WTO members by one member may provide one solution to this problem. *Harmonization* of regulation, also called 'positive integration' is another. However, the potential for harmonization through the WTO seems limited. Still, interaction with other international standards may prove useful in this regard. The principles and regulatory standards developed by the Basel Committee on Banking Supervision can play a role in the application of the obligations of the GATS.

144. The structure of Part II is as follows. We first address the relevant legal sources that set out the international approach to regulation and liberalization of banking (Chapter 7). As indicated, the main source is the GATS. However, we also discuss the supervisory principles and regulatory standards that are developed by the Basel Committee on Banking Supervision. Thereafter, the degree to which the GATS restricts the right of the WTO members to regulate (Chapter 8) and supervise (Chapter 9) the market for banking services is examined. For both regulation and supervision, we shall consider what measures are within the scope of the GATS and examine the obligations and exceptions that are relevant for these measures. In this regard, the standards and principles of the Basel Committee play a role.

7

Sources of international banking liberalization and regulation

145. This chapter provides an overview of the different sources relevant to international trade in banking services. We examine the GATS and its annexes (the main sources of legally binding international obligations for liberalizing trade in banking services), on the one hand, and the principles and standards developed by the Basel Committee on Banking Supervision (the main source of non-binding harmonization of banking regulation and supervisory principles), on the other hand.

7.1 The GATS and its annexes: relevant sources and further negotiations

7.1.1 Uruguay Round documents

146. The sources of WTO law relevant to banking services extend beyond the GATS in a strict sense (the GATS framework agreement).[136] Important additional sources are the GATS Annex on Article II Exemptions,[137] which specifies the conditions under which WTO members are exempted from the obligation in Article II:1,[138] and the Annex on Financial Services[139] that sets out definitions (especially a broad definition of 'financial service') as well as

[136] General Agreement on Trade in Services, Annex 1B to the Agreement Establishing the World Trade Organization, done at Marrakesh on 15 April 1994, UNTS No. 31874. The text is available in WTO, *The Results of the Uruguay Round of Multilateral Trade Negotiations. The Legal Texts* (Cambridge University Press, 1999) 284.

[137] WTO, above n. 136, at 308.

[138] The WTO members were indeed allowed, on accession, to inscribe certain exceptions to the MFN obligation in their list of MFN exemptions.

[139] WTO, above n. 136, at 310. The first drafts of the Annex on Financial Services were elaborated by the so-called 'Fu Lung' group, an informal group of negotiators who met in a restaurant of that name. This group consisted of major OECD countries, some Latin American countries and the SEACEN countries (a collaboration between South East Asian Central Banks). The drafts were later taken up by the Working Group on Trade in Financial Services and thereafter by the 'Sectoral Ad-hoc Working Group' (combining the work of all the sectoral working groups). It became clear that the developing countries

a number of rules specifically for the financial services sector. The Annex on Financial Services indeed adds two specific exceptions to the GATS for measures that are taken for 'prudential reasons' and for measures that protect confidential information. It also provides a financial service-specific definition of 'services supplied in the exercise of governmental authority' and has some specific rules for 'recognition' of prudential regulation. Finally, it also indicates that for disputes relating to prudential regulation and other financial matters, dispute settlement panels should have the necessary expertise in the field. The precise content of the Annex on Financial Services is discussed in the next sections.

147. All annexes are an integral part of the GATS.[140] Since the Annex on Financial Services contains a number of provisions that specifically apply to 'measures affecting the supply of financial services', it can be considered a *lex specialis* in relation to the GATS framework agreement. Unless the Annex excludes the application of a provision in the GATS,[141] the provisions of the Annex and the GATS apply simultaneously. However, if these provisions were to conflict, the Annex as *lex specialis* would apply.[142]

148. With regard to the principles of market access, national treatment and some other GATS obligations that involve 'progressive liberalization', one should consult the schedules of specific commitments of each WTO member for a definition of the extent to which they have undertaken liberalization commitments.[143] These schedules are specific to each member and include

were opposed to a text that included specific commitments in an annex. World Trade Organization, Committee on Specific Commitments, Additional Commitments under Art. XVIII of the GATS, Note by the Secretariat, S/CSC/W/34, 16 July 2002, para. 68. In 1991, a draft was submitted by the co-chair of the Group of Negotiations on Services that separated, on the one hand, specific issues relating to financial services, such as on prudential regulation and recognition (to be included in an annex), and, on the other hand, issues relating to specific commitments (which became the Understanding on Commitments in Financial Services – see below para. 149).

140 Art. XXIX GATS.

141 For instance, the application of paragraph 4(b) of Art. VII GATS (which involves an obligation to notify the Council for Trade in Services as far in advance as possible when negotiations on a recognition agreement are started or when unilateral recognition is considered) is excluded in paragraph 3(c) of the Annex.

142 During the negotiations, the representative of the European Communities stated, 'All the provisions of the draft framework proposal would apply fully in the financial services area, except where specific provisions were established in the proposed sectoral annex.' Working Group on Financial Services Including Insurance, Note on the Meeting of 12–13 July 1990, MTN.GNS/FIN/2, 10 August 1990, para. 18.

143 However, this does not give a complete and correct picture of the openness of the WTO member's market to foreign financial services or providers. First, the commitments are

commitments that are specific to financial services as well as horizontal (non-sector-specific) commitments. The commitments are split into four columns, one setting out the services sector in question and three others corresponding to the three obligations for which such commitments are made (market access – Article XVI; national treatment – Article XVII; additional commitments – Article XVIII). The commitments of the European Union and its member states are combined in a single schedule.[144] Like the annexes, the schedules are an integral part of the GATS.[145]

149. Furthermore, we should also consider the Understanding on Commitments in Financial Services.[146] This Understanding provides a so-called 'alternative approach' to GATS commitments and becomes

often less far-reaching than real market openness. The difference between the bound access in the Schedule and the actual openness is called a 'binding gap'. Second, the member's schedule does not say anything about the restrictions a foreign supplier may be faced with for the types of financial services for which no commitments were made. See A. Gkoutzinis, 'International Trade in Banking Services and the Role of the WTO: Discussing the Legal Framework and Policy Objectives of the General Agreement on Trade in Services and the Current State of Play in the Doha Round of Trade Negotiations', (2005) 39 *International Lawyer* 877, at 893.

144 The European Union (before the Lisbon Treaty entered into force referred to by the WTO as the European Communities (EC)) conducts the negotiations in the World Trade Organization. The EU submitted a schedule of specific GATS commitments in 1995, covering the twelve states that were members of the EC at that time. The EC submitted two modifications (supplements) in 1997 (relating to telecommunications and financial services), which covered its member states. The commitments are contained in European Communities and their Member States, Schedule of Specific Commitments, GATS/SC/31 (15 April 1994), with four supplements. The financial service commitments that are applicable are contained in (Revised) Supplement 4, GATS/SC/31/Supp.4/Rev. (18 November 1999). Moreover, the enlargement of the European Union requires bringing the commitments into line with the EU schedule. The EU has drafted a consolidated Schedule of Commitments, merging all schedules of the member states when the Communities grew to twenty-five members in 2004 and 2005. The results of this process can be found in Communication of the European Communities and its Member States, Draft Consolidated GATS Schedule, 14 and 29 September 2006, S/C/W/273 (9 October 2006). The negotiations on the EC-25 consolidated schedule of commitments, pursuant to Art. XXI (Modification of Schedules) of the GATS, were concluded in September 2006. Certification of the EC-25 schedule was completed in December 2006, and the schedule will enter into force following the completion of the internal decision-making procedure of the EU and its member states, where applicable. However, as at the time of writing, this Consolidated Schedule is not yet in force. Moreover, the accession of Romania and Bulgaria in 2007 and of Croatia in 2013 means that the Schedule again needs an update. The EU has launched negotiations aimed at consolidating the services commitments, pursuant to Art. XXI of the GATS. In the meantime, one should consult the individual schedules of those three countries.

145 Art. XX:3 GATS.

146 Understanding on Commitments in Financial Services, LT/UR/U/1, adopted 15 April 1994. The gradual enlargement of the EU has lead to a situation where not all EU member

part of the GATS for those countries that indicate in their schedules of specific commitments that they make commitments according to the Understanding. The Understanding emerged from the difficult negotiations in the Uruguay Round with regard to financial services.[147] Issues relating to specific commitments that could not be included in the Annex on Financial Services (which is an integral part of the GATS and thus applies immediately to all WTO members) were placed in the Understanding (which is part of the Uruguay Round 'package', but does not form an integral part of the GATS). The Understanding is said to provide a 'model'[148] or 'formula approach'[149] for far-reaching commitments in the field of financial services, with regard to market access and national treatment or additional commitments for those WTO members that so desire.

150. The exact legal status of the Understanding on Commitments in Financial Services is unclear. The obligations in the Understanding only apply if the WTO member has indicated this in its schedule of specific commitments. This might be done in the headnote in the section in the Schedule for the Financial Services Sector. By including an entry in the schedule, the obligations in the Understanding become an integral part of the GATS, since a WTO member's schedules are an integral part of the GATS.[150] However, it binds only those members that have made this entry. Nonetheless, other WTO members can still derive rights from it, since the benefits of any of the commitments by means of the

states have commitments based on the Understanding. This was still the case in 1999, the year when the fourth (and last) revision of the EU's schedules was adopted. The Consolidated Schedule of the EU now has a separate section with commitments for those member states that have made commitments with reference to the Understanding (Austria, Belgium, Czech Republic, Denmark, Germany, Spain, Finland, France, Greece, Hungary, Italy, Ireland, Luxembourg, Netherlands, Portugal, Sweden, Slovakia and the United Kingdom), and a section for those member states that have not done so (Cyprus, Estonia, Latvia, Lithuania, Malta, Poland and Slovenia). See Communication of the European Communities and its Member States, Draft Consolidated GATS Schedule, 14 and 29 September 2006, S/C/W/273 (9 October 2006), at 292.

147 See also above para. 146 (n. 139).

148 S. Key, 'Financial Services', in P. Macrory, A. Appleton and M. Plummer (eds.), *The World Trade Organization. Legal, Economic and Political Analysis* (New York: Springer, 2005), Vol. 1, 955–88, at 985.

149 See Committee on Specific Commitments, Additional Commitments under Art. XVIII of the GATS, Note by the Secretariat, S/CSC/W/34, 16 July 2002, para. 72.

150 This is by virtue of Art. XX:3 GATS; see Appellate Body Report, *United States – Measures Affecting the Cross-Border Supply of Gambling and Betting Services* (*US – Gambling*), WT/DS285/AB/R, adopted 20 April 2005, para. 160.

Understanding have to be extended to the other WTO members on a most-favoured-nation (MFN) basis.[151]

151. A further question concerns the relationship between the Understanding and the GATS framework agreement. Trachtman argues that the Understanding 'purports to take the place of the provision of GATS dealing with national treatment and market access'.[152] This seems at first sight to be correct: the introductory paragraph of the Understanding provides that the WTO members can make commitments with respect to financial services 'on the basis of an *alternative* approach to that covered by the provisions of Part III [that includes Article XVI and Article XVII] of the Agreement' (emphasis added). Hence, because the Understanding is an 'alternative', it would apply to *exclusion* of the provisions in Part III of the GATS.[153] In other words, an additional commitment referring to the Understanding makes Article XVI and XVII inapplicable, and replaces it with the provisions in the Understanding.

152. However, this interpretation leads to odd consequences. In certain cases, WTO members that have relied on the Understanding would commit to less than WTO members that have not done so. The Understanding seems in some cases more cautious than the open-ended commitments under Articles XVI or XVII.

153. For instance, with regard to market access in banking and other financial services (excluding insurance) by means of Mode 1, the Understanding sets out commitments that are limited to the transfer of financial information and financial data processing (as in subparagraph 5(a)(xx) of the Annex on Financial Services) and advisory and other financial services, excluding intermediation (as in subparagraph 5(a)(xvi) of the Annex).[154] The market access commitment in the Understanding does not cover other types of 'Banking and other Financial Services' that are defined in the Annex on Financial Services.[155]

[151] Understanding on Commitments in Financial Services, above n. 146, introductory paragraphs item (iii).

[152] J. Trachtman, 'Trade in Financial Services under GATS, NAFTA and the EC: A Regulatory Jurisdiction Analysis', (1996) 34 *Columbia Journal of Transnational Law* 40, at 69.

[153] The *Oxford Compact Dictionary of English* defines 'alternative' as: 'adjective: 1 (of one or more things) available as another possibility. 2 (of two things) *mutually exclusive*. 3 departing from or challenging traditional practices' (emphasis added).

[154] Understanding on Commitments in Financial Services, Section B.3 (c).

[155] See also Key, above n. 148, at 985.

154. Furthermore, also with regard to national treatment, the Understanding imposes only two obligations on the WTO members. First of all, there is an obligation for the WTO member to provide to financial service suppliers from other members that are established in the territory access to 'payment and clearing systems operated by public entities, and to official funding and refinancing facilities available in the ordinary course of business'.[156] Second, the member should ensure that certain organizations or associations for which membership is required to provide financial services provide national treatment to service suppliers from other members that are resident in the territory.[157]

155. Finally, the Understanding even includes exceptions that are not present in the GATS Framework Agreement or in the Annex on Financial Services. For instance, the Understanding indicates that WTO members that make commitments by means of the Understanding are not obliged to extend national treatment to foreign financial service suppliers established in their territory when it concerns 'lender of last resort' facilities.[158]

156. The mentioned examples show that the Understanding cannot apply *to the exclusion* of Part III of the GATS, even if the wording of the introductory paragraph of the Understanding may suggest this. Some WTO members seemed to be aware of the problematic relationship between the Understanding and the GATS. While some WTO members merely included a headnote in their schedule for financial services where they stated that the commitments 'are in accordance

[156] Understanding on Commitments in Financial Services, Section C.1. In this respect, it has been argued that a WTO member that grants support to banks in crisis circumstances and has made commitments by reference to the Understanding is not obliged to respect the national treatment obligation with regard to this crisis support. Such government support would not be covered by the national treatment obligation in the Understanding, since the support is not 'available in the normal course of ordinary business'. See, in this sense, A. Von Bogdandy and J. Windsor, 'Understanding on Commitments in Financial Services', in R. Wolfrum, P. Stoll and C. Feinäugle (eds.), *WTO – Trade in Services* (Leiden: Martinus Nijhoff, 2008) 647–66, at 662–3. If the obligations in the Understanding indeed apply to the exclusion of the obligations in Part III of the GATS, the WTO member that adopts crisis support that is solely available to domestically owned banks would not be violating any obligation in the GATS. However, as argued further in this Chapter, the latter interpretation of the relationship between the Understanding and the Framework Agreement cannot be correct.

[157] Understanding on Commitments in Financial Services, Section C.2.

[158] Ibid., Section C.1.

with the Understanding on Commitments in Financial Services',[159] other members stated that their commitments are in accordance with the GATS, the Annex and the Understanding, thereby ensuring that all three apply.[160] Others explicitly state that the Understanding applies *in addition* to Part III of the GATS.[161]

157. The Understanding indeed indicates explicitly that 'it does not prejudice the right of any Member to schedule its specific commitments in accordance with the approach under Part III of the Agreement'.[162] A pragmatic approach is therefore desirable. The Understanding provides a number of 'pre-cooked' entries ('formulas') for commitments in financial services. It concerns an initial degree of liberalization that is in certain respects far-reaching (for instance the explicit mention of a number of non-discriminatory measures that may produce adverse effects on financial service providers of other members). Yet it would go against the object and purpose of the GATS (which involves progressive liberalization)[163] and the Understanding (which states in the introductory paragraph that commitments on the basis of the Understanding may not conflict with the GATS)[164] to interpret the Understanding as *excluding* the application of obligations in Part III of the GATS.

158. The fact that a WTO member makes commitments by reference to the Understanding does not mean that it cannot limit its commitments (by, for example, scheduling limitations in the columns on market access or national treatment in its schedule). The WTO member still determines the extent to which it accepts liberalizing its market for financial services. The fourth introductory paragraph of the Understanding indeed states that 'no presumption has been created as to the degree of liberalization to which a Member is committing itself under the Agreement'.[165] The explicit reference

159 See, e.g., the headnotes in the schedules of the European Communities and of the United States (GATS/SC/90/Supp 3).

160 See, e.g., the headnote in the schedule of Sri Lanka (GATS/SC/79/Supp 2) or the Slovak Republic (GATS/SC/77/Supp. 3).

161 See, e.g., the headnote in the schedule of Australia (GATS/SC/6/Supp. 1/Rev 1) and the schedule of Japan (GATS/SC/46/Supp. 3).

162 Understanding on Commitments in Financial Services, above n. 146, introductory paragraphs item (ii).

163 See the second introductory paragraph of the GATS.

164 Understanding on Commitments in Financial Services, above n. 146, introductory paragraphs item (i).

165 Understanding on Commitments in Financial Services, above n. 146, introductory paragraphs item (iv).

at the end of the introduction to the Understanding reaffirms this, indicating that the commitments are 'subject to conditions and qualifications where specified'. Such conditions and qualifications can only apply to existing measures. Because of the explicit 'standstill' obligation in Section A of the Understanding, measures adopted after the member has made its commitments (and relied on the Understanding) have to comply in any event with the model commitments.

159. All the above-mentioned documents are part of the Uruguay Round package and were adopted on 15 April 1994, when the Uruguay Round was finished. They entered into force on 1 January 1995.

7.1.2 Post-Uruguay Round documents

160. At the end of the Uruguay Round, several negotiating parties thought that the commitments by other parties with regard to financial services did not go far enough. Therefore the negotiations continued after 15 April 1995. This led to a number of additional sources (of which the most important are two protocols) specifically relating to financial services. The protocols include deeper liberalization commitments, which are member-specific. Indeed, a number of countries (especially the United States) did not want to conclude the negotiations. They felt that they offered far-reaching commitments to market access and national treatment in the financial services sector without receiving sufficient commitments in return. These commitments would be extended to all WTO members through the principle of most-favoured-nation treatment. Hence other WTO members would benefit without having offered something in return.

161. Therefore the United States planned to include an exemption to the obligation of most-favoured-nation treatment that would result in distinguishing between WTO members. More extensive liberalization commitments in the financial services sector would only be offered in return for reciprocity.[166] However, the European Communities managed to convince the negotiating parties to extend the negotiations. A Decision on Financial Services[167] was adopted at the end of the Uruguay Round, which extended the negotiations for six months after the date of entry into force of the WTO Agreement.

[166] Gkoutzinis, above n. 143, at 890; and Trachtman, above n. 152, at 70.
[167] Decision on Financial Services, LT/UR/D-5/2, adopted 15 April 1994.

162. Thus the negotiations continued from 1 January to 30 June 1995. During that period the reciprocity conditions by means of which some members had qualified their obligation of most-favoured-nation treatment could not be applied.[168] The Second Annex on Trade in Financial Services[169] indicated that, during the additional six-month period, the WTO members were allowed to list additional most-favoured-nation exemptions relating to financial services. Furthermore, WTO members could 'improve, modify or withdraw' commitments without the obligation to provide compensatory adjustment, as normally required under Article XXI:1 GATS. Because the negotiations were still not finalized within the additional six months, the Council for Trade in Services adopted a Decision on the Application of the Second Annex on Financial Services,[170] which further extended the period for notifying changes to the specific commitments and the most-favoured-nation exemptions from 30 June 1995 to 28 July 1995. Eventually, the Council for Trade in Services adopted the Second Protocol to the General Agreement on Trade in Services on 21 July 1995.[171] The modified commitments and exemptions of twenty-nine WTO members (the European Communities counted as one) were annexed to this protocol. It entered in force for all these members on 1 September 1996.[172]

163. The negotiations on financial services were far from finished. A Decision by the Council for Trade in Services, adopted on the same date as the Second Protocol, already indicated that further negotiations on

[168] Ibid., para. 1. [169] WTO, *Legal Texts*, above n. 136, at 313.

[170] Council for Trade in Services, Decision on the Application of the Second Annex on Financial Services, S/L/6, adopted 30 June 1995.

[171] Second Protocol to the General Agreement on Trade in Services, S/L/11, adopted by the Council on Trade in Services on 21 July 1995. On that same date two other decisions were adopted by the Council for Trade in Services. First, the Decision on Commitments in Financial Services, S/L/8, adopted 21 July 1995, indicated that if the Second Protocol were not adopted, WTO members had sixty days beginning 1 August 1996 to modify and withdraw commitments and to revise MFN exemptions. Second, the Decision on Financial Services, S/L/9, adopted 21 July 1995, indicated that if the Second Protocol were adopted, WTO members concerned had sixty days beginning 1 November 1997 to modify or withdraw commitments and to revise MFN exemptions. Hence a plan for further negotiations in the sector of financial services was already envisaged.

[172] The Second Protocol was open for acceptance until 30 June 1996 and would enter into force thirty days after the acceptance of all WTO members concerned. All members that signed the Second Protocol did so before the set deadline. Three WTO members, including the United States, did not wish to sign it, but made unilateral commitments. J. Simser, 'GATS and Financial Services: Redefining Borders', (1996) 3 *Buffalo Journal of International Law* 34, at 60.

trade in financial services would take place from 1 November 1997. For this reason, the Second Protocol was often referred to as an 'Interim Agreement'. The Fifth Protocol to the General Agreement on Trade in Services (also called the 'Financial Services Agreement') was adopted on 14 November 1997.[173] The Fifth Protocol had an annex with further liberalization commitments of seventy WTO members.[174] Members concerned would have until 29 January 1999 to accept the Fifth Protocol. It would then enter into force on the thirtieth day after acceptance by all members concerned. Nonetheless, by the deadline only fifty-two of the seventy members had accepted the Protocol. Therefore these members agreed to let the Protocol enter into force on 1 March 1999. At the time of writing, two members still have to accept the Fifth Protocol: Brazil and Jamaica.

164. Further negotiations on the liberalization of trade in financial services are still ongoing. Article XIX:1 GATS requires WTO members to restart services negotiations not later than five years after the entry into force of the WTO Agreement. In February 2000, new negotiations on trade in services started (GATS 2000). The ambition and expectations were very high. There was 'no *a priori* exclusion of any service sector or mode of supply'.[175] Hence further financial services liberalization was again on the agenda.

165. With the adoption of the Doha Ministerial Declaration, services negotiations were incorporated in the Doha Development Agenda.[176] Negotiations proceeded on a 'request–offer' approach: individual WTO members make lists of requests for further liberalization commitments by specific members and offer commitments in return. By 31 March 2003, ninety-six initial offers for commitments had been made.

166. The negotiations suffered a major setback when the Ministerial Conference of Cancún in September 2003 failed. The subsequent July

[173] Fifth Protocol to the General Agreement on Trade in Services, S/L/45, adopted by the Committee on Trade in Financial Services on 14 November 1997, S/L/44.

[174] The negotiations on these modified commitments were finalized on 12 December 1997. There is thus no separate Agreement on Financial Services, but only further liberalization commitments indicated in the Schedules of Commitments of a number of WTO members. Key, above n. 148, at 957.

[175] Special Session of the Council for Trade in Services, Guidelines and Procedures for the Negotiations on Trade in Services, S/L/39, adopted 28 March 2001, para. 5.

[176] Ministerial Declaration of Doha, WT/MIN(01)/DEC/1, adopted 14 November 2001, para. 12.

Package urged further progress in the services negotiations.[177] Revised offers for commitments were introduced by thirty members by 19 May 2005. The Hong Kong Ministerial Declaration of December 2005 equally urged further negotiations and introduced an important aspect for negotiations.[178] While the main approach remains bilateral negotiations on a 'request–offer' basis, a plurilateral approach was also suggested. Members or a group of members may present their requests in a service sector or mode of supply to other members, thereby identifying goals of negotiations. Members to whom such requests were made must then consider these requests.[179] These plurilateral requests allow for focused, sector-based discussions among experts and also help to identify a 'critical mass' of WTO members that was necessary for a deal to be struck.[180]

167. Negotiations were suspended in May 2006 because of lack of progress in agriculture negotiations. However, they were resumed in 2008 and the target was to strike a deal in that year. On 26 July 2008, a so-called 'signalling conference' took place, to 'signal' and discuss the offers and requests with regard to service commitments.[181] Nonetheless, the WTO members were unable to strike a deal at the Ministerial Conference that took place in Geneva in July 2008. The seventh Ministerial Conference did not address the Doha negotiations, but rather involved a political discussion of the role and functioning of the WTO in the light of the global economic crisis.

168. In April 2011, the chair of the Council for Trade in Services issued a report giving the state of play in services negotiations. With regard to financial services, the report made it clear that the offers members had

177 Decision adopted by the General Council on 1 August 2003, WT/L/579, para. 1 (e) and Annex C.

178 Ministerial Declaration of Hong Kong, WT/MIN(06)/DEC, adopted 18 December 2005, paras. 25–27. It was the first time that services took more than one paragraph in a ministerial declaration.

179 Ibid., Annex C.7.

180 Presentation by J. Marchetti, 'Recent Developments in the Doha Round Talks on Financial Services', British Institute of International and Comparative Law (BIICL), 12 May 2008. He identified as 'demandeurs' Australia, Canada, Chinese Taipei, EU, Ecuador, Hong Kong China, Japan, South Korea, Norway, Panama and the United States. The 'target countries' would be Argentina, Brazil, China, Costa Rica, Egypt, India, Indonesia, Israel, Kuwait, Malaysia, Morocco, Nigeria, Pakistan, Philippines, Singapore, South Africa, Thailand, Tunisia, Turkey, United Arab Emirates and Uruguay.

181 Services Signalling Conference, Report by the Chairman of the TNC (Trade Negotiations Committee), JOB(08)/93, 30 July 2008.

made clearly fell below the level of the autonomous liberalization that had taken place in this sector.[182]

169. The eighth Ministerial Conference recognized the impasse in the Doha Round negotiations and paid no specific attention to negotiations in financial services. It merely provided some political guidance for the negotiations.[183] The ninth Ministerial Conference in December 2013 did

Table 7.1. *Chronological overview of relevant WTO legal sources relating to financial services*

Date	Source	Content
15 April 1994	GATS Framework Agreement	Scope, definitions, general obligations, specific commitments, future liberalization agenda
	Annex on Financial Services	Definitions, prudential exception, protection of confidential information, recognition, dispute settlement, definitions
	GATS Understanding on Commitments in Financial Services, LT/UR/U/1	'Alternative approach': farther-reaching commitments
	Decision on Financial Services, LT/UR/D-5/2	Extends negotiations for max. six months from date of entry into force of WTO Agreement: 1 January 1995 to 30 June 1995.
	Second Annex on Financial Services	During six-month additional negotiation period, commitments may be modified and MFN exemptions may be revised. Reciprocity cannot be applied in the meantime.

182 Special Session of the Council for Trade in Services, Negotiations on Trade in Services, Report by the Chairman, Ambassador Fernando de Mateo, to the Trade Negotiations Committee, TN/S/36, 21 April 2011, paras. 30–31.

183 Chairman's Concluding Statement to the Eighth Ministerial Conference, WT/MIN(11)/11, 17 December 2011.

Table 7.1. (*cont.*)

Date	Source	Content
30 June 1995	Decision on the Application of the Second Annex on Financial Services, S/L/6	Further extends negotiation period from 30 June 1995 to 28 July 1995.
24 July 1995	Second Protocol to the General Agreement on Trade in Services (Interim Agreement), S/L/11	Has an annex with all the improved commitments of twenty-nine WTO members (EC counted as one) achieved during the 1 January–28 July 1995 period. Entered into force 1 September 1996.
14 November 1997	Fifth Protocol to the General Agreement on Trade in Services, S/L/45	Has an annex with all improved commitments of seventy WTO members (negotiations finalized on 12 December 1997). Entered into force 1 March 1999 for fifty-two members.
February 2000	Start of new GATS negotiations (GATS 2000)	
14 November 2001	Doha Ministerial Declaration, WT/MIN(01)/DEC/1	GATS negotiations incorporated in Doha Development Agenda
18 December 2005	Hong Kong Ministerial Declaration, WT/MIN(05)/DEC	Suggestion for plurilateral 'request–offer' negotiations
21 April 2011	Report by the Chairman of the Council for Trade in Services, TN/S/36	Conclusion that members' offers fall below level of autonomous liberalization in the sector.
17 December 2011	Chairman's Concluding Statement to the Eighth Ministerial Conference, WT/MIN(11)/11	Recognition of the impasse in the negotiations.

not address financial services at all. Further efforts to liberalize trade in financial services take place among a more limited group of WTO members as part of a Trade in Services Agreement (TiSA). It is still uncertain how TiSA will relate to the GATS.

7.2 Supervisory principles and regulatory standards of the Basel Committee

170. As discussed in Part I, regulation to avoid the private and social costs of market failures plays an essential role in the banking services sector. Policymakers need to make a trade-off between competition and financial stability and can influence the outcome of this trade-off through regulation. Efforts that seek to intensify international trade in banking services by removing protectionist barriers to such trade must happen in tandem with regulatory adjustments that take into account the reality of banking activity that spans different jurisdictions.

171. At the same time, many regulatory burdens will only disappear if host countries agree that they will not apply their own regulation and supervisory assessments to foreign banks that seek to pursue activities in the host markets and accept the regulations and assessments made by the home country. This may happen if supervisory authorities in the host countries are sufficiently satisfied with regard to the quality of the regulation and supervision in the home countries of the banks. International coordination of supervisory techniques and regulatory standards is thus an essential precondition.

172. The GATS does not contain any substantive regulatory requirements for banking services. Even the Disciplines on Domestic Regulation that are being developed on the basis of the mandate laid down in Article VI:4 will not result in the harmonization of substantive requirements for access to and performance of banking activities. WTO negotiations are mainly conducted by trade officials, and therefore the WTO is not the appropriate body for such efforts. Efforts towards international coordination and harmonization can only be made by a body in which specialists in the service sector at stake are represented. The Basel Committee on Banking Supervision (Basel Committee) is the body that since 1975 has been engaged in international standard-setting for regulation and supervision in the banking sector.

173. At the end of 1974, in response to the Herstatt Bank collapse and the Franklin National Bank failure, the central bank governors of the G10 set up the Basel Committee. The Basel Committee aims to 'enhance understanding of key supervisory issues and improve the quality of banking supervision worldwide'.[184] In fact, the Basel Committee has no formal founding document; this founding mandate lies only in a

[184] Basel Committee on Banking Supervision, 'About the Basel Committee', available at www.bis.org/bcbs/index.htm.

press communiqué from the central bank governors of the G10 issued in the framework of the Bank for International Settlements on 12 February 1975.[185] This makes its status under international law uncertain. It is not a public international organization with international legal personality, but rather an informally constituted group, whose members are not states, but representatives of their central banks or supervisory authorities.[186] Its secretariat is located in the Bank of International Settlements.

174. Because the Group of 20 largest economies (G20) played a prominent role in determining international policy responses to the global financial crisis, the membership of the Basel Committee was broadened on 10 July 2009 to include all G20 WTO members (some of which were not previously represented on the Committee) as well as Hong Kong and Singapore (with important emerging financial markets).[187] The decision making of the Basel Committee takes place informally and by consensus. The standards that are developed are not binding, but mere recommendations.

175. The global financial and macroeconomic crisis gave rise to important adjustments to the international financial architecture. The leaders of the G20[188] met at regular times to determine the appropriate policy response to the global crisis. The communiqués of the G20 summits in Washington (October 2008), London (April 2009) and Pittsburgh (September 2009) set out recommendations to tackle the crisis and to reform global financial regulation and supervision.[189] Therefore the

[185] D. Zaring, 'International Law by Other Means: The Twilight Existence of International Financial Regulatory Organizations', (1998) 33 *Texas International Law Journal* 281, at 287.

[186] S. Ghosh, 'Evolving International Supervisory Architecture: Design, Rationale and Policy Reform', (2005) 6 *Journal of Banking Regulation* 246, at 248–9.

[187] It is now composed of senior officials responsible for banking supervision or financial stability issues in central banks or the banking supervisory authorities (if the banking supervision is not performed by the central bank) of Argentina, Australia, Belgium, Brazil, Canada, China, France, Germany, Hong Kong SAR, India, Indonesia, Italy, Japan, South Korea, Luxembourg, Mexico, Netherlands, Russia, Saudi Arabia, Singapore, South Africa, Spain, Sweden, Switzerland, Turkey, United Kingdom and United States.

[188] There are nineteen countries represented in the G20: Argentina, Australia, Brazil, Canada, China, France, Germany, India, Indonesia, Italy, Japan, Mexico, Russia, Saudi Arabia, South Africa, South Korea, Turkey, United Kingdom and United States. In addition, the EU is represented by the President of the European Council and the European Central Bank. The G20 is said to 'represent around 90 per cent of global gross national product, 80 per cent of world trade (including EU intra-trade) as well as two-thirds of the world's population'. G20, 'About G-20', available at www.g20.org/about_G20. A G20 meeting normally assembles finance ministers and central bank governors of the G20 members.

[189] Later meetings of the G20 took place in Toronto (June 2010), Seoul (November 2010), Cannes (November 2011) and Los Cabos (June 2012). At the Cannes meeting, the G20

United Kingdom's former prime minister Gordon Brown called the G20 'the world's main economic governing council'.[190] However, the G20 meetings only set out general policy lines and make recommendations. Regulatory work happens at national (or European) levels as well in international financial organizations.

176. One of the recommendations of the G20 Washington summit was to expand the Financial Stability Forum (FSF) to include other emerging economies.[191] The Financial Stability Forum, set up by the G7 in order to enhance cooperation among the various national and international supervisory bodies and international financial institutions so as to promote stability in the international financial system, was re-formed in April 2009 into the Financial Stability Board (FSB), with a broader membership and mandate. All G20 members are represented in the FSB, in addition to a number of international organizations[192] and international standard-setters (including the Basel Committee).[193]

177. The role of the FSB is to coordinate work at the international level and to monitor and assess developments and risks relating to the global financial system, rather than to engage in international standard-setting.[194] The Basel Committee thus remains in principle the international body that develops regulatory standards and supervisory principles for the banking sector. Nonetheless, on the basis of its mandate, the FSB developed a series of principles, including Principles for Cross-border

agreed to meet annually. Further meetings are planned in Saint Petersburg (September 2013) and Brisbane (November 2014).

[190] 'G20 Will Become Main Economic Council: UK's Brown', Reuters, 25 September 2009, available at www.reuters.com/article/idUSTRE58O13S20090925.

[191] See G20 Declaration, 'Summit on Financial Markets and the World Economy', 15 November 2008, available at www.g20.org/Documents/g20_summit_declaration.pdf, para. 9.

[192] These are the EU, the European Central Bank, the Bank of International Settlements, the IMF, the OECD and the World Bank.

[193] These are the Basel Committee, the Committee on the Global Financial System, the Committee on Payment and Settlement Systems, the International Association of Insurance Supervisors, the International Accounting Standards Board and the International Organization of Securities Commissions.

[194] The FSB has as its objective 'to coordinate at the international level the work of national financial authorities and international standard setting bodies (SSBs) in order to develop and promote the implementation of effective regulatory, supervisory and other financial sector policies. In collaboration with the international financial institutions, the FSB will address vulnerabilities affecting financial systems in the interest of global financial stability.' Financial Stability Board Charter, Art. 1, available at www.financialstabilityboard.org/about/mandate.htm.

Cooperation on Crisis Management[195] and the Principles for Sound Compensation Policies.[196] Arguably, this reflects the fact that much of the financial regulation that nowadays is developed at the national and international level must cover several financial sectors at the same time. Hence, representatives of other, non-bank financial institutions should be represented in the standard-setting.

178. Still, the basic principles on effective banking supervision and supervision of cross-border banking groups emerge from the Basel Committee. Moreover, the Basel standards on capital requirements are still the primary source of international harmonization of capital requirements.

7.2.1 The Basel principles and standards on banking supervision

179. The Basel Committee developed influential standards with regard to banking supervision. The initiatives by the Basel Committee were most often in response to banking crises, which pointed to the inadequacies of prudential supervision for international banking.[197] As explained in Part I (above paras. 120–126), if banks operate across borders through branches and subsidiaries, it becomes crucial to supervise the large cross-border banking group adequately and to coordinate the role of the authority in the home country of the bank and that of the authorities in the countries where subsidiaries or branches are located or where the bank offers activities without a commercial presence (host countries).

180. Therefore, in 1975, the Basel Committee drafted the Basel Concordat, which included a basic rule that divided supervisory responsibilities between host and home authorities. After revision in 1983,[198] the revised Concordat established the principle of 'consolidated supervision', meaning that the home country supervisory authority was responsible for ensuring the supervision of all operations of a bank, both at home and abroad. It also introduced the principle of 'dual key' supervision, meaning that home and

[195] FSF Principles for Cross-border Cooperation on Crisis Management, 2 April 2009, available at www.financialstabilityboard.org/publications/r_0904c.pdf.

[196] FSF Principles for Sound Compensation Practices, 2 April 2009, available at www.financialstabilityboard.org/publications/r_0904b.pdf.

[197] For a discussion see D. Alford, 'Core Principles for Effective Banking Supervision: An Enforceable International Financial Standard?', (2005) 28 *Boston College International and Comparative Law Review* 237, at 240–69.

[198] In 1983 the Basel Concordat was revised in response to the Latin American debt crisis and the collapse of the Italian Banco Ambrosiano.

host supervisors need to be satisfied with each other's supervision. If not, the home supervisor is urged to discourage the foreign expansion of the bank. The host supervisor, for its part, must either prohibit the establishment or may allow it while in the meantime imposing the necessary regulatory conditions and restrictions.[199]

181. In 1992, again in response to a bank failure,[200] the Basel Committee drafted the Minimum Standards for the Supervision of International Banking Groups and their Cross-Border Establishments.[201] These Minimum Standards state clearly that international banks and banking groups need to be supervised on a consolidated basis by the home supervisor.[202] Further, if an international bank wants to open foreign establishments, both home and host authorities need to approve this. The home and host authorities have to give specific consideration to two factors. It concerns, first, the strength of the capital of the bank or banking group and, second, the appropriateness of the risk management of the bank or banking group. If one of the competent authorities considers that the system of supervisory competences proposed by the Basel Concordat (i.e. that home authorities are responsible for consolidated supervision) would be inadequate because of the bank's activities, location or structure of its management, it has the responsibility to consult with the other relevant authorities to establish a better division of responsibilities.[203] This may, for instance, be important when the banking group's activities are not concentrated in the country of incorporation.[204] In that case, the authority of the country where the main activities are taking place may need to perform the consolidated

[199] Basel Committee on Banking Supervision, Principles for the Supervision of Bank's Foreign Establishments, Bank for International Settlements, May 1983, available at www.bis.org/publ/bcbsc312.pdf, especially Section III.

[200] In 1992, after the failure of the Bank of Credit and Commerce International (BCCI), it became clear that defining the supervisor (home supervisor) responsible for the entire group was far from obvious, especially in case of financial holding companies. BCCI was owned by a holding company that was incorporated in Luxembourg. Nevertheless, the main operations of BCCI were administered from London. The Bank of England claimed that the Luxembourg authority was responsible for the consolidated supervision of BCCI, while the Luxembourg authority claimed the opposite.

[201] Basel Committee on Banking Supervision, Minimum Standards for the Supervision of International Banking Groups and Their Cross-Border Establishments, July 1992, available at www.bis.org/publ/bcbsc314.pdf.

[202] Minimum Standard 1. [203] Minimum Standard 2.

[204] K. Leigh Case, 'The Daiwa Wake-Up Call: The Need for International Standards for Banking Supervision', (1996) 26 *Georgia Journal for International and Comparative Law* 215, at 224. This was indeed the problem for BCCI.

supervision. The Minimum Standards also proposed that host and home authorities conclude an agreement on information exchange.[205] Finally, the Minimum Standards reiterated that, if a host supervisor in the country where the bank seeks to expand felt that the requirements of the Minimum Standards were not met, it should block the establishment or only allow it under restrictive conditions.[206]

182. A recurring element in these initiatives of the Basel Committee is that host supervisors should be careful in allowing the expansion of foreign banks in their own territory. They should always reassure themselves of the adequacy of the prudential framework and supervision in the home country. In order to provide a benchmark for assessing supervision,[207] the Basel Committee in 1997 developed the Core Principles for Effective Banking Supervision.[208] The twenty-five Core Principles set out best practices for banking supervision and thereby go beyond the mere coordination of supervisory tasks. Specifically with regard to cross-border banking, they stress that the home supervisor must ensure consolidated supervision and, as a part of this, must establish information exchange with supervisors. On the other hand, the host supervisor must apply to local operations of foreign banks the same prudential, inspection and reporting requirements as to domestic banks (Core Principle 25). The Principles recognize, however, that relevant differences need to be taken into account, for instance the fact that branches are not separately capitalized.

183. In order to avoid divergent interpretations of the core principles, the Basel Committee drafted in 1999 the Core Principles Methodology.[209] The Methodology sets out clear criteria for assessing compliance with the Core Principles. For instance, with regard to Principle 25 (on the role of host supervisors), the Methodology states that a host country must assess whether the home country of a bank performs consolidated supervision and must obtain a statement by the home supervisor that it

[205] Minimum Standard 3. [206] Minimum Standard 4.

[207] This initiative by the Basel Committee was again triggered by a crisis, this time the 1997 financial crisis that spread across Asia. It was the G7 who called for further action at its summit in Lyon in June 1996. Alford, above n. 197, at 260.

[208] Basel Committee on Banking Supervision, Core Principles for Effective Banking Supervision, September 1997, available at www.bis.org/publ/bcbs30a.pdf.

[209] Basel Committee on Banking Supervision, Core Principles Methodology, October 1999, available at www.bis.org/publ/bcbs61.pdf?noframes=1.

does not object to the foreign expansion of the bank's activities in the host country.

184. In 2006, the Core Principles[210] as well as the Methodology[211] were revised in the light of new developments. In the Methodology on Principle 5, relating to major acquisitions, it is now explicitly stated that, when a bank wishes to acquire a significant holding in a financial institution in another country, the parent supervisor must consider the quality of supervision in that foreign country and assess its ability to perform consolidated supervision.

185. In 2012, the Core Principles were again revised,[212] whereby the Principles and the Methodology were merged into one document and the developments during the financial crisis taken into account. The 2012 Core Principles point out that particular attention was paid to the need for greater intensity and resources to deal effectively with systemically important banks;[213] the importance of applying a system-wide, macro perspective to the microprudential supervision of banks to assist in identifying and analysing systemic risk and taking pre-emptive action to address it;[214] the increasing focus on effective crisis management, recovery and resolution measures in reducing both the probability and the impact of a bank failure;[215] and good corporate governance,[216] disclosure and transparency.[217]

[210] Basel Committee on Banking Supervision, Core Principles for Effective Banking Supervision, October 2006, available at www.bis.org/publ/bcbs129.pdf?noframes=1.

[211] Basel Committee on Banking Supervision, Core Principles Methodology, October 2006, available at www.bis.org/publ/bcbs130.pdf?noframes=1.

[212] Basel Committee on Banking Supervision, Core Principles for Effective Banking Supervision, September 2012, available at www.bis.org/publ/bcbs230.pdf.

[213] It was decided not to adopt a principle that is specific to systemically important banks, since all principles were considered to apply to all banks, with systemically important banks at one end of the spectrum.

[214] As for systemically important banks, no specific principle was introduced for introducing the macroeconomic perspective to supervision. Nevertheless, Principle 15, on the supervisory control of a financial institution's risk management process, Principle 16, on capital adequacy, Principle 17, on credit risk, Principle 22, on market risk, Principle 23, on interest rate risk, Principle 24, on liquidity risk, and Principle 25, on operational risk, refer to the assessment of macroeconomic conditions.

[215] The Core Principles now contain references to the importance of supervisory authorities and banks having contingency arrangements in place to deal with situations where a bank failure could occur, in particular Principle 15, on the supervisory control of a financial institution's risk management process. They also pay particular attention to crisis management and the resolution of cross-border banks.

[216] A new Core Principle (Principle 14) was introduced to this effect.

[217] A new Core Principle (Principle 28) was introduced to this effect.

7.2.2 The Basel Capital Adequacy Framework

186. A second area in which the Basel Committee has contributed to international regulatory convergence is that of capital adequacy requirements for banks. In Part I we examined the role of capital adequacy requirements to influence the behaviour of credit institutions (above, paras. 74–77). National differences in capital requirements constitute important obstacles to competition between banks from different countries.

187. The first capital framework was adopted in 1988 (Basel I).[218] It called for a minimum capital ratio of 8 per cent of the 'risk-weighted assets'[219] of a bank. Basel I set out a definition of capital, consisting of two types (Tier I or core capital, involving equity and disclosed reserves, and Tier II or supplementary capital, involving undisclosed reserves, asset revaluation reserves, general provisions, hybrid instruments and subordinated term debt),[220] as well as rules for measuring the risk weights of the bank's asset- and off-balance-sheet exposure (i.e. banking business that does not generate liabilities or assets on the balance sheet of a bank, such as letters of credit offered by the bank).[221]

188. This capital framework gradually showed major problems. The framework was mainly criticized as applying a 'one size fits all' approach.[222] The capital requirement would not take into account sufficiently the very diverse risk profiles of banks.[223] Basel I also considered only credit risk, while banks are exposed to many other sources of risk – besides the chance of a debtor not being able to repay its loan – such as market risk and operational risk.

[218] Basel Committee on Banking Supervision, International Convergence of Capital Measurement and Capital Standards (July 1988, updated to April 1998), available at www.bis.org/publ/bcbsc111.pdf?noframes=1 (hereinafter 'Basel I'). See H. Scott, *International Finance: Law and Regulation* (London: Sweet and Maxwell, 2008) 282–93.

[219] The 'risk-weighted assets' of a bank are calculated by multiplying the outstanding credits by certain risk weights. These weights ranged from 0 to 100 per cent.

[220] See Section I, Basel I. From this capital, certain deductions should be made, consisting of goodwill and investments in subsidiaries engaged in banking and financial activities which are not consolidated in national systems. The national authorities could decide at their discretion whether or not to include certain elements of Tier II capital, but the amount of Tier II capital could not exceed 100 per cent of the amount of Tier I capital.

[221] Basel II (below n. 224), Section II. These off-balance-sheet items are converted into credit risk equivalents by multiplying them by a conversion factor. Para. 42, Basel II.

[222] E. Wu, 'Basel II: A Revised Framework', (2005) 24 *Annual Review of Banking and Financial Law* 150, at 151.

[223] European Central Bank, 'The New Basel Capital Framework and Its Implementation in the European Union', ECB Occasional Paper Series No. 42, 2005, 8.

189. The new capital framework (Basel II), adopted in June 2004, set out a number of more sophisticated principles that seek to ensure that banks maintain an adequate amount of capital.[224] This would improve bank soundness and the stability of the global financial system.[225] It is intended to be applied to 'internationally active banks', but, when implementing Basel II, states can make the requirements applicable to all banks.[226] The new capital framework consists of three aspects ('pillars').

190. The first pillar of Basel II concerns the *minimum capital ratio itself*, as well as rules with regard to the different components that can be considered capital and the measurement of the risk-weighted assets. Improved techniques for risk measurement have been elaborated in order to apply more sophisticated risk weightings. Basel II not only covers credit risk, but also operational risk and market risk.[227] For the calculation of the ratio for *credit risk*, banks can choose between a standardized approach (Basel II lays down specific risk weights for assets by referring to ratings by credit rating agencies),[228] or an internal-ratings-based approach. The latter approach allows banks themselves to determine the credit risk by means of internal rating systems. The use of this approach must be approved by the competent supervisory authorities.[229]

[224] Basel Committee on Banking Supervision, International Convergence of Capital Measurement and Capital Standards: A Revised Framework, June 2004, available at www.bis.org/publ/bcbs107.pdf?noframes=1. In June 2006, a Comprehensive Version of Basel II was enacted by the Basel Committee because some aspects of capital and risk weight calculation were still determined by older documents (especially Basel I): Basel Committee on Banking Supervision, International Convergence of Capital Measurement and Capital Standards. A Revised Framework. Comprehensive Version (June 2006), available at www.bis.org/publ/bcbs128.pdf?noframes=1 (hereinafter Basel II).

[225] R. Ayadi and F. Musch, 'Basel II Implementation in the Midst of Turbulence', CEPS Task Force Reports, 2008; D. Heremans, 'Financial Regulation and Supervision of Banks. The Basel II Capital Framework', in D. Heremans et al. (eds.), *Current Developments in European Integration: Financial Services, Transport Policy: Legal and Economic Contributions to the Fortis Bank Chair 2001–2003* (Leuven: Universitaire Pers Leuven, 2004) 115–133; M. Malloy, 'Emerging International Regime of Financial Services Regulation', (2005) 18 *Transnational Lawyer* 329; and Scott, above n. 218, at 294–323.

[226] This was done, for instance, in the European Union.

[227] Capital requirements for market risk were already designed by the Basel Committee by January 1996; they were modified in September 1997 and in November 2005. They are now included in the comprehensive version of the capital framework.

[228] Part 2, Section II of Basel II.

[229] Part 2, Section III of Basel II. The internal-ratings-based approach can be further subdivided into the 'foundation' and 'advanced' internal-ratings-based approach. The foundation approach allows the bank in question only to estimate the probability of

Basel II further specifies the treatment of securitization transactions.[230] For the calculation of the ratio for *operational risk*,[231] Basel II provides three different approaches. Banks can make use of the Basic Indicator Approach (the requirement to maintain own funds at a level that is at least 15 per cent of an indicator based on net income), the Standardized Approach (different required percentages of income split over different business lines) or the Advanced Measurement Approach (competent authorities permit the credit institution to use their own operational risk measurement systems).[232] Finally, Basel II provides capital charges for *market risk*.[233] It describes two alternative approaches to the measurement of market risk, a standardized method and an internal models approach.[234]

191. The second pillar concerns the *supervisory review process*. National supervisors are expected to review how well banks are assessing their capital needs. Hence banks should not only comply with the capital requirements, but should also have effective risk monitoring and management techniques in place.[235] In order to create a level playing field among states, it was necessary to pursue convergence in these national supervisory practices.[236]

192. Finally, the third pillar deals with *market discipline*. In order to allow market forces to come into play and to reward banks that adopt a prudent risk profile, it is necessary to ensure sufficient disclosure of a bank's business profile, risk exposure and risk management. Disclosure would in principle enable market participants to compare banks and to discipline these banks if the market participants are of the opinion that the bank engages in excessively risky conduct. Therefore Basel II imposes a number of disclosure requirements.[237]

193. The global financial crisis prompted the Basel Committee to revise a number of aspects of the Basel II capital framework. Enhancements

default of each grade of assets, but, further, allows the supervisory authorities to estimate the other risk components.

230 Part 2, Section IV of Basel II.

231 Basel II defines operational risk as 'the risk of loss resulting from inadequate or failed internal processes, people and systems or from external events. This definition includes legal risk, but excludes strategic and reputational risk.' Basel II, para. 644.

232 Part 2, Section V of Basel II.

233 Basel II defines market risk as 'the risk of losses in on and off-balance-sheet positions arising from movements in market prices.' Basel II, para. 683 (i).

234 Part 2, Section VI of Basel II. 235 Basel II, para. 720. 236 Part 3 of Basel II.

237 Part 4, Section II of Basel II.

were adopted in July 2009.[238] In Pillar I, the revision involved especially higher risk weights for resecuritization exposures and imposing specific operational requirements for banks when they make an assessment of securitization transactions. With regard to Pillar II, banks should have enhanced risk management processes in place,[239] and competent supervisors are responsible for monitoring these processes. Finally, with regard to Pillar III, disclosure requirements were especially strengthened for securitization transactions. These enhancements took effect on 1 January 2012. Furthermore, the Basel Committee adopted a revision of requirements relating to market risk in the trading book.[240]

194. In December 2009, the Basel Committee made further proposals to revise the capital framework. These proposals sought to strengthen the Tier I capital base, enhance the risk coverage of the capital framework (including operational risk as well as counterparty credit risk arising from repos, derivatives and securities financing), introduce a 'leverage ratio' that is meant to prevent banks from building up excessive leverage, and adopt countercyclical capital requirements[241] and a minimum liquidity standard for internationally active banks.[242] The consultation on these proposals ended on 16 April 2010. Finally, in July 2010, the Basel Committee published a consultative document on a proposal for countercyclical capital buffers.[243] Consultations ended on 10 September 2010. This process resulted in December 2010 in the Basel III capital framework. A final change was made in June 2011 to take into account risks of losses in case of changes in the credit quality of a counterparty.[244]

[238] Basel Committee on Banking Supervision, Enhancements to the Basel II Framework (July 2009), available at www.bis.org/publ/bcbs157.pdf?noframes=1.

[239] This involves firm-wide governance and risk management; capturing the risk of off-balance-sheet exposures and securitizations activities; managing risk concentrations; providing incentives for banks to manage better risk and returns over the long term; and sound compensation practices.

[240] Basel Committee on Banking Supervision, Revisions to the Basel II Market Risk Framework (July 2009), available at www.bis.org/publ/bcbs158.pdf?noframes=1.

[241] Basel Committee on Banking Supervision, Strengthening the Resilience of the Banking Sector, Consultative Document, December 2009, available at www.bis.org/publ/bcbs164.pdf.

[242] Basel Committee on Banking Supervision, International Framework for Liquidity Risk Measurement, Standards and Monitoring. Consultative Document (December 2009), available at www.bis.org/publ/bcbs165.pdf.

[243] Basel Committee on Banking Supervision, Countercyclical Capital Buffer Proposal (July 2010), available at www.bis.org/publ/bcbs172.pdf.

[244] Basel Committee on Banking Supervision, Basel III: A Global Regulatory Framework for More Resilient Banks and Banking Systems, December 2010 (rev. June 2011), available at www.bis.org/publ/bcbs189.pdf.

In January 2013, a standard on the liquidity coverage ratio as well as on liquidity risk monitoring tools was adopted.[245]

195. Basel III includes a new capital definition and higher minimum ratios,[246] a new leverage ratio,[247] countercyclical capital buffers,[248] a systemic add-on,[249] adjustment of risk-weights for counterparty credit risk, and a global liquidity standard (consisting of (i) a liquidity coverage ratio[250] and (ii) a net stable funding ratio[251]). The members of the Basel Committee should put the new rules in place by 1 January 2019, except for the phasing out of certain capital instruments, such as hybrid capital and Tier II capital instruments. The latter need only be completed by 1 January 2022.

7.2.3 The legal status of the Basel principles and standards

196. Since the principles and standards of the Basel Committee are not legally binding, the Basel Committee members will only implement them in their domestic legal orders if they feel that it is useful or if there is sufficient international pressure to do so.

197. The IMF and the World Bank have established a Financial Sector Assessment Program (FSAP) that assesses the strengths and weaknesses of the financial sector of those IMF members that agree to subject themselves to such assessment.[252] Submitting a country to the FSAP is

[245] Basel Committee on Banking Supervision, Liquidity Coverage Ratio and Liquidity Risk Monitoring Tools, January 2013, available at www.bis.org/publ/bcbs238.pdf.

[246] The minimum ratio of common equity will rise from 2 per cent to 7 per cent (4.5 per cent plus a conservation buffer of 2.5 per cent).

[247] The leverage ratio is a non-risk-based ratio. A minimum Tier I leverage ratio of 3 per cent is tested during a period from 1 January 2013 to 1 January 2017. The basis of calculation is the average of the monthly leverage ratio over the quarter based on capital and total exposure.

[248] When supervisory authorities consider that credit growth is resulting in an unacceptable build-up of systematic risk, they can impose a minimum ratio up to 2.5 per cent.

[249] For systemically important financial institutions, supervisory authorities can impose capital surcharges.

[250] This ratio aims to ensure that banks hold a capital buffer to allow them to be self-sufficient for up to thirty days, should a bank-specific stress event and a market downturn occur at the same time.

[251] This ratio seeks to encourage banks to better match the funding characteristics of their assets and liabilities beyond a one-year period.

[252] In the light of the global financial crisis, the IMF and the World Bank revised the Program in September 2009. It remains voluntary, but more sophisticated assessment techniques are introduced, paying more attention to liquidity risk, and cross-border and cross-market linkages. IMF and World Bank, 'The Financial Sector Assessment

thus voluntary.[253] The assessment includes an evaluation of the financial stability in the IMF member under scrutiny, as well as an evaluation of how international standards and codes for financial services are implemented in the state's national law.[254]

198. The results of the assessment of compliance with international standards and codes are laid down in the Reports on Observance of Standards and Codes, which are made public. The results are also used as an input for the periodic surveillance performed by the IMF (so-called Article IV consultations, in which the monetary and financial policies of each IMF member is evaluated in the light of the need for domestic and international stability). This surveillance in any case pays attention to financial sector policies, even if the IMF member under surveillance has not accepted being subject to the FSAP.[255]

199. In addition, the Financial Stability Forum in 1999 established a special Task Force on Implementation of Standards.[256] When the Financial Stability Forum was re-formed as the Financial Stability Board, the members of the FSB committed themselves to implement international financial standards and to undergo periodic peer review.[257] Such pressure coming from international institutions may thus provide

Program After Ten Years: Experience and Reforms for the Next Decade', 28 August 2009, available at www.imf.org/external/np/pp/eng/2009/082809B.pdf.

253 The IMF and the World Bank note, 'More than three-quarters of the membership have volunteered for FSAP assessments or agreed to do so in the near future, including almost all the G20 countries.' IMF and World Bank, above n. 252, at 4. In the Declaration of Washington of 15 November 2008, the leaders of the G20 declared that 'all G-20 members commit to undertake a Financial Sector Assessment Program (FSAP) report and support the transparent assessments of countries' national regulatory systems'. G20 Declaration, 'Summit on Financial Markets and the World Economy', 15 November 2008, available at www.g20.org/Documents/g20_summit_declaration.pdf. At the time of writing, the G20 countries that have not been subject to an FSAP are Argentina, Brazil, China, India, Indonesia, South Korea and United States. However, assessments of China, Indonesia and the United States are being performed.

254 Alford, above n. 197, at 269–92, and L. Lee, 'The Basle Accords as Soft Law: Strengthening International Banking Supervision', (1998) 39 *Virginia Journal of International Law* 1, at 36.

255 IMF, 'Surveillance Policies for the International Monetary Fund 2008–2011', 8 October 2008, revised in September 2009, available at www.imf.org/external/np/pdr/surv/2008/index.htm.

256 M. Giovanoli, 'Architecture for the Global Financial Market: Legal Aspects of International Standard Setting', in M. Giovanoli (ed.), *International Monetary Law. Issues for the New Millennium* (Oxford University Press, 2000) 3–59, at 49.

257 Art. 5(1)(c) and (d), Financial Stability Board Charter, available at www.financialstabilityboard.org/about/mandate.htm.

strong incentives for states to implement the Basel principles and standards. Further, on 21 September 2010, the Executive Board of the IMF decided to make financial stability assessments under the FSAP a *mandatory part* of the IMF's surveillance under Article IV of the IMF Articles of Agreement when it concerns IMF members with systemically important financial sectors.[258]

200. Besides such international institutional pressure, incentives may also originate in the market itself. Adhering to international standards may be a way to secure access to the domestic financial sector to other markets (especially the markets of the countries that are represented in the Basel Committee).[259] Hence, when the regulatory conditions and supervisory practices that WTO members impose on foreign banks and services are examined in the light of the obligations in the GATS, the Basel principles and standards will play a role (especially when the prohibitions of discrimination and the exceptions are applied).

201. The GATS and its Annexes and Understanding, as well as the Basel principles and standards, together define the legal framework that must be considered to determine the extent to which the right of WTO members to regulate and supervise their banking sector is restricted. In the next chapters, the right to regulate is considered first. Thereafter, we focus on the right to supervise.

[258] The financial stability assessments consist of: (i) an evaluation of the source, probability, and potential impact of the main risks to macro-financial stability in the short term, based on an analysis of the structure and soundness of the financial system and its interlinkages with the rest of the economy; (ii) an assessment of each country's financial stability policy framework, involving an evaluation of the effectiveness of financial sector supervision against international standards; and (iii) an assessment of the authorities' capacity to manage and resolve a financial crisis should the risks materialize, looking at the country's liquidity management framework, financial safety nets, crisis preparedness and crisis resolution frameworks. The twenty-nine IMF members considered to have a systemically important financial sector are Australia, Austria, Belgium, Brazil, Canada, China, Denmark, Finland, France, Germany, Hong Kong SAR, India, Ireland, Italy, Japan, India, Ireland, Luxembourg, Mexico, Netherlands, Russia, Singapore, South Korea, Spain, Sweden, Switzerland, Turkey, United Kingdom, and United States. Decision by the Executive Board of the IMF, Integrating Stability Assessments under the Financial Sector Assessment Program into Art. IV Surveillance (Revised Proposed Decision), 21 September 2010, available at www.imf.org/external/np/pp/eng/2010/082710b.pdf and Update of 15 November 2013.

[259] Alexander, Dhumale and Eatwell, above n. 9, at 143–144.

8

Limitations on the right of WTO members to regulate the banking sector

8.1 Introduction

202. In Part I, we discussed the importance of regulation and supervision in the banking sector to prevent the private and social costs of banking failures. Further, we addressed the economic literature arguing that intensified international competition in the banking sector can lead to efficiency gains. However, economists are far from unanimous on the question whether competition improves or threatens financial stability. Therefore national policymakers must define the balance between regulation and liberalization of the market for banking services. The international project of liberalizing trade in services influences the WTO members' regulatory leeway.

203. The GATS contains the legally binding international obligations with regard to liberalization of trade in banking services. Still, in the application of these obligations, the Basel principles and standards can play a role. Given the fact that the GATS involves a project in which 159 WTO members are involved, often with very different levels of economic development, it is no surprise that the application of a number of obligations in the GATS is very flexible. Moreover, especially in the area of financial services, there exists a broad exception for measures taken for prudential reasons. In the following sections we analyse the international obligations WTO members must respect when they want to regulate the market for banking services. Before considering the different obligations, we determine the extent to which banking regulation falls within the scope of the GATS.

8.2 Banking regulation falling within the scope of the GATS

204. The GATS applies to 'measures by Members affecting trade in services'.[260] This is a threshold question that needs to be addressed

[260] Art. I:1 GATS.

before consistency with any of the substantive provisions of the GATS can be examined.[261] It is an important question not only for determining the extent to which the GATS restricts the right of WTO members not only to *regulate* the market for banking services, but also to *supervise* it. The latter question is discussed in Chapter 9 below.

205. We must consider three issues in order to determine the general scope of application of the GATS: (a) what actions qualify as 'measures'; (b) what is necessary in order for measures to 'affect' trade in services; and (c) what exactly concerns 'trade in services' and specifically in 'financial services'. In principle, *any* policy intervention in the banking sector falls within the scope of the GATS, *provided* that it affects trade in services.

8.2.1 'Measures'

206. A broad range of measures may affect trade in services. Article XXVIII(a) GATS defines 'measure' as 'any measure by a Member, whether in the form of a law, regulation, rule, procedure, decision, administrative action, or any other form'.

207. When a dispute is brought under the dispute settlement system, it is important to determine precisely the measure that is challenged (the 'measure at issue'), since this determination defines the jurisdiction ('terms of reference') of the panel.[262] Moreover, it is important for the responding member to know exactly against what challenge it has to defend itself.[263] Finally, determining the measure at issue is crucial for the implementation

[261] Appellate Body Report, *Canada – Certain Measures Affecting the Automotive Industry* (*Canada – Autos*), WT/DS139/AB/R, WT/DS142/AB/R, adopted 19 June 2000, paras. 151–152.

[262] Art. 7.1 DSU. See Appellate Body Report, *China – Measures Relating to the Exportation of Various Raw Materials* (*China – Raw Materials*), WT/DS394/AB/R, WT/DS395/AB/R and WT/DS398/AB/R, adopted 22 February 2012, para. 219.

[263] Arts. 3.3 and 6.2 DSU. The link with the rights of the defendant was clearly made by the Appellate Body in *Thailand – H-Beams*. There, the Appellate Body stated, 'Article 6.2 of the DSU calls for sufficient clarity with respect to the legal basis of the complaint, that is, with respect to the "claims" that are being asserted by the complaining party. A defending party is entitled to know what case it has to answer, and what violations have been alleged so that it can begin preparing its defence. Likewise, those Members of the WTO who intend to participate as third parties in panel proceedings must be informed of the legal basis of the complaint. This requirement of due process is fundamental to ensuring a fair and orderly conduct of dispute settlement proceedings.' Appellate Body Report, *Thailand – Anti-Dumping Duties on Angles, Shapes and Sections of Iron or Non-Alloy Steel and H-Beams from Poland* (*Thailand – H-Beams*), WT/DS122/AB/R, adopted 5 April 2001, para. 88.

once the panel has made its findings in a report.[264] The report will address the measure at issue and, if this measure is found to be WTO-inconsistent, only this measure will need to be modified. Other aspects of a WTO member's regulatory framework will remain unaffected.

208. Measures that are challenged before the WTO can be subdivided in measures that are challenged 'as such' and measures that can be challenged 'as applied'.[265] Only once the 'measure at issue' is defined, one can embark upon the substantive analysis on the consistency of a measure with the relevant WTO provision.[266]

209. Policy intervention to shape the market for banking services has two important aspects. First, it involves the regulation of the market. Second, it also involves the assessment of the compliance of a bank with regulatory requirements at the moment the bank applies to obtain a bank licence and continuously during the operation of the bank. While banking regulation that imposes minimum capital requirements leaves not much discretion to competent authorities when applying the requirements (the bank complies with the ratio or not, be it that there may be some discretion in the risk ratings that banks are allowed to use), many banking regulations often leave discretion to the competent authorities to determine the practical meaning of regulatory requirements and thus depend on discretionary assessments by these authorities (e.g. whether persons are 'fit and proper' as bank managers). Supervisory assessments thus involve an indispensable aspect of policy towards the banking sector.

210. The fact that the practical meaning of certain banking regulation depends to a large extent on assessments by authorities also means that one can often only determine whether such banking regulation violates GATS obligations if one considers the *application* of this regulation. It is thus sometimes difficult to maintain a strict distinction between regulatory and supervisory measures. In the paragraphs that directly follow here, we examine how WTO law makes a distinction between claims brought against measures 'as such' and 'as applied'. We examine the

[264] A. Yanovich and T. Voon, 'What is the Measure at Issue?', in A. Mitchell (ed.), *Challenges and Prospects for the WTO* (London: Cameron May, 2005) 115–63, at 117.

[265] Ibid., at 125–7; and WTO, *A Handbook on the WTO Dispute Settlement System* (Cambridge University Press, 2004) 44.

[266] Appellate Body Report, *United States – Laws, Regulations and Methodology for Calculating Dumping Margins ('Zeroing')* (*US – Zeroing (EC)*), WT/DS294/AB/R, adopted 9 May 2006, para. 203.

extent to which supervisory assessments by competent authorities *in individual cases* (e.g. a foreign bank applies for a licence for a local subsidy in a host country, but the supervisory authorities in the host country consider that there are insufficient guarantees that the banking group will be adequately supervised on a consolidated basis) fall within the scope of the GATS in Chapter 9 (below, paras. 472–556).

8.2.1.1 The general scope of the GATS and the normative scope of individual GATS obligations

211. The broad definition of the word 'measure' in Article XXVIII(a) GATS implies that WTO members may challenge a wide range of measures as a violation of the GATS provisions. However, some provisions in the GATS narrow down the range of measures that are envisaged by a provision. This depends on the 'normative scope' of the provision. For instance, Articles VI:4 and VI:5, on domestic regulation, apply only to qualification requirements and procedures, technical standards and licensing requirements. Furthermore, Article XVI, on market access, applies only to the six types of market access restrictions listed in Article XVI:2.[267] The normative scope of the individual GATS provisions thus imposes a limitation on the measures that can be challenged.

8.2.1.2 Challenging measures 'as such' or 'as applied'

212. Furthermore, measures can be challenged 'as such' or 'as applied'. Deciding whether to challenge a measure 'as such' or 'as applied' determines the outcome of the dispute. Depending on the result envisaged, the complainant must consider carefully whether to phrase the complaint against the measure 'as such' or 'as applied'. Often, the claim is brought against both.

213. Still, if the panel or the Appellate Body decide that there is a violation, it makes an important difference whether the findings concern the measure 'as such' or 'as applied'. If a measure is challenged 'as such', the complainant seeks to prevent WTO members *ex ante* from engaging in certain conduct.[268] If a measure is challenged 'as such', the complainant

[267] See below, para. 246.

[268] Appellate Body Report, *United States – Sunset Reviews of Anti-Dumping Measures on Oil Country Tubular Goods from Argentina* (*US – Oil Country Tubular Goods Sunset Reviews*), WT/DS268/AB/R, adopted 17 December 2004, para. 172; repeated in Appellate Body Report, *US – Zeroing (EC)*, para. 243.

asserts 'that a Member's conduct – not only in a particular instance that has occurred, but in future situations as well – will necessarily be inconsistent with that Member's WTO obligations'.[269] In contrast, when a measure is challenged 'as applied', what the complainant wants to achieve is preventing a future *application* of the measure in a WTO-inconsistent way, as has allegedly been done in the past. It does not seek the elimination or modification of the measure itself but only of a certain application of it. The Appellate Body stressed the seriousness of 'as such' claims by noting that 'implications of such challenges are obviously more far-reaching than "as applied" claims'.[270]

214. A measure is often challenged 'as applied' in a specific situation. The distinction is especially relevant when a law or regulation leaves discretion on how it must be applied in practice. Individual applications of a measure that seems 'as such' not WTO-inconsistent may nevertheless in these practical instances constitute a violation.[271] For instance, a particular interpretation of a law or regulation by the administrative authorities may be inconsistent with WTO obligations. A WTO member may then challenge the law or regulation 'as applied' to prevent this interpretation being used in the future.

8.2.1.3 Mandatory versus discretionary measures

215. The question whether an action constitutes a measure that should be challenged 'as such' or should rather be challenged 'as applied' is linked to the characterization of the measure as 'mandatory' or 'discretionary'. Given the fact that many bank regulations provide room for discretionary assessments by supervisory authorities, this distinction is of particular importance here.

216. Arguably, in the case of banking services, a claim against *the law or regulation 'as such'* will often be unsuccessful. Banking laws and regulations often leave discretion to the supervisory authorities that will determine whether the banking regulation is being complied with. The

[269] Appellate Body Report, *US – Oil Country Tubular Goods Sunset Reviews*, para. 172.

[270] Ibid.

[271] See Panel Report, *Canada – Measures Affecting the Export of Civilian Aircraft* (*Canada – Aircraft*), WT/DS70/R, adopted 20 August 1999, upheld by Appellate Body Report, WT/DS70/AB/R, para. 9.124, referring to the GATT case: *United States – Measures Affecting the Importation, Internal Sale and Use of Tobacco*, BISD 41S/131, adopted on 4 October 1994 (*United States – Tobacco*), para. 118.

authorities will thus interpret the conditions in the regulations. Whether a measure that leaves discretion may violate the GATS will probably depend on the GATS obligation at stake. As explained below (paras. 521–530), measures that leave broad discretion may violate Article VI:1, Article VI:5 or the disciplines developed on the basis of Article VI:4 if they are not based on 'objective and transparent' criteria. Equally, such broad discretion may be problematic in the light of Article VII, which requires a WTO member that recognizes another member's standards as equivalent to its own to afford adequate opportunity to other WTO members to show that they also should deserve the benefit of recognition (below, para. 360).

217. In contrast, it appears more difficult to establish clearly that a regulation that leaves discretion violates 'as such' GATS provisions that prohibit discrimination (most-favoured-nation treatment and national treatment). Arguably, a panel will only find a violation if a complainant can prove convincingly that the discretionary measure involves a risk of discrimination that has a 'chilling effect' on economic operators.[272] These operators may not want to conduct business any more in the member state that has adopted the measure because of the unpredictable discriminatory application. Consistent application of this measure (the 'practice' linked to the measure) may provide proof of this risk. Because it may not always be easy to establish that a discretionary measure violates a GATS provision, the challenge would rather be directed at the measure 'as applied'. A discretionary measure that 'as such' does not violate a GATS provision that prohibits discrimination might nevertheless 'as applied' violate this obligation, if it is consistently applied in a discriminatory manner.

8.2.1.4 Measures attributable to a government

218. Measures may be taken by central, regional or local governments and authorities, as well as by non-governmental bodies in the exercise of powers delegated by central, regional or local governments or authorities.[273] It is essential that the measures that are challenged can be attributed to the government of a WTO member. 'Self-regulation' by professional bodies may also be challenged for violating the GATS as far as the government has delegated competences to the regulatory body.[274]

[272] Panel Report, *US – Section 301 Trade Act*, para. 7.81–7.85. [273] Art. I:3(a) GATS.
[274] Art. I:3(a)(ii) GATS.

8.2.2 *'Affecting'*

219. WTO case law has clarified that a measure may directly govern the supply of a service, or may regulate other matters but nevertheless affect trade in services.[275] The GATS thus has a broad scope of application and there is no *a priori* exclusion of any measures from it.[276] This broad scope of application is intended to 'ensure that the disciplines of the GATS would cover any measure bearing upon conditions of competition in supply of a service, regardless of whether the measure directly governs or indirectly affects the supply of the service'.[277]

8.2.3 *'Trade in (financial) services'*

220. The concept of 'service' in the GATS is a broad one, and covers 'any service in any sector *except* services supplied in the exercise of governmental authority'. The GATS thus applies a negative definition of 'service'. Services supplied in the exercise of governmental authority are services which are supplied *neither* on a commercial basis *nor* in competition with one or more service suppliers.[278] However, the Annex on Financial Services provides a more specified definition in the case of financial services.[279]

221. The Annex excludes the following activities from the scope of the GATS: (i) activities conducted by a central bank or monetary authority or by any other public entity in pursuit of monetary or exchange rate

275 Panel Reports, *European Communities – Regime for the Importation, Sale and Distribution of Bananas* (*EC – Bananas III*), WT/DS27/R/ECU *(Ecuador)*, WT/DS27/R/GTM, WT/DS27/R/HND *(Guatemala and Honduras)*, WT/DS27/R/MEX *(Mexico)*, and WT/DS27/R/USA *(US)*, adopted 25 September 1997, as modified by Appellate Body Report, WT/DS27/AB/R, para. 7.285.

276 Appellate Body Report, *European Communities – Regime for the Importation, Sale and Distribution of Bananas* (*EC – Bananas III*), WT/DS27/AB/R, adopted 25 September 1997, para. 220. See also Panel Report, *United States – Measures Affecting the Cross-Border Supply of Gambling and Betting Services* (*US – Gambling*), WT/DS285/R, adopted 20 April 2005, as modified by Appellate Body Report, WT/DS285/AB/R, para. 6.174.

277 Panel Report, *EC – Bananas III*, para. 7.281.

278 Art. I:3(b) and (c) GATS (emphasis added). See E. Leroux, 'What Is a "Service Supplied in the Exercise of Governmental Authority" Under Art. I:3(b) and (c) of the General Agreement on Trade in Services?', (2006) 40 *Journal of World Trade* 345. VanDuzer has noted that Art. I:3(b) is 'not an exception, but rather a provision that defines the scope of the Agreement's application'. J. VanDuzer, 'Health, Education and Social Services in Canada: The Impact of the GATS', in J. Curtis and D. Ciuriak (eds.), *Trade Policy Research 2004* (Ottawa: Trade Policy Canada, 2004) 303–505, at 393.

279 Paragraph 1(d) Annex on Financial Services.

policies; (ii) activities forming part of a statutory system of social security or public retirement plan; and (iii) other activities conducted by a public entity on account of or with the guarantee of or using the financial resources of the government.[280] Hence these services do not fall within the scope of the GATS because of their special nature.[281] A WTO member is not required to open up these services to competition by suppliers from other WTO members. However, if the WTO member allows services of types (ii) and (iii) to be supplied 'in competition with a public entity or a financial service supplier', they are no longer excluded from the scope of the GATS.[282]

222. Furthermore, the Annex specifies that a 'financial service supplier' 'means any natural or juridical person of a Member wishing to supply or supplying financial services'. Nevertheless, this 'does not include a public entity'.[283] Measures that apply to a financial service provider that is a 'public entity' fall outside the scope of the GATS. 'Public entity' is further defined in two ways. First, a public entity is a 'government, a central bank or a monetary authority, of a Member, or an entity owned or controlled by a Member, that is principally engaged in carrying out governmental functions or activities for governmental purposes'.[284] This first definition focuses on the nature of the entity. The Annex immediately adds that this does not include 'an entity principally engaged in supplying financial services on commercial terms'.[285] The second definition considers the situation where a private entity is nevertheless considered to be a public entity. It focuses rather on the functions that an entity performs. A private entity is considered to be a public entity when it is 'performing functions normally performed by a central bank or monetary authority, when exercising those functions'.[286]

[280] Ibid., paragraph 1(b). Von Bogdandy and Windsor consider the activities described in paragraph 1(b)(iii) to be 'a broadly phrased catch-all'. See A. Von Bogdandy and J. Windsor, 'Annex on Financial Services', in Wolfrum, Stoll and Feinäugle, above n. 156, 618–39, at 631.

[281] Importantly, the focus is on the special nature of the services *in the country where the foreign service supplier seeks access*. Therefore it does not matter that a service supplier that seeks access is in the home country performing an activity of the type listed in paragraph 1(b). Hence the fact that a public entity from a certain WTO member (using the financial resources of the government) seeks to gain access to another member to provide services is not a reason to exclude the application of the GATS. Only when this entity would seek to provide services of the type listed in paragraph 1(b) in the host country would the exclusion apply.

[282] Paragraph 1(c) Annex on Financial Services. [283] Ibid., paragraph 5(b).

[284] Ibid., paragraph 5(c)(i). [285] Ibid. [286] Ibid., paragraph 5(c)(ii).

223. The exception in paragraph 1(c) (when services supplied in the exercise of governmental authority (normally excluded from the GATS) are nevertheless provided in competition with other suppliers, they are still included in the scope of the GATS) does not apply to functions performed by a central bank or monetary authority.[287] Hence the services by a private entity that performs such functions are *never* subject to the GATS.

224. The GATS does not define precisely what a 'service' is, or where the exact difference regarding 'good' lies.[288] It only defines forms ('modes') of 'trade in services'. The GATS applies to four different modes of providing services.[289]

225. The first mode (Mode 1) concerns the *cross-border supply* of services. This means that the service crosses the border without any movement of the service provider or consumer.

226. The second mode (Mode 2) concerns the *consumption of services abroad* by a service consumer who to this end moves abroad. In the case where a WTO member has made a commitment under Mode 2, the member undertakes not to prevent its own citizens from going abroad to receive services there. This is because the service sector of the member making the commitment is opened up to foreign competition. Foreign competition also emerges from the fact that consumers can easily move abroad to consume services provided by foreign suppliers.

227. The third mode (Mode 3) is *commercial presence*. Mode 3 covers two situations, depending whether the presence takes the form of a legal person or not. First, commercial presence means 'any type of business

[287] Paragraph 1(c) only refers to the activities in subparagraphs (b)(ii) and (iii) of paragraph 1(b). Hence the activities in subparagraph (b)(i) will never be subject to the GATS.

[288] For an extensive discussion of the distinction between goods and services see F. Smith and L. Woods, 'A Distinction without a Difference: Exploring the Boundary between Goods and Services in the World Trade Organization and the European Union', (2005) 12 *Columbia Journal of European Law* 1. In *China – Publications and Audiovisual Products*, the Appellate Body focused on the physical nature of a product to determine whether it should be classified as a good or a service. Since films are carried by physical delivery materials, restrictions on their imports must also be considered under the GATT. The Appellate Body confirmed that certain measures affect both goods and services and that a distinction between the content (the film) and the good (the physical carrier) is artificial. Appellate Body Report, *China – Measures Affecting Trading Rights and Distribution Services for Certain Publications and Audiovisual Entertainment Products* (*China – Publications and Audiovisual Products*), WT/DS363/AB/R, adopted 19 January 2010, paras. 188 and 195.

[289] Art. I:2 GATS.

or professional establishment, including through . . . the constitution, acquisition or maintenance of a juridical person'.[290] One can create such a juridical person by establishing a new subsidiary (legal person), but also by taking a controlling interest (de jure or de facto)[291] in an existing financial service provider.[292] Second, there may be commercial presence without creating a separate legal person in the host country, through 'the creation or maintenance of a branch or a representative office'.[293]

228. Finally, the fourth mode (Mode 4) is the *presence of a natural person* in the territory of another member state in order to offer services. It may concern self-employed service suppliers who travel abroad, as well as natural persons who, employed by a service supplier, travel abroad to offer a service. However, the GATS only applies to measures affecting the 'temporary' presence of natural persons.[294]

229. The distinction between the different modes of supply is first of all based on the origin of the supplier and receiver of the service as well as on

[290] Art. XXVIII(d)(i) GATS.

[291] Art. XXVIII(m)(ii) GATS indicates that a commercial presence by a 'juridical person of another Member' is a juridical person that is 'owned or controlled by' (natural or legal) persons of that member. A person from another WTO member state thus does not necessarily have to have a majority stake in a company (that is a service supplier) to be able to control this service supplier.

[292] See the discussion by Crosby, demonstrating that China cannot validly claim that it made only market access commitments for *establishing new* companies and not for *acquisition of equity* in existing Chinese companies. D. Crosby, 'Banking on China's WTO Commitments: "Same Bed, Different Dreams" in China's Financial Services Sector', (2008) 11 *Journal of International Economic Law* 75, at 95.

[293] See Art. XXVIII(d)(ii) GATS.

[294] See paragraph 2 of the Annex on Movement of Natural Persons Supplying Services under the Agreement. It is far from clear how the concept 'temporary' (or 'non-permanent') needs to be interpreted. There is no available case law on this subject. The temporal nature is most likely related to the time needed for providing the service. Nonetheless, this depends greatly on the service that is at stake. Bast suggests that a presence of more than one year involves permanent employment. He bases this on the IMF *Balance of Payment Manual* that indicates that 'if the employees are from other economies but are employed for one year or more, they are treated as residents of the economies of location, and their compensation is classified in the same manner. Thus, in the case of employees from other economies who are employed for less than one year, no payments to residents are involved.' IMF, *Balance of Payments Manual*, 5th edn (Washington, DC: IMF, 1993) 70, para. 270; also J. Bast, 'Annex on Movement of Natural Persons', in Wolfrum, Stoll and Feinäugle, above n. 156, 573–95, at 587. It nevertheless seems very difficult to accept such a general rule; rather, a case-by-case assessment seems appropriate for defining the 'temporal nature'.

the place where they are physically present.[295] Because of the quick development of telecommunications technology and the emergence of e-commerce, it is often very difficult to define the exact difference between the separate modes of supply, especially between modes 1 and 2.[296] In particular, how does one define the place where a service is received when no physical movement is involved, but a consumer 'virtually' visits the website of a bank abroad? For instance, when money is lent by a bank to a consumer, the bank and the consumer do not necessarily need to meet each other physically.

230. An informal note by the WTO Secretariat suggested alternative criteria for defining the place where such a service is received: the place where the borrowed funds are provided, the place where the service was purchased or the place where repayment is due.[297] These criteria have never been applied in a dispute.

231. The Panel Report in *US – Gambling* has confirmed the principle of the 'technological neutrality' of the GATS. In this dispute, the US prohibition on providing 'remote gambling and betting services' was challenged. According to the panel, the GATS does not distinguish between the different 'means of delivery' to determine whether Mode 1 or Mode 2 is at stake. Trade in services through electronic means can thus be qualified within any mode of supply.[298] The panel accepted that online gambling activities concern cross-border service provision (Mode 1) and not the consumption of services abroad (Mode 2). This decision was not clarified by means of further arguments and the Appellate Body did not reconsider it.[299] On this basis, it seems that a panel will likely consider opening a bank account online or concluding a loan agreement via the Internet as service provision by means of cross-border supply (Mode 1).

[295] WTO, Guidelines for Scheduling of Specific Commitments under the General Agreement on Trade in Services (GATS), adopted by the Council for Trade in Services on 23 March 2001, S/L/92, 28 March 2001, para. 26.

[296] See, e.g., the comments by the representative of Brazil in Committee on Trade in Financial Services, Report of the Meeting Held on 23 June 2005, Note by the Secretariat, S/FIN/M/49, 24 August 2005 at para. 15.

[297] Committee on Trade in Financial Services, Technical Issues Concerning Financial Services Schedules, S/FIN/W/9, 29 July 1996, para. 10.

[298] See also Panel Report, *US – Gambling*, para. 6.285.

[299] Ibid., para. 6.29. See also on this matter S. Zleptnig, 'The GATS and Internet-Based Services: Between Market Access and Domestic Regulation', (2007) 20 *Cambridge Review of International Affairs* 133, at 139–40.

232. The Annex on Financial Services seeks to clarify further the concept of financial service as 'any service of a financial nature offered by a financial service supplier of a Member. Financial services include all insurance and insurance-related services, and all banking and other financial services (excluding insurance).'[300] The Annex then provides a non-exhaustive list of insurance and insurance-related services and of banking and other financial services:[301]

Insurance and insurance-related services

(i) direct insurance (including co-insurance):
  (A) life
  (B) non-life;
(ii) reinsurance and retrocession;
(iii) insurance intermediation, such as brokerage and agency;
(iv) services auxiliary to insurance, such as consultancy, actuarial, risk assessment and claim settlement services.

Banking and other financial services (excluding insurance)

(v) acceptance of deposits and other repayable funds from the public;
(vi) lending of all types, including consumer credit, mortgage credit, factoring and financing of commercial transaction;
(vii) financial leasing;
(viii) all payment and money transmission services, including credit, charge and debit cards, travellers' cheques and bankers' drafts;
(ix) guarantees and commitments;
(x) trading for own account or for account of customers, whether on an exchange, in an over-the-counter market or otherwise, the following:
  (A) money market instruments (including cheques, bills, certificates of deposits);
  (B) foreign exchange;
  (C) derivative products including, but not limited to, futures and options;

[300] This definition is arguably tautological, because it states that financial services include all insurance and insurance-related services, and all banking *and other financial services* (excluding insurance).

[301] This list follows the UN Central Product Classification (United Nations Central Product Classification System, Version 1.1, UN Doc. ST/ESA/STAT/SER.M/77/Ver.1.1, March 2002, available at http://unstats.un.org/unsd/cr/registry/regcst.asp?Cl=16&Lg=1). See also Appellate Body Report, *Canada – Autos*, para. 157.

(D) exchange-rate and interest-rate instruments, including products such as swaps and forward rate agreements;
(E) transferable securities;
(F) other negotiable instruments and financial assets, including bullion;

(xi) participation in issues of all kinds of securities, including underwriting and placement as agent (whether publicly or privately) and provision of services related to such issues;
(xii) money broking;
(xiii) asset management, such as cash or portfolio management, all forms of collective investment management, pension fund management, custodial, depository and trust services;
(xiv) settlement and clearing services for financial assets, including securities, derivative products and other negotiable instruments;
(xv) provision and transfer of financial information, and financial data-processing and related software by suppliers of other financial services;
(xvi) advisory, intermediation and other auxiliary financial services on all the activities listed in subparagraphs (v) to (xv), including credit reference and analysis, investment and portfolio research and advice, and advice on acquisitions and on corporate restructuring and strategy.

8.2.4 Macroeconomic policy management and prudential measures

233. A 1997 WTO special study identified two types of policy interventions that would not be touched by the GATS: macroeconomic policy management and prudential measures.[302] However, it seems that these two types of policy intervention are not per se outside the scope of application of the GATS.

8.2.4.1 Macroeconomic policy management

234. As an example of macroeconomic policy management, the study refers to open market operations by central banks. However, the WTO special study does not indicate the legal basis for such general exclusion.

[302] WTO, 'Opening Markets in Financial Services and the Role of the GATS', WTO Special Studies, 1997, at 3.

235. As discussed in paragraph 222 above, there exists an exception from the scope of the GATS for 'services supplied in the exercise of governmental authority'. Such services include 'activities conducted by a central bank or monetary authority or by any other public entity in pursuit of monetary or exchange rate policies'.[303] Arguably, this does *not* mean that the measures taken by a central bank or monetary authority or other public entity are outside the scope of the GATS. What the specific exception in the Annex on Financial Services provides is that activities conducted by a central bank, monetary authority or any other public entity in pursuit of monetary or exchange-rate policies must not be considered 'services' within the scope of the GATS. Hence, if a government adopts a measure that affects such activities, this measure cannot be scrutinized under the GATS.[304] However, if the 'measure' at issue emerges from the central bank, monetary authority or other public entity, and this measure 'affects trade in financial services', this measure falls within the scope of the GATS. In other words, the exception with regard to the scope of the GATS focuses on the services that are affected by a measure at issue and thus does not consider the *nature* of the measure (macroeconomic policy management) or its *origin* (e.g. a measure emerging from the central bank) to be relevant.

236. It is clear that measures of macroeconomic policy management may affect trade in banking services. The WTO special study indicates that 'When a central bank conducts open market operations, for example, conditions in the financial sector could be affected through the impact of such interventions on the money supply, interest rates or exchange rates.'[305] For instance, these actions by the central bank may be discriminatory (e.g. excluding local subsidiaries or branches that are owned by banks established in another WTO member from the benefit of emergency assistance by the central bank of the WTO member where the subsidiaries or branches are located).[306] If the drafters of the Annex wanted to exclude these measures *ab initio* from the scope of

303 See Paragraph 1(b)(i) Annex on Financial Services.

304 However, it should be repeated that as soon as the WTO member in question allows one of the activities mentioned to be provided by private suppliers in competition with the public entities, these services are no longer excluded from the definition of 'service'. Paragraph 1(c) GATS Annex on Financial Services.

305 WTO, above n. 302, at 3.

306 WTO, OECD and UNCTAD, Report on G20 Trade and Investment Measures, 14 September 2009, available at www.wto.org/english/news_e/news09_e/trdev_dg_report_14sep09_e.doc, at 15. One example is the US Temporary Liquidity Guarantee Program (TLGP) of the Federal

the GATS, they should have explicitly stated that macroeconomic policy management measures, such as open-market operations by central banks, are excluded from the scope of the GATS, rather than make a confusing reference to 'services supplied in the exercise of governmental authority'.

237. Even if macroeconomic policy measures are within the general scope of the GATS, this does not necessarily mean that the GATS obligations impose a significant restriction on such measures. The GATS is a flexible agreement. For important obligations the WTO members can determine to what extent certain GATS obligations apply in the banking sector and to what types of measures. In this respect, note that section C.1 of the Understanding on Commitments in financial services states explicitly that when a WTO member that makes use of the Understanding when making national treatment commitments in financial services, this does not mean that it is obliged to provide access by foreign banks to the WTO member's lender-of-last-resort facilities. Under these circumstances, the national treatment obligation in Article XVII GATS does not affect this type of measure by a central bank. What is more, the exception in the GATS Annex on Financial Services for measures for prudential reasons would also be available to certain macroeconomic policy management measures when these measures seek to maintain financial stability.

8.2.4.2 Measures for prudential reasons

238. The second example of policy interventions that, according to the WTO special study, are not touched by the GATS are measures for prudential reasons.

239. Paragraph 2(a) of the GATS Annex on Financial Services indicates that WTO members 'shall not be prevented from taking measures for prudential reasons'. This is the so-called prudential 'carve-out'. A WTO Secretariat background note of 2 December 1998 on financial services noted that measures for prudential reasons must not be scheduled under the GATS, since they are not trade restrictions that could violate the

Deposit Insurance Corporation. Under that programme, branches of foreign banking institutions are not eligible for such a guarantee, even if they are insured with the FDIC (12 CFR §370.2(b)). It is indicated that 'insured depositary institutions' are eligible for the guarantee. These 'insured depositary institutions' are in turn defined in Section 3(c)(d) of the Federal Deposit Insurance Act, 12 USC 1813(c)(2), but 'insured branch[es]' of a foreign bank are excluded.

obligations of market access and national treatment.[307] However, as far as they do not pursue prudential objectives (e.g. licensing restrictions for foreigners with the objective of developing a domestic financial industry) they must be scheduled. The note indicates that this explains why some WTO members have scheduled measures that are at first sight prudential: they want to prevent any of these measures being challenged under the market access and national treatment obligations in the GATS.[308]

240. Because of the prudential 'carve-out', a panel that considers a dispute in respect of a measure that is allegedly prudential might quickly dismiss these claims. The panel may immediately accept that it is a prudential measure. It would thus consider the prudential exception before considering the GATS obligations that are allegedly violated. Nevertheless, since it is extremely difficult to determine the dividing line between prudential and non-prudential measures, one cannot exclude the possibility that such measures will be scrutinized under the GATS obligations. Moreover, it is more logical to assess first whether a regulation violates an obligation and only thereafter to consider whether the prudential exception applies.

241. In fact, the so-called prudential 'carve-out' does not remove prudential measures from the scope of the GATS, but merely exempts these measures from the obligations, subject to the conditions of the exemption. As a consequence, the common reference to paragraph 2(a) of the Annex on Financial Services as 'carving out' the scope of the GATS is not correct. It is an *exception*, to be applied once obligations with regard to the GATS are violated. Indeed, the paragraph starts with the phrase

[307] WTO Council for Trade in Services, Financial Services, Background Note by the Secretariat, S/C/W/72, 2 December 1998, at para. 35 *in fine*. Some major GATS obligations (market access and national treatment) are only applicable if the WTO member in question has decided to make them applicable to the banking sector. This can be consulted in the Schedule of Commitments of the WTO member. However, if this WTO member wants to maintain specific measures that violate the market access and national treatment obligations, it can inscribe these measures in the schedule as a 'limitation' to the commitment. If prudential measures are not touched by the GATS anyway, there would be no reason to inscribe them as a limitation.

[308] WTO Council for Trade in Services, Financial Services, Background Note by the Secretariat, S/C/W/72, 2 December 1998, para. 41. It is interesting that the Secretariat notes: 'As such licensing requirements are liberalized and are made purely prudential, they may no longer need to be scheduled as trade restrictions, but there may still be an issue of whether they constitute unnecessary barriers to trade in financial services.' In a footnote, the Secretariat states: 'Although technically, Article VI:4 and 5 may not be applicable to prudential measures, questions may remain as to whether they are based on objective and transparent criteria, or are not more burdensome than necessary.'

'Notwithstanding any other provisions of the Agreement'. This language clearly shows that it *is* an exception. The word 'notwithstanding' is indeed used elsewhere in the GATS to express an exception to an obligation.[309] The scope and content of paragraph 2(a) are discussed further in detail later in this chapter (para. 452).

8.2.5 Conclusion on banking regulation and the scope of the GATS

242. In the previous paragraphs we examined the extent to which banking regulation falls within the scope of the GATS. Any action affecting trade in banking services falls within the general scope of the GATS, provided it can be attributed to the government of a WTO member. Hence it appears that the GATS imposes an important restriction on the right of policymakers to determine the balance between regulation and liberalization of the market for banking services. Nonetheless, for the reasons discussed in the following sections, the opposite is true. Because of the limited normative scope (i.e. scope of application) of specific GATS obligations and the specific normative content (i.e. actual requirement imposed) of the obligations, it is not easy to show that a banking regulation violates an obligation. The many flexibilities and important prudential exception included in the GATS imply that the restriction imposed by the GATS is in fact rather limited.

243. Because the general scope of the GATS covers any government action affecting trade in services, we will now analyse the GATS obligations relating to banking services. One can distinguish three types of obligation: first, the obligation not to impose restrictions on market access that are mostly of a quantitative nature; second, obligations based on the prohibition of discrimination (subdivided between the obligation of most-favoured-nation treatment and national treatment); and, third, obligations imposing specific disciplines on domestic regulation.

8.3 GATS and market access

8.3.1 Introduction

244. In general, liberalization of trade in banking services seeks to create access for foreign banks to foreign markets. However, the market access

[309] See for instance, Art. V:3(b) of the GATS, Art. XXI:4(b) of the GATS or Paragraph 1 of the Second Annex on Financial Services. See also Art. XII:1 of the GATT 1994.

obligation in Article XVI GATS has a limited scope. Article XVI involves the obligation of WTO members not to impede market access in a services sector if the WTO member in question has made a commitment not to do so. Article XVI:2 lists six types of market access restrictions that cannot be maintained in the case of a commitment. The explicit listing of the prohibited market access restrictions is intentional, since it forms a guarantee against an overly intrusive application of Article XVI. One might indeed interpret a prohibition of market access restrictions as a prohibition against restricting economic freedom in general. Any regulation of the activity of service suppliers may form a restriction on their access to the services market of a state. Such an approach to Article XVI would imply a serious restriction on the competence of WTO members to adopt and apply banking regulation in general. However, Article XVI is more limited.

245. Article XVI GATS imposes on WTO members a requirement that they do not accord a treatment to services and service suppliers from other WTO members that is less favourable than the treatment to which a WTO member has committed in its schedule of market access commitments. The obligation of market access only applies as far as specific commitments were made by the member in question. WTO members are allowed to include limitations in their schedules of commitments, indicating what market access restrictions they still want to maintain. However, contrary to what is the case for the GATS provisions on most-favoured-nation treatment and national treatment (below, paras. 307–379), Article XVI is not based on discrimination. In other words, while in the case of Articles II and XVII discrimination is used as a 'proxy' for establishing protectionism, this is not necessary as far as Article XVI is concerned. As soon as a WTO member makes a relevant market access commitment, this prevents the member from adopting one of the measures that qualify as market access restrictions, unless a limitation was inscribed.

246. The types of measure that WTO members cannot adopt if they have made a full market access commitment are listed in Article XVI:2 GATS. The panel in *US – Gambling* stated that this list of six types of measure is an exhaustive one.[310] The majority of these measures are of a

[310] Panel Report, *US – Gambling*, paras. 6.298 and 6.318. This statement by the panel was not reviewed by the Appellate Body.

quantitative nature, like, for instance, measures that limit the number of service suppliers.[311] Other measures are of a different nature, namely measures which restrict or require specific types of legal entity or joint venture through which a service supplier may supply a service.[312]

247. The prohibition on adopting one of the measures listed in Article XVI:2 GATS is absolute. If a full market access commitment was made, the listed measures are prohibited outright, without further enquiry into whether or not the measure is discriminatory or is more restrictive than necessary.[313] The only way of justifying the measures in question would be to rely on Article XIV GATS or the prudential exception in the Annex on Financial Services.

248. Because of the absolute nature of the prohibition, it is essential to delineate clearly the scope of application of Article XIV. The wider the scope, the more the national regulatory autonomy of the WTO members is restricted. It is also important to define the scope of application of Article XVI in order to answer the question whether there exists overlap with Article XVII on national treatment and with Article VI on domestic regulation, all of which have a different normative content. When determining the scope of application of the different GATS provisions, one should make sense of the structure of the GATS, which contains sections that provide more intensive scrutiny than others. The Appellate Body has acknowledged that any interpretation on the basis of Article 31 of the Vienna Convention on the Law of Treaties (VCLT, which is recognized as customary international law[314]) must give meaning and effect to all the terms of the treaty. According to the Appellate Body, 'an interpreter is not free to adopt a reading that would result in reducing whole clauses or paragraphs of a treaty to redundancy or inutility'.[315]

[311] Art. XVI:2(a) GATS. [312] Art. XVI:2(e) GATS. See Zleptnig, above n. 299, at 142.

[313] F. Ortino, 'Treaty Interpretation and the WTO Appellate Body Report in *US – Gambling*: A Critique', (2006) 9 *Journal of International Economic Law* 117, at 138.

[314] The International Court of Justice has recognized repeatedly that Art. 31 VCLT reflects customary international law. See *Case Concerning the Territorial Dispute (Libyan Arab Jamahiriya/Chad)*, Judgment, [1994] ICJ Rep. 21, para. 41; *Case Concerning Oil Platforms (Islamic Republic of Iran/United States of America)*, Preliminary Objections, Judgment, [1996] (II) ICJ Rep. 812, para. 23 and, specifically on Art. 31.3, *Case Concerning Kasikili/Sedudu Island*, Judgment, [1994] ICJ Rep. 1045, para. 48.

[315] Appellate Body Report, *United States – Standards for Reformulated and Conventional Gasoline* (*US – Gasoline*), WT/DS2/AB/R, adopted 20 May 1996, p. 21.

8.3.2 *Quantitative restrictions and absolute prohibitions*

249. A first question relating to the scope of the application of Article XVI is how the types of measures that are listed in Article XVI:2 must be interpreted. The wider the range of measures that are subsumed under the six categories of measures, the more intense the scrutiny imposed by the market access obligation. This issue was of major concern in the *US – Gambling* case. In this dispute, Antigua and Barbuda challenged a number of US federal and state rules that imposed restrictions on suppliers of gambling services that were located outside the United States. The restrictions prevented these suppliers from providing gambling and betting services to consumers in the United States. The panel and Appellate Body both agreed that these federal and state measures constituted violations contrary to the market access commitments made by the United States. However, contrary to the panel, the Appellate Body accepted that these measures were justified under Article XIV(a) GATS.

250. After having decided that the United States had indeed made a market access commitment with regard to gambling and betting services under the entry 'Other recreational services',[316] the panel and the Appellate Body addressed the question whether the measures fell under one of the types of measure listed in Article XVI:2. The panel concluded that the list of measures in Article XVI:2 is exhaustive.[317] Some authors have nevertheless suggested that the list cannot be exhaustive. The Appellate Body did not address this question in *US – Gambling*.[318]

251. The specific types of measure at stake in the dispute were limitations on the number of service suppliers, in the form of numerical quotas,

[316] Panel Report, *US – Gambling*, para. 6.134, and Appellate Body Report, *US – Gambling*, para. 213.

[317] Panel Report, *US – Gambling*, para. 6.318. Hence Art. XVI:1 has no 'residual' application. In this respect, Leroux has stated dramatically: 'This provided a sigh of relief, as any other interpretation would have disastrous consequences for the WTO membership as a whole.' E. Leroux, 'Eleven Years of GATS Case Law: What Have We Learned?', (2007) 10 *Journal of International Economic Law* 749, at 769.

[318] Ortino argues that there may nevertheless be some indication that the Appellate Body would disagree with the conclusion of the panel. He states that this can be derived from the fact that the Appellate Body concluded that both Art. XVI:2(a) and Art. XVI:2(c) apply to the US measures. In his view, 'If the list were really exhaustive in nature, the limitations listed in subparagraphs (a) to (f) would not apply cumulatively.' See Ortino, above n. 313, at 137. See also, disagreeing that the list is exhaustive, Leroux, above n. 317, at 770–1; P. Mavroidis, 'Highway XVI Revisited: The Road from Non-discrimination to Market Access in GATS', (2007) 6 *World Trade Review* 1, at 6 (n. 15).

monopolies, exclusive service suppliers or an economic needs test (Article XVI:2(a)), as well as limitations on the total number of service operations or total quantity of service output expressed in terms of numerical units in the form of quotas or an economic needs test (Article XVI:2(c)). The main question in this respect was whether the measures amounted to limitations 'in the form of' numerical quotas. The measures in dispute did not express their limitations explicitly in the form of numerical restrictions. Rather, they involved the imposition of fines or prison sentences on whoever engaged in offering online gambling and betting services. It was thus clear that no service supplier (be it a domestic or foreign one) was permitted to engage in such activities and that no service operations consisting of such activities were allowed. Still, Antigua argued that these measures, which impose a total prohibition, are numerical restrictions of zero.[319] Thus, even though the measures at issue did not literally refer to numerical restrictions, they certainly had the *effect* of imposing a zero quota. The panel accepted that these measures were indeed of the type listed in Article XVI:2(a)[320] and (b).[321]

252. The statements by Appellate Body on this issue do not excel in clarity. The Appellate Body noted that it did not agree that 'the words "in the form of" should be ignored or replaced by the words "that have the effect of"'.[322] Nevertheless, it noted that the thrust of the measures listed in Article XVI:2(a) and (c) 'is not on the *form* of limitations, but on their *numerical*, or *quantitative*, nature'.[323] Even if the drafters of the GATS might have had in mind numerical restrictions above zero, nothing in the text of the provision prevents limitations amounting to zero from also being considered quantitative limitations within the scope of Article XVI:2(a) and (c).[324] Hence, without explicitly accepting that a national measure that has the *effect* of one of the measures listed in Article XVI:2 is also caught in its scope, the Appellate Body nevertheless stretched the meaning to something that is very close to that. Still, it did not use the word 'effect' but rather the words 'amounting to' or 'resulting in'. Even so, such interpretation implies that a wide range of measures may be captured under the absolute prohibition of Article XVI.

[319] Panel Report, *US – Gambling*, para. 4.130. This argument was also made by the European Communities, ibid., para. 5.35.
[320] Ibid., para. 6.338. [321] Ibid., para. 6.355.
[322] Appellate Body Report, *US – Gambling*, para. 232.
[323] Ibid. (emphasis in original).
[324] Appellate Body Report, *US – Gambling*, paras. 233, 238 and 251.

253. The Appellate Body's approach has been widely criticized as intruding too much into national regulatory autonomy.[325] If the types of measure listed in Article XVI:2 also cover measures that do not take the exact form of those listed but nevertheless 'amount to' or 'result in' such a listed measure, it becomes unclear where the limits of the scrutiny through Article XVI are. To be sure, the Appellate Body was aware of this and therefore left the door open for such limitation by stressing that it did *not* replace the words 'in the form of' by 'having the effect of' and that the thrust of the measures in Article XVI:2(a) and (c) is on the quantitative nature. Because the *quantitative* nature of the listed measures was seen as determinative, national measures that might restrict market access but would not impose a quota will arguably be excluded from the scope of the prohibition. At the same time, it makes sense not to limit the prohibition to measures that literally impose a numerical restriction.[326] Arguably, only when one can translate these measures *ex ante* (i.e. when placing oneself at the moment when the measure was adopted) into numbers are they caught by Article XVI:2(a) or (c). This of course leads to the inclusion of measures that express the quantitative limitation in advance, but also of measures that do not do this explicitly but for which this can clearly be determined in advance. If that is not possible, they may still be considered under Article XVII or Article VI. In fact, such translation into specific numbers will quite often be impossible, since the quantitative effect of a national measure will often only be clear once the measure has entered into effect. This already limits seriously the impact of the statements by the Appellate Body.[327]

[325] D. Irwin and J. Weiler, 'Measures Affecting Cross-Border Supply of Gambling and Betting Services (DS 285)', (2008) 7 *World Trade Review* 71; M. Krajewski, 'Playing by the Rules of the Game? Specific Commitments after *US – Gambling and Betting* and the Current GATS Negotiations', (2005) 32 *Legal Issues of Economic Integration* 417; Mavroidis, above n. 318; Ortino, above n. 313; J. Pauwelyn, '*Rien ne Va Plus?* Distinguishing Domestic Regulation from Market Access in GATT and GATS', (2005) 4 *World Trade Review* 131; and J. Trachtman, 'United States – Measures Affecting the Cross-Border Supply of Gambling and Betting Services', (2005) 99 *American Journal of International Law* 861.

[326] See also Leroux, above n. 317, at 774.

[327] For instance, to use the example of Pauwelyn, if a WTO member requires taxi drivers to submit themselves to a driving test, it would not be possible to 'translate' this requirement into specific quantitative restrictions that are set on the moment of adopting such prohibition. It would thus not be a measure that falls within the scope of Art. XVI, but should rather be assessed under Arts. XVII or VI GATS. Trachtman has stated that the Appellate Body did not seem to reject the reasoning of the panel that a measure that results in a quota above zero is also covered by Art. XVI (Appellate Body Report,

254. It is also logical that a measure that imposes an absolute prohibition is considered to be a zero quota and, therefore, has a quantitative nature. In fact, such a zero quota, in the form of a nationality requirement, is explicitly mentioned in the Guidelines on the Scheduling of Specific Commitments, drafted by the WTO Secretariat (Scheduling Guidelines), as an example of a measure under Article XVI:2(a).[328] Since zero is a number, the above-mentioned approach of translating a measure into a quantitative measure will be self-evident for measures that impose prohibitions. States impose prohibitions for all kinds of public policy reasons and it is not acceptable that all these measures would be caught by the prohibition of Article XVI. In fact, any measure regulating a services market restricts market access. One can think of measures that prohibit certain medical treatments, or measures that impose limits on the exposures banks can build up with regard to one single client. Such measures could then only be justified on the basis of Article XIV GATS or the exception for prudential measures. There should thus be limits to the scope of application of Article XIV in the case of measures that contain prohibitions.

255. Leroux argued that one should assess these measures while taking into account the regulatory aim of these measures.[329] However, this is very difficult to square with the text of Article XVI. This provision precisely concerns an absolute prohibition of market access restrictions without further test. It provides no legal basis for considering the goals of the measure. If certain policy concerns would justify certain measures, these measures should be indicated in the members' schedules, thereby shielding them from a violation of Article XVI. Therefore the scope of Article XVI should be limited in other ways.

256. Abu-Akeel suggested that the measures falling within the scope of Article XVI GATS are in fact pre-establishment measures, while the measures falling under Article XVII GATS are post-establishment measures.[330] This seems at first sight intuitively correct: a market *access*

US – Gambling, para. 234). He notes that 'It is difficult to see the limits of Art. XVI under this interpretation'; because of the absolute prohibition contained in Art. XVI, such limits are clearly necessary to safeguard the regulatory autonomy of the WTO members. Trachtman, above n. 325, at 866, n. 32.

328 Guidelines on the Scheduling of Specific Commitments under the General Agreement on Trade in Services (GATS), S/L/92, 28 March 2001, para. 12(a), fourth indent.

329 Leroux, above n. 317, at 774.

330 A. Abu-Akeel, 'The MFN as It Applies to Service Trade: New Problems for an Old Concept', (1999) 33 *Journal of World Trade* 103, at 126.

obligation would concern measures that affect the *access* of service suppliers to the market.[331] In turn, national treatment would concern the treatment of services and service suppliers *once they are present* in the market. However, this interpretation would mean that Article XVI has no relevance for market access of services in the case where the supplier does not maintain a 'physical' presence (by means of a subsidiary, branch, representative office or presence of natural persons) in the market (Modes 1 and 2). It is indeed not possible to identify exactly the point at which a service crosses the border, contrary to what is the case for goods. This interpretation of the scope of Article XVI cannot be correct. WTO members make commitments for market access in all four modes of supply. Furthermore, Article XVI:2(b) has a clear reference to *service transactions*. This does not necessarily involve an establishment of the provider in the market.

257. Still, one could of course argue that a distinction on the basis of pre- or post-establishment does not relate to the question whether or not a service supplier wants to create a presence in the market, but rather whether the measure concerns an *entry* condition or a condition *after entry*. In that case, service provision beyond Modes 3 and 4 would also be covered.[332] However, it is extremely difficult to define whether a measure concerns in fact a condition of entry of the service or rather a mere modality of the provision in the market, once entered. Does a prohibition against publicizing a service affect the entry of a service or only the way of providing the service, once entered? What about a measure that allows a tax exemption on the first €1,600 of interest on savings accounts *only if* this savings account is held with a domestic bank? The latter measure may in fact amount to an absolute prohibition against foreign banks offering savings account services and thus fall under Article XVI; however, it is also a discriminatory measure, as prohibited by Article XVII.

258. In a similar fashion, Pauwelyn argued that the measures that are covered should be real market access measures and not measures of *domestic regulation*. This distinction is again difficult to apply in practice. It is not

[331] Mattoo notes that the distinction 'has the appeal of creating a neat division of disciplines between Articles XVI and XVII'. A. Mattoo, 'National Treatment in the GATS. Cornerstone or Pandora's Box?', (1997) 31 *Journal of World Trade* 107, at 116.

[332] In the case of Mode 2, it in fact concerns not entry of the service or supplier, but rather the possibility of a service receiver exiting the domestic market to receive a service and then returning to his country.

at all clear what types of measure are domestic regulations and what are not. One would need to make a distinction between measures that are domestic regulations falling within the scope of Article XVI and those that fall within the scope of Article VI.

259. One possibility is to limit the prohibitions that are caught by Article XVI to those that are really a zero quota, in the sense that they *entirely* prohibit trade in services in a particular sector or mode of supply. This could then be contrasted with those that are of a qualitative nature. In this respect, Pauwelyn stresses that the *qualitative* nature of the *online* gambling ban (prohibiting one mode of *how* one can provide gambling services) makes the ban a domestic regulation, rather than a *quantitative* market access restriction of zero.[333] This depends, of course, on how broad the general rule is seen as being: is the prohibition part of a general regulation on gambling (in which case the prohibition against gambling online is a qualitative measure, not amounting to a zero quota), or is it the only rule at issue (namely a prohibition *tout court*)? In the latter case, the measure would be covered by Article XVI. If the measure is only part of a more general rule, it is of a qualitative nature and is caught by Article XVII or Article VI.

260. The panel and the Appellate Body in *US – Gambling* in fact decided that the measures in dispute amounted to an absolute prohibition on *online provision* of gambling services. Trachtman suggested that the United States should, rather, have challenged on appeal the fact that the panel had found that a *way* of providing gambling services (being part of the sector 'other recreational services' and being only one means of providing cross-border gambling services) was prohibited.[334] Hence, the United States could have argued that the measure at issue did not amount to an absolute prohibition and thus to a zero quota, but rather to a qualitative measure defining the *way* in which gambling and betting services could be supplied across borders. Zleptnig makes a similar argument. He notes that when no means of delivery are possible at all, there is a market access restriction that falls within the scope of Article XVI. However, if only one or some means of delivery are foreclosed, this may not be a market access restriction because market access is still

[333] Pauwelyn, above n. 325, at 164–166.

[334] Trachtman, above n. 325, at 866. These were arguments that the United States seemed to have advanced at the panel stage. Panel Report, *US – Gambling*, paras. 4.132–133.

possible through other means of delivery.[335] Measures that only impose some conditions on service provision (e.g. not to sell to minors) or that prohibit a specific means of delivery (e.g. door-to-door selling) would therefore not fall within the scope of Article XVI.

261. In sum, the measures covered are (i) those that explicitly impose quantitative (maximum) restrictions (e.g. a limit of five new bank licences per year); (ii) those that *ex ante* can be translated into numerical quotas (e.g. a regulatory requirement set in such manner that only five banks are able to comply with it); and (iii) those that lead to a zero quota for trade in services in the entire scheduled sector (or sub-sector) or mode of supply (i.e. a total prohibition) – for example, a prohibition against providing loans over the telephone, by means of written correspondence or by means of the Internet, even if a commitment under Mode 1 to such banking services was made.

8.3.3 *'Indistinctly applicable' measures*

262. A second question relating to the scope of application of Article XVI is whether the measures in question concern only those that apply to foreign suppliers or services *or* whether they also include measures that apply to foreign suppliers or services *at the same time as* to domestic suppliers or services. Clearly, the impact of Article XVI on regulatory autonomy is much less when the six listed measures are limited to those that apply *only* to imported services or foreign suppliers rather than when they also include measures that are 'indistinctly applicable'.

263. Some authors, most prominently Mavroidis, consider the former to be the case. This would mean that Article XVII on national treatment has a wider scope of application than Article XVI; Article XVII would cover measures that apply *only* to imported services and foreign suppliers *as well as* measures that apply to imported services and foreign suppliers *at the same time as* to domestic services and suppliers. Such measures would not fall under the absolute prohibition of Article XVI and therefore Article XVI would show deference to all types of domestic

[335] Zleptnig, above n. 299, at 152. However, he agrees with the reasoning of the panel and the Appellate Body in *US – Gambling*, since the prohibition on online gambling prevented the only means of supply possible under Mode 1. Ibid., at 153–154. In fact, an entire mode of supply was foreclosed.

regulation that apply indistinctly to domestic and foreign services.[336] In other words, under this interpretation, Article XVI would have a narrower scope of application than Article XVII. Three arguments are advanced to support such a limited approach to the scope of Article XVI.

264. First, the text of Article XVI:1 GATS is explicit in imposing an obligation on WTO members to accord to 'services and service suppliers of any *other* Member' the treatment specified in the schedule of specific market access commitments.[337] The obligation would thus not concern treatment accorded to *domestic* services and suppliers. What is more, the text in Article XVI:1 also refers to market access 'through the modes of supply identified in Article I'. These modes of supply only concern service provision by *foreign* suppliers.

265. Second, the very purpose of GATS is to liberalize trade with foreign countries; it is not concerned with the enhancement of the economic freedom of all market participants.[338] If one were to interpret the absolute prohibition in Article XVI:1 as applying also to measures that are indistinctly applicable, a wide range of measures might need to be eliminated.[339]

266. Third, trade liberalization would actually be served by such an interpretation of Article XVI. If the measures listed in Article XVI:2 GATS include measures that are indistinctly applicable, a limitation indicated in the schedules of specific commitments would also concern domestic services or suppliers. The example provided by Mavroidis is a market access commitment that involves a limitation by a numerical quota of five banks. If the measures within the scope of Article XVI:2

[336] Mavroidis, above n. 318, at 9. See also J. Marchetti and P. Mavroidis, 'Walking the Tightrope between Domestic Policy and Globalization: Market Access, Discrimination and Regulatory Intervention under the GATS', mimeo, 2006.

[337] Art. XVI:1 GATS (emphasis added).

[338] For a completely opposed position see Krajewski, who argues that the GATS was negotiated against the background of the liberalization and deregulation agenda of the 1980s in the United States. He states that Art. XVI 'reflects the intentions of the drafters of GATS to provide for the opening of domestic markets to foreign services and service suppliers even if – one could almost say: especially if – these markets were also restricted for domestic suppliers.' Krajewski, above n. 325, at 430–1.

[339] This can be compared with the criticism in the field of EU law towards the wide scope of application of the provisions on free movement of goods (Art. 34 TFEU), freedom of establishment (Art. 49 TFEU) and freedom to provide services (Art. 56 TFEU). See inter alia E. Spaventa, 'From Gebhard to Carpenter: Towards a (Non-)Economic European Constitution', (2004) 41 *Common Market Law Review* 743.

GATS also concerned measures that apply to domestic *as well as* foreign services and suppliers, both foreign and domestic suppliers would need to compete for these five banking licences. If Article XVI concerned only measures applicable to foreign suppliers, the five licences would all be issued to foreign banks, thus leading to an increase in competition.

267. Under this interpretation, measures that are 'indistinctly applicable' would need to be considered under Article XVII on national treatment. The 'normative content' of this provision is a discrimination test. If the measures under scrutiny are de jure or de facto discriminatory, they violate Article XVII. Moreover, these measures may also violate Article VI:4 or VI:5 GATS, depending on whether they fall within the scope of application of these provisions and fail to satisfy the test set out. Measures that violate Article XVI (i.e. measures that apply only to imported services or foreign suppliers) at the same time violate Article XVII, since they treat imported services or foreign suppliers less favourably. According to Mavroidis, because of the overlap between the scope of Articles XVI and XVII, Article XVI only becomes relevant if no commitments were made under Article XVII.

268. Other authors do not see any basis for such limited scope of Article XVI. In their view, Article XVI disciplines measures that apply solely to foreign services and providers *as well as* measures that are indistinctly applicable.[340] Under this approach, measures that are indistinctly applicable and *that are of the type* listed in Article XVI:2 will be immediately prohibited (of course as far as Article XVI commitments have been made, and unless justified under one of the GATS exceptions).

269. There are good arguments supporting the position that Article XVI does *not* apply solely to measures that concern *only* foreign services or suppliers. Only the final type of measure in the list included in Article XVI:2, concerning limitations on the participation of foreign capital, has an explicit reference to foreign origin. All other listed measures may also include measures that are indistinctly applicable. The Scheduling Guidelines provide further support. They mention as examples of the types of measure in Article XVI:2 measures that are indistinctly

[340] Pauwelyn, above n. 325, at 148–49. See also P. Delimatsis and M. Molinuevo, 'Article XVI GATS', in Wolfrum, Stoll and Feinäugle, above n. 156, 367–95, at 370; and R. Adlung, P. Morrison, M. Roy and W. Zhang, 'Fog in GATS Commitments – Boon or Bane?', WTO Staff Working Paper ERSD-2011-04, 31 March 2011, 4–5.

applicable as well as measures that draw a distinction between foreign and domestic services or suppliers. Mavroidis argues that the references in some examples in the Scheduling Guidelines to the foreign origin of services or services suppliers show clearly that the drafters of the GATS intended to limit the application of Article XVI to measures that apply only to foreign services or suppliers.[341] The examples of measures where no reference is made to origin can also be interpreted as measures that apply only to foreigners.[342] However, the contrary seems equally valid. The fact that examples of measures are mentioned that apply only to foreigners, next to measures where no such specific origin is indicated, may support the argument that Article XVI applies to both sets of measures.

270. Furthermore, limiting the scope of application of Article XVI to a number of measures that apply only to foreigners reduces Article XVI to merely an 'explication' of a number of discriminatory measures. They would be the 'most frequent violations of national treatment'.[343] One may wonder what such a provision would add to the GATS. If a measure that applies only to foreigners is considered under the GATS, such measures would almost immediately violate Article XVII. To be sure, it would be necessary to establish discrimination. Yet the fact that the measure makes a distinction according to the origin of the measure almost immediately satisfies this test.

271. Finally, the argument that Article XVI would only cover measures that apply only to imported services and foreign suppliers seeks to introduce a similar relationship between Articles XVI and XVII GATS as

[341] See, as examples of measures that explicitly refer to the foreign origin, (a) annually established quotas for foreign medical practitioners; (b) foreign bank subsidiaries limited to *x* per cent of total domestic assets of all banks; (c) restrictions on broadcasting time available for foreign films; (d) foreign labour should not exceed *x* per cent and/or wages *xy* per cent of total; (e) foreign companies required to establish subsidiaries; and (f) foreign equity ceiling of *x* per cent for a particular form of commercial presence. Scheduling Guidelines, para. 12.

[342] See, as examples of measures that do not explicitly refer to foreign origin, (a) licence for a new restaurant based on an economic needs test (it is not clear whether this licence hereby may also concern a licence required for a domestic restaurant services-supplier) and nationality requirements for suppliers of services (equivalent to zero quota) (one may argue that the nationality requirement obviously also applies to domestic suppliers); as well as (e) commercial presence excludes representative offices (again, one may argue that this measure also applies to domestic suppliers). Scheduling Guidelines, para. 12.

[343] Mavroidis, above n. 318, at 9.

between Articles III and XI GATT. With regard to trade in goods, the note *Ad* Article III GATT indicates that any internal tax or regulation that applies to an imported good and to the like domestic good, but for this imported good is collected or enforced at the time or point of importation, is nevertheless to be considered as a tax or regulation subject to Article III. Such measures thus do not fall within the scope of Article XI GATT. To distinguish between the scope of Article III and Article XI GATT, it is therefore essential to determine whether the measure in question applies also to the domestic like product (in which case Article III will be applicable) or not (in which case Article XI applies).[344] Nevertheless, the GATS does not contain such interpretative note and neither does it contain any explicit provision indicating such a distinction between measures that apply only at the border to imported services or foreign service suppliers and those that are indistinctly applicable. Indeed, in the case of services it is much less clear than for goods to determine the time or point of importation.

272. For all these reasons, Article XVI covers measures that apply *only* to foreign services and providers *as well as* to measures that are indistinctly applicable.

8.3.4 The overlap of Article XVI and Article XVII

273. Linked to the question of what types of measure are included in Article XVI is a third question with regard to the overlap between Article XVI and Article XVII. One may wonder whether measures that are consistent with Article XVI *must still comply with* Article XVII (and thus be non-discriminatory). In other words, how should the overlap between Article XVI and XVII be dealt with? Arguably, when considering the text of the GATS, Article XVII on national treatment would have a broader scope of application than Article XVI, since the latter applies only to the limited list of measures in Article XVI:2 whereas Article XVII applies to '*all measures affecting the supply of a service*' (emphasis added). When focusing on this very general wording, it seems that the scope of Article XVII includes that of Article XVI and, in fact, the *scope* of any

[344] Panel Report, *European Communities – Measures Affecting Asbestos and Asbestos-Containing Products (EC – Asbestos)*, adopted 5 April 2001, as modified by Appellate Body Report, WT/DS135/AB/R, paras 8.91–8.92.

provision in the GATS.[345] The overlap is especially important when different commitments are scheduled for market access and national treatment.

274. The question of how to deal with this overlap has been the subject of discussions before the Committee on Specific Commitments,[346] and the Swiss delegation on this committee has submitted a study of this issue.[347] The chair of this committee identified *five approaches* to the relation between Article XVI and Article XVII.

8.3.4.1 First approach: the six listed types of measure in Article XVI:2 are excluded from the scope of Article XVII

275. The first approach excludes the six types of measure listed in Article XVI:2 from the scope of Article XVII. The problem with this approach is that nowhere in the GATS is there an indication that measures listed in Article XVI:2 are excluded from the scope of Article XVII.

276. Krajewski derives from Article XX:2 GATS (which states that measures inconsistent with both articles but which a member nevertheless wants to maintain even though commitments are made, must be inscribed in the column relating to Article XVI) that once a measure falls within the scope of Article XVI, Article XVII does not apply.[348]

277. Nevertheless, the text of Article XX:2 and its location in the GATS (in Part IV on 'progressive liberalization', which deals with negotiation of specific commitments, the content of schedules of specific commitments and modification of schedules) seem to indicate that this provision is a scheduling convention rather than a provision setting out a

[345] Additional commitments under Art. XVIII thus cover the same range of measures as Art. XVII, but the *normative content* of Art. XVIII is different: if an additional commitment is made, the measure at stake is prohibited *even if it is not discriminatory*.

[346] Committee on Specific Commitments, Consideration of Issues Relating to Art. XX:2 of the GATS, Report by the Chairman, S/C/W/237, 24 March 2004. The Committee on Specific Commitments is a subsidiary body of the Council for Trade in Services.

[347] Communication from Switzerland, Consideration of Issues Relating to Article XX:2 of the GATS, JOB (03)/214, 27 November 2003, Annex II to S/C/W/237, above n. 346.

[348] M. Krajewski, *National Regulation and Trade Liberalization in Services: The Legal Impact of the General Agreement on Trade in Services (GATS) on National Regulatory Autonomy* (The Hague: Kluwer, 2003), 115. The argument based on Art. XX:2 was first made by Mattoo, above n. 331, at 114–19.

hierarchy of provisions in the GATS.[349] What is more, the existence of Article XX:2 in fact shows that there must be an overlap between the scope of Article XVI and XVII. If not, it would make no sense to require measures that are inconsistent with *both* to be inscribed only in the column of Article XVI. This does not mean that the distinction between the scope of Article XVI and XVII is irrelevant. If a measure can already be qualified as one of the types of measure listed in Article XVI:2, it is immediately prohibited, without a further test (as discussed above para. 245).

8.3.4.2 Second approach: only non-discriminatory measures are within the scope of Article XVI

278. The second approach limits the application of Article XVI to measures that are non-discriminatory. Once one of the measures listed in Article XVI:2 is discriminatory, Article XVI becomes irrelevant and Article XVII is applicable. The principle of discrimination would then always apply in its entirety.[350] Besides the fact that it is hard to find a legal basis in the GATS to support such interpretation, this approach is problematic, since the measures specified in Article XVI:2(f) are necessarily discriminatory.

279. The third and fourth approaches focus on the relation between the commitments that are made under both provisions. As long as the commitments made under Articles XVI and XVII are the same, there is no problem that the provisions overlap.[351] A 'none' in both columns means that no limitations are imposed and that the principles of market access and national treatment apply to their full extent. Measures of the type listed in Article XVI:2 are prohibited, be they discriminatory or not. An entry 'unbound' in both columns means that the WTO member can still adopt measures that are listed in Article XVI:2. These measures can be discriminatory.

[349] See the comments of the representative of Switzerland on issues relating to Art. XX:2. WTO Document S/CSC/M/31, para. 33, included as Annex IV to S/C/W/237, above n. 346.

[350] See the comments of Hong Kong, China, on issues relating to Art. XX:2. WTO Document S/CSC/M/31, para. 48, Annex IV to S/C/W/237, above n. 346.

[351] Committee on Specific Commitments, Consideration of Issues Relating to Art. XX:2 of the GATS, Note by the Chairman, JOB (03)/213, 20 November 2003, para. 5, Annex I to S/C/W/237, above n. 346.

8.3.4.3 Third approach: limitations prevail over commitments

280. Incompatibilities are caused by the overlap of Articles XVI and XVII once the entries in both columns differ (possible combinations of entries are indicated in Table 8.1, below). The third approach suggests that an 'unbound' entry in one column prevails over a commitment in another column. This would mean that an entry 'unbound' in the market access column, in parallel with a full national treatment commitment ('none'), would allow the WTO member to adopt any of the measures listed in Article XVI:2, even if they were discriminatory. A full market access commitment ('none'), in combination with a full limitation ('unbound') in the national treatment column would imply that the WTO member would be allowed to adopt the measures listed in Article XVI:2 *as long as they are discriminatory.*

281. This last implication indicates that the third approach may lead to odd results, affecting the expectations of the other WTO members with regard to the commitments made by one member. As the Swiss delegation has noted, 'under approach 3, Article XVI-type measures that are non-discriminatory could no longer be introduced, but if the Member concerned still wanted to introduce an Article XVI-type measure, it could do so by devising it in a discriminatory way'.[352]

8.3.4.4 Fourth approach: commitments prevail over limitations, except when Article XX:2 applies

282. These problems seem to be absent in case of the fourth approach, which considers that a full commitment ('none') prevails over a full limitation ('unbound'). An 'unbound' entry in the market access column combined with a full national treatment commitment leads to a situation where a WTO member is still allowed to adopt one of the measures listed in Article XVI:2, as long as it is not discriminatory. A full market access commitment in combination with a full limitation on national treatment means that a WTO member can still adopt discriminatory measures, as long as these are not of the type listed in Article XVI:2. This approach seems to take more account of the expectations WTO members may

[352] Communication from Switzerland, Consideration of Issues Relating to Art. XX:2 of the GATS, JOB (03)/214, 27 November 2003, para. 10, included in Annex II to S/C/W/237, above n. 346. The Swiss delegation suggested that a limitation on the participation of foreign capital (see Art. XVI:2(f)) would be allowed, in spite of the full commitment under Art. XVI.

have when another member makes commitments and also favours liberalization through the GATS.[353] It also seems a logically consistent approach towards the issue. The question remains, however, of what elements in the GATS may provide an indication that the fourth approach also has a *legal basis*. One may argue that this basis lies in the structure and wording of the GATS provisions relating to market access and national treatment. In the preamble of the GATS, the wish of the WTO members is expressed that trade in services be expanded 'under the conditions of transparency and progressive liberalization'.[354] The fourth approach contributes most to such transparency and progressive liberalization.

283. One should recall that the possible entries into WTO members' schedules of specific commitments are not only 'none' and 'unbound', but that WTO members may also, when making a commitment, explicitly list measures to which they wish to limit this commitment. Therefore, besides the four possible combinations of entries in the market access and national treatment columns, five other combinations of entries should be considered under the fourth approach.

284. A fifth possible combination of entries is one where specific limitations are inscribed in both the market access and national treatment

Table 8.1. *Possible combinations of commitments and limitations for market access and national treatment*

	Market access	National treatment
1	None	None
2	Unbound	Unbound
3	Unbound	None
4	None	Unbound
5	Specific limitation	Specific limitation
6	None	Specific limitation
7	Specific limitation	None
8	Specific limitation	Unbound
9	Unbound	Specific limitation

353 P. Delimatsis, 'Don't Gamble with GATS – The Interaction between Articles VI, XVI, XVII and XVIII GATS in the Light of the *US – Gambling* Case', (2006) 40 *Journal of World Trade* 1059, at 1074.

354 Paragraph 2 of the Preamble to the GATS.

columns. Here, no specific problems seem to arise. A specific limitation in the market access column also extends to measures that are at the same time a violation of national treatment. This is by virtue of Article XX:2. Under the fourth approach, a specific limitation in the national treatment column will not prevail over a market access limitation. Hence such a specific limitation will not lead to Article XVI:2-type measures being allowed if they take a discriminatory form. If that were the intention of the WTO member, it would need to inscribe the measure as a specific limitation in the market access column.

285. Combinations of a full commitment ('none') and a specific limitation lead to the sixth and seventh possible situations. In that case WTO members may be induced to be clear and specify the measure for which limitations are introduced. In these cases, Article XX:2 may play its full role. If a full market access commitment is made ('none'), in combination with a specific limitation in the national treatment commitment, the WTO member is prohibited from adopting one of the measures listed in Article XVI:2. It does not matter whether the measure is discriminatory or not, since, under the fourth approach, the market access commitment prevails over the national treatment limitation. If a specific limitation is inscribed in the market access column and a full national treatment commitment is made, the WTO member is allowed to adopt the measure that is exempted from the market access commitment, as long as this measure is not discriminatory. However, even if the Article XVI:2-type measure is also discriminatory, the measure could be maintained by virtue of Article XX:2: the specific limitation in the market access column also extends to national treatment. Hence, if a WTO member were, for instance, to want to maintain restrictions on the participation of foreign capital, this limitation should be inscribed in the market access column and it would also avoid this discriminatory measure violating Article XVII.

286. Finally, the eighth and ninth combinations – where one of the entries is 'unbound' and the other one concerns a specific limitation – may show the inadequacy of current Article XX:2. If a specific limitation is inscribed in the market access column while the entry in the national treatment column is 'unbound', the specific measure that is exempted from the market access obligation may be maintained, even if it is discriminatory. If the entry in the market access column is 'unbound' and there is a specific limitation in the national treatment column, the WTO member may adopt any measure listed under Article XVI:2, *as* *long as* this measure is not discriminatory *except when* this measure is the specific discriminatory one that is exempted from the discipline of Article XVII. This would mean that, for instance, a limit on the participation of foreign capital is allowed under Article XVI, but will be prohibited under Article XVII, except when this measure was inscribed as a specific limitation of the national treatment commitment. Nevertheless, since this measure is incompatible with both Article XVI and Article XVII, this limitation would need to be inscribed in the market access column by virtue of Article XX:2.

287. One may wonder whether it would already be excluded through the 'unbound' commitment inscribed in the market access column.[355] This is probably not the case, because the principle in Article XX:2 only deals with *specific* measures that are inscribed as a limitation in the market access column and, where this measure also violates national treatment, also extends the limitation to the latter principle. If one were to interpret the 'unbound' entry as also including a specific limitation of national treatment for this specific measure, the 'fourth approach' would be turned upside down: the limitation would again prevail over the commitment. To avoid such a situation it would thus be necessary to inscribe *either* the specific limitation in the national treatment column *or* specify the limitation in the market access column. The former is difficult to reconcile with the wording of Article XX:2 GATS. There is an obligation (Article XX:2 uses the word 'shall') to inscribe measures inconsistent with both articles in the market access column. The latter may lead to situations where, next to an entry 'unbound', a specific limitation in the market access column is also inscribed. One should be careful, however, since such technical *ex post* interpretations may lead to a reinterpretation of WTO members' schedules.[356] Some WTO members may now be faced with the reality that the effect of an 'unbound' entry in the market access column is negated by the fact that they would not have included a limitation for this measure in its discriminatory form[357] in the national treatment column.

[355] The representative of the United States on the Committee on Specific Commitments has noted that 'the questions was whether 'Unbound' was equivalent to what Art. XX:2 described as measures inconsistent with both Art. XVI and Art. XVII, if it was inscribed in either place'. WTO Document S/CSC/M/31, para. 55, Annex IV to S/C/W/237, above n. 346.

[356] This was indeed noted by the representative of Japan in the discussions on Art. XX:2. WTO Document S/CSC/M/31, para. 53, Annex IV to S/C/W/237, above n. 346.

[357] Note that Art. XVI:2(f) will necessarily be discriminatory.

8.3.4.5 Fifth approach: clarify the intended scope of commitments and limitations in WTO members' schedules

288. To avoid such unintended effects, several WTO members suggested relying on a possible 'fifth approach', which is of a procedural nature. This would involve a clarification in the schedules of individual members as to the intended scope of the commitments.[358] This approach also fits with the Guidelines on the Scheduling of Specific Commitments. The Guidelines suggest that a WTO member could indicate for measures that are inconsistent with both Article XVI and XVII that a limitation in the market access column 'also limits national treatment'.[359] This may also prove useful to avoid problems in the ninth situation, mentioned above. It is unclear whether an 'unbound' entry in the market access column also exempts Article XVI:2-type measures that are discriminatory. An indication in the market access column whether this is the case or not would greatly improve transparency and predictability. However, this would not help for the present schedules, which are most likely not always drafted with these considerations in mind.

289. Nonetheless, the panel in *China – Electronic Payment Services* provided the necessary clarification, confirming – with reference to Article XX:2 GATS – that an inscription 'unbound' in the market access column also provides a qualification to the national treatment commitment.[360] The panel noted that 'with an inscription of "Unbound" for subsection (d) in mode 1 under Article XVI, and a corresponding "None" for Article XVII, China has indicated that it is free to maintain the full range of limitations expressed in the six categories of Article XVI:2, whether discriminatory or not'.[361]

[358] Committee on Specific Commitments, Consideration of Issues Relating to Art. XX:2 of the GATS, Report by the Chairman, S/C/W/237, 24 March 2004, para. 20.

[359] Guidelines on the Scheduling of Specific Commitments under the General Agreement on Trade in Services (GATS), S/L/92, 28 March 2001, para. 18. On the other hand, para. 40 of the Guidelines indicates: 'Given the legal nature of a schedule, it should contain only descriptions of bound commitments. Any additional information for transparency purposes should not be entered in the schedule.' Nonetheless, the specifications at stake here are precisely the detailed descriptions of the commitments.

[360] Panel Report, *China – Measures Affecting Electronic Payment Services*, WT/DS413/R, adopted 31 August 2012 (*China – Electronic Payment Services*), para. 7.660.

[361] Ibid., para. 7.661.

8.3.5 *Market access in the Understanding on Commitments in Financial Services*

290. The Understanding on Commitments in Financial Services (by reference to which a part of the EU has made commitments (see above para. 150 (footnote 146)) has a number of specific provisions on market access. The WTO members that make commitments on the basis of the Understanding in fact accept a number of obligations with regard to market access as specified in the Understanding.

291. First of all is an obligation with regard to monopoly rights that a member may have granted to certain financial service suppliers in its territory. While Article VIII GATS already requires that each WTO member ensures that actions by monopoly suppliers are not inconsistent with the member's most-favoured-nation obligation and its specific commitments,[362] section B.1 of the Understanding requires members to list the existing monopoly rights of service suppliers in their schedules. There is, further, a 'best endeavour' obligation to eliminate these monopolies or reduce their scope. If this is done, financial service suppliers from other WTO members will be able to access the market and provide these financial services. Remarkably, this obligation also applies to activities by a public entity using financial sources of the government, or acting on the government's account or with its guarantee. Measures that affect the latter services are normally excluded from the scope of the GATS by virtue of subparagraph 1(b)(iii) of the Annex on Financial Services.

292. The Understanding further provides 'an exception to the exception' in Article XIII GATS. The latter article excludes government procurement[363] from the obligations of most-favoured-nation treatment, market access and national treatment. Section B.2 requires WTO members that have relied on the Understanding to ensure that government procurement of financial services complies with the obligations of most-favoured-nation treatment and national treatment. Financial service suppliers from other

[362] It only concerns service suppliers with a government-granted monopoly and not with a 'natural' monopoly. This provision was invoked once by the United States against Belgium concerning practices by Belgacom (the largest telecoms operator) on telephone directory services. No panel was established in this case, and consultations do not seem to be pursued further. *Belgium – Measures affecting Commercial Telephone Directory Services – Request for Consultations by the United States*, WT/DS80/1, 13 May 1997.

[363] The procurement is to be done by government agencies and concerns 'services purchased for governmental purposes and not with a view to commercial resale or with a view to use in the supply of services for commercial sale'.

WTO members *that have an establishment* in the territory of the WTO member in question thus benefit from these obligations. This does not extend to service suppliers that provide services across-border (Mode 1 or Mode 2). Remarkably, although the general title of section B refers to market access, this is not repeated in provision B.2 itself. There should first be a possibility for the financial service suppliers to establish themselves in the territory of the WTO member in question, before they can benefit from section B.2. A model commitment for providing market access by means of establishing a commercial presence (Mode 3) is included in section B.5 of the Understanding.

293. The remaining paragraphs of section B (market access) of the Understanding provide model commitments for market access. They are distributed over the four modes of service supply. The first obligation concerns 'cross-border trade'. This involves both Mode 1 service provision (cross-border supply) and Mode 2 service provision (consumption abroad).

294. The content of a market access commitment for Mode 1 supply under the Understanding is specified in section B.3. It involves allowing non-resident suppliers[364] of financial services 'to supply, as a principal, through an intermediary or as an intermediary, and under terms and conditions that permit national treatment', a number of specific insurance services[365] and, more importantly for the purpose of the present analysis, the 'provision and transfer of financial information and financial data processing as referred to

[364] Section D.1 of the Understanding defines a non-resident supplier of financial services as 'a financial service supplier of a Member which supplies a financial service into the territory of another Member from an establishment located in the territory of another Member, regardless of whether such a financial service supplier has or has not a commercial presence in the territory of the Member in which the financial service is supplied'. Von Bogdandy and Windsor suggest that the definition of 'non-resident supplier' aims to stress that 'any inscribed restrictions on commercial presence (mode 3) do not affect the tradability of cross-border services or consumption of services abroad'. Indeed, the fact that limitations are made for Mode 3 does not imply that Mode 1 would necessarily be restricted. Von Bogdandy and Windsor, above n. 156, 647–666, at 665.

[365] It involves first of all (i) insurance of maritime shipping and commercial aviation and space launching and freight, covering the transport vehicle as well as the goods that are being transported and any liability that arises and (ii) insurance of international transit. (See Understanding on Commitments in Financial Services, Section B.3(a).) Next, it also concerns 'reinsurance and retrocession and the services auxiliary to insurance as referred to in subparagraph 5(a)(xvi) of the Annex.' (See Understanding on Commitments in Financial Services, Section B.3(b).)

in subparagraph 5(a)(xv) of the Annex[[366]] and advisory and other auxiliary services, excluding intermediation, relating to banking and other financial services as referred to in subparagraph 5(a)(xvi) of the Annex[[367]]'. Note that 'intermediation' relating to banking and other financial services, while being present in the description in the Annex, is explicitly excluded from the Understanding. One can observe that the model market access commitment in section B.3 of the Understanding does not go very far. Only a limited selection of the 'banking and other financial services' as described in subparagraphs 5(a)(v) to (xvi) are covered by the commitment. The EU has indeed explicitly indicated in the headnote to its Schedule on Financial Services that the 'market access commitments in respect of modes (1) and (2) apply only to the transactions indicated in paragraphs B.3 and B.4 of the market access section of the Understanding respectively'.

295. With regard to market access commitments for Mode 2, the Understanding is much more far-reaching than for Mode 1. A WTO member that makes a market access commitment must 'permit its residents to purchase in the territory of any other Member the financial services' already mentioned for Mode 1. However, it extends the scope of the commitment to *all* banking and other financial services (excluding insurance). Hence, for Mode 2 (consumption abroad), the Understanding provides a very broad market-access model commitment when it concerns banking and other financial services that are not insurance services.[368] This difference in scope points again to the difficult distinction between Mode 1 and Mode 2 service provision. However, the Understanding puts

[366] Subparagraph 5(a)(xv) of the Annex equally refers to 'provision and transfer of financial information and financial data processing', but adds also 'related software'. By means of a cross-reference to the Annex, the Understanding avoids deviating interpretations of the scope the specific services to which the Annex and the Understanding refer.

[367] Subparagraph 5(a)(xvi) of the Annex refers to 'Advisory, intermediation and other auxiliary financial services on all the activities listed in subparagraphs (v) through (xv) [i.e. banking and other financial services (excluding insurance)], including credit reference and analysis, investment and portfolio research and advice, advice on acquisitions and on corporate restructuring and strategy.'

[368] Von Bogdandy and Windsor suggest a reason for this broader scope. They argue that there is 'apparently lesser need to supervise and regulate consumption abroad as opposed to cross-border supply'. Von Bogdandy and Windsor, above n. 156, at 656. However, since this broad commitment does not cover insurance, is there, then, more need to supervise insurance services than banking?

the stress on the place where the service is 'purchased' as a criterion for making the distinction between both modes of supply.[369]

296. When a WTO member makes a market access commitment for Mode 3 by reference to the Understanding, it is prevented from adopting any possible measure that restricts financial service providers of any other WTO member from establishing a commercial presence in its territory. The measures the WTO member is prevented from adopting are not limited to those specified in the exhaustive list in Article XVI:2 GATS. A market access commitment by reference to the Understanding thus involves very broad access to the territory of the member making the commitment, provided the access comes about by means of establishing a commercial presence.[370] The techniques for obtaining an establishment (or expanding an existing establishment) include (but are not limited to) the 'acquisition of existing enterprises'.[371] Nonetheless, this broad commitment is immediately qualified by the acknowledgement that each member 'may impose terms, conditions and procedures for authorization of the establishment and expansion of a commercial presence in so far as they do not circumvent the Member's obligation under paragraph 5 and they are consistent with the other obligations of the Agreement'. Hence the mere fact that a WTO member requires foreign banks to obtain an authorization before establishing or expanding a commercial presence should not be considered to be a violation of the market access commitment. Nevertheless, when the WTO member adopts and applies such an authorization requirement, it should make certain to comply with the other obligations (non-discrimination and the disciplines on domestic regulation) in the GATS.

297. Section B.6 further makes it explicit that market access commitments under the Understanding also involve an obligation to allow the supply of any 'new' financial service by the suppliers from other members that have an establishment in the territory. This is an important addition, since technological evolution and financial innovation may give rise to new financial services that were not thought of when the

[369] See the discussion of the criteria that have been suggested by the WTO Secretariat, above para. 229.

[370] Key, above n. 148, at 985.

[371] Understanding on Commitments in Financial Services, Section B.5. Gkoutzinis has noted that a study has found that 'banks like Citibank, JP Morgan Chase and Deutsche Bank usually establish new branches or subsidiaries, while ABN Amro, Commerzbank and HSBC tend to purchase existing franchises'. Gkoutzinis, above n. 143, at 894, n. 68.

member's schedule was drafted. A 'new financial service' is 'a service of a financial nature, including services related to existing and new products or the manner in which a product is delivered, that is not supplied by any financial service supplier in the territory of a particular Member but which is supplied in the territory of another Member'. It seems not to be necessary that the service is already supplied in the home country of the foreign service supplier. In theory, the foreign service supplier can thus use a WTO member's market as a 'testing ground' of this new service that it is not yet supplying in its own territory, but that is supplied already by other suppliers in other WTO members. However, measures that prevent this will most likely be justified on the basis of the prudential exception.

298. It may be important for foreign service providers to be able to transfer personal data on clients from one country to the other. Furthermore, in financial services markets, financial information is an important asset. Section B.8 provides that as far as the transfer of information, processing of financial information or the transfer of equipment is necessary for the conduct of the ordinary business of the service supplier, WTO members that rely on the Understanding are prevented from restricting these transfers. Hence there needs to be a close link between the ordinary business of the provider and the information or equipment, such that the provider would not be able to provide its services without having the transfers available. The *transfers of information and processing of financial information* include 'transfers of data by electronic means'. Nevertheless, section B.8 still permits WTO members to apply measures to 'protect personal data, personal privacy and the confidentiality of individual records and accounts so long as such right is not used to circumvent the provision of the Agreement'. In addition, the financial service provider may want to have specific *equipment* available in the territory of the other member in order to provide its services. Here, also, WTO members that have made a commitment by reference to the Understanding shall not restrict the transfer of equipment.[372] However, importation rules that are consistent with international agreements (including the GATT) can be applied. The Understanding thus makes

[372] The WTO Secretariat has noted that the Understanding thereby 'goes beyond what could be scheduled under item 5(xv) of the classification contained in the Annex on Financial Services.' Committee on Specific Commitments, Additional Commitments under Art. XVIII of the GATS, Note by the Secretariat, S/CSC/W/34, 16 July 2002.

a bridge between trade in goods and trade in services, and indicates that service commitments may also require the liberalization of trade in specific goods that are necessary for the service provision.

299. Finally, also with regard to Mode 4 (temporary presence of natural persons), the Understanding provides model commitments. The temporary presence of natural persons is closely linked to the possibility of market access by means of commercial presence (Mode 3). Just as it is often required to move capital goods that are necessary for conducting the business of service provision (see above, para. 298, the discussion with regard to transfers of equipment), it is also often important for a financial service supplier to move 'human capital' to the country where the service will be provided. Article I:2(d) of the GATS in conjunction with paragraph 1 of the GATS Annex on Movement of Natural Persons Supplying Services under the Agreement, which describe the meaning of Mode 4 service provision, indicate that Mode 4 service supply may involve *independent* natural persons who supply services *as well as* natural persons who supply services abroad *employed* by a foreign service supplier that is established abroad or in the country where the service is supplied. Nevertheless, the presence of natural persons to which the Understanding is referring concerns solely the presence of natural persons who are in one way or another connected to the commercial presence of a financial services supplier from a WTO member with a commercial presence in a host country. Natural persons who are *independent* service suppliers and seek to enter a market of another WTO member are not covered by the model commitment in Section B.9 of the Understanding. Moreover, in the model commitment, the Understanding refers only to 'personnel', which has been interpreted by Jarreau as requiring an employer–employee relationship and thus probably excludes 'independent contractors'.[373]

300. It is far from clear what 'temporary' presence means exactly. There is no case law yet on this concept. The 'temporariness' is probably related to the duration of the provision of the specific service. This varies from case to case.[374]

[373] S. Jarreau, 'Interpreting the General Agreement on Trade in Services and the WTO Agreements Relevant to the International Trade of Financial Services: The Lawyer's Perspective', (1999) 25 *North Carolina Journal of International Law and Commercial Regulation* 1, at 61.

[374] Above n. 294.

301. Section B.9 has two subparagraphs. Section B.9(a) requires WTO members that have relied on the Understanding to permit temporary entry of '(i) senior managerial personnel possessing proprietary information essential to the establishment, control and operation of the services of the financial supplier' and '(ii) specialists in the operation of the financial service supplier'. As for the transfer of information and the equipment mentioned above, there must be a clear link between the need for the personnel and the financial service at stake.[375] The financial service supplier in question is a service supplier of another WTO member that 'is establishing or has established a commercial presence in the territory of the Member'. Section B.9(b) involves the temporary entry of personnel that is less essential (in the sense that it is less essential that they come from the country of origin of the financial service provider) for the operation of the service supplier than the personnel referred to in Section B.9(a). It only concerns personnel 'associated with a commercial presence'. Moreover, the Understanding indicates that a service supplier should first consider whether there are qualified personnel available in the territory of the host member.[376] The relevant personnel consist of '(i) specialists in computer services, telecommunication services and accounts of the financial service supplier', and '(ii) actuarial and legal specialists'.

8.3.6 Conclusion on market access

302. This section provided a legal analysis of the obligation of market access in Article XVI GATS. It is important to define carefully the scope of Article XVI because the normative content of Article XVI is such that as soon as a measure falls within its scope, the measure is violating the obligation not to impede market access (as committed to in the schedule of specific commitments). Potentially, any regulatory measure in the field of banking services affects market access. Hence the question with regard to the scope of Article XVI is of essential importance.

303. As discussed, Article XVI:2 lists six types of measure, most of them of a quantitative nature. They comprise measures that explicitly impose

[375] Von Bogdandy and Windsor note that it 'seems reasonable to assume that the specialization must be, to some degree, peculiar to the company in question or to the activity it carries out, and this based on objective, articulable criteria.' Von Bogdandy and Windsor, above n. 156, at 659.

[376] The first sentence of Section D.9(b) indicates that the access must be permitted 'subject to the availability of personnel' in host country. Jarreau, above n. 373, at 61.

quantitative maximum restrictions, those that *ex ante* can be translated into numerical quotas and those that involve an absolute prohibition of trade in the entire scheduled sector or mode of supply.

304. The analysis further addressed the question whether Article XVI only applies to measures that apply to foreigners (hence per definition discriminatory measures) or also to indistinctly applicable measures. The panel and Appellate Body in *US – Gambling* found that the latter type of measures is also included within the scope of Article XVI. We concluded that the approach taken by the panel and Appellate Body in *US – Gambling* is based on (mainly textual) arguments that are perfectly sound, be it that this approach may be more difficult to reconcile with the idea of progressive liberalization and regulatory autonomy.

305. We also examined the Understanding on Commitments in Financial Services. The use of the Understanding with regard to market access lies mainly in the fact that it makes it easier for WTO members to make clear liberalization commitments in the field of financial services. It thus reduces the need for WTO member to specify exactly the extent of a commitment, but at the same time also implies that the WTO member accepts the level of liberalization as specified in the Understanding. This level of liberalization is in principle high, be it that this is a too general statement. One should consider carefully the conditions inscribed in the Understanding. Moreover, WTO members can still inscribe limitations to the commitments and rely on the exceptions available in the GATS.

306. In sum, the complexities and uncertainties with regard to the interpretation of Article XVI and the Understanding make it very difficult to provide a clear and general appreciation of the extent to which this obligation restricts the right of WTO members to regulate their banking services markets. Article XVI *of itself* constitutes an important restriction: any indistinctly applicable banking regulation will fall within its scope. However, the extent to which Article XVI applies in this sector depends on the commitments and limitations made by the WTO member in question in its schedule of commitments. Moreover, we shall consider further that a broad prudential exception is available. Hence the threat of Article XVI to regulatory autonomy may still be limited in practice. WTO members that have made market access commitments based on the Understanding have accepted an important restriction on their right to regulate. However, the model commitments do not imply for all modes of supply the same degree of liberalization (especially with regard to the financial services covered) and important qualifications are included (most importantly the explicit right to require a licence before trade by means of Mode 3 can be carried out).

8.4 GATS obligations based on discrimination

8.4.1 Introduction

307. The primary goal of the international trade regime is to eliminate protectionism.[377] Defining 'protectionism' requires a number of tools or 'proxies' to prevent the adjudicator from getting entangled in the difficult process of defining the *mens rea* of a regulator. A major proxy for determining whether protectionism is at issue is to define whether the measure at stake 'discriminates'. Nevertheless, discrimination is a proxy that is in many aspects flawed. Even if a measure has a discriminatory effect, it may not necessarily be protectionist.

308. To discipline protectionism in the area of services, GATS provisions prohibit WTO members from applying measures that discriminate.[378] To the extent that banking regulation gives rise to discrimination on the basis of the origin of banking services or suppliers of banking services, there may be a violation of the GATS. Despite some commonalities, the two main principles prohibiting discrimination – most-favoured-nation treatment and national treatment – apply to a different extent. They involve two different situations of discrimination. The principle of most favoured nation concerns discrimination by a WTO member between different trading partners. The principle of national treatment addresses discrimination between domestic services or suppliers, on the one hand, and foreign services or suppliers on the other. Moreover, the provisions also do not apply to the same extent to WTO members. The principle of most favoured nation is included in Part II of the GATS, containing general obligations and disciplines. This means

[377] G. De Búrca, 'Unpacking the Concept of Discrimination in EC and International Trade Law', in C. Barnard and J. Scott (eds.), *The Law of the Single European Market. Unpacking the Premises* (Oxford: Hart, 2002) 181–95, at 181.

[378] On the choice of discrimination as the cornerstone of global trade liberalization, see A. Sykes, 'Regulatory Protectionism and the Law of International Trade', (1999) 66 *University of Chicago Law Review* 1; and N. Diebold, 'Non-discrimination and the Pillars of International Economic Law. Comparative Analysis and Building Coherency', Society of International Economic Law Working Paper No. 2010/24, July 2010, available at http://papers.ssrn.com/sol3/papers.cfm?abstract_id=1632927.

that this most-favoured-nation obligation applies immediately to all WTO members. In contrast, the national treatment obligation is included in Part III of the GATS, entitled 'Specific Commitments'. As for market access, the national treatment obligation only applies as far as the WTO member in question has made a specific commitment to subject the relevant sector to the national treatment obligation.

309. Before examining the particularities of the most-favoured-nation and national treatment provisions in greater detail, we examine two issues that are common to most-favoured-nation and national treatment: the concept of 'likeness' and the phrase 'less favourable treatment'. It is not always obvious whether a regulation at issue gives rise to a violation of the provisions prohibiting discrimination or whether it creates a barrier to trade without being discriminatory, in which case the provisions on non-discriminatory barriers apply (Article VI GATS and any future Disciplines on Domestic Regulation). Still, because both sets of provisions set out different tests of scrutiny, it is important to categorize banking regulation under one or the other. It is through the interpretation of the concept of 'likeness' and the phrase 'less favourable' that case law and authors have tried to define this boundary.

8.4.2 Likeness and less favourable treatment

310. Since the principles of most-favoured-nation treatment and national treatment are both expressions of the more general principle of non-discrimination, it is in both cases necessary to perform a two-step analysis. The first step requires a consideration of the extent to which the services or service suppliers are like. The second step involves a determination to what extent certain services (or suppliers) are treated less favourably than others.

8.4.2.1 Likeness

311. The concept of 'likeness' is one that has been interpreted extensively in the field of trade of goods,[379] but it is also a cornerstone of the

[379] The criteria that are used are the so-called 'Border Tax Adjustment' criteria. Three criteria were suggested: (i) the end-use of the product on the market; (ii) consumers' tastes and habits; and (iii) the product's properties, nature and quality. Working Party Report on Border Tax Adjustments, BISD, 18S/97 (2 December 1970), para. 18. A further criterion to determine 'likeness' is the tariff classification in the Harmonized System. If two products are included in the same classification, they may be considered

provisions that prohibit discrimination in the GATS. Indeed, if one applies a non-discrimination standard, it is necessary to determine whether like situations are treated in the same way and different situations in a different way. Defining 'likeness' of services or service suppliers is thus the first step in the analysis. To the extent that the services or service suppliers are not considered 'like', there is no need for further assessment of whether some are treated less favourably than others.

312. The principles of most-favoured-nation treatment and national treatment in the GATS concern the treatment of both services and service suppliers. This stands in contrast with the GATT, where Article I and Article III GATT concern only the treatment of goods. One can also contrast this with the EU, where separate provisions exist for the freedom of establishment of service suppliers and for the free movement of services.[380] The simultaneous reference to services and service suppliers seriously broadens the scope of the disciplines on discrimination in the GATS, but is understandable, given the way in which the service is often closely intertwined with the service provider itself.

'like'. See W. M. Choi, *'Like Products' in International Trade Law: Towards a Consistent GATT/WTO Jurisprudence* (Oxford University Press, 2003).

[380] Tison states that different objectives can be attributed to the separate freedoms in the EU law. The free movement of services, much like the free movement of goods, is concerned with mobility of (immaterial) products and ancillary the temporary moment of the person providing the service. In contrast, freedom of establishment is concerned with the mobility of natural or legal persons across borders, largely unrelated to the mobility of the services themselves. M. Tison, 'Unravelling the General Good Exception: The Case for Financial Services', in M. Andenas and W. Roth (eds.), *Services and Free Movement in EU Law* (Oxford University Press, 2002) 321–81, at 328; and P. Eeckhout, 'Constitutional Concepts for Free Trade in Services', in J. Scott and G. De Búrca (eds.), *The EU and the WTO: Legal and Constitutional Issues* (Oxford: Hart, 2001) 211–35, at 212. Wouters has suggested that the scrutiny of measures affecting the mere movement of services and temporary presence of service suppliers should be more intense than that of measures that regulate the relatively permanent presence of foreign service suppliers in the territory of a state. In the latter case, the argument in favour of regulatory jurisdiction of host states is much stronger. J. Wouters, 'Freedom of Establishment, Freedom to Provide Services and Aspects of Conflict of Laws Concerning Financial Services', in D. Heremans et al. (eds.), *Current Developments in European Integration* (Leuven University Press, 2004) 15–91, at 52, 57; C. Barnard, *The Substantive Law of the EU*, 2nd edn (Oxford University Press, 2007) 643, 397; V. Hatzopoulos, 'Recent Developments of the Case Law of the ECJ in the Field of Services', (2000) 37 *Common Market Law Review* 43, at 74; and see, for a criticism, L. Daniele, 'Non-discriminatory Restrictions to the Free Movement of Persons', (1997) 22 *European Law Review* 191, at 191.

8.4.2.1.1 Likeness of services **313.** The criteria that are used to determine the likeness of *services* are not much elaborated on in dispute settlement on trade in services. The panel in *EC – Bananas III* mentioned the nature and characteristics of the services as criteria.[381] This suggests that the same criteria are used as for goods, namely end-uses, consumer tastes and habits, and product characteristics (the so-called 'Border Tax Adjustment criteria'). A further criterion used for determining likeness of goods is the classification of the goods in the Harmonized Commodity Description and Coding System, developed by the World Customs Organization.[382] Nevertheless, several authors have noted that the criteria for goods are of limited use for services. Indeed, it often makes no sense to define the physical characteristics of something immaterial like a service. Neither is the classification of a service in the Central Product Classification System (CPC, created by the United Nations)[383] of much use, since this system is much less developed than the Harmonized System for goods.[384]

314. The existing case law on non-discrimination indicates that when defining likeness for the purpose of assessing regulation, one should rather focus on the *interchangeability* of the services by applying a *cross-price elasticity test.*[385] In *Japan – Alcoholic Beverages II*, the panel stated explicitly that 'the appropriate test to define whether two products

[381] Panel Report, *EC – Bananas III*, para. 7.322.

[382] International Convention on the Harmonized Commodity Description and Coding System, done at Brussels on 14 June 1983, and the Protocol of Amendment thereto of 24 June 1986, entered into force 1 January 1998, OJ 2003 L198/3–10. This system classifies goods using a four-digit code (indicating a product group) and a two-digit code (indicating a specific product line).

[383] United Nations Central Product Classification System, Version 1.1, UN Doc. ST/ESA/STAT/SER.M/77/Ver.1.1, March 2002, available at http://unstats.un.org/unsd/cr/registry/regcst.asp?Cl=16&Lg=1. On 31 December 2008, a second version of the CPC was finalized: United Nations Central Product Classification System, Version 2, 31 December 2008, available at http://unstats.un.org/unsd/cr/registry/cpc-2.asp.

[384] Mattoo, above n. 331, at 127–8; and W. Zdouc, 'WTO Dispute Settlement Practice Relating to the General Agreement on Trade in Services', in F. Ortino and E.-U. Petersmann (eds.), *The WTO Dispute Settlement System 1995–2003* (Antwerp: Kluwer, 2004) 381–420, at 395–7.

[385] Focusing on the substitutability of banking services, through the application of a cross-price-elasticity test, may provide a predictable test for determining likeness. According to Choi, economic analysis can provide 'objective criteria of judgement, by enhancing the consistency, predictability and transparency of the dispute settlement system, which thereby increases the acceptability of decisions made by the WTO tribunal'. Choi, above n. 379, at 10. For further support in favour of a 'market-based' approach to likeness, see M. Bronkers and N. McNelis, 'Rethinking the "Like Product" Definition in

are "like" or "directly competitive or substitutable products" is the marketplace'.[386] This was cited with approval by the Appellate Body[387] and repeated in later reports.[388] The marketplace is 'the forum where consumers choose between different products'.[389] While these statements related to internal taxation in the framework of Article III:2 GATT, the Appellate Body in *EC – Asbestos* also noted that 'a determination of "likeness" under Article III:4 [of GATT] is, fundamentally, a determination about the nature and extent of a competitive relationship between and among products'.[390] If one can establish, for example through consumer surveys, that a sufficiently large number of consumers will switch to a substitute if the price of the product under consideration increases by a small but significant amount, this shows that the consumers consider the services as interchangeable and thus as substitutes.

315. Nevertheless, one may wonder whether the finding of low cross-price elasticity between two services is due to the fact that the services are not interchangeable or, rather, because the consumers only *perceive* the services as different because of years of indoctrination through regulatory distinctions in government regulation and information provision.[391] One may for instance think of situations where governments have for years consistently warned of the dangers of certain foreign banking services. Furthermore, consumers may have a bias against banks from certain countries merely because of their origin, even if the

GATT 1994: Anti-Dumping and Environmental Protection', in M. Bronkers (ed.), *A Cross-Section of WTO Law* (London: Cameron May, 2000) 15–56.

[386] Panel Report, *Japan – Taxes on Alcoholic Beverages* (*Japan – Alcoholic Beverages II*), WT/DS8/R, WT/DS10/R, WT/DS11/R, adopted 1 November 1996, as modified by Appellate Body Report, WT/DS8/AB/R, WT/DS10/AB/R, WT/DS11/AB/R, para. 6.22.

[387] Appellate Body Report, *Japan – Alcoholic Beverages II*, p. 20.

[388] See Appellate Body Report, *Korea – Taxes on Alcoholic Beverages* (*Korea – Alcoholic Beverages*), WT/DS75/AB/R, WT/DS84/AB/R, adopted 17 February 1999, para. 114; and Appellate Body Report, *United States – Transitional Safeguard Measure on Combed Cotton Yarn from Pakistan* (*US – Cotton Yarn*), WT/DS192/AB/R, adopted 5 November 2001, para. 96.

[389] Appellate Body Report, *Korea – Alcoholic Beverages*, above n. 388.

[390] Appellate Body Report, *European Communities – Measures Affecting Asbestos and Asbestos-Containing Products (EC – Asbestos)*, WT/DS135/AB/R, adopted 5 April 2001, para. 99.

[391] Verhoosel states that '[c]onsumer behaviour is naturally exposed to influence by the government' and that there 'are boundaries to consumer autonomy'. G. Verhoosel, *National Treatment and WTO Dispute Settlement. Adjudicating the Boundaries of Regulatory Autonomy* (Oxford: Hart, 2002) 57.

regulatory framework in which the banks operate is largely similar. Consumers may prefer ('trust more') banking services of a certain origin (especially domestic) over services of another origin. If that is the case, different credit institutions will be considered by consumers as 'unlike' and consequently, following the reasoning that dissimilar situations can be treated differently, the national regulator may discriminate between them. In other words, this may result in the test to determine discrimination being 'under-inclusive'.

316. This argument was considered by the Appellate Body in *Korea – Alcoholic Beverages* and *EC – Asbestos*, in the context of trade of goods. The Appellate Body stated that a complainant may produce evidence of latent consumer demand that is suppressed by regulatory barriers.[392] The problem, however, is how to construct this 'latent demand'. One thus needs to construct a reasonable argument that there is, in fact, potential competition, even if this is not immediately seen in present consumer behaviour.[393] Furthermore, the Appellate Body noted that it is also possible to submit 'evidence of substitutability from some relevant third market'.[394] This would arguably lead to an objective and abstract test of determining likeness from the perspective of a 'reasonable consumer'. Howse and Türk note that the Appellate Body in *EC – Asbestos* applies a test from the perspective of consumer tastes and habits in an 'ideal' marketplace, where consumers have full information and negative externalities have already to some extent been internalized. They argue that this brings back into the picture the regulatory aims, which in the GATT 1947 cases were considered under the 'aim and effects' test. However, this approach has been rejected in the case law since the WTO was established (below, para. 319). The only difference is that the perspective of consumer behaviour is taken.[395] Hoekman and Mavroidis have argued that the Appellate Body in *EC – Asbestos* implicitly applied a

[392] Appellate Body Report, *EC – Asbestos*, para. 123, which refers to Appellate Body Report, *Korea – Alcoholic Beverages*, paras. 115–121.

[393] Choi states, referring to *Korea – Alcoholic Beverages*, that potential substitutability should also be considered, since 'the GATT is, after all, an instrument used to protect the expectation of competitive opportunities in the market. The instrument should be capable of extending to the potential market as well as to the current one, as long as it aids global market governance'. Choi, above n. 379, at 31 and see Appellate Body Report, *Korea – Alcoholic Beverages*, paras. 114–15.

[394] Appellate Body Report, *Korea – Alcoholic Beverages*, paras. 114–15. Verhoosel notes that this is problematic since every state should be able to determine its own level of protection. Verhoosel, above n. 391, at 58.

[395] R. Howse and E. Türk, 'The WTO Impact on Internal Regulations – A Case Study of the Canada–EC Asbestos Dispute', in Scott and De Búrca, above n. 380, 283–328, at 301.

'reasonable consumer' test, which had as an implication that it was not necessary to look for factual evidence of such consumer perceptions in the market.[396]

317. Eventually, as a consequence of such a test, more services and service providers will be considered as 'like'. This stretches the scrutiny of the provisions that prohibit discrimination in the GATS. However, since the WTO Agreements are concerned with equality of competitive opportunities, the focus on a broader test of likeness, which includes also potential competition, seems appropriate. If over-inclusiveness were to follow from this 'stretching', this may be remedied through the second tier of the non-discrimination test. A mere detrimental effect on certain 'like' services or service suppliers is not sufficient to find a violation.

318. Another problem related to relying on consumer perceptions to define the 'likeness' of services is that most consumers may not be aware of the risks linked to a particular foreign service. For instance, with regard to a service provided by a foreign bank, the consumer may not be aware of the quality of the regulatory framework in which this bank is operating and of the supervision performed in the home country. Hence they often cannot give due account to this fact in their decisions on the purchase of the banking service. Financial services are a sector par excellence where information asymmetries play an important role (see above, paras. 37–49). Hence, since consumers would consider the services offered by, for example, a US and Chinese banking service supplier as 'like', the non-discrimination obligations in the GATS would prevent the national authorities from treating the suppliers as different, even if the authorities consider that they give rise to different risks. However, regulatory intervention draws distinctions precisely because some characteristics are not reflected in the marketplace and are *not* perceived by consumers.[397] One can argue that the result is an 'over-inclusive' outcome of the likeness test: too many services are considered 'like' by the consumers, even if there are, arguably, pertinent differences.

319. During the GATT era, a GATT panel developed the so-called 'aim and effects' test, which implied that the aim and the effect of a measure

[396] They also argue that it makes not much sense, from an economical viewpoint, only to consider criteria on the demand-side of the market. B. Hoekman and P. Mavroidis, *The World Trade Organization. Law, Economics, and Politics* (London: Routledge, 2007) 41–2.

[397] A. Porges and J. Trachtman, 'Robert Hudec and Domestic Regulation: The Resurrection of Aim and Effects', (2003) 37 *Journal of World Trade* 783, at 791.

would be considered when comparing domestic and imported products.[398] Hence two products would not be considered to be 'like' when the regulatory aim underlying the distinction is taken into account. Nevertheless, once the WTO was established, the Appellate Body rejected the use of intent to determine whether the products are different.[399] The main reason stated by the Appellate Body for the rejection was that panels could not sort through all the subjective reasons a national regulator might have. Also with regard to trade in services, the Appellate Body in *EC – Bananas III* saw 'no specific authority either in Article II or in Article XVII of the GATS for the proposition that the "aims and effects" of a measure are in any way relevant in determining whether that measure is inconsistent with those provisions'.[400] The Appellate Body stated that the 'aims and effects' doctrine in GATT was based on the statement in Article III:1 GATT that national measures (taxation and regulation) 'should not be applied to imported or domestic products so as to afford protection to domestic production'. According to the Appellate Body, the absence from the GATS of a reference to 'so as to afford protection', made it clear that the aim of a measure should not be considered here.

320. Nevertheless, when the determination of 'likeness' is made on the basis of consumer perceptions with regard to the characteristics of goods or services, the regulatory objective may in fact be closely linked to the characteristics. In *EC – Asbestos*, the Appellate Body stated that the health risk linked to asbestos fibres makes these fibres different from other fibres. According to the Appellate Body, the health risk of a

[398] GATT Panel Report: United States – Measures Affecting Alcoholic and Malt Beverages, DS23/R (19 June 1992), BISD 39S/206, paras. 5.73–5.74; and GATT Panel Report: United States – Taxes on Automobiles, DS31/R (29 September 1994, unadopted), paras. 5.9–5.10. On the 'aim and effects' test, see R. Hudec, 'GATT/WTO Constraints on National Regulation: Requiem for an "Aim and Effects" Test', (1998) 32 *International Lawyer* 619, at 624. Farber and Hudec have noted that the 'aim and effects' decision in *US – Taxes on Automobiles* (rendered in 1994) may not be a decision from which general statements may easily be derived. According to these authors, 'the decision was rendered under extreme pressure due to the much noted danger that a finding of violation against the United States might impede congressional ratification of the WTO Charter and the Uruguay Agreements'. D. Farber and R. Hudec, 'GATT Legal Restraints on Domestic Environmental Regulations', in J. Bhagwati and R. Hudec (eds.), *Fair Trade and Harmonization: Prerequisites for Free Trade?, Vol. 2 Legal Analysis* (Cambridge, MA: MIT Press, 1996) 59–94, at 74. Moreover, this GATT panel report was never adopted.

[399] Appellate Body Report, *Japan – Alcoholic Beverages II*, pp. 18–19.

[400] Appellate Body Report, *EC – Bananas III*, para. 241.

product is a characteristic that consumers will take into account when they consider whether two products are substitutes.[401] Consumers are aware of the health risk and thus treat asbestos and non-asbestos fibres as different. Therefore they are not in a competitive relationship. Still, it is precisely because the government wants to avoid the health risk that the products receive different regulatory treatment. Nevertheless, the statement by the Appellate Body links the risks clearly to the perceptions of consumers.[402]

321. The close link between the characteristics of services and the nature and characteristics of the service providers also raises the question whether services may be considered 'unlike' because the providers are different. Case law relating to the GATT draws a strict distinction between the product itself and the production process for this product is maintained. WTO members are not allowed to differentiate between goods on the basis of the differences in production process that do not affect the quality (or characteristics) of the product.[403] This distinction, which has been criticized in the field of trade of goods, is in the case of services very difficult to apply, because the nature and characteristics of a service may be intertwined with the provider supplying the service.

322. Indeed, when applying the cross-price elasticity test, in the case of a hypothetical price increase of the service under consideration, a large number of consumers may refrain from switching to another service

[401] Appellate Body Report, *EC – Asbestos*, paras. 114–117.

[402] In a concurring opinion in *EC – Asbestos*, one Appellate Body member expressed agreement with the 'likeness' conclusion but disagreement with the fundamentally economic approach taken which focused solely on the competitive relationship between the products. Appellate Body Report, *EC – Asbestos*, paras. 149–154.

[403] This is the so-called product/process distinction, which dates from the pre-WTO GATT period. (See GATT Panel Report, *United States – Restrictions on Imports of Tuna* (*US – Tuna (Mexico)*), DS21/R, 3 September 1991, unadopted, BISD 39S/155, para 5.11; and GATT Panel Report, *United States – Restrictions on Imports of Tuna* (*US – Tuna (EEC)*), DS29/R, 16 June 1994, unadopted, paras 5.8 and 5.9.) The distinction has been criticized for not having a basis in the text of the GATT. S. Charnovitz, 'The Law of Environmental "PPMs" in the WTO: Debunking the Myth of Illegality', (2002) 27 *Yale Journal of International Law* 59; R. Howse and D. Regan, 'The Product/Process Distinction – An Illusory Basis for Disciplining "Unilateralism" in Trade Policy', (2000) 11 *European Journal of International Law* 249; and D. Kysar, 'Preferences for Processes: the Process/Product Distinction and the Regulation of Consumer Choice', (2004) 118 *Harvard Law Review* 525. For a brief criticism on this position, stating that abolishing the product/process distinction opens the door for abuses and hidden protectionism, see J. Jackson, 'Comments on Shrimp/Turtle and the Product/Process Distinction', (2000) 11 *European Journal of International Law* 303.

which at first sight may be like, because it is provided by a service supplier that is considered to be unlike the other one.[404] Some characteristics of the supplier may influence the quality of the service that is supplied. The problem is, of course, to determine what characteristics of the provider influence indirectly the qualities of the service and what characteristics do not. Arguably, the characteristics that play a role in the decision of consumers whether to consider the services as substitutes are such characteristics that indirectly define the service. Other characteristics that are considered in the regulatory distinction, but are not reflected in the decision by consumers, are not part of the analysis of whether the services are like.

8.4.2.1.2 Likeness of service suppliers **323.** The case law on likeness of services is thus far from settled. It seems even less clear what criteria should be applied for determining whether *service suppliers* are like. The panel in *Canada – Autos* has merely noted with regard to 'likeness' of service suppliers in Article II GATS (MFN) that 'to the extent that the service suppliers concerned supply the same services, they should be considered "like"'.[405] Despite its concise formulation, the impact of this statement may be wide-ranging.[406] As soon as services are like, the service providers are also considered like. Hence it seems that there is no possibility of treating two service providers as different if the services they provide are like. This seriously curtails the leeway states have to regulate their services markets (e.g. the market for banking services).[407]

[404] According to Hudec, for goods regulatory distinctions can only be based on the qualities of the products themselves. This would involve the product qualities themselves *or* other characteristics *that indirectly govern product qualities.* He cites as examples of the latter slaughterhouse cleanliness or possession of a licence certifying certain requisite skills. This may be similar to considering e.g. the qualifications and reputation of a service provider in determining whether two services are like. Hudec, above n. 398, at 624.

[405] Panel Report, *Canada – Autos*, para. 10.248, and see also Panel Report, *EC – Bananas*, para. 7.322.

[406] Zdouc, above n. 384, at 398.

[407] Therefore Nicolaïdis and Trachtman argue that a disjunctive test needs to be applied: one has to define whether the measure concerns services or service suppliers and then define whether they are like. This would lead to more deference to regulatory autonomy, because the service suppliers would be considered unlike even if the services they provide are like (e.g. a bank and an insurance company offering 'like' banking services and thus having to comply with minimum capital requirements are not like). K. Nicolaïdis and J. Trachtman, 'From Policed Regulation to Managed Recognition: Mapping the Boundary of GATS', in J. Trachtman (ed.), *The International Economic Law Revolution and the Right to Regulate* (London: Cameron May, 2006) 281–321, at

The panel in *China – Electronic Payment Services* provided some clarification. The panel noted that 'the fact that service suppliers provide like services may in some cases raise a presumption that they are "like" service suppliers'. Yet, 'in the specific circumstances of other cases, a separate inquiry into the likeness of the suppliers may be called for'.[408]

324. Might one conclude that service providers can be treated as different only if the services are *not* like? This way, the characteristics of the service define the likeness of service providers and only these characteristics will be relevant in the analysis of the likeness of providers. Arguably, from a trade perspective, different characteristics of providers are irrelevant, as long as they do not constitute a comparative advantage, in which case they would have been reflected in the characteristics of the services. Hence, because of the fact that services and service providers are so much intertwined in the view of consumers, the services will not be considered interchangeable and, consequently, the service providers will also be considered to be different. It is indeed difficult to apply a cross-price elasticity test when considering the service suppliers only. A consumer does not pay a price for a supplier, but rather for the service that is supplied. When a cross-price elasticity test is applied to the service, and interchangeability is found, the providers may be considered like. Thus service providers are like, unless their different characteristics are reflected in consumer decisions on the interchangeability of the services they provide.

325. As has been noted with regard to likeness of services (above, para. 318), it should again be acknowledged that governments often regulate and draw distinctions because consumers are not sufficiently aware of the risks that certain providers run. If consumer perception is the determining criterion for establishing likeness (as is the case under existing case

294–5. See also, approving this approach, Krajewski, above n. 348, at 106–7. Verhoosel argues that it is difficult to separate them. Verhoosel, above n. 391, at 62 (footnote 30). See also M. Cossy, 'Determining "likeness" under the GATS: Squaring the Circle?', WTO Staff Working Paper ERSD-2006-08, September 2006, available at www.wto.org/english/res_e/reser_e/ersd200608_e.pdf, 9. As is argued further, since the characteristics of the service suppliers and of the services are so intertwined, the question is rather to what extent the consumer sees the characteristics of service suppliers as relevant for the characteristics of services and vice versa.

[408] See Panel Report, *China – Electronic Payment Services*, para. 7.705. A situation where such presumption of likeness could apply is where the service suppliers are the same in all material aspects – including business scope – except for origin (see Panel Report, *China – Publications and Audiovisual Products*, para. 7.795). In a case where no such presumption applies, it needs to be determined whether the different suppliers are in a competitive relationship (Panel Report, *China – Electronic Payment Services*, para. 7.700).

law) such regulatory distinctions will not be taken into account. Hence two suppliers will be considered 'like', even if the government had good reasons to consider them different. In such cases one might wonder whether a panel or the Appellate Body would look beyond consumer perceptions and also consider objective criteria that pointed to differences between the providers. This may be a translation to services of the criterion of 'physical characteristics' used as a criterion for distinguishing between different goods. For instance, the differences in the regulatory frameworks in which banks of a different origin operate may be such objective criteria (especially when they are based on international standards, such as the Basel principles and standards). Hence, it is not unthinkable that a panel will consider that a banking service originating in a country that has implemented the Basel principles and standards is not 'like' a banking service originating in a country that has not done so. However, once distinctions involve a determination of 'adequacy' or 'riskiness' of a framework, one cannot talk any more about objective product characteristics that can be taken into account in the determination of 'likeness'. The service providers (e.g. banks) will be considered 'like' and the focus then shifts to the second tier of the test (namely whether there is 'less favourable treatment').

326. On the other hand, when one focuses on the cross-price elasticity of services to determine the interchangeability of service providers, and finds that consumers do not consider them interchangeable, one may wonder whether the fact that consumers do consider the characteristics of the providers as relevant for the non-interchangeability of the services is not due to government regulation itself. Regulatory distinctions may then in fact determine the perceptions of consumers. The same remarks as those with regard to likeness of services are applicable here. The adjudicator may need to have recourse to an objective test that looks at other, similar markets or considers likeness from the perspective of a reasonable consumer. This is not necessarily incompatible with a facts-based determination. Filtering out consumer bias can be done by including specific questions in the questionnaire that is drafted to assess consumer preferences. It is then necessary to single out 'neutral' consumers.[409]

8.4.2.1.3 Summary of likeness **327.** As case law stands now, one should determine the likeness of services first of all on the basis of a

[409] Choi, above n. 379, at p. 80.

cross-price elasticity test, applied on the basis of consumer perceptions. This would allow defining whether services are in a competitive relationship. Because the characteristics of services and service suppliers are so much intertwined, it is appropriate to consider to what extent the characteristics of service suppliers are reflected in the consumer perceptions of the characteristics of the services. Only these characteristics of the suppliers can be taken into account.

328. However, it is recognized that the focus on consumer perceptions may be problematic if these perceptions are influenced by government policies. By relying on evidence from relevant other markets (as the Appellate Body in *EC – Asbestos* has suggested), the perceptions of a 'reasonable consumer' can be constructed. Yet consumers are very often unaware of certain risks and this is precisely the reason why a government wants to make a regulatory distinction. Hence, because consumers will often perceive banks or banking services to be like, the services or suppliers are considered in a competitive relationship.

329. Nonetheless, we considered that in the case of services or service suppliers other criteria besides consumer perceptions could be used to determine likeness, provided that these criteria are objective. The fact that a banking service is supplied by a bank originating in a country that applies standards and principles laid down by the Basel Committee may be such an objective criterion for distinction. However, as soon as they involve some value judgement on 'riskiness' of services, the criteria can no longer be labelled 'objective'. The Appellate Body has clearly rejected taking into account the regulatory aim when determining likeness. Admittedly, this will lead to some 'over-inclusiveness' of the test, which should, however, be remedied in the second tier of the test or when addressing grounds of justification. Only in the latter situation is there a textual basis in the GATS for allowing panels or the Appellate Body to consider the non-protectionist aim of a measure as a justification for a regulatory distinction.

8.4.2.2 Less favourable treatment

330. Once it is established that the services or service suppliers are 'like', one must consider whether the regulatory distinction leads to less favourable treatment. Article II:1 GATS requires that the services and service suppliers of one WTO member receive treatment no less favourable than the like services and service suppliers of any other country. Article XVII:1 GATS requires that the services and service suppliers of any WTO member receive treatment no less favourable than the like domestic services and service suppliers. The phrase 'treatment no less favourable' also figures in the national treatment provision in Article III:4 of the GATT, for which much more case law is available. With regard to trade in goods, this has been interpreted as imposing an enquiry into whether the conditions of competition are modified,[410] and this explanation of the phrase is made explicit in Article XVII:3 GATS. The question is thus whether the regulatory distinction between the like services or service suppliers produces an actual or potential effect[411] of modifying the conditions of competition to the detriment of certain services or service suppliers.

8.4.2.2.1 De jure and de facto discrimination **331.** The most obvious cases of a violation of the provisions on discrimination are regulatory distinctions based on the origin of the service or service supplier. In such cases of de jure discrimination, the fact that a regulatory distinction is based on the specific national origin may suggest that there is obviously a violation of the principles of most-favoured-nation or national treatment. Yet a complainant must always show that the conditions of competition are modified because of the distinction. Hence formally different treatment does not per se violate the GATS provisions prohibiting discrimination.[412]

332. Arguably, today the majority of cases with regard to trade in services that could lead to a violation of these provisions are cases where a national regulation does not make a formal distinction on the basis of the national origin of services or service suppliers, but nevertheless leads in practice to such a distinction and results in a disadvantageous treatment for certain services or service suppliers. Other elements, besides the *effect* of the measure, are necessary to establish such a case of de facto discrimination. Almost any measure affecting trade in services or service suppliers may have the effect of modifying the conditions of competition. The mere existence of regulatory diversity across borders imposes on some service providers a

[410] Appellate Body Report, *Korea – Various Measures on Beef*, para. 144.

[411] It should be noted that the Appellate Body stated that the question is not whether there is protective effect, in the sense that certain trade *volumes* are guaranteed. The question is rather whether competitive *opportunities* are guaranteed. The regulatory distinction may thus lead to less favourable treatment, even if there are no actual changes in trade volumes noticeable. Appellate Body Report, *Japan – Alcoholic Beverages II*, p. 15, repeating the statements of the GATT Panel Report, *United States – Taxes on Petroleum and Certain Imported Substances* (*US – Superfund*), adopted 17 June 1987, BISD 34S/136, para. 5.1.9.

[412] Appellate Body Report, *Korea – Various Measures on Beef*, paras. 135–137.

higher burden than on others. Nonetheless, if such measures apply without making any distinction at all this cannot be sufficient to violate a provision that prohibits discrimination. It is difficult to reconcile such an approach with the provisions in the GATS that specifically aim at disciplining non-discriminatory measures. The distinction between both sets of provisions would become blurred.[413]

8.4.2.2.2 Considering the 'intent' of a measure when applying provisions that prohibit discrimination **333.** In the previous paragraphs we considered that the regulatory objective that underlies the distinctions made by WTO members is not taken into account when determining 'likeness'. Likeness is determined on the basis of consumer perceptions with regard to the interchangeability of services. However, in case law relating to the GATT, the Appellate Body in *Chile – Alcoholic Beverages* has stressed that 'the measure's purposes, objectively manifested in the design, architecture and structure of the measure, *are* intensely pertinent to the task of evaluating whether or not that measure is applied so as to afford protection to domestic production'.[414]

334. The phrase 'so as to afford protection' is absent in Articles II and XVII GATS, and one may wonder whether a panel or the Appellate Body will, without a textual basis, accept the same analysis when considering whether the treatment is 'less favourable'.[415] The absence of this phrase

[413] One should note the contrast with the situation within the European Union, where the Court of Justice has defined that Art. 49 TFEU (freedom of establishment) and Art. 56 TFEU (free movement of services) covers not only measures that discriminate on the ground of nationality, but any restriction, even if it applies without any distinction when it is liable to create a barrier to the exercise of the freedom of establishment or free movement of services. See, for a criticism of the European move from discrimination towards market access, G. Davies, *Nationality Discrimination in the European Internal Market* (The Hague: Kluwer, 2003) 93–115. See, with regard to establishment, CJEU, Case C-55/94 *Gebhard/Consiglio dell'Ordine degli Avvocati e Procuratori di Milano*, [1995] ECR I-4165, para. 37; and, with regard to free movement of services, CJEU, Case C-76/90 *Säger* v. *Dennemeyer*, [1991] ECR I-4221, para. 12. See, on the limits of the application of Art. 43 and Art. 49, inter alia Tison, above n. 380, at 321–81; and Wouters, above n. 380, at 15–91.

[414] Appellate Body Report, *Chile – Taxes on Alcoholic Beverages* (*Chile – Alcoholic Beverages*), WT/DS87 and 110/AB/R, adopted 12 January 2000, para. 71 (emphasis in original).

[415] The Appellate Body in *EC – Asbestos* has noted: 'The term "less favourable treatment" expresses the general principle, in Art. III:1 [GATT], that internal regulations "should not be applied . . . so as to afford protection to domestic production".' Appellate Body Report, *EC – Asbestos*, para. 100. Even if Art. III:4 GATT did not refer to Art. III:1, it considered Art. III:1 to express a general principle.

has been stressed by the Appellate Body in *EC – Bananas III*.[416] On the other hand, it can easily be argued that the wish to expand trade in services by means of 'progressive liberalization' (as expressed in the second paragraph of the Preamble to the GATS) involves the removal of protectionist measures (be it only gradually).

335. If such an approach is taken, the question arises of when a measure's purpose can be said to be 'objectively manifested'. With regard to Article III:2 GATT (which concerns internal taxation), the Appellate Body in *Japan – Taxes on Alcoholic Beverages II* has stated that the protective application of a measure can sometimes be discerned *objectively* from the design, architecture and revealing structure of the measure.[417]

336. In practice, factual evidence of intent will have some impact on the analysis of whether the measure is 'so as to afford protection'.[418] This is exactly what was done by the Appellate Body in *Canada – Periodicals*, where the Appellate Body referred to declared policy objectives in preparatory works by Canada.[419] Moreover, in *Mexico – Soft Drinks*, the panel noted that 'the declared intention of legislators and regulators of the Member adopting the measure should not be totally disregarded, particularly when the explicit objective of the measure is that of affording protection to domestic production'.[420] Hence it seems that the factual evidence of protectionist intent will probably have impact on the analysis of whether the measures violate a provision that prohibits discrimination. However, these cases concerned evidence of *protectionist* intent and not the consideration of *non-protectionist* objectives in the determination of whether a measure is discriminatory.[421]

416 Appellate Body Report, *EC – Bananas III*, para. 241.

417 Appellate Body Report, *Japan – Taxes on Alcoholic Beverages II*, p. 29. This was repeated in Appellate Body Report, *Korea – Various Measures on Beef*, para 150, and Appellate Body Report, *Chile – Taxes on Alcoholic Beverages* (*Chile – Alcoholic Beverages*), WT/DS87 and 110/AB/R, adopted 12 January 2000, para 62. On the difficulty of making such an 'objective' assessment, see H. Horn and P. Mavroidis, 'Still Hazy after All These Years: The Interpretation of National Treatment in the GATT/WTO Case-Law on Discrimination', (2004) 15 *European Journal of International Law* 39, at 58.

418 Porges and Trachtman, above n. 397, at 791.

419 Appellate Body Report, *Canada – Periodicals*, p. 30.

420 Panel Report, *Mexico – Tax Measures on Soft Drinks and Other Beverages* (*Mexico – Taxes on Soft Drinks*), WT/DS308/R, adopted 24 March 2006, as modified by Appellate Body Report, WT/DS308/AB/R, para. 8.91.

421 According to some authors, the Appellate Body in *EC – Asbestos*, in an enigmatic formulation, left the door open for fully considering the aim of measures also under Art. III:4 GATT (concerning internal regulation). The Appellate Body noted that treating

8.4.2.2.3 Considering the non-protectionist intent of a measure when applying provisions that prohibit discrimination **337.** While factual evidence of protectionist intent can play a role when applying the provisions that prohibit discrimination, whether a *non-protectionist* objective can be considered at that stage is still another issue. Should a panel or the Appellate Body consider here the claim by a respondent that a measure that has an adverse effect on banking services of a certain origin does not violate the prohibition to discriminate on the basis of origin because this measure pursues a non-protectionist objective? In other words, could national regulations be saved on the basis of other regulatory objectives *not mentioned* in the limitative lists of general exceptions in the GATS? Some authors have suggested considering the intent of a measure that is already under scrutiny at the moment of applying the provisions that prohibit discrimination.[422]

338. In two cases where Article III:4 GATT was interpreted, the analysis also seemed to suggest that even though a measure has the effect of modifying the conditions of competition, it still does not violate the prohibition of discrimination because of other considerations. In *Dominican Republic – Cigarettes*, the Appellate Body noted that 'the existence of a detrimental effect on a given imported product resulting from a measure does not necessarily imply that this measure accords less favourable treatment to imports if the detrimental effect is explained by factors or circumstances unrelated to the foreign origin of the product'.[423] Pauwelyn has argued that 'a non-protectionist explanation – here market share, but possibly in other cases a non-protectionist alternative purpose – may demonstrate that the regulation is not de facto discriminatory based on origin'.[424] In the *EC – Biotech* dispute, the panel noted that, in order to violate Article III:4 GATT,

like products different does not necessarily lead to a violation of the provisions on discrimination, but that it is also necessary that some products are treated 'less favourably'. According to the Appellate Body, the 'term "less favourable treatment" expresses the general principle, in Art. III:1, that internal regulations "should not be applied . . . so as to afford protection to domestic production"'. Porges and Trachtman, above n. 397, at 796.

422 See Cossy, above n. 407, at 39; and A. Mattoo and A. Subramanian, 'Regulatory Autonomy and Multilateral Disciplines. The Dilemma and a Possible Resolution', (1998) 1 *Journal of International Economic Law* 303, at 314.

423 Appellate Body Report, *Dominican Republic – Measures Affecting the Importation and Internal Sale of Cigarettes* (*Dominican Republic – Import and Sale of Cigarettes*), WT/DS302/AB/R, adopted 19 May 2005, para. 96.

424 J. Pauwelyn, 'The Unbearable Lightness of Likeness', in M. Panizzon, N. Pohl and P. Sauvé (eds.), *GATS and the Regulation of International Trade in Services* (Cambridge University Press, 2008) 358–69, at 365.

the less favourable treatment of imported products must be 'explained by the foreign origin of these products rather than' some other cause, such as, for example, a different perception of the safety of the products.[425] All this may point to the need to make a careful analysis of the effects of a measure before it can be considered as 'so as to afford protection'. However, these statements do not seem to introduce an enquiry into the non-protectionist aim of the measure as a justification in combination with an assessment whether the restrictions of trade are necessary to achieve this goal. In this regard it can be noted that the Appellate Body has, in footnote 372 of its report in *US – Clove Cigarettes*, sought to qualify its earlier statement in *Dominican Republic – Cigarettes*. The Appellate Body stated that its findngs should *not* be viewed as requiring a further enquiry into the rationale of the detrimental impact under Article III:4 of the GATT. The Appellate Body stressed that no such enquiry was made in *Dominican Republic – Cigarettes*.

339. Considering the non-protectionist aim of a measure when already applying the provisions that prohibit discrimination is far from evident when looking at the GATS. There are three arguments for this.

340. First, there is a need for a textual basis for engaging in such analysis. As already indicated (above, para. 334), the Appellate Body in *EC – Bananas III* stated firmly that, in contrast to Article III:1 GATT, there is no reference to 'so as to afford protection' in the provisions on discrimination in the GATS.

341. Because the GATS aims at the progressive liberalization of trade in services (as stated in the second paragraph of the Preamble of the GATS) (above, para. 334), the goal of the GATS is clearly to remove protectionist measures. Therefore one can argue that the provisions on discrimination in the GATS only prohibit measures that are protectionist on the basis of origin. This may in fact provide the textual support for not only considering the expressed *protectionist* intent of a measure, but also paying attention to the *non-protectionist aim* of the measure at issue. However, while the non-protectionist aim of a measure may play a role in the assessment under Article II and XVII GATS, this may not amount to a subjective assessment of justification grounds invoked by a defendant and an analysis of whether there are less restrictive means to achieve this goal. This would run contrary to the statements by the Appellate Body in

[425] Panel Report, *European Communities – Measures Affecting the Approval and Marketing of Biotech Products* (*EC – Approval and Marketing of Biotech Products*), WT/DS291/R, WT/DS292/R, WT/DS293/R, Corr.1 and Add.1, 2, 3, 4, 5, 6, 7, 8 and 9, adopted 21 November 2006, para. 7.2411.

Chile – Alcoholic Beverages and *Japan – Taxes on Alcoholic Beverages II* that the aim of the measure must be 'objectively manifested'.

342. Verhoosel suggested that, for national treatment, the textual basis for such a far-reaching test lies in footnote 10 to Article XVII GATS. The footnote places a limit on the scrutiny of the national treatment provision. It provides that the commitments by WTO members under the national treatment provision of the GATS 'shall not be construed to require any Member to compensate for any inherent competitive disadvantages which result from the foreign character of the relevant services or service suppliers'. This footnote defines what the obligation of national treatment is *not* about.[426] WTO members that made a national treatment commitment are not required to compensate for disadvantages that are merely due to the foreign character of the service or service supplier. It 'does not provide cover for actions which might modify the conditions of competition against services and service suppliers which are already disadvantaged due to their foreign character'.[427] Verhoosel suggested that this implies a consideration of the aim of the measure and whether the measure at hand is the least restrictive means of achieving the aim. If an alternative measure can be designed that results in less restrictive effects, the disadvantage felt by the foreign services or service suppliers is caused not by the foreign character alone, but by the measure itself.[428] While this is certainly a strong argument, it is difficult to reconcile this reading of the footnote with its wording. The focus is on the *effects* of the measure and not on its aim. Moreover, as Krajewski has argued, the footnote is clearly meant to be *limiting* the scope of the national-treatment obligation in the GATS and not to allow for a proportionality test within the *wide* scope of the obligation.[429] Ortino argues that footnote 10 imposes only a requirement of *causation*.[430] The measure

[426] See Krajewski, above n. 348, at 111.

[427] Panel Report, *Canada – Autos*, para. 10.300. The problem is, of course, how to distinguish in practice the inherent competitive disadvantages from those created by the regulatory measure. Zdouc has elaborated a theoretical test on how to compare, on the one hand, the restrictive impact of the measure on the foreign service or provider with, on the other hand, the restrictive effect of the regulation on the domestic service or provider *plus* the inherent competitive advantages from being a foreign service or provider. This test is difficult to apply in practice because the restrictive impact needs to be quantified somehow. This is recognized by Zdouc himself. Zdouc, above n. 384, at 412.

[428] Verhoosel, above n. 391, at 91. [429] See Krajewski, above n. 348, at 111.

[430] F. Ortino, 'The Principle of Non-discrimination and Its Exceptions in GATS: Selected Legal Issues', Working Paper presented at Conflict and Crises? – The WTO After Hong Kong, Vienna, 24–25 April 2006, available at http://ssrn.com/abstract=979481, 7. Note that Farber and Hudec stated that 'by introducing the all-purpose concept of causation, the draftsmen of the Uruguay Round Services Agreement may in fact have found

at stake needs to have *caused* the adverse effects. One thus needs to consider to what extent the effects would have manifested themselves *but for* the measure. Footnote 10 to Article XVII arguably does not provide a textual basis for introducing a test that considers the non-protectionist aim under the non-discrimination obligation.

343. Second, while one may disagree on whether it is possible to find a textual basis in the GATS, there is another reason why such a far-reaching test seems difficult. If progressive liberalization of trade in (banking) services is the objective of the GATS, it is hardly acceptable that a WTO member can invoke any non-protectionist measure as a justification of a discriminatory effect under Article II or XVII without any assessment of the acceptability of this objective or of the manner in which achieving this objective is attempted. Therefore the inclusion of such a test in the non-discrimination obligation is sometimes suggested.[431] Arguably, this may be inspired by the 'rule of reason' approach developed in the EU by the Court of Justice towards measures that have an 'equivalent effect to quantitative restrictions'.[432] In Article XIV GATS, which provides specific exceptions to obligations in the GATS, such an assessment is provided through a so-called 'necessity test'.[433] A measure that violates one of the GATS provisions is nonetheless justified if it is 'necessary' for the achievement of a specific objective. This involves a 'weighing and balancing' of (a)

another way of introducing the issue of valid regulatory purpose into the legal definition of "less favourable treatment".' Farber and Hudec, above n. 398, at 77.

[431] Verhoosel, above n. 391, at 91; and Mattoo and Subramanian, above n. 422, at 314. Panourgias also argues for a 'necessity test' in the provisions on non-discrimination. However, he reads this test in the first prong of the analysis (on 'likeness'). Panourgias, above n. 1, at 74.

[432] The Court of Justice of the EU has defined Art. 49 TFEU (ex 43 EC Treaty) (freedom of establishment) and Art. 56 TFEU (ex 49 EC Treaty) (free movement of services) as covering not only measures that discriminate on the ground of nationality, but any restriction, even if it applies without any distinction, when it is liable to create a barrier to the exercise of the freedom of establishment or free movement of services. Such barriers do not violate Art. 49 *c.q.* 56 on condition that they (i) are applied in a non-discriminatory manner; (ii) are justified by imperative requirements in the general interest; (iii) are suitable for securing the attainment of the objective which they pursue; and (iv) do not go beyond what is necessary to attain the objective. See, with regard to establishment, CJEU, Case C-55/94 *Gebhard/Consiglio dell'Ordine degli Avvocati e Procuratori di Milano*, [1995] ECR I-4165, para 37; and, with regard to free movement of services, CJEU, Case C-76/90 *Säger* v. *Dennemeyer*, [1991] ECR I-4221, para. 12.

[433] It should be noted that depending on the policy objective at issue in Art. XX GATT, the test involves a requirement of 'necessity' or 'related to'. However, in Art. XIV GATS, the main paragraphs only refer to 'necessity'. Paragraphs (d) and (e) of Art. XIV GATS do not mention necessity. These paragraphs provide exceptions from Arts. XVII and II respectively for measures pursuing tax purposes.

the importance of the interests that are protected; (b) the extent to which the measures contribute to achieve the end pursued; and (c) the respective trade impact of the measures.[434]

344. However, it would upset the structure of the GATS if a test of a similar level of intensity is included in the provisions that prohibit discrimination.[435] If a measure were to fail the 'necessity test' in these obligations regarding discrimination, how could it ever satisfy the already intensive necessity test in the exception in paragraphs (a)–(c) of Article XIV? Following this reasoning, the test under the former provisions would thus need to be stricter than that in Article XIV. Nevertheless, this does not fit with the statement of the Appellate Body in *Chile – Alcoholic Beverages*. In that report, the Appellate Body stated that it would be inappropriate to introduce into the provisions that prohibit discrimination an examination of whether a discriminatory measure is necessary to achieve its objectives.[436] Furthermore, introducing a test into the provisions that prohibit discrimination that would engage in a fully fledged 'weighing and balancing' (and thus be more intensive than 'necessity' in Article XIV by balancing the value of a goal against the costs to free trade) would introduce a very important limit on the regulatory autonomy of WTO members, based on a very narrow textual basis.

345. Third, invoking a necessity test under the provisions that prohibit discrimination also blurs the distinction from other provisions in the GATS. Indeed, under Article VI:4 GATS, disciplines are being developed that would apply to measures that are non-discriminatory. The main point of discussion in these negotiations concerns the inclusion of a necessity test. Pauwelyn has noted that if the provisions that prohibit discrimination already contain a necessity test, it would be strange for

434 The necessity requirement in Art. XIV GATS was for the first time interpreted in *US – Gambling*. Appellate Body Report, *US – Gambling*, paras 300–327. On the 'weighing and balancing' see also Appellate Body Report, *Korea – Various Measures on Beef*, para. 178; and Appellate Body Report, *EC – Asbestos*, para. 172. For a critical discussion of this test, arguing that no real balancing of trade and other interests takes place, see D. Regan, 'The Meaning of "Necessary" in GATT Art. XX and GATS Art. XIV: the Myth of Cost-Benefit Balancing', (2007) 6 *World Trade Review* 347, at 347–69.

435 The invocation of all kinds of regulatory objectives under Arts. II and XVII GATS (or the corresponding provisions in GATT) could make the provisions that allow for exemptions redundant. Indeed, the measures would already satisfy the test under Art. II (or XVII), and there would no longer be any need to justify them under the exceptions. The exceptions may then only be relevant for the measures that are de jure discriminatory.

436 Appellate Body Report, *Chile – Alcoholic Beverages*, para. 72. Note that the statement concerned the second sentence of Art. III:2 GATT.

this still to be a point of discussion in the negotiations under Article VI:4 GATS.[437]

346. In sum, there is a clear tendency in the legal literature that argues in favour of considering the non-protectionist aim of a measure when analysing whether a measure that adversely affects services from a certain origin is in fact violating the provisions that prohibit discrimination.[438] Nonetheless, as the case law stands at present, it is difficult to find any recognition by a panel or the Appellate Body of the existence of a possible analysis within the non-discrimination provisions that would consider the non-protectionist aim of a measure invoked by a defendant and would assess whether the measure is necessary to achieve the objective, much in the same way as is done in the 'rule of reason' analysis in the EU.

8.4.2.2.4 Linking the 'adverse effect' of a measure to the origin of banking services **347.** A final way to limit the application of the prohibition on discrimination is to specify in greater detail the way the discriminatory effect is measured. One can find a violation of the prohibition as soon as *one* service or service supplier is (actually or potentially) treated less favourably than another. Clearly, this would often lead to a violation of the provisions. It will almost always be possible to find a service or service supplier that is placed in a less advantageous competitive position than another because of the measure. Therefore Ehring has suggested requiring that the effect is based on an 'asymmetric impact' analysis. This way, only if the impact of the measure on a *group* of services or service suppliers is asymmetric with the impact on another group would there be a violation.[439] This is what the Appellate Body has declared (as an *obiter dictum*) in *EC – Asbestos*. The Appellate Body noted that, for establishing a violation of Article III:4 GATT, a comparison must be made between the group of like imported and the group of

[437] Pauwelyn, above n. 424, at 369.

[438] For another account of the tendencies that argue in favour or against including the consideration of the regulatory purpose in the determination of whether a discrimination provision is violated, see M. Trebilcock and R. Howse, *The Regulation of International Trade*, 3rd edn (London: Routledge, 2005), at 108–11, and see J. Flett, 'WTO Space for National Regulation: Requiem for a Diagonal Vector Test', (2013) 16 *Journal of International Economic Law* 37, at 37–40.

[439] L. Ehring, '*De Facto* Discrimination in World Trade Law. National and Most-Favoured-Nation Treatment – or Equal Treatment?', (2002) 36 *Journal of World Trade* 921, at 921–77.

like domestic products.[440] Thus an *aggregate* rather than an individual test should be performed. Such an approach to the effects of a measure limits the application of the non-discrimination provisions. However, this qualification may not be useful for cases where an individual application of a measure is scrutinized (see below, para. 506).[441]

348. Nevertheless, one is still left with the statements in the abovementioned *Dominican Republic – Cigarettes* and *EC – Biotech* decisions. These statements may imply that a complainant needs to establish a link between the effects of the measure and the origin of the specific group of goods, services or service suppliers that is adversely affected. This is not that difficult for de jure discriminatory measures. Measures would only amount to de facto discrimination if the criteria that are used to make a distinction can be convincingly related to origin. This is obviously clear when the complainant can produce evidence of the protective intent of the measure.[442] Yet, if this is not available, a plausible argument will need to be constructed as to how the distinctions in the measure are linked to origin. Examples are residence requirements, language requirements, local qualification requirements or geographical characteristics.[443] Therefore a licence requirement that produces adverse effects on a specified group of service suppliers will not fall under the prohibition on non-discrimination if no plausible link can be established with the origin of the service suppliers that are adversely affected. Such an analysis is a fact-intensive one and will allow for the consideration of counter-arguments that could rebut the arguments by the complainant on the link between the origin and the effects. As Pauwelyn has argued with regard to national treatment, 'it will be for the adjudicator to weigh everything together and to decide whether the complainant has met its burden of proving that the regulation treats imports less favourably as opposed to domestic production'.[444] Such counter-arguments can be that the detrimental effect is not *caused* by the measure, but is due to

440 Appellate Body Report, *EC – Asbestos*, para. 100.

441 As will be explained, below Chapter 9, individual applications of regulations may also be scrutinized under the GATS.

442 See, as explained earlier (above n. 419 and accompanying text), Appellate Body Report, *Canada – Periodicals*, p. 30; and Panel Report, *Mexico – Soft Drinks*, para. 8.91.

443 See the examples mentioned in F. Ortino, 'From "Non-discrimination" to "Reasonableness": A Paradigm Shift in International Economic Law?', Jean Monnet Working Paper 01/05, April 2005, at 11–12, available at www.jeanmonnetprogram.org.

444 Pauwelyn, above n. 424, at 12.

the inherent disadvantage of being foreign.[445] An argument may also involve proof that the market share of a foreign producer is so small that the effect of the measure is felt more intensely.[446]

349. Nevertheless, no panel nor the Appellate Body has accepted an alleged non-protectionist aim of a measure that might rebut the claim that the measure is discriminatory. To be sure, the Appellate Body in *Chile – Alcoholic Beverages* admitted that 'the measure's purposes, objectively manifested in the design, architecture and structure of the measure, *are* intensely pertinent to the task of evaluating whether or not that measure is applied so as to afford protection to domestic production'.[447] However, the alleged non-protectionist aim needs to be examined in the practical context of the operation of the measure. The fact that the defending party each time failed to advance convincing evidence on how the regulatory distinctions are in practice linked to the non-protectionist aim, left the Appellate Body with no other choice than to find a violation of the prohibition of discrimination.[448] This is *not* to say that the defendant needs to show that the measure is *necessary* to achieve the non-protectionist aim.[449] Yet the defendant will need to make the link between the regulatory distinction and the objective pursued plausible. How plausible will depend on the broader weighing exercise.[450]

8.4.2.2.5 Summary on less favourable treatment **350.** It is useful to summarize the practical test to define whether a measure that applies to like services or service suppliers of different origins is violating the

[445] Footnote 10 to Art. XVII GATS.

[446] Appellate Body Report, *Dominican Republic – Import and Sale of Cigarettes*, para. 96.

[447] Appellate Body Report, *Chile – Alcoholic Beverages*, para. 71.

[448] In *Chile – Alcoholic Beverages*, the Appellate Body noted that explanations of the structure of the new Chilean tax system 'might have been helpful in understanding what *prima facie* appear to be anomalies in the progression of tax rates'. Ibid.

[449] See also the statements of the Appellate Body in *Chile – Alcoholic Beverages*: 'At the same time, we agree with Chile that it would be inappropriate, under Art. III:2, second sentence, of the GATT 1994, to examine whether the tax measure is *necessary* for achieving its stated objectives or purposes.' Ibid., para. 72.

[450] Pauwelyn notes that 'the nexus required within national treatment itself could vary depending on the "relative importance" of the non-protectionist objective put on the table by the defendant. In that event, the required nexus could be "necessity", "related to" or "rational relationship" or any other test, depending on the non-protectionist objective in question'. Pauwelyn, above n. 424, at 14.

provisions prohibiting discrimination. The question is whether the measure leads to 'less favourable treatment'. This requires, first of all, that the complainant shows that the measure has the actual or potential effect of treating one group of services or service suppliers less favourably than another group of like services or service suppliers. Yet, the unfavourable effect is not sufficient to establish a violation of non-discrimination. This distinct group must be identifiable on the basis of origin. Obviously, this can be shown by the use of direct evidence of the protectionist intentions of the defending party, but will more often need to be shown on the basis of indirect evidence linking the origin to the regulatory distinction. This may already narrow down the scope of the prohibitions on discrimination. Yet inventive litigants[451] may always manage to construct arguments that link the measure to origin. Indeed, to give an extreme example, the mere existence of a regulation may have the effect of treating foreign service suppliers less favourably than like domestic suppliers. The complainant could then argue that the distinction is based on the origin of a service or service supplier, since national suppliers (e.g. domestic-owned banks) would find it easier to comply than foreign suppliers (e.g. foreign-owned banks). The defendant should then advance factual counter-arguments such as the fact that this disadvantage is inherent in the foreign character of the suppliers and thus is not caused by a measure that singles out the origin of the supplier. One could also argue that the measure is pursuing an objective on the basis of regulatory distinctions that happen to coincide largely with the origin of suppliers (e.g. because no non-European banks use a particular accounting standard). In that case, the defendant should make a plausible argument that the structure of the measure is linked to the objective of the measure. It will then be for the panel or the Appellate Body to weigh the arguments against each other.

351. We now turn to the two main principles in the GATS that are based on discrimination: the principle of most-favoured-nation treatment and the principle of national treatment.

[451] It is interesting to see how the Court of Justice in its *Keck and Mithouard* decision referred to the 'increasing tendency of traders to invoke Art. 30 of the Treaty as a means of challenging any rules whose effect is to limit their commercial freedom even where such rules are not aimed at products from other Member States', as the reason for the re-examination of its previous case law tried and its attempt to limit the scope of the fundamental freedoms in EU law. See CJEU, Cases C-267 and C-268/91, *Keck and Mithouard* [1993] ECR I-6097, para. 14.

8.4.3 *Most-favoured-nation treatment*

8.4.3.1 The principle

352. The principle of most-favoured-nation treatment, laid down in Article II GATS, is contained in Part II of the GATS ('General Obligations and Disciplines') and therefore applies to its full extent, except when explicit exemptions are made by the WTO members in their lists of Article II exemptions ('negative list' approach).[452] In its Schedule of Article II Exemptions, the EU has no specific most-favoured-nation exemptions for banking services.[453] Some of its member states, however, may have adopted specific most-favoured-nation exemptions.[454]

353. Mattoo has suggested that a most-favoured-nation exception, coexisting with full liberal (market access and) national treatment commitments has little meaning, unless a member wants to treat foreign banks *better* than domestic banks and make a differentiation from the better treated foreign banks.[455] Indeed, once a national treatment commitment is made,

[452] Art. II:2 GATS; and see GATS Annex on Art. II Exemptions. In principle, these exemptions could not have a duration of more than ten years (Para. 6 GATS Annex on Article II Exemptions) and would thus have expired in December 2005. Yet, because their expiration is subject to negotiations and the Hong Kong Ministerial conference could not agree upon this expiration, these exemptions are still applicable. On the MFN principle in GATS and with regard to financial services see Y. Wang, 'Most-Favoured-Nation Treatment under the General Agreement on Trade in Services – And Its Application in Financial Services', (1996) 30 *Journal of World Trade* 91, at 91–124.

[453] European Communities and their Member States, Final List of Article II (MFN) Exemptions, GATS/EL/31, 15 April 1994, p. 7.

[454] In order to support certain countries in transition to a market economy, Italy has adopted measures granting favourable tax treatment in Italy to service suppliers trading with specific countries in central, eastern and south-eastern Europe. This favourable tax treatment is not extended to service suppliers from other countries. It should also be noted that Hungary has a requirement for reciprocal MFN treatment for financial institutions that seek access to the Hungarian market: specific commitments made under Mode 3 may be subject to the reciprocity requirement. Hungary Final List of Article II (MFN) Exemptions, Supplement 1, GATS/EL/40/Suppl. 1, 26 February 1998, p. 1. A similar exemption exists for the Slovak Republic. Slovak Republic Final List of Article II (MFN) Exemptions, Supplement 1, GATS/EL/77/Suppl. 1, 28 July 1995, p. 1. Furthermore, Austria has an exemption providing for more favourable treatment than provided in specific commitments for financial service suppliers of countries that offer competitive opportunities and effective market access to Austrian services suppliers equivalent to those offered by Austria. Austria Final List of Article II (MFN) Exemptions, GATS/EL/7, 15 April 1994, p. 4.

[455] See A. Mattoo, 'MFN and the GATS', in T. Cottier, P. Mavroidis and P. Blatter (eds.), *Regulatory Barriers and the Principle of Non-discrimination in World Trade Law* (Ann Arbor: University of Michigan Press, 2000) 51–99, at 56.

the treatment of the domestic bank becomes the benchmark: every foreign bank must be treated *at least* as well as the domestic bank. Differentiation among foreign banks can then only happen in the sense of *better* treatment. We shall examine in Part III whether this combination of the most-favoured-nation and the national treatment obligations plays an important role in the interaction between the European and international liberalization of banking services. Even if there exists an exception to Article II GATS for the preferential trade integration within the EU, the treatment of banks from WTO members that are not EU member states and that seek access to the EU market may in principle not be less favourable than the treatment of European banks, unless exceptions are available (below, paras. 689–709).

354. On the basis of Article II GATS, WTO members are required, with respect to any measure covered by the GATS, to accord immediately[456] and unconditionally[457] to services and service suppliers of any other WTO member treatment no less favourable than what it accords to like services and service suppliers of any other country.[458] Hence measures affecting trade in services should not treat services or service suppliers originating in one WTO member worse than those like services or service suppliers from other trading partners.

8.4.3.2 Recognition

8.4.3.2.1 Recognition is problematic in the light of the most-favoured-nation obligation in Article II GATS **355.** The principle of most-favoured-nation treatment also plays a role in a number of other GATS provisions that are relevant to the liberalization of banking services. An important modification of the most-favoured-nation obligation concerns the recognition of the equivalence of foreign regulations that are applicable to foreign services and service suppliers. The principle of 'recognition' implies that a WTO member accepts that when a good or service can lawfully be sold in the home country, it can also be sold in the host country, without having to comply with the regulations in this host

[456] This implies that a WTO member acquires the right to MFN treatment as soon as another WTO member grants a benefit to a country. This extends both to existing and future benefits. Wang, above n. 452, at 96.

[457] The WTO members thus cannot limit the benefit of MFN treatment to certain countries because of some specific circumstances in these countries.

[458] Note that the benefits do not need to be given to a WTO member in order for another WTO member to claim this same benefit on the basis of MFN treatment in the GATS. It may thus also concern benefits granted to third countries.

country.[459] However, recognition can cover the substantive standards that are applied to a banking service supplier (such as, for example, minimum capital requirements), but can also cover the *supervision* of the compliance with substantive standards.[460] For instance, if a supervisory authority in a member state of the EU accepts the equivalence of the regulation or supervision by third-country authorities, no additional regulation or supervision will be applied by the European authorities, which implies fewer information requirements and related burdens for the foreign service or service supplier. Hence banking service suppliers from certain third countries will receive better treatment than some other banks. This may lead to trade diversion in favour of the banks from the countries for which the 'equivalence' of regulation or supervision is recognized. Hence recognition appears problematic in the light of the most-favoured-nation obligation in Article II GATS.

356. There are, however, specific provisions in Article VII GATS and Paragraph 3 of the Annex on Financial Services that deal with recognition arrangements.[461] Mathis has argued that these provisions in fact

[459] See K. Nicolaïdis, 'Non-discriminatory Mutual Recognition: An Oxymoron in the New WTO Lexicon?', in Cottier, Mavroidis and Blatter, above n. 455, 267–301, at 268.

[460] While it is not entirely clear whether Art. VII:1 also covers recognition of *supervision procedures* (it only refers to 'the education or experience obtained, requirements met, or licenses or certifications granted in a particular country'), Paragraph 3(a) of the Annex of Financial Services refers to the recognition of 'prudential measures'. This broad concept also covers prudential supervision procedures. Mathis has also suggested that Art. VII covers recognition of both conformity assessment and equivalency aspects (of substantive standards). J. Mathis, 'Mutual Recognition Agreements: Transatlantic Parties and the Limits to Non-tariff Barrier Regionalism in the WTO', (1998) 32 *Journal of World Trade* 5, at 22.

[461] The GATT itself does not contain a provision specifically dealing with recognition arrangements and the role of MFN in Art. I GATT. (To be sure, Arts. 2.7 and 6.3 TBT Agreement encourage recognition and Art. 4 SPS Agreement requires WTO member to accept the equivalence of other Members' SPS measures, subject to conditions.) In the context of trade in goods, Mavroidis argues that 'any interpretation of the WTO agreements that the MFN principle precludes [Mutual Recognition Agreements] must be rejected, because it runs counter to the principle of "effective interpretation" of the treaties as laid down in the Vienna Convention on the Law of Treaties'. P. Mavroidis, 'Transatlantic Regulatory Cooperation: Exclusive Club or "Open Regionalism"?', in G. Bermann, M. Herdegan and P. Lindseth (eds.), *Transatlantic Regulatory Cooperation: Legal Problems and Political Prospects* (Oxford University Press, 2001) 263, 266; and see W. Davey and J. Pauwelyn, 'MFN Unconditionality: A Legal Analysis of the Concept in View of Its Evolution in the GATT/WTO Jurisprudence with Particular Reference to the Issue of "Like Product"', in Cottier, Mavroidis and Blatter, above n. 455, 13–50, at 23–24.

constitute a specific application of the most-favoured-nation principle: a 'conditional MFN'.[462] One could thus argue that these provisions do not constitute exceptions to the most-favoured-nation obligation in Article II GATS. Article VII GATS and paragraph 3(b) of the Annex do not use the phrase 'nothing in this Agreement shall prevent', common to exception provisions.[463] Such an interpretation may also solve the question with regard to the relationship between Article V (the exception for preferential trade agreements on services) and Article VII GATS. If Article VII GATS is a specific application of the most-favoured-nation obligation, Article V can still be available for recognition arrangements that do not comply with the conditions imposed in Article VII GATS.

357. In any event, these provisions impose a number of conditions on mutual or unilateral recognition in an effort to reduce the trade-diversion effects of recognition. Article VII GATS provides specific conditions for unilateral or mutual recognition of 'the education or experience obtained, requirements met, or licences or certifications granted in a particular country'.[464] This provision tries to find a balance between, on the one hand, allowing further trade integration through recognition and, on the other hand, ensuring that discrimination against services and service suppliers from other countries is minimized.[465] Specifically with regard to financial services, paragraph 3(a) of the Annex on Financial Services states that a 'Member may recognize prudential measures of any other country in determining how the Member's measures relating to financial services shall be applied'. The recognition can take the form of an arrangement between WTO members (e.g. the United States and the EU), but can also be autonomous (i.e. unilateral). Three conditions are imposed to ensure that recognition does not overly impede multilateral trade liberalization.

8.4.3.2.2 Notification of recognition arrangements **358.** First of all, WTO members must notify the Council for Trade in Services of existing

[462] Mathis, above n. 460, at 25.

[463] See Art. V:1 GATS, the introductory paragraph of Art. XIV GATS and Paragraph 2(a) of the Annex on Financial Services.

[464] Art. VII:1 GATS.

[465] Mattoo, above n. 455, at Section. 3.3; Mathis, above n. 460, at 23; and A. Zampetti, 'Market Access through Mutual Recognition: The Promise and Limits of GATS Article VII', in P. Sauvé and R. Stern (eds.), *GATS 2000. New Directions in Services Trade Liberalization* (Washington, DC: Brookings Institution Press, 2000) 283–306, at 305.

recognition measures[466] or the adoption of new measures.[467] Remarkably, the Annex on Financial Services excludes the obligation in Article VII:4(b) GATS to notify as far in advance as possible the fact that a member is *contemplating* recognition.[468] It may be noted that New Zealand has asked that same Council whether Article VII:4(b) also extends to autonomous recognition. Since it refers to 'an agreement or arrangement of the type referred to in paragraph 1 [of Article VII]', this must be the case.

359. To date, only two mutual recognition agreements were notified that apply between EU member states and third countries and that relate to financial services. First, there is an agreement between Switzerland and the EU that involves reciprocal recognition of each other's evidence relating to the solvency of insurance companies having their head office in the territory of the EU or Switzerland.[469] Second, there have also been notified two bilateral recognition agreements between Germany and the United States, and Germany and Japan. These recognition agreements exempt branches established in Germany of credit institutions which have their registered office in the United States and in Japan respectively from the provisions of the German Banking Act concerning limits on credit volume, price risk and certain investments, as well as availability of additional capital.[470] In the Council for Trade in Services, India has reiterated several times its concerns on the lack of notification of recognition arrangements under Article VII. In this respect, the European Union recognized the importance of transparency, but has also noted that one should not conclude that the absence of notifications would mean that members were not complying with their obligations under Article VII.[471]

[466] Para. 3 (c) GATS Annex on Financial Services in conjunction with Art. VII:4(a) GATS.

[467] Para. 3 (c) GATS Annex on Financial Services in conjunction with Art. VII:4(c) GATS.

[468] Nonetheless, Colombia has proposed to implement Art. VII:4(b) also for financial services. Council for Trade in Services, Special Session, Communication of Colombia, S/CSS/W/96, 9 July 2001, para. 11.

[469] Council for Trade in Services, Notification Pursuant to Art. VII:4 of the General Agreement on Trade in Services, S/C/N/43, 24 March 1997.

[470] Council for Trade in Services, Notification Pursuant to Art. VII:4 of the General Agreement on Trade in Services, S/C/N/50, 28 January 1997.

[471] Council for Trade in Services, Report of the Meeting Held on 3 and 7 July 2003, S/C/M/67, 17 September 2003, para. 19 (India) and 38 (EC); and see R. Adlung, 'Services Negotiations in the Doha Round: Lost in Flexibility', (2006) 9 *Journal of International Economic Law* 865, at n. 18.

8.4.3.2.3 'Open' recognition **360.** Second, WTO members must afford adequate opportunity for other interested members to negotiate their accession to a multilateral recognition agreement or to negotiate comparable agreements. In the case of unilateral recognition, other WTO members must have an adequate opportunity to demonstrate that they also deserve to benefit from the recognition.

361. Even if an interested member were to know of the existence of a recognition arrangement (thanks to the notification of such arrangements), that member might find it difficult to become successfully involved in the process. Allowing or rejecting recognition often depends on a wide range of factors beyond mere equivalence of the substantive rules of the states in question. Much depends on mutual trust and familiarity among the institutions that perform the assessment of conformity with the substantive rules.[472] The Annex on Financial Services seems to point to this fact by noting that the opportunity to become part of a recognition agreement will need to be considered 'under circumstances in which there would be equivalent regulation, oversight, implementation of [the national] regulation, and, if appropriate, procedures concerning the sharing of information between the parties to the agreement or arrangement'.[473] What is more, Nielson has noted that, while the GATS requires members to provide an *opportunity* to demonstrate that they also meet required standards, it does not include a *requirement* eventually to *extend recognition* after negotiations.[474] Marchetti and Mavroidis argue that the level of persuasion necessary for a WTO member to show that it must also benefit from recognition provides incumbents 'with an effective legal shield against requests for extension of their recognition agreement'. They conclude, 'The original choice of partners is thus cemented.'[475] However, at a minimum, the articles on recognition would provide an obligation to be transparent in the recognition decisions, which would enable other interested parties to take the necessary steps also to be included.[476]

[472] Nicolaïdis, above n. 459, at 294–297; and Zampetti, above n. 465, at 301.

[473] Paragraph 3(b) Annex on Financial Services.

[474] J. Nielson, 'Trade Agreements and Recognition', in OECD, *Quality and Recognition in Higher Education* (Paris: OECD Publishing, 2004), 159.

[475] J. Marchetti and P. Mavroidis, 'I Now Recognize You (and Only You) as Equal. An Anatomy of (Mutual) Recognition Agreements in the GATS', in I. Lianos and O. Odudu (eds.), *Regulating Trade in Services in the EU and the WTO: Trust, Distrust and Economic Integration* (Cambridge University Press, 2012) 415–43.

[476] Nicolaïdis, above n. 459, at 296.

362. One might wonder how one should assess recognition arrangements existing between states that are parties to a preferential trade agreement. We shall see (below, para. 627) that Article V GATS provides an exception for preferential trade agreements for services. Does Article V GATS permit recognition when this recognition is not open to service suppliers from WTO members that are not a party to the preferential arrangement? In other words, can such a closed recognition arrangement that would normally not comply with the obligation in Article VII or paragraph 3(b) of the Annex to be 'open' to other WTO members still be justified by virtue of Article V? This is arguably the case. However, one needs to consider whether such closed recognition would be *necessary* for the formation of the preferential arrangement. This is clear from case law with regard to Article XXIV GATT, which is the provision that provides an exception for preferential trade agreements in the GATT. The Appellate Body in *Turkey – Textiles* stated that in order to benefit from the defence under Article XXIV, a defendant 'must demonstrate that the formation of that customs union would be prevented if it were not allowed to introduce the measure at issue [i.e. violating an obligation in the GATT]'.[477]

363. One could argue that a closed recognition arrangement is necessary for preferential trade arrangements in services. Regulations restrict trade in services. Hence, once a discriminatory regulation is removed, 'deeper' integration can only be achieved by reducing regulatory diversity. Recognition of each other's regulation and supervisory assessments is an essential tool for reducing regulatory diversity. It is very difficult to open up recognition achieved in such a trade integration project. 'Open' recognition would constitute a (less trade restrictive) alternative, but is an alternative that is not reasonably available. It would be too complicated to open this recognition to other WTO members. The recognition arrangements can be part of a broader 'package deal' struck within the preferential trade agreement and are based on lengthy negotiations, building long-term trust among the parties to such an agreement. Hence it can clearly be argued that 'closed' recognition is necessary for the preferential trade agreement.[478]

[477] Appellate Body Report, *Turkey – Restrictions on Imports of Textile and Clothing Products* (*Turkey – Textiles*), WT/DS34/AB/R, adopted 19 November 1999, para. 58.

[478] J. Trachtman, 'Embedding Mutual Recognition at the WTO', 11 August 2006, available at http://papers.ssrn.com/sol3/papers.cfm?abstract_id=923903, 16. See also, suggesting that members to a recognition agreement that want to exclude the benefit of recognition

8.4.3.2.4 Recognition cannot constitute a means of discrimination or a disguised restriction of trade **364.** Finally, recognition cannot constitute a means of discrimination between countries in the application of the standards or criteria for authorization, licensing or certification of suppliers by the member who provides for recognition, or constitute a disguised restriction of trade.[479] This is a difficult condition, since recognition arrangements necessarily treat the beneficiaries of the recognition differently from others. As explained, recognition is a process involving sensitive consideration of another country's regulation and supervision. Therefore authors construct this as a narrow obligation, not imposing the same constraint as most favoured nation in Article II.[480] As long as it is shown that the recognition is based on criteria that are not biased towards one country or another and is part of an assessment procedure following due process, the recognition may be considered to be non-discriminatory.

365. Remarkably, the Annex on Financial Services does not mention this condition of non-discrimination and, according to Key, thereby seems to provide a fully fledged exception to the principle of most-

might choose for regional trade agreements legalized under Art. XXIV GATT and Art. V GATS, Mavroidis, above n. 461, at 267. Marchetti and Mavroidis defend a different opinion. In their view, the conclusion of a preferential trade agreement does not provide for a 'shield against all claims for extension of recognition'. They argue that recognition arrangements are 'not a *legal requirement* for the conclusion of [a preferential trade agreement]' (emphasis in original), and thus such recognition arrangements are not justified on the basis of Art. V GATS. However, the outcome of their analysis is the same as the outcome of the analysis in this book. Because of the burden of persuasion required for non-parties to a recognition arrangement to show that they should also benefit from recognition, it will be very difficult to bring such a successful claim. Recognition in the framework of the preferential arrangement will thus most often remain closed. Marchetti and Mavroidis, above n. 475, at 15–17.

479 Art. VII:3 GATS.

480 Nielson interprets this obligation as essentially meaning that 'WTO members can apply whatever standards they want in according recognition, but they must apply the same standards to all WTO members'. Nielson, above n. 474, at 159. Nicolaïdis and Trachtman argue that the obligation concerns 'procedural MFN', in the sense of requiring Members not to discriminate among WTO members when applying the criteria for including them in the recognition process. In their view, this obligation cannot mean that panels 'would be able to decide that third parties ought to be allowed to participate simply by assessing the equivalence of its standards to any of the parties to the [Recognition Agreement]'. (See Nicolaïdis and Trachtman, above n. 407, at 315.) In contrast, in the discussions in the Working Party on Domestic Regulation, Egypt supported a stronger interpretation of Art. VII:3, but did not further clarify what this would mean. (See Working Party on Domestic Regulation, Report on the Meeting Held on 24 February 2003, S/WPDR/M/20, 31 March 2003, para. 43.)

favoured-nation treatment.[481] This would provide more flexibility for recognition in the field of financial services. However, it is not clear whether the fact that the non-discrimination obligation in Article VII:3 is not repeated in Paragraph 3(a) of the Annex on Financial Services also means that the obligation is not applicable in case of financial services. Indeed, one can argue that only the obligation to notify in advance the fact that recognition is contemplated is explicitly excluded (see paragraph 3(c)). Therefore, since the Annex does not explicitly exclude the non-discrimination obligation, it may still be applicable. In any case, some authors have suggested that the difficult determination of discrimination can be informed by Article VII:5 GATS, which encourages basing recognition on multilaterally agreed criteria.[482] Even if this provision only 'encourages' the use of international standards,[483] the combination with the obligations of openness and non-discrimination may give a strong incentive to base recognition on international standards.

366. Hence, if the fact that a banking service or bank originates in a country that has implemented the Basel supervisory principles and capital standards is a criterion on which recognition is based, this recognition arrangement would arguably comply with the condition in Article VII:3. However, this does not mean that a bank originating in a WTO member that has implemented these international principles and standards must necessarily benefit from the recognition arrangement. As explained, this depends also on further trust and familiarity among the regulatory and supervisory authorities of the WTO members in question.

8.4.4 National treatment

8.4.4.1 The principle

367. According to Article XVII:1 GATS, a member 'shall accord to services and service suppliers of any other Member, in respect of all measures affecting the supply of services, treatment no less favourable than that it accords to its own like services and service suppliers'. Contrary to what is the case for most-favoured-nation treatment, the principle of national treatment in the GATS applies only to the extent

[481] Key, above n. 148, at 966.

[482] M. Matsushita, T. Schoenbaum and P. Mavroidis, *The World Trade Organization: Law, Practice, and Policy* (Oxford University Press, 2006) 630–1.

[483] Cf. Art. 2.4 Agreement on Technical Barriers to Trade and Art. 3 Agreement on Sanitary and Phytosanitary Measures, which include a more pressing obligation.

that specific commitments have been taken in the schedules of specific commitments of the members.[484] What is more, even if a services sector is inscribed in the schedule of a WTO member, the member may indicate limitations on these commitments. The word 'none' in the column of limitations of the scheduled sector indicates that a member makes commitments without any limitations. The word 'unbound' means that the member reserves to itself the right to adopt further restrictions. Sometimes the specific restrictions that the member wants to maintain are indicated as 'limitations' to the commitments.

368. The principle of national treatment prohibits discrimination between domestic services or service suppliers and like services or service suppliers of other WTO members. One must define again, *first*, whether the services or service suppliers at stake are 'like' and, *second*, whether there is 'less favourable treatment'. The scope of this provision determines the extent of scrutiny imposed by the principle of national treatment. Both situations of de jure and de facto discrimination are caught by Article XVII GATS, as is clear from the reference in Article XVII:2 GATS. Nevertheless, in situations where a regulatory distinction is made on the basis of origin, protectionism is not always the motivation that lies behind all of them, and a trade regime should only discipline those measures that are protectionist.[485] This delimitation of the provisions prohibiting discrimination and the provisions disciplining non-discriminatory measures is subject to much debate and was discussed for most-favoured-nation treatment and national treatment together (above, paras. 310–351).

8.4.4.2 National treatment in the Understanding on Commitments in Financial Services

369. The Understanding on Commitments in Financial Services also specifies some aspects of national treatment in the financial sector. Section C.1 of the Understanding indicates that a WTO member that has made commitments on the basis of the Understanding must grant to financial service suppliers that are established in the territory of that member 'access to payment and clearing systems operated by public entities and to official funding and refinancing facilities available in the normal course of ordinary business'. This specification only covers one

[484] Commitments can be made sector-specific or horizontal. Jarreau, above n. 373, at 40–8.
[485] De Búrca, above n. 377, at 182.

mode of supply: commercial presence. There is thus no obligation to extend the access on a national treatment basis for financial service suppliers that provide services by means of the other modes of supply, unless of course further commitments were to have been made in this sense.

370. Von Bogdandy and Windsor have argued that when a WTO member makes commitments by reference to the Understanding, 'it need not afford national treatment to a foreign supplier of financial services with respect to extraordinary or emergency funding', since these measures are not 'available in the normal course of ordinary business'.[486] Arguably, this interpretation supposes that when a WTO member has made commitments by reference to the Understanding it means that for financial services the scope of the national treatment obligation is entirely determined by section C.1, and the national treatment obligation in Part III of the GATS framework agreement no longer applies. However, as argued above (paras. 152–157), this interpretation is not correct. Even though the Understanding provides specifications of the national treatment obligation in the financial services sector, that does not mean that one should no longer consider the general application of Article XVII of the GATS. However, section C.1 of the Understanding does exclude lender of last resort facilities from the benefit of national treatment on the basis of the Understanding. Hence the national treatment obligation will apply only for lender of last resort facilities where the WTO member had made this explicit in its schedules of commitments. It is remarkable, however, that the Understanding provides here an explicit exception on which WTO members that made commitments by reference to the Understanding can rely, whereas other WTO members will have to specify this limitation (or make no national treatment commitment in this respect at all).

371. Finally, section C.2 of the Understanding also specifies that where a WTO member requires financial service suppliers to be a member of, participate in or have access to 'any self-regulatory body, securities or futures exchange or market, clearing agency, or any other organization or association' or when a WTO member attaches privileges or advantages to such participation, the WTO member must ensure that financial service providers of another WTO member resident in the territory of the member are granted national treatment. Von Bogdandy and

[486] Von Bogdandy and Windsor, above n. 156, at 662–3.

Windsor have argued that attention should be paid to the fact that section C.2 refers to service providers 'resident' in the territory of the WTO member and not to providers 'established' there. In their view, the different wording may mean that this obligation also covers a situation where a financial service supplier is present in the territory of the WTO member and does not yet have a commercial presence in this territory, but is seeking to become established.[487]

8.4.5 Conclusion on GATS provisions prohibiting discrimination

372. In this section we have sought to determine the extent to which the GATS provisions that prohibit discrimination restrict the right of WTO members to regulate their market for banking services. We considered that the prohibition to discriminate has two manifestations, the obligation of most-favoured-nation treatment and the national treatment obligation.

373. The impact on the regulatory autonomy of WTO members of a prohibition on discrimination depends to a large extent on the interpretation of the concepts of 'like' services or suppliers and 'less favourable treatment'. With regard to the concept of 'likeness', the current WTO case law seems to take a market-based approach. Since the obligations are about equality of competitive opportunities, banking services with a different origin will be considered 'like' if consumers consider them to be in competition. We saw that the case law with regard to the provisions that prohibit discrimination does not consider the regulatory aim of a distinction as a relevant criterion to determine whether two services are 'like', except when the non-protectionist reason for the distinction is taken into account by consumers in their perception of the characteristics of the services. This is often difficult because the regulatory distinction will be made precisely because consumers fail to see the relevant difference between the banking services (market failure).

374. The GATS provisions prohibiting discriminatory measures focus on the treatment not only of services, but also of service suppliers. In Part I, we discussed how much the characteristics of banking services are intertwined with the characteristics and qualities of the banks providing these services. It is in this light that the statement by the panel in *Canada – Autos* (to the

[487] Ibid., at 664.

extent the services they supply are like, the suppliers should be considered to be like) must be understood. As far as consumers consider the characteristics of the suppliers to be relevant in their decision on whether different services are 'like', these characteristics determine whether the suppliers are like.

375. However, it is not unthinkable that, besides consumer perceptions, objective characteristics of banking services may also be taken into account as criteria for considering them as 'like' or not. The fact that a bank originates in a country that implements the Basel principles and standards may be such an objective criterion. In any event, the fact that the primary criterion for determining 'likeness' is consumer perceptions means that banking services with a different origin will often be considered to be 'like', even if a regulatory distinction was not intended to be protectionist at all. Such regulatory distinctions could thus violate the prohibitions on discrimination.

376. At first sight, it appears that these provisions thus impose an important restriction on the regulatory autonomy of the WTO members. They would be called on to justify, on the basis of the general exceptions in the GATS or the prudential exception, all regulatory distinctions drawn between banking services that are not perceived by consumers as relevant in making a decision on whether the services are substitutable. However, this danger is to a certain extent mitigated because, in order to violate one of the provisions that prohibit discrimination, one should determine not only whether the banking services/banks are 'like' but also whether the treatment granted by the measure at issue leads to 'less favourable treatment'. Yet, because such 'less favourable treatment' has been interpreted as meaning a situation where the conditions of competition are *actually or potentially* modified, the danger to regulatory autonomy may appear far from mitigated. Almost any measure that treats 'like' banking services or suppliers with a different origin differently will modify their conditions of competition.

377. Nonetheless, factual evidence of protectionist intent may be considered in order to decide whether the measure is providing 'less favourable treatment'. It is much more problematic to consider the *non-protectionist* intent of a measure when applying the provisions that prohibit discrimination. This might easily result in a situation where a panel or the Appellate Body have to make a subjective assessment of non-protectionist aims invoked by a defendant to justify the adverse impact of the measure at issue on banking services of a certain origin. This is difficult to reconcile with the statements by the Appellate Body in *Chile – Alcoholic Beverages* and *Japan – Taxes on Alcoholic Beverages II* that the measure's intent must be 'objectively manifested'. Moreover, this would raise questions on the relationship to the general exceptions and the role of other provisions in the GATS. Nonetheless, since the prohibitions of discrimination seek to prohibit protectionist measures, it is clearly necessary that a complainant proves convincingly that the measure's adverse impact is linked to the origin of the affected services or suppliers. It is, then, not sufficient to find only one or a few adversely affected banks of a certain origin. One should compare the group of banking services or banks of a certain origin with the group of other 'like' services or banks of another origin (e.g. domestic) and prove that the impact of the measure is asymmetrical. The defendant will then probably advance counter-arguments based on the regulatory structure of the scheme and seek to show that the distinction is not based on origin. It will be for the panel to consider these factual arguments. However, this may not involve a subjective evaluation of the possible justifications for the distinction on the basis of the objectives that are pursued.

378. The analysis shows that the application of the GATS provisions that prohibit discrimination will greatly depend on the circumstances of the case. Even if the existing case law does not recognize a 'rule of reason' analysis such as exists in EU law, the impact of these provisions on the regulatory autonomy of the WTO members may not be as dangerous as would appear at first sight. It is indeed important for the complainant to show convincingly the link between the adverse impact of the measure and the origin. What is more, some particularities of the obligations of most-favoured-nation treatment and national treatment still limit their impact. With regard to most-favoured-nation treatment, WTO members were allowed to inscribe exceptions to the obligation and the obligation has been specified for recognition arrangements. With regard to national treatment, this obligation only applies as far as the WTO member has made a commitment regarding the banking sector and the mode of supply at issue. Moreover, limitations to the commitments can be inscribed.

379. The Understanding on Commitments in Financial Services specifies the national treatment obligation. Most importantly, it provides an explicit exclusion of the benefit of lender of last resort facilities from the application of the national treatment obligation.

8.5 Domestic regulation

8.5.1 Introduction

380. When the restrictions listed in Article XVI GATS as well as discriminatory measures affecting trade in banking services are removed, this does not necessarily mean that foreign banks no longer face any legal hurdles to providing services in other WTO member states. The mere fact of regulatory diversity constitutes a cost for a bank from one country to operate in other countries. Because of the prevalence of domestic regulation in the banking sector, addressing regulatory diversity is an important challenge for international liberalization of trade in banking services. The WTO does not engage in harmonization of banking regulation, and neither does it constitute a forum for the negotiation of recognition arrangements. However, the GATS contains a provision that is meant specifically to address the impact of domestic regulation on international trade in services. It concerns Article VI GATS on domestic regulation. Article VI contains a number of obligations that affect measures that impose certain requirements on service providers and the services they provide. To a certain extent this article is a 'sleeping beauty' (or rather 'sleeping dragon'), because its real impact may only become clear as soon as the disciplines – developed on the basis of Article VI:4 – are adopted.

381. The underlying rationale of Article VI is that domestic regulation may impede market access, even if it is not of a type listed in Article XVI:2 and even if it is not discriminatory in the sense of Article XVII GATS.[488] Hence Article VI aims to minimize the costs of accessing a market and operating in this market.

382. The precise scope of application of Article VI remains unclear. Nevertheless, the panel in the *US – Gambling* case gave some guidance on its relationship to the GATS provisions on market access and national treatment. The scope of application of the separate sections of Article VI depends on several factors: (i) whether specific commitments are made for a certain service sector or not; (ii) whether specific types of domestic

[488] Mattoo and Sauvé have described Art. VI 'as the third complementary dimension of a three-pronged approach to effective access to services markets'. The two other prongs would be Art. XVI and Art. XVII. A. Mattoo and P. Sauvé, 'Domestic Regulation and Trade in Services: Key Issues', in A. Mattoo and P. Sauvé (eds.), *Domestic Regulation and Service Trade Liberalization* (Washington, DC: World Bank, 2003) 1–6, at 3.

regulation are specified or not; and (iii) whether the fact that certain measures fall within the scope of other GATS provisions means that they are excluded from the scope of a section of Article VI. For each section of Article VI the scope will be indicated. In general, the sections can be divided into two parts: some sections impose obligations with regard to the *administration* of regulations and some other sections rather impose obligations with regard to the *content* of regulations.

8.5.2 Procedural obligations relating to the administration of domestic regulation

383. There are first of all a number of disciplines in Article VI that have a procedural nature. Note that Article III GATS also includes a general procedural obligation of transparency.[489] However, whereas Article III is focused on making all regulation publicly available, the procedural obligations in Article VI are, rather, focused on the *application* of domestic regulation.

384. These procedural obligations are of particular importance to trade in banking services, since foreign banks are generally obliged to obtain a licence before they can establish themselves in the host country. In the

[489] It requires WTO members to publish promptly (at least by the time of their entry into force) all relevant measures of general application which pertain to or affect the operation of the Agreement. Also, international agreements pertaining to or affecting trade in services to which a member is signatory must be published (Art. III:1 GATS). If publication is not practically possible, the information on the measures of general application or international standards must be made otherwise publicly available (Art. III:2). Furthermore, members are required to inform the Council for Trade in Services promptly and at least annually of new (or modifications to) laws, regulations or administrative guidelines that significantly affect trade in services covered by the specific commitments of that member (Art. III:3). Hence, it seems that this obligation only covers services sectors for which a member has made specific commitments. What is more, there is still some further margin of appreciation for WTO members, since they should only inform the Council for Trade in Services on measures that *significantly* affect trade in services. WTO members may request a member to provide specific information of their measures of general application or international agreements. If such requests are made, it is required by Art. III:4 that the member responds promptly. Note that these requests need to be made by (the government of) a WTO member. Requests made by the traders themselves (e.g. a service supplier) do not fall under the obligation of a prompt response. Members are also required to establish one or more enquiry points to provide specific information to other members. Finally, a possibility of so-called 'cross-notification' is included. Any WTO member may notify the Council for Trade in Services on any measure by another WTO member, if the former considers that it affects the operation of the GATS (Art. III:5).

process of applying the conditions for a licence, it is important that the supervisory authorities comply with a number of conditions set out in Article VI:1, 2 and 3. However, they will be discussed in Chapter 9, where the limits imposed by the GATS on supervisory competence are addressed (below, paras. 511–554).

8.5.3 Substantive and procedural obligations relating to the content of domestic regulation

385. With regard to the *regulatory* autonomy of WTO members in the field of banking services, the most important sections of Article VI GATS are arguably Articles VI:4 and VI:5 GATS. These provisions go beyond mere procedural requirements and also provide a test on the *substance* of domestic regulation. Article VI:4 provides a mandate to develop 'disciplines for domestic regulation'. Until such disciplines are developed and have entered into force, Article VI:5 will provide for some limited scrutiny. Before addressing the tests contained in Articles VI:4 and VI:5, the scope of application of these important sections of Article VI need further clarification.

8.5.3.1 The scope of the disciplines based on Article VI:4 and the scope of Article VI:5

8.5.3.1.1 Qualification requirements and procedures, technical standards and licensing requirements **386.** First of all, Articles VI:4 and VI:5 do not apply to *any* type of domestic regulation. They cover only *specified* measures that relate to qualification requirements and procedures, technical standards and licensing requirements.[490] The GATS does not define these types of measure. However, the WTO Secretariat has provided

[490] These measures may also be covered by Art. XVIII, but the latter article has a wider scope than Art. VI, since it is not limited to qualification requirements and procedures, technical standards and licensing requirements. It has been argued that this article is a much more realistic way to ensure further market access for financial services rather than developing disciplines under Art. VI:4 GATS. S. Key, *The Doha Round and Financial Services Negotiations* (Washington, DC: AEI Press, 2003) 47–9, 50–1. One may wonder what measures may fall outside the scope of Art. VI:4. Delimatsis suggests the following measures: 'the question of the independence of the regulatory authority, universal service provisions, and access to networks as well as to essential facilities'. P. Delimatsis, *International Trade in Services and Domestic Regulation* (Oxford University Press, 2007) 190. See also J. Bigos, 'Contemplating GATS Art. XVIII on Additional Commitments', (2008) 42 *Journal of World Trade* 723.

useful descriptions of the different categories of measures in a note.[491] The note indicates that it is not meant to be an authoritative interpretation of the provisions of the GATS.[492] Nevertheless, the draft text for Horizontal Disciplines on the basis of Article VI:4 that was developed by the chair of the Working Party on Domestic Regulation (WPDR), copies these definitions to a large extent.[493]

387. *Licensing requirements* are described as 'substantive requirements, other than qualification requirements, with which a natural or juridical person is required to comply in order to obtain, amend or renew authorization to supply a service'. *Licensing procedures* are 'administrative or procedural rules that a natural or a juridical person, seeking authorization to supply a service, including the amendment or renewal of a licence, must adhere to in order to demonstrate compliance with licensing requirements'. *Qualification requirements* are 'substantive requirements relating to the competence of a natural person in relation to the supply of a service, and which are required to be demonstrated for the purpose of obtaining authorization to supply a service'. *Qualification procedures* are 'administrative or procedural rules that a natural person must adhere to in order to demonstrate compliance with qualification requirements, for the purpose of obtaining authorization to supply a service'. Finally, *technical standards* are 'measures that lay down the characteristics of a service or the manner in which it is supplied'. They also include 'the procedures relating to the enforcement of such standards'.[494]

388. Although the disciplines in Articles VI:4 and VI:5 apply only to these types of domestic regulation, they seem to catch a wide range of domestic regulations in the services sector. Moreover, Articles VI:4 and

[491] Working Party on Professional Services, The Relevance of the Disciplines of the Agreements on Technical Barriers to Trade (TBT) and on Import Licensing Procedures to Article VI:4 of the General Agreement on Trade in Services, S/WPPS/W/9, 11 September 1996, para. 4.

[492] Ibid., para. 1.

[493] The draft Horizontal Disciplines provide an update of the definitions since these disciplines do not apply only to professional services.

[494] See Section II (Definitions) of the Working Party on Domestic Regulation, Disciplines on Domestic Regulation Pursuant to GATS Art. VI:4, Second Revision, Informal Note by the Chairman, 20 March 2009, available at www.tradeobservatory.org/library.cfm?refID=106851. The latest state of play of the negotiations on the text can be found in Working Party on Domestic Regulation, Disciplines on Domestic Regulation Pursuant to Article VI:4 of the GATS, Chairman's Progress Report, S/WPDR/W/45, 14 April 2011.

VI:5 also cover measures *relating to* qualifications, licensing and technical standards. Hence the scope of Articles VI:4 and VI:5 is potentially very broad.[495] Still, the Horizontal Disciplines will arguably not cover visa requirements for natural persons who are a service supplier. The same can probably be said about building permits for service suppliers that need to set up infrastructure (e.g. large supermarkets). Yet measures that do not fall within the scope of Articles VI:4 and VI:5 may still be caught by the additional commitments made under Article XVIII GATS.[496]

389. Requirements for obtaining an authorization to start providing banking services in a market (e.g. initial capital requirements, declaration of a programme of operations, 'fit and proper' tests for management, requirements for important shareholders etc.) are 'licensing requirements' in the sense of Articles VI:4 and VI:5. Further, the procedures legal persons have to follow to obtain such authorization are 'licensing procedures'.

390. One may wonder whether the requirements imposed by members with regard to the characteristics of the banking services that are provided (e.g. obligatory contract terms, limits on interest rates etc.) can qualify as 'technical standards'. Banking services are contracts. Hence the characteristics of banking services are to a large extent determined by the clauses and conditions that are laid down in the contract. The discussions in the Working Party on Domestic Regulation on the definition of 'technical standards' in the draft Horizontal Disciplines have mainly focused on the question whether mandatory technical standards shall be covered by the definition of 'licensing requirements' or that of 'technical standards'.[497] Defining 'technical standards' is thus a threshold question for the application of the Horizontal Disciplines in general and for the application of Article VI:5 in particular. While examples of 'technical standards' are rarely given in the documents on the discussions of the definitions, the discussions show that it is clearly not meant that the Horizontal Disciplines cover *any possible substantive requirements*.[498] Therefore mandatory rules of contract law for banking services

495 Delimatsis, above n. 490, at 190. 496 Bigos, above n. 490.

497 Working Party on Domestic Regulation, Disciplines on Domestic Regulation Pursuant to GATS Article VI:4, Annotated Text, Informal Note by the Chairperson, RD/SERV/10, 14 March 2010, at para. 49 and paras. 61–67.

498 For instance, it was suggested that the definition of 'licensing requirements' be amended 'such that it also covered technical standards that need to be complied with in order to "maintain" a license'. Nonetheless, the chair of the WPDR warned:

are arguably not meant to be covered by the definition of 'technical standards'. Deciding otherwise would unduly expand the scope of the disciplines and Article VI:5.

391. Further, it is not entirely certain whether the requirements imposed on banks during their operations once authorized (reporting requirements, minimum capital requirements, conditions imposed on changes in shareholdings, exposure limits, limits on remuneration of management, etc.), would be covered by the disciplines. Since these are requirements that need to be fulfilled by banks in order to *maintain* their licence, the absence of a reference to 'maintaining' in the definition of 'licensing requirement' means that they are not covered by this definition. Could they be considered to be 'technical standards'? At first sight, these requirements do not seem to lay down the 'characteristics of a service or the manner in which it is supplied'. However, as indicated (above, paras. 33, 321), the characteristics of a banking service are very much intertwined with the characteristics of the bank that provides these services. The quality and characteristics of services are to a large extent determined by the characteristics (and daily conduct) of the banks that provide the services. Therefore the requirements imposed on the banks once authorized can be considered 'technical standards', and are thus within the scope of Articles VI:4 and VI:5 GATS and the future disciplines.

8.5.3.1.2 Sectors where specific commitments are made **392.** Second, the provisions of Article VI:5 apply only in sectors where specific commitments are made. It is less clear whether the existence of commitments

'[A]dding the word "maintain" to the definition of licensing requirement may give rise to another concern, as it would expand the scope of licensing requirements such that not only compliancy with mandatory technical standards would henceforth be covered by the definition of licensing requirement, but also non-compliance with *any* [emphasis in original] substantive requirement which might lead to the cancellation of the license. For example, cancellation of a taxi license for repeated violation of traffic rules would mean that the traffic rules were deemed to be part of the licensing requirements (as they are substantive requirements that need to be adhered to in order to maintain a license), even though they would not be considered mandatory technical standards. This *might be seen to unduly expand the scope of application of the disciplines* [emphasis added] with regard to the general provisions requiring licensing requirements to be based on objective criteria, or relevant to the supply of the service' (ibid., para. 64). The United States also proposed a definition of the concept 'authorization' that would exclude certain government measures, such as general conduct of business or governing the safety or impact on human, animal or plant life or health of the service, that did not necessarily relate to services, although they might impact a service supplier. Working Party on Domestic Regulation, Proposed Definition of 'Authorization', RD/SERV/33, 17 January 2011.

is also necessary for the application of the disciplines that are developed under Article VI:4. The latter article has no such indication. The only disciplines that have been developed until now are disciplines specifically addressing accountancy services.[499] Notably, when the Council for Trade in Services approved the disciplines, it decided that these disciplines will, once they enter into force, only apply to those sectors where WTO members have made specific commitments.[500] Currently, negotiations are ongoing within the Working Party on Domestic Regulation to develop Horizontal Disciplines. It remains to be seen how the scope of application of these disciplines may be limited, but it seems that here also a preference for limiting the application to scheduled sectors is prevailing.[501]

8.5.3.1.3 Relation to Articles XVI and XVII **393.** Third, and related to the previous point, we should consider the relation between Articles VI:4 and VI:5 and Articles XVI and XVII.

8.5.3.1.3.1 *Relation to Article XVI* **394.** In *US – Gambling*, the panel stated that the provision on market access, on the one hand, and Articles VI:4 and VI:5, on the other, are mutually exclusive.[502] Some authors have confirmed this position.[503] Nonetheless, the Appellate Body in *US – Gambling* did not address this question, and several other authors[504] have questioned the mutual exclusivity of Article VI and Articles XVI

[499] Working Party on Professional Services, Disciplines on Domestic Regulation in the Accountancy Sector, S/WPPS/W/21, 30 November 1998, adopted by the Council on Trade in Services Decision S/L/63 of 14 December 1998 (Accountancy Disciplines). They have not at the time of writing entered into force. In the decision by which the Council on Trade in Services adopted the disciplines, it was stated that they are meant to become integral part of the GATS 'no later than at the conclusion of the forthcoming round of services negotiations'. Since the Doha Round is clearly not yet about to be finished, the entry into force of the disciplines seems also not to be happening very soon.

[500] Council on Trade in Services Decision adopting the Accountancy Disciplines, S/L/63, 14 December 1998, para. 1.

[501] Working Party on Domestic Regulation, Disciplines on Domestic Regulation Pursuant to GATS Art. VI:4. Second Revision, para. 10, above n. 494.

[502] Panel Report, *US – Gambling*, paras. 6.305 and 6.308.

[503] See, e.g., M. Hilf and S. Oeter, *WTO-Recht. Rechtsordnung des Welthandels* (Baden-Baden: Nomos, 2005), 406.

[504] See, e.g., Pauwelyn, above n. 325, at 150; and E. Vranes, 'The WTO and Regulatory Freedom: WTO Disciplines on Market Access, Non-discrimination and Domestic Regulation Relating to Trade in Goods and Services', (2009) 12 *Journal of International Economic Law* 953, at 967, 974.

and XVII.[505] The panel also recognized that domestic regulations that are scrutinized under Articles VI:4 and VI:5 GATS may amount to restrictions on market access, since foreign services and service suppliers that do not comply with the national rules of a WTO member will not be able to obtain access to the market of this member. Nevertheless, the panel stated that the tests under Articles VI:4 and VI:5 and Article XVI GATS are clearly different. While measures that fall within the scope of Article XVI (as explained above, para. 247) are prohibited and must be removed (subject to the application of Article XIV GATS or other exceptions), measures that fall within the scope of Articles VI:4 and VI:5 can be maintained if they comply with the test set out in Article VI:5 (or the disciplines adopted on the basis of Article VI:4). Besides referring to the different set-up of Articles VI:4 and VI:5 and XVI GATS, the panel also referred to the Scheduling Guidelines for GATS commitments,[506] which specifically state that (non-discriminatory) measures that do *not* fall within the scope of Article XVI are subject to Article VI:5 GATS.[507] Yet even the Scheduling Guidelines do not state explicitly that measures falling within the scope of Article XVI GATS are *outside* the scope of Article VI:5.

395. The confusion that may exist with regard to the overlap between Article XVI (and Article XVII), on the one hand, and Article VI:5 and

[505] Compare this to the relationship between the GATT, on the one hand, and the SPS and TBT Agreements, on the other hand. First, this concerns provisions in separate agreements. Second, the General Interpretative Note to Annex 1A of the WTO Agreement (i.e. the Multilateral Agreements on Trade in Goods) states that in case of conflict between a provision of the GATT and a provision in another multilateral agreement on trade in goods (like the SPS or TBT Agreement), the provision in the other agreement shall prevail.

[506] The panel considers the Scheduling Guidelines as 'context' for the GATS provisions (see Art. 31:2 VCLT). This was rejected by the Appellate Body, which considered the Guidelines as 'supplementary means of interpretation' (see Art. 32 VCLT).

[507] *US – Gambling*, para. 6.307–308. See Scheduling of Initial Commitments in Trade in Services, Explanatory Note, MTN.GNS/W/164, 3 September 1993, para. 5 and (revised) Guidelines for the Scheduling of Specific Commitments under the General Agreement on Trade in Services (GATS), S/L/92, 28 March 2001, para. 11. The panel also referred to the Working Party on Professional Services, Discussion of Matters Relating to Arts. XVI and XVII of the GATS in Connection with the Disciplines on Domestic Regulation in the Accountancy Sector, Job No. 6496, 25 November 1998, paras. 2 and 3, included in Annex 4 to the (revised) Guidelines for the Scheduling of Specific Commitments, above this note. It should be noted, however, that the latter document of the Working Party on Professional Services concerned specifically with the development of the Accounting Disciplines, where the mutual exclusivity of Arts. XVI and XVII was *explicitly* recognized.

the disciplines developed on the basis of Article VI:4, on the other, may be caused by mixing up the question whether a measure is within the *scope* of the provisions with that of whether a measure *violates* one or the other provision. In the case of Article XVI, the fact that a measure is of the type listed in Article XVI:2 immediately means that it also violates the provision, unless the measure benefits from a limitation to the market access commitment. The question is then *whether the measure, even if within the scope of Article XVI, but not violating it, should still be assessed under Article VI:5 or the disciplines.*

396. This problem has only been addressed explicitly for the disciplines already developed under Article VI:4: indeed, the Accountancy Disciplines exclude their application for measures that are subject to scheduling under Articles XVI and XVII.[508] Since only measures that violate Articles XVI or XVII can be scheduled as limitations, the accountancy disciplines apply only to measures that do not violate Article XVI or are non-discriminatory. The Horizontal Disciplines that are currently under discussion will most likely also include such limitation.

397. On this basis, one can discern the following situations:

(i) Measures that violate Article XVI or XVII are outside the scope of the disciplines. This is logical: in the case of measures that are not explicitly scheduled as limitations and violate Article XVI or XVII, there is arguably no need to scrutinize them under the disciplines.
(ii) Measures that do not violate Article XVI because they benefit from an explicit limitation to the market access commitment are also outside the scope of both sets of disciplines. For instance, if a member inscribes in its market access column that it limits the market access obligation to ten new bank licences each year, the disciplines will only be applicable to the application and administration of this licensing measure. The market access commitment only extends to these ten licences. However, other measures that are

[508] Nicolaïdis and Trachtman state that the Accountancy Disciplines do not apply to national measures that are listed as exceptions under Arts. XVI and XVII. See Nicolaïdis and Trachtman, above n. 407, at 302. This seems to mean that *only* those measures *explicitly listed as exceptions* under the market access or national treatment column would be excluded from the scope of the Disciplines. Other measures, that violate Art. XVI or Art. XVII but are *not listed as exceptions*, would then still be possibly considered under the Accountancy Disciplines.

of the type listed in Article XVI:2 do not violate Article XVI. The market access commitment does not cover these measures and thus they are not subject to the disciplines.

(iii) However, the question remains whether measures that would normally violate Article XVI, but for which the WTO member in question has inscribed 'unbound', can still be scrutinized under the disciplines. These measures were not explicitly scheduled. However, since the WTO member inscribed 'unbound', in such a case it would probably not have been the intention of the WTO member in question to subject these measures to further scrutiny under the disciplines. The entry 'unbound' in the market access column shows that the WTO member wanted to maintain full policy discretion.

398. When it concerns the relation to Article XVI, the scope of the Accountancy Disciplines and the future Horizontal Disciplines thus seems clear. They only apply to measures as far as they are covered by the market access commitment. Measures that are outside the scope of the commitment (because they benefit from an explicit limitation or because the market access commitment was 'unbound') are outside the scope of the disciplines.

399. However, with regard to Article VI:5, the GATS does not contain any clear reference to mutual exclusivity. Hence, where market access commitments are made, when a measure falls within the scope of Article XVI, it may also fall within the scope of Article VI:5. However, as soon as a measure falls within the scope of Article XVI (i.e. is of the type listed in Article XVI:2), the measure violates Article XVI. It is then no longer necessary to consider whether Article VI:5 has also been violated and the panel or the Appellate Body will refrain from so considering by virtue of the principle of judicial economy. If no market access commitments have been made for the sector at stake or if the measure benefits from the limitation to the commitment, it seems that Article VI:5 will not apply either.

8.5.3.1.3.2 *Relation to Article XVII* **400.** The panel in *US – Gambling* did not explicitly state that Article XVII on national treatment and Articles VI:4 and VI:5 are also mutually exclusive. However, the panel did refer to the 1993 Scheduling Guidelines that indicate that measures that are not of the types listed in Article XVI:2, and are discriminatory, fall within the scope of Article XVII. If these measures are not discriminatory they would fall within the scope of Article VI:5.[509] This reference to the 1993 Scheduling Guidelines shows that the dividing line between measures that fall within the scope of Article VI or of Article XVII is whether or not the measures are discriminatory.

8.5.3.1.4 Summary of the scope of Articles VI:4 and VI:5 **401.** In sum, the scope of Articles VI:4 and VI:5 is quite restricted. First of all, the measures under consideration must be of the types described (qualification requirements and procedures, licensing requirements or technical standards). All regulations that impose conditions on becoming authorized as a bank or that set requirements to perform activities as a bank, once authorized, are within the scope of Articles VI:4 and VI:5, as far as they influence the characteristics of the services. Even if this might mean that a wide range of measures would come within the scope of the disciplines, the other aspects of Articles VI:4 and VI:5 seriously limit their application. Indeed, second, Article VI:5 and the already existing disciplines on domestic regulation (Accountancy Disciplines) only apply as far as specific commitments have been made. The Horizontal Disciplines will most likely also include such a restriction. Finally, while the scope of Articles VI:4 and VI:5 and that of Articles XVI and XVII seem to overlap, the Accountancy Disciplines developed under Article VI:4 make it clear that they do not apply to measures that are subject to scheduling under the latter articles. Hence only non-discriminatory measures that are not of the type listed in Article XVI:2 will be scrutinized under the disciplines.

8.5.3.2 Normative content of the disciplines based on Article VI:4 and of Article VI:5

402. Article VI:4 GATS first of all provides a *mandate* for the development of disciplines that would ensure that qualification requirements and procedures, technical standards and licensing requirements 'do not constitute unnecessary barriers to trade in services'. The disciplines should ensure that the mentioned measures are inter alia (a) based on objective and transparent criteria; (b) not more burdensome than is necessary to ensure the quality of the service; and (c) in the case of licensing procedures, not in themselves a restriction on the supply of the service. Delimatsis has noted that these three elements constitute only an

[509] Ibid., para. 6.307.

'indicative list of minimum standards' and thus that future disciplines can include additional elements.[510]

403. WTO members, through the Working Party on Professional Services, developed disciplines specifically addressing accountancy services (Accountancy Disciplines).[511] These disciplines will, once they enter into force, only apply to those sectors, subsectors and modes of supply where WTO members have made specific commitments.[512] The chairperson's draft text for Horizontal Disciplines indicates also that their purposes is

> to facilitate trade in services by ensuring that measures relating to licensing requirements and procedures, qualification requirements and procedures, and technical standards are based on objective and transparent criteria, such as competence and the ability to supply the services, and do not constitute disguised restrictions on trade in services.[513]

They thus elaborate on some elements of Article VI:4, but do not refer in a general manner to the requirement that domestic regulation should 'not be more burdensome than necessary', as stated in Article VI:4(b).

8.5.3.2.1 Objective criteria **404.** The fact that members must base domestic regulation on objective criteria (Article VI:4(a)) implies that the requirements for the foreign service supplier or imported service cannot merely depend on a subjective evaluation of the national authority. Neither can the criteria be prejudiced towards the service suppliers or services from one or the other country. To be sure, the *application* of any criteria remains always a subjective action of an authority, but this application is addressed by Article VI:1, discussed below (paras. 512–531).

[510] P. Delimatsis, 'Due Process and "Good" Regulation Embedded in the GATS – Disciplining Regulatory Behaviour in Services through Art. VI of the GATS', (2007) 10 *Journal of International Economic Law* 13, at 36.

[511] Working Party on Professional Services, Disciplines on Domestic Regulation in the Accountancy Sector, S/WPPS/W/21, 30 November 1998, adopted by the Council on Trade in Services Decision S/L/63 of 14 December 1998. They have not yet entered into force. In the decision by which the Council on Trade in Services adopted the disciplines, it was stated that they are meant to become integral part of the GATS 'no later than at the conclusion of the forthcoming round of services negotiations'.

[512] Council on Trade in Services Decision adopting the Accountancy Disciplines, S/L/63, 14 December 1998, para. 1.

[513] Working Party on Domestic Regulation, Disciplines on Domestic Regulation Pursuant to GATS Art. VI:4, Second Revision, above n. 494, para. 2.

8.5.3.2.2 Transparency 405. Transparency of the criteria must allow the service suppliers to adapt in advance to the regulatory requirements, and may also make other WTO members aware of certain differences between rules that lead to unnecessary barriers. To this end, the Accountancy Disciplines require that qualification and licensing requirements and procedures and technical standards need to be made publicly available.[514] In fact, this is an obligation that has already been imposed by Article III:1. Such transparency can further be enhanced through enquiry and contact points, and such transparency requirements are also under consideration in the discussions on Horizontal Disciplines; many WTO members, however, object to requirements that would oblige them to include foreign suppliers in the preparatory process of domestic regulation. Developing countries in particular are afraid that such procedures will impose a heavy administrative burden on them.[515] On the other hand, the developing countries might benefit by making it less costly to obtain information about applicable requirements in other WTO members. Other countries stress the importance of this measure, making it a measure of good governance that the rule-making process is transparent. This in turn avoids informal pressure from interest groups.

8.5.3.2.3 Not more burdensome than necessary 406. The requirement in Article VI:4 that domestic regulation cannot be 'more burdensome than necessary to ensure the quality of the service' is probably the most contested condition. The test reflects a trade-off between, on the one hand, the important right of the WTO members to regulate their services markets and, on the other hand, the goal of increasing trade in services by removing barriers to trade. Several authors have analysed the elements that are part of the test,[516] and also the WTO Secretariat has drafted a note on 'necessity

[514] Accountancy Disciplines, para. 4.

[515] Alexander, Dhumale and Eatwell, above n. 9, at 115.

[516] See, especially, D. Akoth Osiro, 'GATT/WTO Necessity Analysis: Evolutionary Interpretation and Its Impact on the Autonomy of Domestic Regulation', (2002) 29 *Legal Issues of Economic Integration* 123; M. Andenas and S. Zleptnig, 'Proportionality: WTO Law in Comparative Perspective', (2007) 42 *Texas International Law Journal* 371; A. Desmedt, 'Proportionality in WTO Law', (2001) 4 *Journal of International Economic Law* 441; M. Djordevic, 'Domestic Regulation and Free Trade in Services – A Balancing Act', (2002) 29 *Legal Issues of Economic Integration* 305; M. Hilf and S. Puth, 'The Principle of Proportionality on Its Way into WTO/GATT Law', in A. Von Bogdandy, P. Mavroidis and Y. Meny (eds.), *European Integration and International Coordination.*

tests' in the WTO.[517] These tests express a required relation between the aim of regulatory measures and (the content and effect of) the measures themselves. The stricter the test that is applied to this relation, the more the regulatory autonomy of the WTO members will be questioned through the WTO dispute settlement system. It must therefore also be noted from the outset that any trade-off device in the GATS will in the end be applied by the WTO panels and the Appellate Body. Depending on the elements that are included in the test, the WTO panels and the Appellate Body will have more or less authority to intervene in the regulatory autonomy of the WTO members.

407. The fact that Article VI:4 refers to the 'necessity' of the regulatory measures leads several authors to talk about the 'necessity test'. Since any national regulatory measure restricts trade somehow, the question is to what extent the measure is 'necessary' to achieve its aim. Furthermore, the necessity test also figures in Article VI:5 GATS and in the Accountancy Disciplines.[518] The draft Horizontal Disciplines do not contain such a general test, but only specify that for *licensing requirements* the WTO members 'shall consider whether less restrictive means could be employed to achieve the purposes for which these requirements were established'.[519] Hence, while one can disagree on whether this test amounts to 'necessity testing', the latter test would in any event not apply to qualification requirements and technical standards.

408. The necessity test exists next to other trade-off devices[520] in the GATS that define whether a measure is acceptable from the perspective of the GATS

Studies in Transnational Economic Law in Honour of Claus-Dieter Ehlermann (The Hague: Kluwer, 2002) 199–218; J. Neumann and E. Türk, 'Necessity Revisited: Proportionality in World Trade Organization Law after Korea – Beef, EC – Asbestos and EC – Sardines', (2003) 37 *Journal of World Trade* 199; J. Trachtman, 'Trade and . . . Problems, Cost-Benefit Analysis and Subsidiarity', (1998) 9 *European Journal of International Law* 32; J. Trachtman, 'Lessons for GATS Art. VI from the SPS, TBT and GATT Treatment of Domestic Regulation', 29 January 2002, available at http://ssrn.com/abstract=298760; and J. Waincymer, 'Reformulated Gasoline under the Reformed WTO Dispute Settlement Procedures: Pulling Pandora out of a Chapeau?', (1996) 18 *Michigan Journal of International Law* 141.

517 Working Party on Domestic Regulation, 'Necessity Tests' in the WTO, S/WPDR/W/27, 2 December 2003, and the Addendum that provides an update: S/WPDR/W/27/Add. 1, 17 January 2011.

518 Accountancy Disciplines, Para. 2.

519 Working Party on Domestic Regulation, Disciplines on Domestic Regulation Pursuant to GATS Art. VI:4, Second Revision, above n. 494, para. 16.

520 For a taxonomy of trade-off devices, see Trachtman, 'Trade and . . . Problems', above n. 516, at 35–6.

(which aims to achieve progressively higher levels of liberalization). Indeed, measures may be scrutinized in respect of their discriminatory nature or the fact that they block market access. However, in the case of the necessity test, the aim of the measure and the relation of this measure towards the achievement of this aim come into play. Another provision where the aim of the measure is relevant, but nevertheless no test of 'necessity' of the measure is applied, is the prudential exception in the GATS Annex on Financial Services. As will be discussed (below, paras. 450–471), measures taken for prudential reasons can be maintained, even if they violate GATS provisions, as long as they are not used for avoiding the commitments and obligations of the WTO member under the GATS.[521] The aim of the measure is again relevant, but the scrutiny of the relation between the aim and the measure does not go as far as requiring that the measure is *necessary* to achieve the prudential aim.

409. The 'necessity test' does not exclusively figure in Article VI:4 and the related disciplines on domestic regulation. It also exists in Article XIV GATS, which sets out a number of exceptions to the obligations included in the GATS. However, the necessity test in Article XIV is part of an *exception*, whereas the necessity test in the disciplines developed on the basis of Article VI:4 and in Article VI:5 is part of an *obligation* imposed on the WTO members. This is similar to the obligations imposed by the WTO Agreement on the Application of Sanitary and Phytosanitary Measures (SPS Agreement) and the Agreement on Technical Barriers to Trade (TBT Agreement) in the field of trade in goods. Article 5.6 of the SPS Agreement requires WTO members to 'ensure that [sanitary or phytosanitary] measures are not more trade-restrictive than required to achieve their appropriate level of sanitary or phytosanitary protection'.[522] Likewise, Article 2.2 TBT Agreement requires WTO members to ensure that their technical regulations are not 'prepared, adopted or applied with a view to or with the effect of creating unnecessary obstacles to international trade'.[523] Nevertheless, the 'necessity test' in each of the mentioned provisions is not necessarily the same. Depending on what elements are brought to the test, the test will be more or less intrusive into national regulatory autonomy.

521 Para. 2(a) GATS Annex on Financial Services.

522 See also Art. 2.2 SPS Agreement, which requires that the SPS measures are *applied* only to the extent necessary to protect human, animal or plant life or health.

523 See also Art. 2.5 TBT Agreement for the presumption of necessity when the measure is in accordance with international standards. See also below para. 426.

410. A major technique for making a 'trade-off' between financial stability and competition in the banking sector is the 'proportionality' test *sensu lato*.[524] This technique leaves the jurisdiction to regulate activities of foreign-owned banks with the host country, but subjects the exercise of its competence to a proportionality test. The proportionality analysis consists of three elements. First, one should consider whether the measure is suitable for achieving the aim. Second, one must examine whether the measure is necessary for achieving the aim. Third, one must consider whether the importance of the value pursued by the measure is proportionate to the limitations (costs) imposed by the measure on free trade. This last element is proportionality *sensu stricto*, and involves a balancing of the value of the *goals* pursued. In contrast, the second element of the proportionality *sensu lato* is the necessity test and would compare alternative *measures* for achieving the goal.

411. It is important to note that nowhere does the GATS explicitly use the word 'proportionality'.[525] However, the fact that the word 'proportionality' is not used explicitly does not mean that the three steps of this test are not somehow included. Interpreting the word 'necessity' against the background of this theoretical proportionality test allows making an assessment of the extent to which the GATS intrudes into the regulatory autonomy of the WTO members when they want to determine a trade-off between competition and stability in the market for banking services.

412. The most general, and most cited, statement on the elements included in the 'necessity test' in WTO law is that of the Appellate Body in *Korea – Various Measures on Beef*. There, the Appellate Body noted (with regard to Article XX(d) GATT) that

> [T]he term 'necessary' refers, in our view, to a range of degrees of necessity. At one end of this continuum lies 'necessary' understood as 'indispensable'; at the other end, 'necessary' is taken to mean as 'making a contribution to'. We consider that a 'necessary' measure is, in this

[524] For a detailed analysis see Andenas and Zleptnig, above n. 516, and see the other references in n. 516.

[525] More generally, Desmedt identifies only two instances in the WTO Agreements where the word 'proportionality' is explicitly mentioned. First, Art. 46 of the Agreement on Trade-Related Aspects of Intellectual Property Rights (TRIPS Agreement) obliges national judicial authorities to take into account the proportionality between the seriousness of an infringement of intellectual property rights and the remedies ordered. Second, footnote 9 to the Agreement on Subsidies and Countervailing Measures talks about the proportionality of countermeasures. Desmedt, above n. 516, at 443.

> continuum, located significantly closer to the pole of 'indispensable' than to the opposite pole of simply 'making a contribution to'.[526]

Thus a measure that is 'indispensable' is clearly necessary. Measures that are not 'indispensable' may still be necessary, but need further testing. With regard to this testing, the Appellate Body clarified that the necessity of a measure should be determined through

> a process of weighing and balancing a series of factors which prominently include the contribution made by the compliance measure to the enforcement of the law or regulation at issue, the importance of the common interests or values protected by that law or regulation at issue, and the accompanying impact of the law or regulation on imports or exports.[527]

The analysis of these three factors will then assist in determining whether there are reasonably available alternatives to the measure at issue.[528]

413. Based on the above-mentioned 'theoretical' proportionality test *sensu lato*, we can determine what elements of the test exist in WTO law. However, before the proportionality *sensu lato* of the measure is determined, one must assess to what extent the measure pursues a legitimate goal. Whereas tests in *obligations* in the WTO agreements contain open lists of objectives, the *exemptions* from WTO obligations contain closed lists of acceptable objectives.[529] It is somewhat unclear to what extent the test in Articles VI:4 and VI:5 (which is an *obligation*) contains such open list. The qualification requirements and procedures, technical standards and licensing requirements should be 'no more burdensome than necessary to *ensure the quality of the service*'.[530] On this basis Nicolaïdis and Trachtman suggest that the test may be very interventionist. The acceptable aim could be limited to the *quality of the service.*[531] Other goals, such as the stability of the financial services sector or environmental protection, would not be allowed. However, it can also be argued that the quality of the service can also encompass wider notions of quality, including health or environmental impacts of the service or of its delivery.[532]

526 Appellate Body Report, *Korea – Various Measures on Beef*, para. 161.
527 Ibid., para. 164. 528 Ibid., para. 166.
529 Working Party on Domestic Regulation, 'Necessity Tests' in the WTO, above n. 517, at 2.
530 Art. VI:4(b) GATS (emphasis added).
531 Nicolaïdis and Trachtman, above n. 407, at 300.
532 See also Neumann and Türk, above n. 516, at 224 (n. 171), referring to Council for Trade in Services, Art. VI:4 of the GATS: Disciplines on Domestic Regulation Applicable to All Services, Note by the Secretariat, S/C/W/96, 1 March 1999, para. 26.

414. Once it has been determined that the measure achieves a legitimate objective, one can undertake the proportionality analysis. The *first* element of the scrutiny involves the suitability of the measure itself. Desmedt has noted that there must be a 'causal link between the measure and the aim'.[533] According to Trachtman, most 'trade-off devices' (i.e. tests in the WTO Agreements that determine the appropriate relation between trade values and other societal values) include simple means–end rationality testing. This last considers 'whether the means chosen is a rational means to a purported end'.[534] Suitability was mentioned by the Appellate Body in *Korea – Various Measures on Beef* as one of the factors that need to be taken into account in the 'weighing and balancing' process, and was further clarified in the *Brazil – Retreaded Tyres* case. The Appellate Body stated that there is a contribution by the measure to the achievement of the objective 'when there is a genuine relationship of ends and means between the objective pursued and the measure at issue'.[535] There is no requirement to express the contribution of the measure to the objective in *quantitative* terms.[536]

415. The *second* element in the proportionality test is the determination of the necessity of the measure to achieve the aim. This is distinct from the 'suitability' of the measure, since it determines to what extent there exist reasonably available *alternative* measures that are *less trade restrictive* to achieve the objective. Based on the analysis of the three factors mentioned in the *Korea – Certain Measures on Beef* case ((i) the contribution of the measure to the aim, (ii) the importance of the interests and values at stake, and (iii) the trade restrictiveness of the measure), the panel or the Appellate Body will already be able to make a preliminary conclusion whether the measure is necessary.[537] Subsequently, one should consider possible alternative measures.[538] Even if a less trade-restrictive measure

[533] Desmedt, above n. 516, at 454–5 (with regard to the SPS Agreement) and 465–6 (with regard to Art. XX GATT).

[534] Trachtman, 'Trade and . . . Problems', above n. 516, at 35.

[535] Appellate Body Report, *Brazil – Measures Affecting Imports of Retreaded Tyres* (*Brazil – Retreaded Tyres*), WT/DS332/AB/R, adopted 17 December 2007, para. 145. The panel had merely said that the measure is 'capable' of making a contribution to the end. The Appellate Body disagreed. The elements the Appellate Body refers to in order to determine 'genuine relationship' are the nature of risk, objective pursued, level of protection sought and ultimately nature, quantity and quality of the evidence.

[536] Ibid., para. 147. [537] Ibid., para. 156.

[538] Note that while the defendant bears the burden of proof of establishing that the measure is contributing to one of the legitimate objectives and of making a prima facie case that

could be devised, one should determine whether the measure is 'reasonably available' to the WTO member. In assessing whether the alternative measure is reasonably available, the extent to which the alternative is able to contribute to the realization of the end pursued is considered. In the case of vital or extremely important objectives, it will be easier to accept that the measure is necessary and that the alternative is not able to contribute in the same way.[539] The alternative measure may not be 'merely theoretical in nature'.[540] Therefore 'reasonable availability' of the measure is further determined by the cost, technical difficulties and technical expertise of the WTO member in question.[541] Account should be taken of the level of development of the WTO member.[542]

416. The *third* aspect of the proportionality analysis involves a balancing of the value of the objectives against the cost to trade. It appears that the panels or the Appellate Body have until now never engaged in the analysis of such proportionality *sensu stricto*. Weighing the value of the regulatory goal against the costs of trade will involve an important intrusion into the regulatory autonomy of the WTO members. Before engaging in a necessity analysis, it is always clearly stated by the panels and the Appellate Body that it is up to the WTO members to set the objective they seek to achieve as well as the level of protection they want to obtain.[543] Therefore several authors have argued that the 'weighing and balancing' which is famously referred to

the measure is 'necessary', it is the complainant who has to identify possible alternative measures that are reasonably available to achieve the aim. Once this has been done, the burden of proof shifts again to the defendant to show that the measures are not reasonably available. See Appellate Body Report, *US – Gambling*, paras. 309–311.

539 Appellate Body Report, *EC – Asbestos*, para. 172.

540 Appellate Body Report, *US – Gambling*, para. 308.

541 Working Party on Domestic Regulation, 'Necessity Tests' in the WTO, S/WPDR/W/27, 2 December 2003, para. 35; and Panel Report, *EC – Asbestos*, paras 8.207–8.216. Trachtman has suggested that in defining 'reasonableness', it could be considered whether the costs of the alternative, less restrictive measure do not exceed the benefits to trade (i.e. the degree to which the alternative is less restrictive to trade). This is a cost–benefit analysis, and implies that as soon as the costs of the alternative measure are higher than the benefits to trade, the alternative is not reasonably available. Alternatively, it could be considered whether the costs of the alternative, less restrictive measure are not disproportionately high. Even if the costs of the alternative exceed the benefits to trade, it may still be reasonably available when the costs are not disproportionate to the benefits. This is a proportionality analysis, and it is clearly more intrusive into regulatory autonomy than the cost–benefit approach to 'reasonableness' mentioned before. Trachtman, 'Trade and . . . Problems', above n. 516, at 70.

542 Delimatsis, above n. 490, at 219.

543 Appellate Body Report, *EC – Asbestos*, para. 168; Appellate Body Report, *Brazil – Retreaded Tyres*, paras. 140 and 210.

in *Korea – Certain Measures on Beef* does not involve balancing the value of a goal against the costs to trade.[544] If a real weighing and balancing of the value of the goal against the costs to trade were to take place, the panels or the Appellate Body would need to make a certain quantification of the value of the interest that is pursued. This would mean that they in fact substitute their judgement for that of the national authorities. Nevertheless, one could argue that in making their assessment under the two other elements of the proportionality *sensu lato*, panels and the Appellate Body implicitly perform such a balancing exercise. They have nevertheless always recognized the high importance of the goal that was pursued, and therefore they have never had to conclude that the costs to trade are too high when compared with the value of the non-trade goal. If a panel or the Appellate Body found that a measure did not comply with the exception provisions, this was mostly because there were fewer trade-restrictive alternatives reasonably available or because the measure was applied in a manner that led to arbitrary or unjustifiable discrimination.

417. With regard to the necessity test in Article VI:5 and the Disciplines on the basis of Article VI:4, it is also important to take into account the structure of the GATS, where necessity tests figure at the same time in obligations and in exceptions.[545] Applying the same test in each of the provisions may lead to odd results. Indeed, if a strict (i.e. very intrusive into regulatory autonomy) test is applied in an obligation, how can a measure that violates this strict obligation be saved by an exemption, if in

544 See, e.g., Desmedt, above n. 516, at 478 and Regan, above n. 434, at 365. *Contra*, Andenas and Zleptnig, above n. 516, at 373, where they argue that 'balancing within Art. XX needs to be undertaken several times in order to determine the necessity, reasonableness or proportionality of a particular measure. The question in those cases is to determine which rights or interests need to be balanced against each other, and it would be misleading to reduce this balancing act solely to general trade versus non-trade concerns.'

545 This stands in contrast with the necessity tests in the obligations in the TBT and SPS Agreements, on the one hand, and the necessity test in the exception in Art. XX GATT, on the other hand. Here the tests are set out in separate agreements. Japan has submitted an informal paper to the WPDR discussing the relation between disciplines on the basis of Art. VI:4 and the exceptions provisions in the GATS. It was stated that 'the application of Art. VI:4 should not prevent measures under the exceptions of Art. XIV'. Communication from Japan, Coverage of Disciplines to be Developed on Domestic Regulation, JOB(02)/150, 22 October 2002, mentioned in Working Party on Domestic Regulation, Report of the Meeting held on 22 October 2002, S/WPDR/M/18, 3 December 2002, para. 12. On the one hand, this may imply that measures that violate Art. VI:4 should be able to be justified under Art. XIV. On the other hand, this may imply that the test in Art. VI:4 should be the same as in Art. XIV: measures that would be exempted under Art. XIV should also be acceptable under Art. VI:4.

the latter a stricter or equally strict test applies? In other words, if a measure is more trade-restrictive than is necessary to achieve the aim and thereby violates Article VI:5(a) or a necessity test in the Disciplines on the basis of Article VI:4, it seems difficult also to justify these measures on the basis of Article XIV, which also includes in its first three subparagraphs a requirement that the measure is not more trade restrictive than necessary to achieve the aim. This leads to a remarkable situation. A complainant has to prove under Article VI that the measure is not necessary. Where a panel or the Appellate Body concludes that the complainant has met the burden of proof, the defendant then has to prove that the measure was *not* necessary to meet one of the listed objectives in Article XIV.

418. One could argue that it is not sensible still to apply the exception provision when a similar test is already performed under the obligation in Article VI. When addressing the obligation in Article VI, it is most likely that the defendant will also argue that the measure is in fact necessary. In the case of a violation, it may then be no longer of any use to apply the exception. The tests in the obligation and the exception in the GATS would then be one and the same.

419. In sum, the 'necessity test', initially elaborated through case law relating to trade in goods, considers whether a particular measure is necessary to achieve the aim or whether alternative measures should have been used. Exactly how 'necessary' the measure must be and what elements are included in the test are the questions under consideration and they must be laid down in the wording of the Disciplines and clarified through its interpretation. If a necessity test is included in the Disciplines, the coexistence with the necessity test in the exceptions in Article XIV raises the question whether measures that violate the necessity requirement in the Disciplines may still be justified under the exception. While it is in theory possible to construct variations in the intensity of the necessity tests, the better argument may be that measures that fail the necessity test in the Disciplines will no longer be assessed under Article XIV, since the similar necessity test would apply here.[546]

[546] This would also be in line with the argument by Japan that that 'the application of Art. VI:4 should not prevent measures under the exceptions of Art. XIV' (above n. 545). Since the tests in both the obligation and the exception are the same, measures that would fail the test under Art. VI would in any case also fail the test under Art. XIV. Hence the application of Art. VI:4 does not prevent measures that would be justified under Art. XIV.

The exception will, of course, remain relevant in all cases where provisions in Article VI or the disciplines that do not include a necessity test are violated.

8.5.3.2.4 The necessity test in the draft Horizontal Disciplines

420. Paragraph 2 of the chair's draft text for Horizontal Disciplines states that the purpose of the disciplines is to ensure that 'measures relating to licensing requirements and procedures, qualification requirements and procedures, and technical standards are based on objective and transparent criteria . . . and do *not constitute a disguised restriction on trade*'.[547] This appears to have been interpreted in the area of Article XX GATT as involving an enquiry into the *intent* of the measure: it must be assessed whether, despite the fact that an exception is available to justify a violation of a GATS obligation, this exception is not abused by the member for protectionist reasons.[548]

421. The draft Horizontal Disciplines are developed on the basis of Article VI:4, where it is clearly indicated that the Disciplines 'shall aim to ensure that [qualification requirements and procedures, technical standards and licensing requirements] are, *inter alia* . . . not more burdensome than necessary to ensure the quality of the service'. The object and purpose of this provision was thus that the Horizontal Disciplines should elaborate the necessity test referred to in Article VI:4(b). Therefore it may possibly be argued by future litigants before WTO panels or the Appellate Body that the underlying rationale of the Disciplines is a necessity test and that the Disciplines provide elements for such necessity testing.[549]

547 Working Party on Domestic Regulation, Disciplines on Domestic Regulation Pursuant to GATS Art. VI:4, Second Revision, above n. 494, para. 2 (emphasis added).

548 The Appellate Body in *US – Gasoline* has noted: 'We consider that "disguised restriction", whatever else it covers, may properly be read as embracing restrictions amounting to arbitrary or unjustifiable discrimination in international trade taken under the guise of a measure formally within the terms of an exception listed in Art. XX'. Appellate Body Report, *US – Gasoline*, above n. 315, p. 25. And in *Brazil – Retreaded Tyres* it noted that '[a]nalyzing whether discrimination is arbitrary or unjustifiable usually involves an analysis that relates primarily to the cause or the rationale of the discrimination'. Appellate Body Report, *Brazil – Retreaded Tyres*, para. 225.

549 See also the remark by Delimatsis that when the panels or Appellate Body apply any horizontal disciplines that do not include a necessity test, such a principle 'will be creeping into the disciplines anyway'. He notes that it was suggested during negotiations that it be reiterated in the Preamble of the Horizontal Disciplines that the

422. However, since this paragraph in the draft Horizontal Disciplines only indicates the *purpose of the Disciplines*, it could also be argued that the *devices* to determine this disguised protection are to be discerned for each type of domestic regulation, as set out in the Horizontal Disciplines, separately (licensing requirements, qualifications requirements and technical standards). For none of the types of domestic regulation is an explicit necessity test provided in the Disciplines.

423. Nonetheless, even if there is no explicit 'necessity test', there are some expressions in the draft that use language that nevertheless can be interpreted to include elements of such a test. Still, it remains to be seen what language will eventually be adopted.

8.5.3.2.4.1 *Relevant criteria* **424.** The requirement in paragraph 11 that the measures of domestic regulation must be based on 'relevant' criteria, may still indicate that that at least the 'first step' in a proportionality test *sensu lato* will be applied: a consideration of the 'suitability' of the criteria in the light of the goal pursued by the domestic regulation.

8.5.3.2.4.2 *Technical standards* **425.** The Disciplines do not provide requirements relating to the *content* of technical standards, except for general paragraph 11, which requires that measures relating to licensing requirements and procedures, qualification requirements and procedures, and technical standards are 'pre-established, based on objective and transparent criteria and relevant to the supply of the services to which they apply'. The specific chapter on technical standards rather focuses solely on the standard-setting processes of non-governmental bodies. WTO members are encouraged to ensure the maximum transparency in the relevant processes of development and application of

measures falling within the scope of the disciplines should not constitute *unnecessary* barriers to trade in services (thereby repeating what is said in the introductory paragraph of Art. VI:4 GATS). The panels or the Appellate Body may then construct their own test. Hence WTO members 'will [have missed] the opportunity to design themselves a necessity test that would encompass concepts and elements on which Members could reach a consensus'. Delimatsis, above n. 490, at 254 and n. 351. The draft Horizontal Disciplines do *not* refer explicitly to the fact that the mandate under Art. VI:4 was to develop disciplines to ensure that the covered measures 'do not constitute unnecessary barriers to trade'. They now only refer to the requirement that they 'do not constitute a disguised restriction on trade in services'. Hence there is no longer an explicit reference to necessity. This may indeed avoid the panels or the Appellate Body reading a necessity test into the disciplines.

domestic and international standards by non-governmental bodies.[550] In the banking sector, one thinks inevitably of the Basel Committee. While the membership of the Basel Committee has already been broadened, one may wonder whether the Disciplines will induce the members of the Basel Committee to adapt their procedures further. Further, WTO members should take into account (existing or imminent) relevant international standards in formulating technical standards.[551] Hence, when WTO members develop technical standards relating to banking services, they should take into account the Basel standards (e.g. on capital adequacy). The Draft Horizontal Disciplines would thus to a certain extent provide an incentive to WTO members to use the Basel standards. This is not necessary, however, if these international standards were to be ineffective or inappropriate in achieving the national policy objectives.

426. The formulation 'should take into account' again makes this provision not very strong. Contrary to what is the case for the SPS Agreement, where SPS measures that conform to international standards are refutably presumed to be consistent with other obligations in the SPS Agreement and the TBT Agreement, where TBT measures that are in accordance with international standards are refutably presumed not to create unnecessary obstacles to trade, the disciplines make no such connection to other aspects of the Horizontal Disciplines.

8.5.3.2.5 The necessity test in Article VI:5 **427.** Even though there may at present be no further disciplines on qualification requirements and procedures, technical standards and licensing procedures beyond those on accountancy services, Article VI:5 still puts such measures under scrutiny. Nonetheless, the application of this discipline is subject to a number of conditions. Article VI:5 again applies only in service sectors in which WTO members have made specific commitments. Article VI:5 will be violated if there is nullification or impairment of the specific commitments that have been made.[552] This nullification and

550 Hence no further scrutiny is applied to these standards developed by non-governmental bodies. There is only a 'soft obligation for transparency'. Delimatsis, above n. 490, at 201.

551 Working Party on Domestic Regulation, Disciplines on Domestic Regulation Pursuant to GATS Art. VI:4, Second Revision, above n. 494, para. 41.

552 The question whether the measure at stake regulates a service that is part of a sector for which specific commitments have been made may be quite controversial. The schedules of commitments will need to be interpreted to define the delimitation of the

impairment must, first, happen through a violation of the criteria (a)–(c) of Article VI:4 mentioned above (paras. 404–419). Second, the nullification and impairment could not have been reasonably expected by the member at the time the specific commitments were made in this sector. Since the second element further limits the application of Article VI:5, we examine this element first.

428. According to Article 3.8 of the Dispute Settlement Understanding (DSU),[553] there is prima facie nullification and impairment when an obligation in one of the WTO Agreements is breached. Remarkably, Article VI:5 incorporates nullification and impairment as a condition for finding a violation of the obligation.[554] It is therefore necessary for a complainant to show the trade effects of the measure.[555] This leads to a serious hurdle for bringing a claim that Article VI:5 is violated. Moreover, the nullification and impairment of the commitments must not have been reasonably expected by the complainant. Trachtman has stated that this means that Article VI:5 is in fact only a 'standstill' obligation.[556] Indeed, if the measures that are challenged existed at the moment the commitments were made, they cannot lead to 'nullification and impairment in a manner that could not reasonably be expected' because the members were aware of the existence of the measures. On the contrary, for measures that are adopted *after* the commitments are

commitment. The issue of interpreting schedules of commitments was at stake in the *US – Gambling* dispute. Appellate Body Report, *US – Gambling*, paras. 158–213.

553 Understanding on Rules and Procedures Governing the Settlement of Disputes, Annex 2 to the Final Act Embodying the Results of the Uruguay Round of Multilateral Trade Negotiations, done in Marrakesh on 15 April 1994.

554 Some have argued that by including this element, Art. VI in fact introduces the concept of *non-violation* nullification and impairment into services trade. See, e.g., P. Sauvé and A. Mattoo, 'Domestic Regulation and the GATS: Untangling the Issues', in P. Sauvé (ed.), *Essays on Services, Investment and the New Trade Agenda* (London: Cameron May, 2003) 113–130, at 125. Arts. XXIII:1 (b) GATT and 26 DSU provide for the possibility of bringing a complaint alleging that benefits under the WTO Agreements are nullified or impaired by a measure that is nevertheless consistent with the obligations under the WTO Agreements. In the present author's opinion, Art. VI:5 is a not provision that deals with non-violation complaints. Rather, the concept of nullification and impairment becomes part of the *obligation* in Art. VI:5, and thus a *violation* of this provision is conditional on the proof of nullification and impairment.

555 J. Trachtman, 'Accounting Standards and Trade Disciplines. Irreconcilable Differences?', (1997) 31 *Journal of World Trade* 63, at 84.

556 J. Trachtman, 'Negotiations on Domestic Regulation and Trade in Services (GATS Art. VI): A Legal Analysis of Selected Current Issues', in E.-U. Petersmann (ed.), *Reforming the World Trading System. Legitimacy, Efficiency and Democratic Governance* (Oxford University Press, 2005) 205–219, at 213.

made, it is (refutably) presumed that they could not reasonably be anticipated.[557] Newly adopted measures are thus subject to the discipline of Article VI:5.

429. Therefore one should not underestimate that at present, there already exists an important discipline on newly adopted measures of domestic regulation: the obligation that they are based on reasonable and objective criteria and, most importantly, must not be more burdensome than is necessary to ensure the quality of the service. Arguably, once horizontal disciplines are adopted, Article VI:5 will lose its importance. If the Disciplines were not to include a 'necessity test', the discipline would at first sight be more limited. Nonetheless, the different separate obligations in the Disciplines can also be considered to be specific elements in ensuring that measures are 'not more burdensome than necessary'. The difference would then be that there is no general, abstract, necessity test imposed.

430. With regard to *existing* measures of domestic regulation, the focus lies much more on eliminating them through further negotiations. If such measures do not fall within the scope of Article XVI on market access or if they do not violate Article XVII on national treatment because they are not discriminatory, they may still be inscribed under the additional commitments column pursuant to Article XVIII GATS.

431. Thus measures relating to qualification requirements and procedures, licensing requirements or technical standards that apply within a services sector for which commitments were made and that are adopted *after* the date of making these commitments, may be challenged on the basis of Article VI:5. A complainant will further need to show that the measure does not comply with either one of the criteria in Article VI:4(a) to (c).

432. It is remarkable that Article VI:4(b), to which Article VI:5(a)(i) refers, states that measures 'cannot be more *burdensome* than necessary to ensure the quality of the service'.[558] One may wonder whether the

[557] The panel in *Japan – Film* stated that there is a presumption that measures introduced subsequent to the conclusion of tariff negotiations at issue should not be held to have been anticipated. It is for the WTO member adopting these measures to rebut the presumption. Likewise, there is a presumption that measures that existed prior to the conclusion of tariff negotiations should have been anticipated by the WTO members. It is then for the WTO member claiming that these measures could not reasonably be anticipated to rebut the presumption. Panel Report, *Japan – Film*, paras. 10.79 and 10.80.

[558] Emphasis added.

'burdensomeness' of a measure assesses something different from the impact a measure has on *trade*. At first sight, the fact that a measure is 'burdensome' does not necessarily mean that it is trade-restrictive. The WTO Secretariat noted that there was a difference between 'burdensome' and 'trade restrictive', but did not provide criteria for making the distinction.[559] However, Krajewski notes that, while a test on the 'burdensomeness' of a measure has a potentially greater impact on the regulatory autonomy of the WTO members, the fact that the introductory paragraph of Article VI:4 GATS states that the purpose of the Disciplines is to ensure that specified domestic regulation does 'not constitute unnecessary barriers to trade in services' means that the test is also focused on the degree of trade restriction and does not imply a wider test on the extent to which the measure is burdensome. In the Working Party on Domestic Regulation, South Korea argued that 'not more trade restrictive' refers to cross-border trade and 'not more burdensome' to domestic procedures. This would be because GATS modes of supply do not concern only traditional cross-border trade. Nonetheless, South Korea in the end concluded that 'regardless of the wording that is being used, both phrases – "not more burdensome than necessary" and "not more trade-restrictive than necessary" – appear to imply a need to determine whether there are less burdensome or less restrictive alternatives available'.[560] Delimatsis notes that it is unacceptable that 'WTO adjudicating bodies [would] pronounce on the legality of unduly burdensome domestic regulation measures even in the absence of an international trade restriction, something that would be hardly accepted by the WTO membership'.[561]

8.5.3.2.6 International standards **433.** Regulatory diversity may seriously hamper free trade in banking services. The GATS mainly focuses on negative integration: its provisions define what WTO members must *not* do when regulating their services markets. The disciplines that are developed on the basis of Article VI:4 can in principle go beyond this and may involve some positive integration, by requiring WTO members to

[559] Working Party on Domestic Regulation, Report of the Meeting Held on 29 November 2000, S/WPDR/M/9, 12 March 2001, p. 8. The Secretariat merely stated that 'there was a difference, and that a measure could be more burdensome than necessary, but not to the point of being trade restrictive and vice-versa'.

[560] Working Party on Domestic Regulation, Communication from the Republic of Korea on the Necessity Test, S/WPDR/W/9, 28 September 2000, para. 8.

[561] Delimatsis, above n. 490, at 208.

recognize each other's domestic regulations or even to harmonize domestic regulation in certain service sectors. The chairperson's draft text for Horizontal Disciplines does neither.

434. First of all, *positive* integration through recognition of other members' regulations is useful for improving free trade. Specifically for qualification requirements, the draft disciplines only require members where the competent authority 'finds it relevant' to give 'due consideration' to the relevant professional experience of the applicant as a complement to educational qualification, and, where they consider membership of a professional association in another WTO member as indicative of the competence or experience of a service provider, they must also give due consideration to this fact.[562] It seems easy for a WTO member to 'give due consideration' and then conclude that the foreign professional experience of the applicant is not sufficient. Moreover, the authority is only required to give due consideration 'where it finds it relevant'. The minimal requirement this may impose is that the WTO members indicate why foreign experience would not be sufficiently relevant to be considered and at least show that they have considered the experience, where relevant. A WTO member can thus probably not satisfy the requirement by completely ignoring the foreign experience. If a WTO member were to find that an applicant has deficient professional qualifications, it must identify this deficiency and allow applicants to fulfil requirements of coursework, examinations, training or work experience in the jurisdiction of another WTO member.[563] Nevertheless, this is only required 'where appropriate'. In sum, there is no obligation to accept foreign requirements as equivalent. Finally, *mutual* recognition also contributes to *positive* integration. Nonetheless, the Horizontal Disciplines do not contain paragraphs requiring or encouraging mutual recognition.

435. Second, one could reduce regulatory diversity by harmonizing domestic regulation. However, the Accountancy Disciplines and the draft Horizontal Disciplines do not define the substantive requirements that must be imposed in the measures relating to licensing requirements and procedures, qualification requirements and procedures, and technical standards of the WTO members. This is certainly not the case for the

[562] Working Party on Domestic Regulation, Disciplines on Domestic Regulation Pursuant to GATS Art. VI:4, Second Revision, above n. 494, para. 27.

[563] Ibid., para. 28.

draft Horizontal Disciplines, since the precise content of the requirements necessarily differs from sector to sector. The Horizontal Disciplines therefore only seek to ensure that the measures are *based on* objective and transparent criteria and do not constitute disguised restrictions of trade. However, even in the Accountancy Disciplines, which are sector-specific, and thus would allow for more detail, no specific content for measures relating to the accountancy profession is defined. This comes as no surprise. Every WTO member has the right to regulate the services sector at stake, as recognized in the fourth introductory paragraph of the GATS and also in paragraph 3 of the draft Horizontal Disciplines. Moreover, the WTO is hardly an appropriate forum for negotiating specific requirements. In the Working Group on Domestic Regulation, mainly trade specialists are represented and not specific government officials who are active in regulating the service sector at issue. The technical nature of many service regulations requires bringing together experts in the field at stake, as can for instance be seen in the Basel Committee. The WTO is not fit for such negotiations, since it focuses on trade liberalization. Moreover, the WTO consists of a large group of members with diverging levels of economic development. It is clearly inappropriate to develop regulation that would be the same for all these members. Finally, the decision-making process in the WTO, which is based on consensus, make it highly unlikely that harmonized regulations for service sectors could be adopted.

436. Therefore, real positive integration of an international banking market might only be realized through harmonization of banking regulation *outside* the WTO. Nevertheless, the GATS sometimes includes references to international standards as a point of reference for determining whether a national regulation is acceptable from the perspective of free trade. These provisions can play an important role in strengthening the impact of international standards, even if they were developed as voluntary standards.

437. The first set of provisions in the GATS that might promote the impact of international standards are the obligations prohibiting WTO members from discriminating: Article II (most-favoured-nation treatment) and Article XVII (national treatment). As suggested (above, para. 325), the fact that a service originates in a country that has implemented an international standard on banking regulation or supervision may be considered by a panel as an 'objective characteristic' of the services and thus be taken into account to determine 'likeness'. However, no panel has until now considered international standards in the determination of likeness. Implementing international standards would thus be a way for a WTO member to ensure that, when its banks operate abroad, these banks and the services they supply abroad are treated no less favourably than domestic banks and banking services in other member states that have also implemented these standards.

438. A second provision that strengthens the role of international standards is Article VII:5 GATS. Article VII:5 indicates that WTO members should, wherever appropriate, base recognition on multilaterally agreed criteria. The fact that the word 'should' is used, rather than 'shall', in combination with the phrase 'where appropriate', gives WTO members some leeway in making use of these multilateral criteria. However, as indicated (above, paras. 365–366), the combination of the requirement not to accord recognition in a manner that would constitute a means of discrimination or a disguised restriction of trade,[564] gives an important incentive for using international standards, where they are available. The draft Horizontal Disciplines state that members should take relevant international standards into account (or the relevant parts of these standards) in formulating international standards, except when this would be an ineffective or inappropriate means of fulfilling national policy objectives.[565] The formulation 'should', in combination with the possibility of not using international standards where this would be 'ineffective or inappropriate', may again provide some flexibility to WTO members. However, arguably, WTO members will have to explain why they did not use these standards.

439. Finally, international standards may also play a role in the interpretation of Article XIV GATS, which provides general exceptions to the GATS obligations and, more specifically for the trade in banking services, the prudential exception in paragraph 2(a) of the GATS Annex on Financial Services. When a WTO member claims that a measure that violates one of the obligations in the GATS should be justified because it is used 'for prudential reasons', it will be easier for this member to support its claim if the measure is in fact implementing an international standard. WTO case law has indicated how international standards can be used to interpret concepts in the WTO agreements. Article 3.2 DSU indicates that legal

[564] Art. VII:3 GATS.

[565] Working Party on Domestic Regulation, Disciplines on Domestic Regulation Pursuant to GATS Art. VI:4, Second Revision, above n. 494, para. 41.

interpretations must be made in accordance with customary rules of interpretation of public international law. The Appellate Body has stressed that such interpretations should be based on Articles 31 and 32 of the VCLT.[566] Article 31 VCLT states that provisions in international agreements should be interpreted 'in good faith in accordance with the ordinary meaning to be given to the terms of the treaty in their context and in the light of its object and purpose'. Moreover, subsequent agreements and practices relating to the interpretation of the treaty and any relevant rules of international law applicable in the relations between the parties shall also be taken into account, together with the context.[567] Hence, a panel or the Appellate Body can consider non-WTO agreements to interpret provisions in the WTO Agreements. Nevertheless, these agreements must, at least implicitly,[568] be approved by *all* WTO members (and not solely by the parties to a dispute).[569] The principles and standards of the Basel Committee are clearly not approved by all WTO members. Even after its enlargement, the Committee consists of representatives of only twenty-seven countries.[570]

566 Vienna Convention on the Law of Treaties, done at Vienna on 23 May 1969, *UNTS* no. 18232. See the references in Appellate Body Report, *US – Gasoline*, p. 15; and in Appellate Body Report, *Japan – Alcoholic Beverages II*, pp. 9–10.

567 Art. 31.3 VCLT. The International Court of Justice has recognized repeatedly that Art. 31 VCLT reflects customary international law. See *Case Concerning the Territorial Dispute (Libyan Arab Jamahiriya/Chad)*, Judgment, [1994] ICJ Rep. 21, para. 41; *Case Concerning Oil Platforms (Islamic Republic of Iran/United States of America)*, Preliminary Objections, Judgment, [1996] (II) ICJ Rep. 812, para. 23; and, specifically on Art. 31.3, *Case Concerning Kasikili/Sedudu Island*, Judgment, [1994] ICJ Rep. 1045, para. 48.

568 The fact that the International Law Commission decided to change the phrase 'subsequent practice . . . of *all* the parties' into 'subsequent practice . . . of the parties' does not mean that it is not necessary that all parties should have accepted the practice. It only meant to indicate that it was sufficient that the states had accepted the principles and that it is not essential that each and every state has explicitly followed the principles in practice. The adherence of the state to the principles that are laid down in a certain international instrument can be presumed by the absence of a reaction by this state. Cf. M. K. Yasseen, 'L'interprétation des traités d'après la Convention de Vienne sur le droit des traités', (1976-III) 149 *Rec. des Cours*, at 49. Thus only if a WTO member has explicitly stated disagreement with the principles laid down in the international instrument would it be unacceptable to use the instrument as a tool for interpreting WTO provisions.

569 GATT Panel Report, *US – Tuna (EEC)*; Panel Report, *Canada – Patent Protection of Pharmaceutical Products*, WT/DS114/R, adopted 7 April 2000, para. 4.31. This was confirmed in Panel Report, *EC – Approval and Marketing of Biotech Products*, paras 7.70–7.72.

570 See also R. Bismuth, 'Financial Sector Regulation and Financial Services Liberalization at the Crossroads: The Relevance of International Financial Standards in WTO Law', (2010) 44 *Journal of World Trade* 489, at 501–2.

440. Nevertheless, other WTO case law still leaves open the possibility of using the Basel principles as a tool for interpretation of WTO law. In the *EC – Biotech* case, the panel noted that rules of international law which were *not* applicable to the relations between all WTO members could still be used for interpreting the terms of the WTO Agreements in order to define their 'ordinary meaning'. However, these instruments would then not be considered as legal rules, but would provide evidence of the 'ordinary meaning' of terms in WTO Agreements in the same way as dictionaries, and be considered because of their 'informative character'.[571]

441. That does not mean that the member is obliged to use the international standard or that it cannot impose a measure that is more restrictive than the international standard (after all, these international standards are only minimum standards). Still, in that case, the WTO member may find it more challenging to show that the measure is not used 'as a means of avoiding the Member's commitments or obligations under the [GATS]'. (See further below, paras. 462–468.)

8.5.4 Non-discriminatory measures and the Understanding on Commitments in Financial Services

442. Section B.10 of the Understanding on Commitments in Financial Services requires WTO members that make commitments with reference to the Understanding to 'endeavour' to 'remove or limit any significant adverse effects on financial service suppliers of any other Member of [four specific types of measures]'. The Understanding places this section under the heading 'Market Access'. These measures can restrict market access, but are not necessarily of the type listed in Article XVI:2. They do not concern measures that explicitly impose numerical quotas. However, if they were to amount to an absolute prohibition on providing financial services in a sector or in a mode of supply, they would violate Article XVI (see above, paras. 249–261). Since this is not necessarily so, it is appropriate to discuss these market access limitations under the present section on domestic regulation.

443. The fact that section B.10 indicates that members shall 'endeavour' to remove or limit the adverse effects of the specified measures indicates

[571] Art. 31.1 VCLT. Panel Report, *EC – Approval and Marketing of Biotech Products*, para. 7.92. However, in the end the panel did not apply this statement in practice.

that the WTO member probably has wide discretion whether or not to remove the measures in question. This is all the more the case because the provision is part of an Understanding that already constitutes an effort by those WTO members that wished so to liberalize their market for banking services beyond what is required in the framework agreement.

444. The first category of measures is 'non-discriminatory measures that prevent financial service suppliers from offering in the Member's territory, in the form determined by the Member, all the financial services permitted by the Member'. In a Background Note, the WTO Secretariat suggested that a measure that prohibits banks from engaging in non-banking activities (e.g. insurance or investment services) would be such measure.[572] In the present author's view, given the fact that section B.10(a) of the Understanding only involves a 'best effort' obligation, it does not stand in the way of introducing such a measure. The second category concerns 'non-discriminatory measures that limit the expansion of the activities of financial service suppliers into the entire territory of the Member'. The third category concerns 'measures of a Member, when such Member applies the same measures to the supply of both banking and securities services, and a financial service supplier of any other Member concentrates its activities in the provision of securities services'. Arguably, this encourages WTO members that allow financial institutions to combine banking and securities services, but also apply regulations that focus on a combination of both sets of activities, to consider whether they could exclude the application of the rules relating to banking services in the case where a foreign institution focuses solely on securities services. The application of the measures that relate to banking services may not be appropriate in that case. Finally, members must also endeavour to remove 'other measures that, although respecting the provisions of the Agreement, affect adversely the ability of financial service suppliers of any other Member to operate, compete or enter the Member's market'. This is clearly a very broad category.

445. Section B.10 indicates that it does not require members to exercise 'reverse discrimination'. Members are encouraged to remove or limit the effect of measures that fall into these categories, 'provided that any action

[572] Council for Trade in Services and Committee on Trade in Financial Services, Financial Services: Background, Note by the Secretariat, S/C/W/312 and S/FIN/W/73, 3 February 2010, at para. 45.

taken under this paragraph would not unfairly discriminate against financial service providers of the Member taking such action'.

446. Moreover, the market opportunities and the benefits already enjoyed by financial service suppliers of all other members as a class are in principle guaranteed. When a WTO member adopts a measure that fits in one of the first two categories of non-discriminatory measures, the member must endeavour not to limit the present degree of market opportunities and the benefits already enjoyed, provided that this does not result in unfair discrimination against domestic financial service suppliers of the member applying such measures.[573] Hence, besides removing them, WTO members should also avoid introducing *new* measures that are of the type described in section B.10(a) or (b).

8.5.5 Conclusion on domestic regulation

447. In this section we examined the current and future (possible) GATS disciplines that specifically address the normative content of domestic regulation in the banking sector. Even if a WTO member were to remove market access restrictions of the type listed in Article XVI:2, as well as all discriminatory measures that violate Article XVII, a bank from another WTO member might still be faced with barriers to trade. This is principally due to the fact that banking regulations differ from country to country.

448. Article VI:4 GATS provides a mandate for negotiating the disciplines on domestic regulation 'with a view to ensuring that measures relating to qualification requirements and procedures, technical standards and licensing requirements do not constitute unnecessary barriers to trade in services'. However, judging from the chairperson's draft text, it does not seem that the Horizontal Disciplines that are being prepared by the Working Party on Domestic Regulation will impose an important restraint on WTO members with regard to their right to regulate the market for banking services. Harmonization of banking regulation, reducing regulatory diversity, will need to take place outside the WTO, and even if there are some incentives to make use of international standards, there is no firm obligation in the GATS to rely on them.

449. However, as long as the Horizontal Disciplines on domestic regulation are not adopted, Article VI:5 applies and may still provide some

[573] Section B.11 Understanding.

restriction on the freedom of WTO members to determine the substantive content of banking regulation. This provision already imposes the main obligations announced in Article VI:4. It requires that measures relating to qualification requirements and procedures, technical standards and licensing requirements are based on objective and transparent criteria, are not more burdensome than necessary to ensure the quality of the services, and in the case of licensing procedures must not in themselves be a restriction on the supply of a service. Article VI:5 is thus arguably an important factor for regulators to consider. However, it only applies for new measures taken after the market access and national treatment commitments have been made by the member in question. Moreover, the complainant needs to prove that the measure at issue leads to nullification and impairment of the commitments that were made.

8.6 Prudential exception

8.6.1 Introduction

450. In the previous sections we examined the different obligations in the GATS that restrict the right of WTO members to regulate their market for banking services. The GATS obligations constitute a complex whole, with many nuances. There are clearly obligations that constitute important restrictions on the right to regulate, like Article XVI and XVII GATS. However, the exact extent of their impact much depends on how these obligations are interpreted. In any event, if a banking regulation by a WTO member were found to violate one of the obligations in the GATS, there is still a possibility that this member justifies its measure on the basis of a broad exception in the GATS, specifically designed for the financial sector: the prudential exception in paragraph 2(a) of the Annex on Financial Services.

451. The importance of prudential regulation in the field of financial services markets was acknowledged during the negotiations on the GATS Annex on Financial Services.[574] There was broad consensus that the specific nature of the financial services market (where a balance between efficiency and stability needs to be sought – see above, para. 134) required that WTO members should have sufficient leeway to adopt measures for prudential reasons. This right was considered so important by some states

[574] Working Group on Financial Services Including Insurance, Note on the Meeting of 11–13 June 1990, MTN.GNS/FIN/1, 5 July 1990, paras. 48–95.

that they wanted to exclude such measures entirely from dispute settlement.[575] Other negotiation parties, such as the European Communities (EC) and Canada, opposed this option, which 'appeared to allow almost an unlimited degree of regulatory abuse'.[576]

452. Eventually, the so-called 'prudential carve-out' was included in the Annex on Financial Services. As already indicated (above, para. 240), the commonly used term 'carve-out' is in fact misleading. Paragraph 2(a) of the Annex provides that notwithstanding any other provisions of the GATS, a member shall not be prevented from taking measures for prudential reasons. The fact that the paragraph starts with the phrase 'notwithstanding any other provisions in the GATS' indicates that it concerns an *exception* to the obligations in the GATS. Hence measures for prudential reasons are subject to the obligations, but if they were to violate an obligation, they could still be justified on the basis of this exception. Measures for prudential reasons are thus not 'carved out' of the scope of the GATS. However, this does not mean that the GATS should therefore be considered a threat to such measures. As will be discussed, paragraph 2(a) provides a very broad exception.

453. Given the objective of the GATS progressively to liberalize trade in services, the prudential exception cannot be a cloak for protectionist measures by the WTO members. However, the limits of the exception seem very vague.[577] First, there is no definition of 'prudential' to determine whether a measure is in fact for 'prudential reasons'. Second, the final sentence of paragraph 2(a) states, 'Where such measures do not conform with the provisions of the Agreement, they shall not be used as a means of avoiding the Member's commitments or obligations under the Agreement.' We discuss these two elements in turn.

8.6.2 Measures for prudential reasons

454. The prudential exception in paragraph 2(a) of the GATS Annex on Financial Services does not define the concept 'prudential'. It only provides a non-exhaustive list of examples of measures for prudential

575 Working Group on Financial Services Including Insurance, Communication from the Delegation of Malaysia, MTN.GNS/FIN/W/3, 12 September 1990, p. 7.

576 Working Group on Financial Services Including Insurance, Note on the Meeting of 13–15 September 1990, MTN.GNS/FIN/3, 16 October 1990, paras. 12 and 15.

577 Gkoutzinis argues that 'the rivalry between regulation and liberalization was settled in favor of the regulatory status quo'. Gkoutzinis, above n. 143, at 902.

reasons. These include measures 'for the protection of investors, depositors, policy holders or persons to whom a fiduciary duty is owed by a financial service supplier, or to ensure the integrity and stability of the financial system'. One is left to speculate what other reasons a member might invoke to justify its measure can in fact be considered 'prudential' reasons.

455. The vagueness seems to have been intended by the negotiators. They felt that it was not desirable further to specify and define what should be considered 'prudential' and what not. Only when the prudential exception provided a sufficiently wide 'escape route' were WTO members willing to make liberalization commitments for financial services. Nevertheless, the opposite result seems to have been achieved. In the current Doha Round, many WTO members (especially developing countries) have been hesitant to make further commitments for the financial sector. One of the reasons is that they do not know how wide this exception in fact is and thus how much the GATS nevertheless constrains WTO members to adopt prudential measures. Kono and Yokoi-Arai have argued that an inventory of allegedly prudential measures would seriously increase transparency.[578]

456. A suggestion by Australia that the meaning of 'prudential' be clarified received a mixed response from the other WTO members. The EU, for instance, agreed that it was useful to discuss the subject but that it was too ambitious to develop a definition.[579] Japan stated that 'Members should be cautious in embarking on a discussion that might limit the right of each Member to take regulatory measures for prudential reasons in an appropriate and timely manner'.[580]

457. Definitions in literature mostly limit themselves to providing examples of prudential measures.[581] In Part I we noted that it is very

[578] M. Kono and M. Yokoi-Arai, 'Dissecting Regional Integration in Financial Services from the Competition Policy and Trade Policy Perspectives', BIS Paper No. 42, October 2008, available at www.bis.org/publ/bppdf/bispap42c.pdf, 108. They also refer to the FSAP of the IMF, but note that it is too analytical and does not give a clear overview of the applicable measures.

[579] Committee on Trade in Financial Services, Report of the Meeting Held on 25 May 2000, S/FIN/M/26, 29 June 2000, paras. 21–34.

[580] Council for Trade in Financial Services Special Session, Report of the Meeting held on 3–6 December 2001, S/CSS/M/13, 26 February 2002, para. 267.

[581] For an overview see Panourgias, above n. 1, at 11–15. See also Cranston, above n. 61, at 65–81; and R. Lastra, *Legal Foundations of International Monetary Stability* (Oxford University Press, 2006) 83–90, 92–6.

difficult to define the concept of 'prudential'. Paragraph 2(a) of the Annex sets out that members can adopt measures *for prudential reasons.* Hence the approach that has been taken is to delineate the measures that are exempted by reference to the *objective* that is pursued. We concluded in Part I that a measure is taken for prudential reasons if it pursues financial stability. When banks go bankrupt, private costs are imposed on the individual depositors of the bank and, if the bank in question is 'systemically important', contagion may occur and financial stability will be endangered. Eventually the real economy may be affected. The primary goal of government regulation in the banking sector is therefore to avoid banks going bankrupt.

458. However, such a functional approach could be over-inclusive. Almost any type of regulation in the banking sector may somehow contribute to the objective of financial stability. Besides examples of rules that are traditionally given as examples of prudential regulation, such as rules on capital adequacy requirements of banks and exposure limits, rules of consumer protection law protect consumers against banks exploiting their weak position. Anti-fraud regulation avoids insiders and outsiders of a bank abusing the banking system through illegal activities. To be sure, these types of regulation may contribute to the goal of avoiding banks going bankrupt and thus to financial stability. Very serious fraud may put banks in difficulties. Abuse of consumers may reduce trust in the bank system. It remains to be seen where a panel will draw the line between measures that are prudential and those that are not. Arguably, a panel will be very hesitant to state that a measure is not for 'prudential reasons', even when a member argues that it is.

459. The problem becomes even more delicate when a WTO member takes measures in a situation that it considers to be crisis circumstances. In the case of such 'protective' measures (e.g. emergency support for one or more failing banks), the question will be whether the failure of such bank(s) in fact threatens financial stability. If, for instance, a measure provides for emergency support to a relatively small bank that threatens to go bankrupt because of mismanagement, without there being major linkages with the financial industry in general, it is questionable whether such measure should be considered for prudential reasons.[582] The failure of weak banks is an inherent aspect of competition. What is more, saving

[582] The major GATS obligation that may be violated in the case of emergency support for failing banks is the obligation of national treatment. For a discussion of the role of the

small institutions may increase 'moral hazard' since other banks see that they will be saved, even if they engage in excessively risky activities. Nonetheless, except for very clear situations where financial stability is not threatened (e.g. a failure of a small bank to which only a few other institutions are exposed), it is again questionable whether a panel would be willing to conclude that the protective measure is not for prudential reasons.

460. To be sure, paragraph 4 of the GATS Annex on Financial Services requires that, for disputes on prudential issues and on financial matters, the panels need to have sufficient expertise with respect to the financial service under dispute. There is thus some guarantee that the panel will be sufficiently aware of the specific concerns that underlie financial regulation. Nonetheless, in the present author's view, a panel will rarely conclude that a measure is not for prudential reasons. If a panel does draw limits, it will rather be through the second analytical step in the application of the prudential exception.[583]

461. In Part I of this book we saw that many economists considered that 'appropriate' prudential regulation is regulation that is based on market discipline: rather than determining the structure of the banking services market or specifying the conduct a bank is required to take, regulation should ensure that the market provides incentives to banks to behave prudentially and should facilitate this provision. Measures that distort market discipline (e.g. financial support to banks in financial difficulties because of their own excessively risky behaviour) in fact detract from financial stability and thus should not be considered 'prudential'. According to certain authors, the existence of a government 'safety net' in fact provides exactly the opposite incentives to banks rather than to induce prudent behaviour: because the banks know the government will intervene when their risky behaviour turns bad, they feel fewer incentives to engage in prudent conduct (so-called 'moral hazard'). The existence of protective regulation in fact provides, then, the rationale

GATS with regard to state aid that has been provided to banks during the global financial crisis, see B. De Meester, 'The Global Financial Crisis and Government Support for Banks: What Role for the GATS?', (2010) 13 *Journal of International Economic Law* 27.

[583] Note that Paragraph 4 of the GATS Annex on Financial Services requires that for disputes on prudential issues and on financial matters, the panels need to have sufficient expertise with respect to the financial service under dispute. There is thus some guarantee that the panel will be sufficiently aware of the specific concerns that underlie financial regulation.

for prudential regulation.[584] However, when considering this argument with the structure of the prudential exception in mind, this is an issue on the 'appropriateness' of the measure that is taken for prudential reasons rather than on the question whether the measure is prudential or not. This might need to be assessed under the second step of the test.

8.6.3 Measures cannot be used to avoid commitments

462. Paragraph 2(a) GATS Annex on Financial Services indicates at the end: 'Where such measures do not conform with the provisions of the Agreement, they shall not be used as a means of avoiding the Member's commitments or obligations under the Agreement.' Hence measures that violate one of the obligations in the GATS, but benefit from the prudential exception because they are taken for prudential reasons, must still not be used to avoid the commitments and obligations in the GATS. Would this mean that as soon as a support measure that is 'taken for prudential reasons' violates an obligation in the GATS, the measure cannot be adopted?[585] This cannot be correct. The last sentence of the exception starts from the premise that some prudential measures do not conform to the GATS obligations. If such a measure violates one of the GATS obligations, it can be maintained (and thus is exempted from the obligation) *provided* that it is not used as a means of avoiding the member's commitments and obligations under the GATS.

463. It is important to note that, contrary to the 'general exceptions' provision in Article XIV GATS, the prudential exception does not

[584] See, e.g., Benston, above n. 32, at 45. See also F. Mishkin, 'Prudential Supervision: Why is it Important and What Are the Issues?', in Mishkin, above n. 10, 1–29, at 8. However, Mishkin argues further that there is a case for government regulation to reduce risk taking by banks 'even without the presence of a government safety net such as deposit insurance'. He nevertheless adds: 'the need for restrictions on risky activities is even greater when there is a government safety net which increases the incentives for risky behavior'. Mishkin, this note, at 8–9.

[585] Gkoutzinis has argued that 'if a measure is taken for genuine prudential reasons, the measure is not caught by the GATS commitments unless the measure breaches one of the fundamental GATS disciplines'. Gkoutzinis, above n. 143, at 903. However, in the present author's opinion, the last sentence of the prudential carve-out should not be read as reinstating the relevant GATS obligation. This would be a circular reasoning: if a measure breaches a GATS obligation, it is nevertheless exempted from this obligation because it is prudential. However, if such prudential measure breaches a GATS obligation, it is still subject to it! The test applied to prudential measures that are normally exempted from the GATS should be of a different nature from the one applied in the first assessment whether a measure breaches a GATS obligation in the first place.

require that the measures taken for prudential reasons are 'necessary' to achieve the prudential objective. Hence there is thus no 'necessity test' in the prudential exception that involves a consideration by panels whether there exist less trade-restrictive alternative measures that are reasonably available and that are able to achieve the prudential objective.

464. The requirement in the prudential exception that the measures must not be used to avoid commitments and obligations in the GATS involves a different type of test. This test can be compared to the test applied in the introductory paragraph (the so-called 'chapeau') of the 'general exception' provisions in the GATT and the GATS.[586] This paragraph reads,

> Subject to the requirement that such measures are not applied in a manner which would constitute a means of arbitrary or unjustifiable discrimination between countries where like conditions prevail, or a disguised restriction on trade [in goods or services], nothing in this Agreement shall be construed to prevent the adoption or enforcement by any Member of measures [that pursue one of the objectives listed in the subparagraphs of the Article].

It would be odd to have a provision that provides an exception from one of the obligations (like, for example, the prohibition against discrimination) and then to require again that the obligation of non-discrimination must still be complied with. The Appellate Body has stated that 'the chapeau serves to ensure that Members' rights to avail themselves of exceptions are exercised reasonably, so as not to frustrate the rights accorded to other Members by the substantive rules of the GATS'.[587] The chapeau is in fact

> but one expression of the principle of good faith. This principle, at once a general principle of law and a general principle of international law, controls the exercise of rights by states. One application of this general principle, the application widely known as the doctrine of *abus de droit*, prohibits the abusive exercise of a state's rights . . .[588]

[586] Art. XX GATT and Art. XIV GATS.

[587] Appellate Body Report, *US – Gambling*, at para. 339, referring to the original statement of the Appellate Body with regard to the Chapeau of Art. XX GATT in Appellate Body Report, *US – Gasoline*, at p. 22.

[588] Appellate Body Report, *United States – Import Prohibition of Certain Shrimp and Shrimp Products* (*US – Shrimp*), WT/DS58/AB/R, adopted 6 November 1998, para. 158. See also E. Leroux, 'Trade in Financial Services under the World Trade Organization', (2002) 36 *Journal of World Trade* 413, at 431.

465. While the text of the second sentence of paragraph 2(a) of the Annex and of the chapeau of the general exception provision is not exactly the same, the mentioning of 'avoiding' in the Annex shows that the underlying rationale is in fact the same.[589] Both phrases seek to prevent WTO members abusing their rights under the exception in order to pursue protectionist objectives.

466. The test applied is thus an enquiry into whether the measure in question is *genuinely* for prudential reasons or is, rather, for protectionist reasons – that is, to avoid commitments and obligations. This means that a measure taken for prudential reasons can be discriminatory, provided it has a *rational relationship* with the prudential goal. In order to assess whether a measure is for prudential reasons rather than pursuing protectionist objectives, it can be argued that this test may involve an examination of whether the means is reasonably able to achieve the

[589] The EC submitted in July 1990 a proposal for a draft Annex on Financial Services. Communication from the European Communities, Proposal by the European Community Draft Financial Services Annex, MTN.GNS/FIN/W/1, 10 July 1990. Art. 13.1 of this draft, relating to domestic regulation, read: 'Notwithstanding any other provisions of the Agreement and of this Annex, in order to prevent or to solve a serious economic or financial disturbance, parties may take reasonable measures to safeguard the integrity of the financial system, provided that these measures are not applied in a manner which would constitute a means of arbitrary or unjustifiable discrimination against financial services providers of other parties.' Largely the same wording as in the Chapeau of the general exception provisions in the GATT and GATS was used. The EC clarified during the preparations of the Annex on Financial Services that 'Article 13 on domestic regulation represented an extension of article V of MTN.GNS/W/105 and spelled out the public policy considerations which had to be taken into account in the financial services area, such as the need to ensure an appropriate supervision of the activities of financial institutions, the need to protect depositors, investors and policy holders, the need to secure monetary policy objectives, etc. The EC delegation chose not to draw up a list of public policy considerations strictly for practical reasons; any such list might raise more problems than it solved. The right of authorities to regulate and supervise financial markets and institutions should not be challenged but had nonetheless to be *exercised* in accordance with the provisions of the agreement and should not result in a denial of market access on arbitrary grounds' (emphasis added). Working Group on Financial Services Including Insurance, Note on the Meeting of 12–13 July 1990, MTN.GNS/FIN/2, 10 August 1990, para. 18. The focus was thus rather on compliance with the GATS obligations in the *exercise* of the right to adopt prudential measures rather than on compliance in the measures themselves. While the text of the draft was not maintained in the final, adopted version of the Annex, it is arguable that the same rationale still underlies this provision: it seeks to avoid WTO members abusing the exception for protectionist reasons. There is thus some parallel with the Chapeau to Art. XX GATT and Art. XIV GATS.

end (prudential objective).[590] If a measure is not able to achieve the prudential objective at all, the measure does not comply with the second step in the test.

467. Arguably, such would be the case for emergency support provided by a government in circumstances of a financial crisis but for which only domestically owned banks would be eligible. In such a situation, if foreign-owned banks that are active in the market and are of an equal systemic importance are excluded from the support, the measure is not genuinely contributing to financial stability, but is protectionist. One may wonder whether a similar analysis could be made regarding measures that create moral hazard. Rather than achieving the prudential goal, measures that create moral hazard in fact contribute to further financial instability. It is very questionable, however, that a WTO panel will accept such an analysis. Even if for disputes relating to financial services, the panel members should have specific expertise with regard to the financial sector at issue, it is, in the present author's view, unlikely that a panel will decide that a measure that creates moral hazard is not justified under the 'prudential exception'. As may be clear from the discussion in Part I, economists disagree about the importance of moral hazard and certainly whether the risk of creating moral hazard outweighs the risk (and costs) of financial crises. It will thus be essential for a complainant to show in a convincing manner that protectionism is actually motivating the design of the measure. If not, a panel will arguably not take the risk of concluding that a measure is not saved by the prudential exception. Except for (arguably exceptional) situations where a measure is clearly not able to contribute to financial stability at all, in other situations the complainant may need to find in, for example, legislative history actual evidence of protectionist reasons motivating the measure.

468. A complainant could also argue that the member has applied measures that are stricter than what is provided in international standards, for instance those elaborated by the Basel Committee. In the complainant's argument, this would then be an indication that the member is not just pursuing a prudential objective. However, such an

[590] J. Trachtman, 'Transatlantic Regulatory Cooperation from a Trade Perspective: A Case Study in Accounting Standards', in G. Bermann (ed.), *Transatlantic Regulatory Cooperation: Legal Problems and Political Prospects* (Oxford University Press, 2000) 223–42, at 237. See also Von Bogdandy and Windsor, above n. 156, who state that the carve-out cannot permit 'measures that are purely or primarily protectionist *in effect*' (635–6).

argument is far from evident. The international standards are by definition minimum standards. What is more, the recent global financial crisis has clearly shown that regulators may make important mistakes in their regulatory set-up, with disastrous consequences. Therefore, a panel should not lightly consider that a member that has chosen to apply stricter standards is in fact protecting its own industry.

8.6.4 Conclusion on the prudential exception

469. If a complainant were able to prove that a measure by a WTO member regulating the market for banking services violates one of the GATS obligations, the great majority of the measures in this sector will still be justified under the 'prudential exception' in paragraph 2(a) of the GATS Annex on Financial Services. There exists much uncertainty with regard to this provision, which in fact seems to be intended. However, the uncertainty appears to be an element hampering a discussion on the impact of the GATS on the right of members to undertake measures in pursuit of financial stability. Moreover, it seems to hold back developing country members from making further commitments in the financial sector.

470. As explained in this section, paragraph 2(a) provides an *exception* to the obligations of the GATS, but does not 'carve out' measures taken for prudential reasons from the scope of the GATS. In order to be able to rely on the exception, the defendant has to prove two elements. First, the defendant has to prove that the measure is for prudential reasons. This allows for a broad range of measures to be justified, provided that it is shown that the measure pursues *financial stability*. A panel will be very hesitant to conclude that a measure does not pursue financial stability even though a defendant claims that it does. Certain economic literature may point to a more restrictive approach to the definition of 'prudential', since it considers that only regulation that is based on market discipline must be considered prudential. Regulation that distorts market discipline is not of such a type. However, in the present author's opinion, such an approach to the definition of prudential might rather play a role in the second element of the exception.

471. Indeed, the second element a defendant must show is that the measure, even if taken for prudential reasons, is not used to avoid commitments under the GATS. This second element seeks to prevent WTO members abusing their right under the exception in order to pursue protectionist objective. Therefore the measure must have a rational relationship with the prudential goal. If a measure is not reasonably able to achieve financial stability in any way, the measure does not comply with this condition. Clearly, the argument that a certain measure distorts market discipline may arise here. Nonetheless, a panel may likely not take the risk of concluding that a measure distorts market discipline and thus is not appropriate. As argued, the global financial crisis seriously calls into question the economic arguments in favour of banking regulation that is solely based on market discipline. Therefore, except in exceptional situations where it is clear that a measure does not contribute to financial stability at all, the party claiming that the defendant is abusing its rights under the prudential exception will need to advance clear evidence of protectionist reasons underlying the measure. Therefore the right to regulate seems very strongly safeguarded under the GATS.

9

Limitations on the right of WTO members to supervise the banking sector

9.1 Introduction

472. In Chapter 8 we examined to what extent the GATS, in pursuing progressive liberalization of trade in services, restricts the leeway WTO members have in deciding how to *regulate* the market for banking services. We found that the obligations and exceptions in the GATS find a balance that tends to leave much leeway to members (because of the built-in flexibilities and a broad prudential exception), while disciplining only the most blatant protectionist measures. Even if some obligations are or may be interpreted in a manner that restricts the right to regulate in a manner that must not be underestimated (more particularly the obligation of market access in Article XVI GATS, the prohibition of discrimination in Articles II and XVII, and the future requirement in the disciplines on domestic regulation that measures of domestic regulation must be 'relevant'), the existence of a broad 'prudential exception' will safeguard many measures taken in the banking sector.

473. A further question remains, however, namely how individual supervisory assessments will be dealt with under the GATS. Besides general regulations in the banking sector, the supervisory assessment of the characteristics and conduct of a (candidate) supplier of banking services plays an essential role in the banking sector. It involves the application of the general requirements and criteria (e.g. 'sound and prudent management') laid down in the banking regulations. The question addressed here is to what extent the GATS limits banking supervisors in the WTO members in making such supervisory assessments.

474. It is useful to recall that the Basel Concordat[591] and the Basel Committee's Minimum Standards for the Supervision of International

[591] Basel Committee on Banking Supervision, Principles for the Supervision of Bank's Foreign Establishments, Bank for International Settlements, May 1983, especially Section III, available at www.bis.org/publ/bcbsc312.pdf.

Banking Groups[592] have recommended that the home supervisor of a banking group is responsible for the consolidated supervision over the banking group,[593] but at the same time stressed that *host* supervisors should be careful when allowing a foreign bank to expand activities in the host territory. To this end, the host supervisor should consider the strength of the capital of the bank, the appropriateness of the risk management in place and the adequacy of the prudential framework and supervision in the home country. It also needs to be reminded that these Basel principles are merely recommendations. Hence, in contrast to what is the case in EU law, at the international level there is no firm principle of home country control.

475. In this chapter we consider whether the provisions in the GATS nevertheless restrict the right of host supervisors to make supervisory assessments. It will be explained that such measures fall within the scope of the GATS, but that it is not easy to assess such individual measures under the Agreement. Still, it is not unthinkable that aspects of supervisory assessments will be considered under the GATS.

9.2 Individual supervisory assessments falling within the scope of the GATS

9.2.1 'Measures' within the scope of application of the GATS

476. Individual supervisory assessments by a banking supervisor in a WTO member fall clearly within the scope of the GATS. Article I:1 GATS indicates that the Agreement 'applies to measures by Members affecting trade in services', and paragraph 1.1(a) of the Annex on Financial Services indicates that it applies to 'measures affecting the supply of financial services'. In turn, Article XXVII(a) GATS defines 'measure' as 'any measure by a Member, whether in the form of a law, regulation, rule, procedure, decision, administrative action, or any other form'. Arguably, assessments by the banking supervisor can be considered 'decisions' or 'administrative action'.

477. As explained in Chapter 8 (above, para. 209), these supervisory assessments most often involve the application of general measures.

[592] Basel Committee on Banking Supervision, Minimum Standards for the Supervision of International Banking Groups and Their Cross-Border Establishments, Bank for International Settlements, July 1992, available at www.bis.org/publ/bcbsc314.pdf.

[593] Minimum Standard 1.

Therefore they can provide *evidence* to show that a general measure 'as applied' violates one of the obligations in the GATS. If the supervisory assessments do not involve an application of a general rule, a complainant may seek to establish that several supervisory assessment decisions together constitute a 'practice' (originating with the government of a WTO member, having a sufficiently precise content and having a prospective application) that can be challenged 'as such'. Such challenges were considered in Chapter 8, where the extent to which the GATS restricts WTO members in *regulating* their market for banking services was examined. However, it is also possible that a WTO member challenges certain aspects of a specific decision (supervisory assessment) by a supervisor of another WTO member in an individual case.

478. Administrative decisions, defined as 'determinations by an administrative agency in relation to a specific factual situation', have been challenged before 'as such', be it that it concerned mostly challenges against determinations in the application of trade remedies (antidumping, safeguards or countervailing duties).[594] It seems that individual judicial decisions are also challengeable 'as such' before the WTO.[595] For the application of the GATS, a measure may take the form of a decision.[596] However, such challenges against an individual supervisory decision 'as such' may not always be evident.

479. The ease of making such a claim will depend on the GATS obligation at stake. Until now, no individual administrative decisions have been successfully challenged on the ground that they violate the obligation of most-favoured-nation treatment, market access or national treatment.[597] As indicated in section 9.4, the challenge of an individual

[594] Yanovich and Voon, above n. 264, at 142.

[595] Ibid., at 144–5. In *US – Gambling* Antigua also tried to challenge three court cases as a violation of the GATS. While referring to some ambiguity in the statements of Antigua, the panel concluded that Antigua was in fact not challenging the specific applications of the laws (e.g. in the court decisions), but that these applications could show how the legislative measures that were challenged in fact violated the GATS. Panel Report, *US – Gambling*, para. 6.191–6.192. In *Brazil – Retreaded Tyres*, a number of relevant court injunctions were not considered by the panel to be separate measures, but rather as part of the manner in which an import ban was applied, when assessing this ban under the chapeau of Art. XX GATT. Panel Report, *Brazil – Measures Affecting Imports of Retreaded Tyres* (*Brazil – Retreaded Tyres*), WT/DS332/R, adopted 17 December 2007, as modified by Appellate Body Report, WT/DS332/AB/R, para. 7.107.

[596] Art. XXVIII (a) GATS.

[597] In *US – Gambling*, Antigua also tried to challenge examples of enforcement action of different US federal and state laws that prohibited online gambling, as well as three

decision may not be self-evident when the claim concerns a provision that prohibits discrimination. Making an assessment of whether the individual application of a measure is discriminatory may often be very difficult. There may be several considerations at stake when, for example, supervisory authorities make a decision on an individual application for a banking licence. A comparison with 'like' cases to determine whether there is discrimination will be difficult in this instance. Still, in relation to Article III:4 GATT (containing the national treatment obligation for trade in goods), the GATT panel in *Canada – FIRA* has already stated that 'in judging whether a measure is contrary to the obligations under Article III:4, it is not relevant whether it applies across the board or only in isolated cases'. The panel noted unambiguously that 'any interpretation which would exclude case-by-case action would . . . defeat the purposes of Article III:4'.[598] Individual decisions would then fall under the concept of 'requirements' in Article III:4.[599] However, even though these statements seem to confirm the possibility of challenging individual cases under a discrimination provision, what the United States was actually challenging was the administration of (or 'practice' under) the Foreign Investment Review Act.[600] Therefore, in order to establish that a measure 'as applied' leads to discrimination, a complainant may need to provide proof of a series of individual decisions that apply the measure in a discriminatory fashion.

480. Still, there are other provisions in the GATS that are not based on discrimination. First, Article XVI on market access has been interpreted in *US – Gambling* as prohibiting members from taking measures that 'amount to' a zero quota. It will be examined whether this provision applies also to situations where the market access of just one foreign bank or banking service is restricted. We shall see that individual

court cases. However, it turned out that Antigua was 'not able to point to any specific rejection of its request for a licence to provide cross-border supply of gambling and betting services, despite having effectively asserted as much in its first written submission and first oral statement'. Panel Report, *US – Gambling*, para. 6.191. It appeared to the panel that 'Antigua [was] challenging laws together with related practices rather than specific applications of the relevant laws'. Ibid., para. 6.192.

598 GATT Panel Report, *Canada – Administration of the Foreign Investment Review Act* (*Canada – FIRA*), L/5504, adopted 7 February 1984, BISD 30S/140, para. 5.5. On the possibility of applying GATT regimes to individual decisions by competition authorities, see C.-D. Ehlerman and L. Ehring, 'WTO Dispute Settlement and Competition Law: Views from the Perspective of the Appellate Body's Experience', (2003) 26 *Fordham International Law Journal* 1505, at 1526–32.

599 Ibid., para. 5.4. 600 Ibid., para. 1.1.

decisions (supervisory assessments) can generally not be seen independently from the general criteria that they apply. Hence the challenge is in fact against the general criteria 'as such'. If these criteria can be qualified as market access restrictions, they need to be removed. Only in the exceptional situation where a supervisory authority were to make an ad hoc decision to impose a measure that 'amounts to' a market access restriction, would the challenge be made against the individual decision 'as such'.

481. Further, when considering an individual decision, the lack of the 'reasonable, objective or impartial' administration of a general measure in that instance may amount to a violation of Article VI:1 GATS. Also, the future disciplines on domestic regulation may include relevant obligations. In this case, the distinction between the 'as such' and 'as applied' claim becomes blurred. A complainant challenges the general measure 'as applied' in this specific case. However, what it seeks to achieve is the removal and future non-application of a certain procedural practice. It thus seems to challenge the administration 'as such'. The complainant challenges the manner in which a decision was reached (i.e. the *process*).

9.2.2 Do the obligations in the GATS grant rights to individual service suppliers?

482. A crucial issue to consider when examining the application of the GATS to individual decisions by banking supervisors is to what extent the obligations in the GATS seek to guarantee the *individual* right of a service supplier to trade and thus to deploy activities in another WTO member. In other words, should the difficulties a specific bank experiences when seeking access to the market of another WTO member or when operating in this member state already gives rise to a violation of one of the applicable provision of the GATS? When one considers the impact on a specific bank of supervisory assessments made by competent host country authorities with regard to the application for an authorization (bank licence) or with regard to the operations of this bank, once established in the host country, the comparable situation of the protection of investors under international investment law may spring to mind.

483. Relatively recently, authors have started to pay attention to the overlap between international investment law and international trade law relating to services.[601] States attract and protect investment by means of bilateral investment treaties (BITs). By means of such BITs, a state agrees to grant the investors of another state certain treatment (especially most-favoured-nation treatment, national treatment and fair and equitable treatment, but also a right to investor-state dispute settlement and guarantees against unlawful expropriation).[602] The overlap with the GATS lies in the fact that services provision by means of Mode 3 (commercial presence) may be achieved, according to Article XXVIII(d) GATS, by setting up 'any type of business or professional establishment, including through (i) the constitution, acquisition or maintenance of a juridical person, or (ii) the creation or maintenance of a branch or representative office'. It thus covers 'greenfield' investment, but also the acquisition of a controlling interest in an existing company in the host country.[603] National measures that regulate minority participations thus do not fall within the scope of the GATS if they do not result in an

601 See, for instance, R. Adlung and M. Molinuevo, 'Bilateralism in Services Trade: Is There Fire behind the (BIT-)Smoke?', (2008) 11 *Journal of International Economic Law* 365; N. DiMascio and J. Pauwelyn, 'Non-discrimination in Trade and Investment Treaties: Worlds Apart or Two Sides of the Same Coin?', (2008) 102 *American Journal of International Law* 48; E. Sweeney Samuelson and S. Ebere, 'Could a Foreign Investor Use GATS Disciplines in a BIT Claim?', Harrison Institute for Public Law, Georgetown Law, Discussion Draft of 12 March 2010, on file with the author; J. Trachtman, 'FDI and the Right to Regulate: Lessons from Trade Law', in UNCTAD, The Development Dimensions of FDI and Rule-Making Perspectives, 189 UN Doc. UNCTAD/ITE/IIA/2003/4 (2003), at 189–204; and T. Weiler, 'NAFTA Article 1105 and the Principles of International Economic Law', (2003) 42 *Columbia Journal of Transnational Law* 35.

602 Note that the benefits of such BITs can be reciprocal, when each of the parties to a BIT have investors that invest in the other party. It is also interesting to note, in this respect, that the Treaty of Lisbon seems to give the EU exclusive competence with regard to international investment law. It is likely that the Commission will claim that it can now conclude BITs between the EU and third countries and that the individual member states no longer have this competence. However, it is not entirely clear how far this competence stretches. J. Wouters, D. Coppens and B. De Meester, 'The European Union's External Relations after the Lisbon Treaty', in S. Griller and J. Ziller (eds.), *The Lisbon Treaty. EU Constitutionalism without a Constitutional Treaty* (Vienna: Springer, 2008) 143–203, at 171–2; and see below paras. 674–677.

603 Art. XXVIII(m)(ii) GATS indicates that a 'commercial presence' by a 'juridical person of another Member' is a juridical person that is 'owned or controlled by' (natural or legal) persons of that member. A person from another WTO member does not necessarily need to have a majority stake in a company (that is a service supplier) to be able to *control* this service supplier. Art. XXVIII(n)(ii) indicates that a juridical person is 'controlled' 'if such persons have the power to name the majority of its directors or otherwise to legally direct its actions'. It is not entirely clear whether the foreign entity that acquires a service supplier in another WTO member and thereby provides services through Mode 3 (commercial presence) should already be a service supplier in the home

acquisition of a corporation and thus do not constitute a form of 'commercial presence'.[604] It is of course additionally required that the target corporation provides services.[605]

484. If the obligations in the GATS (inter alia MFN, market access, national treatment, Article VI and the future Disciplines on domestic regulation) apply to measures affecting certain investments, one may

country. In other words, does the GATS apply not only to measures affecting service suppliers creating a secondary establishment in another WTO member for the purpose of supplying a service, *but also* to entities creating a primary establishment in the host country? Art. I:2(c) GATS refers to service supply 'by a *service supplier from one Member*, through commercial presence in the territory of any other Member' (emphasis added). On the one hand, it is arguable that a corporation that is not yet supplying services in the home country is not a 'service supplier from another WTO member'; on the other hand, one could argue that the corporation becomes a service supplier at the moment of acquiring control over a supplier in the recipient country. For instance, a corporation from the United States that acquires control over a bank in the United Kingdom would become a service supplier that supplies a service from the home country of the corporation into the host country (United Kingdom) by means of a subsidiary (the bank in the United Kingdom). Nevertheless, Art. XXVIII(m)(ii)(2) in conjunction with Art. XXVIII(m)(i) indicates that the *juridical person* that is a business or professional establishment for supplying services through commercial presence must be owned and controlled by a juridical person of another member. The latter juridical person must be 'constituted or otherwise organized under the law of that other Member, and [be] engaged in substantive business operations in the territory of that Member or any other Member'. Therefore the acquiring corporation must already be performing 'substantive business operations'; if not, the acquired entity would not be owned by a foreign juridical person. However, these substantive business operations can probably be in any sector, and do not necessarily need to be in the same sector as the one in which the acquired entity is active. Moreover, the existing substantive business operations should not necessarily be performed in the home country of the owning or controlling entity, but can also be performed in another WTO member (i.e. other than the home country or the target country of investment). In contrast, for acquisitions by a *natural person* from another WTO member the GATS does not impose such a requirement for existing substantive business operations. Art. XXVIII(m)(ii)(1) GATS.

[604] A. Mattoo and A. Subramanian, 'Currency Undervaluation and Sovereign Wealth Funds: A New Role for the World Trade Organization', World Bank Policy Research Working Paper No. 4668, July 2008, at 14.

[605] During the discussions in the Working Group on the Relationship between Trade and Investment, a number of WTO members have expressed their view that GATS follows an 'enterprise-based' definition of investment. It was noted that 'the definition was closely linked to the mode 3 of service delivery (commercial presence) which, in the context of GATS, has no other purpose than to facilitate service supply'. Report (2002) of the Working Group on the Relationship between Trade and Investment to the General Council, WT/WGTI/6, 9 December 2002, para. 88; and P. Sauvé and C. Wilkie, 'Investment Liberalization in GATS', in P. Sauvé and R. Stern (eds.), *GATS 2000. New Directions in Services Trade Liberalization* (Washington, DC: Brookings Institution, 2000) 331–63, at 349.

wonder whether obligations imposed in BITs and in the GATS should be interpreted and applied in the same manner.

485. Several authors have stressed the different goals of international investment law and international trade law. For instance, Howse and Chalamish have argued that norms that are 'apparently common both to investor protection law and the multilateral trading system, such as National Treatment and Most-Favoured-Nation, are understood in a different contextual space when used in the investment law regime'. They state that the investment law regime is 'meant to further a variety of different interests, such as promoting the flow of capital and protection of foreign investment, which requires a different legal reasoning than the one used in the WTO adjudication process'.[606] Also Trachtman called for 'caution regarding any efforts to transplant constraints on domestic regulation from the field of international trade law to the field of foreign investment law'.[607] DiMascio and Pauwelyn have compared the objectives and political economy of trade and investment treaties. They argue that in the case of international trade agreements, 'governments exchange trade opportunities; they do not allocate individual rights to exporters'.[608] Hence, '[States] make this exchange not only, or even mainly, to benefit individual exporters, but rather to enable freer trade policies both at home and abroad in the nation's overall interest, including, most specifically, the interest of consumers.' In contrast, investment treaties would seek to attract investment by guaranteeing certain treatment of investors once present in the country.[609]

486. Nonetheless, one may wonder whether this is indeed the case for all obligations in the GATS. This argument may in fact only apply to provisions that prohibit discrimination (national treatment and most-favoured-nation treatment), since the application of such provisions seeks to guarantee equality of competitive opportunities and thus involve a comparison of the treatment of groups of services or service suppliers. For instance, in the case of national treatment, the fact that one or a few suppliers receive unfavourable treatment because of a certain measure should not necessarily mean that there is a violation of the obligation of

[606] R. Howse and E. Chalamish, 'The Use and Abuse of WTO Law in Investor-State Arbitration: A Reply to Jürgen Kurtz', (2009) 20 *European Journal of International Law* 1087, at 1090.

[607] Trachtman, 'FDI and the Right to Regulate: Lessons from Trade Law', above n. 601, at 193.

[608] DiMascio and Pauwelyn, above n. 601, at 54. [609] Ibid., at 54–5.

national treatment as long as there is no 'aggregate asymmetrical impact' of the measure to the disadvantage of services or service suppliers of a certain origin (see above, paras. 347–348). However, in the case of market access and the specific provisions on domestic regulation, no such comparison is made. Therefore these provisions may in fact seek to guarantee the competitive opportunities of each and every individual service supplier. In the next sections whether both the obligation on market access and the provisions on domestic regulation may be violated in the case of a supervisory decision affecting a single bank in an individual case will be examined more specifically.

487. Besides the question whether the obligations in the GATS are meant to guarantee the individual right of a service supplier to trade, a related issue is whether a WTO member will be willing to bring a case on behalf of one single service supplier experiencing difficulties. A major difference between international trade law and international investment law is that there is no right of private companies to bring a dispute before the WTO dispute settlement system and thus to challenge another member's measures. A company or private individual is thus dependent on the willingness of its government to bring a case before the WTO. Therefore, where an individual service supplier (e.g. a bank) experiences difficulties (e.g. it sees its market access rights denied) because of an individual decision made by another government (e.g. the supervisory assessment by the national banking supervisor of a planned acquisition of a domestic bank by this foreign person), this supplier will need to lobby its government to bring a case. For this reason (and also because the investment arbitration may give rise to monetary compensation that is unavailable in the WTO), the supplier may rather decide to start investment arbitration proceedings.

488. Nevertheless, this should not be an argument for not examining the possibility that individual supervisory assessments are challenged under the GATS rules. First, the *US – Gambling* dispute shows that individual companies are able to convince their government to bring a case against another WTO member. Second, the obligations in the GATS may provide opportunities that are not available in investment treaties. More specifically, investment treaties do not always include rights covering the treatment of investors in the *pre-establishment* phase and thus often only cover treatment of investors *once established.*[610] The obligations in the GATS do not

[610] Adlung and Molinuevo, above n. 601, at 371, 379.

make such distinction and thereby may provide tools for actual investment liberalization.

489. A third issue that needs to be taken into account when considering the application of obligations in the GATS to individual supervisory assessments is that WTO dispute settlement can only give rise to remedies that are prospective in nature. Article 19(1) of the Dispute Settlement Understanding indicates that a panel or the Appellate Body can only recommend a defending member to 'bring the measure into conformity' with the applicable WTO agreement. Hence the recommendation a panel can make in a WTO dispute will never be that the applicant must be granted a licence to provide a service (if this was refused before).[611] The recommendation can only be that the authorities of the WTO member in question no longer apply a measure that was

[611] It should be noted that, nonetheless, the implementation panel in *Australia – Automotive Leather II (Article 21.5 – US)* stated that the recommendation to withdraw a prohibited subsidy, based on Art. 4.7 of the Agreement on Subsidies and Countervailing Measures, encompassed in that case the obligation for Australia to require the recipient of the subsidy to repay the subsidy in full. (Note that the United States had argued that the repayment should be limited to the subsidies paid after the panel report was adopted, and thus not the entire amount of the subsidy paid.) Panel Report, *Australia – Subsidies Provided to Producers and Exporters of Automotive Leather, Recourse to Article 21.5 of the DSU by the United States*, WT/DS126/RW and Corr.1, adopted 11 February 2000, para. 6.48. However, this report was heavily criticized; see G. Goh and A. Ziegler, 'Retrospective Remedies in the WTO after Automotive Leather', (2003) 6 *Journal of International Economic Law* 545, at 547–8, 551–61; and P. Grane, 'Remedies under WTO Law', (2001) 4 *Journal of International Economic Law* 755, at 767–9. The panel in *Canada – Aircraft Credits and Guarantees* stated (referring to *Australia – Automotive Leather II (Article 21.5 – US)*): 'In our view, however, it is not entirely clear that the WTO dispute settlement system only provides for prospective remedies in cases involving prohibited export subsidies.' Panel Report, *Canada – Export Credits and Loan Guarantees for Regional Aircraft*, WT/DS222/R and Corr.1, adopted 19 February 2002, para. 7.170. Finally, it is interesting to note that the panel in *US – Cotton (Article 21.5)* found in that dispute no support for the argument that the obligation to withdraw a prohibited subsidy involves an obligation to withdraw or review subsidies that were granted in the past. (However, reference was made to the fact that Brazil itself argued that it did not believe that Art. 4.7 includes a retroactive remedy.) According to the panel, this implied that the obligation to withdraw a prohibited subsidy was not violated when the defending WTO member continued to make payments on the basis of outstanding guarantees found to be in violation of the SCM Agreement. What was prohibited was, rather, to grant *new* guarantees. This point was not appealed before the Appellate Body. Panel Report, *United States – Subsidies on Upland Cotton, Recourse to Article 21.5 of the DSU by Brazil*, WT/DS267/RW and Corr.1, adopted 20 June 2009, as modified by Appellate Body Report, WT/DS267/AB/RW, para. 14.38.

found to be a market access restriction,[612] no longer apply measures in a manner that is motivated by protectionist intent[613] or no longer apply the procedural aspects that were in violation of the GATS.[614] The bank that was faced with the decision may then introduce a new application for a decision (e.g. to obtain a licence). However, it has no guarantee that the decision will now be more favourable (e.g. that the licence will be granted).

9.2.3 Conclusion on the scope of the GATS and supervisory assessments

490. In sum, individual supervisory assessments or the application of general measures in individual cases are within the scope of the GATS. However, whether the GATS will actually restrict the right of WTO members to make their own supervisory assessments with regard to individual banks depends on how the obligations in the GATS would be applied in such instances. In the following analysis we shall first address the application of Article XVI GATS that prohibits restrictions to market access, next the GATS obligations that prohibit discriminatory measures, and finally the application of specific obligations relating to (the administration of) domestic regulation.

9.3 Market access and supervisory assessments

9.3.1 Article XVI and market access rights of individual service suppliers

491. As explained (above, paras. 244–306), in sectors where a member has made specific commitments, Article XVI prohibits the WTO member from taking measures that are of the type listed in Article XVI:2, unless the member has made a specific limitation for the measure at issue.

492. Arguably, an individual supervisory decision whereby the access of a service supplier to the market of another WTO member is refused amounts to a violation of Article XVI. Indeed, in the light of the decision

612 As indicated, the challenge here is against the measure 'as such', be it a measure of general application (a quota or an economic needs test) or an ad hoc measure (a specific decision requiring to set up a specific legal entity in the host country).

613 The challenge here is against the measure 'as applied' in a discriminatory manner.

614 The challenge here is against the measure 'as applied' or the administration 'as such'. The administration is not necessarily linked to content of the general measure.

by the panel and the Appellate Body in *US – Gambling*, one could conclude that the refusal by a banking supervisor to grant an authorization to supply banking services amounts for this individual applicant to a zero quota. The applicant sees its access to the market refused.

493. The essential question thus arises whether Article XVI covers a situation where an individual applicant from a certain WTO member sees its access to the market of the host member restricted, while this may be unrestricted for other applicants from the same WTO member. It can be noted that the text of Article XVI:1 GATS refers to the treatment of services and service suppliers in plural. Hence, it seems to guarantee market access of banks and banking services of a certain WTO member to another WTO member *in general* and not in individual cases. Nevertheless, this textual argument is not fully convincing. It is possible that there is only one or only a small number of banks present in one WTO member. If this single bank then seeks access to the market of another WTO member and this is refused, it is clearly not acceptable that it could be argued that Article XVI is not meant to give rights to individual suppliers. As argued (above, para. 486), contrary to the provisions that prohibit discrimination, the provision on market access does not involve a *comparison* of competitive opportunities.

9.3.2 Supervisory assessments and measures of the type listed in Article XVI:2

494. Nevertheless, the argument that the refusal of a bank licence 'amounts to a zero quota' may focus too much on the *outcome* of an assessment process and ignore the fact that the supervisory assessment involves in fact the *application* of more general criteria. Therefore one must rather consider whether the *criteria* on the basis of which the prudential assessment is made and thus on the basis of which the decision whether to grant a licence or not is made are measures of the type set out in Article XVI:2 GATS. This is also confirmed in the Scheduling Guidelines, which indicate: 'If approval procedures or licensing and qualification requirements contain any of the limitations specified in Article XVI, they should be scheduled as market access limitations'.[615] Such criteria could, for instance, be the consideration of

[615] Guidelines for the Scheduling of Specific Commitments under the General Agreement on Trade in Services (GATS), S/L/92 (28 March 2001), para. 10.

whether all of a limited number of licences have already been allocated, or whether the 'needs of the market' allow for a licence to be granted.

495. This argument applies equally to decisions whereby a candidate acquirer is not allowed to increase its shareholding in a domestic bank in the host member. While such decision *as such* imposes a limit on the participation of foreign capital by the specific foreign bank that is affected (Article XVI:2(f)), it should nevertheless be considered whether the decision is based on *criteria* that are measures within the scope of Article XVI:2. In principle, the bank is allowed to acquire shares, but subject to authorization granted on the basis of specific criteria. If the authorization is nevertheless based on criteria within the scope of Article XVI:2, they must be listed as limitations to the market access commitment. For instance, if the decision is based on the consideration of whether the acquisition does not surpass a certain absolute quantitative limit, this criterion must be listed as a limitation.

496. Finally, when a supervisory decision requires an applicant to set up a specific legal person as a condition for obtaining the licence, it could be argued that this constitutes a measure 'which restrict[s] or require[s] specific types of legal entity or joint venture through which a service supplier may supply a service' in the sense of Article XVI:2(e). However, such a decision may be based on criteria that are not market access restrictions in the sense of Article XVI:2, for instance when this requirement is imposed because the host country authorities believe that this facilitates supervision. Should this decision then still be considered a market access restriction? Where would the difference between this situation and a situation where a licence is refused lie? Arguably, the difference lies in the fact that when a licence is refused on the basis of the application of criteria that are not of the type listed in Article XVI:2, this is merely an application of these general criteria in a specific case. In contrast, in the case of a decision that requires the bank to set up a specific legal person, this imposes at the end of the assessment process a specific requirement of the type set out in Article XVI:2, even if it were to be based on criteria that are not set out in Article XVI:2. If a WTO member had not inscribed a limitation to its market access commitments to reserve the possibility of adopting a decision that imposes such a requirement, the adoption of such a decision would violate Article XVI.

497. To be sure, two remarks may be made with regard to the latter situation. First, one may wonder whether such an individual decision will ever be challenged before a WTO panel. In the present author's view, this possibility cannot be excluded. For instance, if a WTO member had only one bank, which is government-owned, the member might be willing to challenge such a measure. Second, it is quite likely that such a decision can be qualified as a measure taken 'for prudential reasons' and thus be saved by the prudential exemption. Nonetheless, this again cannot be taken for granted. What if the home country of the bank claims that there is no need for requiring the establishment of a specific legal person to improve supervision, since all Basel principles and standards are implemented in the supervisory framework of the home country? What is more, if the decision can be qualified as a market access restriction, the burden of proof shifts immediately to the host country to defend its decision. It is thus important to consider whether such a decision could be qualified as a market access restriction.

9.3.3 Conclusion on supervisory assessments and Article XVI

498. In sum, Article XVI only imposes a limitation on WTO members making supervisory assessments and refusing a licence to a bank from another WTO member or refusing the increase of a shareholding in an existing bank as far as the *criteria* on the basis of which such a decision is made can be qualified as market access restrictions in the sense of Article XVI GATS. If this is the case (e.g. if the criterion is an economic needs test or an assessment whether a quota of licences is already filled), the decisions violate Article XVI. However, in such cases, the complainant in fact challenges the criteria that are applied in the assessment process rather than the outcome of the assessment process (i.e. the decision itself). Article XVI thus, rather, restricts the right to regulate, to adopt such criteria. The only exception would be when the individual decision imposes ad hoc the requirement to set up a specific legal person, while this requirement was not laid down in a rule of general application. In the latter case, it is the supervisory decision itself that violates Article XVI.

499. When a challenge of a supervisory assessment on the basis of Article XVI is successful, the WTO member in question must remove the general measure that is found to violate Article XVI or, where the decision itself was found to constitute a market access restriction, the decision cannot be adopted again. Only in the latter case the challenge is against the supervisory decision itself.

9.4 Non-discrimination and supervisory assessments

9.4.1 Existing case law on non-discrimination and its possible application to supervisory assessments

500. It seems very difficult to apply the GATS provisions that prohibit discrimination to individual supervisory decisions. Even though individual decisions are 'measures' within the normative scope of Article II and XVII of the GATS, these provisions in the GATS do not seem to be suitable for being applied to such individual decisions. As already indicated (above, para. 485), several authors have pointed to the different goals of international investment law and international trade law when they discussed and compared the obligation of national treatment in both areas of law. A brief attempt to apply the national treatment or most-favoured-nation treatment obligation to such individual decisions may point to the difficulties that one may incur.

501. As pointed out, applying provisions in the GATS that require WTO members not to discriminate between services and suppliers with a different origin requires a two-step analysis. First, one needs to determine whether the services or suppliers in question are 'like'. Second, if they are 'like', the question arises whether some are treated 'less favourably' than others because of the measure at issue.

502. As the case law stands at present, when examining whether the services or service suppliers (e.g. banks) are 'like', the focus is mainly on the question whether consumers consider the services to be interchangeable and thus whether the banks or banking services are in a competitive relationship.[616] This implies that different banks will in many cases be considered to be 'like', even if there are differences between them that the authorities find relevant for providing a different treatment, e.g. the financial soundness of an institution. Because of information asymmetries, consumers are often unable to take into account these differences when making decisions. When applying such analysis to individual decisions (e.g. a supervisory assessment of an application for a bank licence), the problem becomes even more pronounced.

503. If a decision affects a certain bank and the WTO member that brings a case argues that this decision violates a GATS provision that prohibits discrimination, the question arises with which other banks the

[616] Appellate Body Report, *EC – Asbestos*, paras. 114–117.

situation of the affected bank should be compared. If the approach is taken that the affected bank is 'like' any other bank that consumers would consider as being in a competitive relationship, the group of banks to be compared is quite large. For instance, banking supervisors may refuse a licence for several reasons (unsuitability of the shareholders or of the management, insufficient initial capital, concerns with regard to the adequate supervision of the bank that is foreign-owned etc.), while consumers are not aware of these aspects of the bank from which they purchase a banking service. This would imply that the bank for which the licence is refused is in a competitive relationship and thus must be considered to be 'like' all banks that have obtained a licence. Taking this analysis further, and also considering the second step of the analysis ('less favourable treatment'), a decision to refuse a licence to an applicant would modify the conditions of competition: the applicant is unable to compete with the banks that have a licence.[617] In conclusion, the mere decision to refuse a licence would be a violation of a provision that prohibits discrimination.

504. The reader may feel quite uncomfortable with this conclusion. On the basis of the current analysis of 'likeness' and 'less favourable treatment', the provisions in the GATS that prohibit discrimination would set a very important limit to the right of host supervisors to make supervisory assessments. It would be quite easy for a complainant to show a violation, and a host state would quickly be obliged to defend its decision. Even if this were not extremely difficult because of the availability of the prudential exception, this exception is not unlimited. Moreover, it is arguably undesirable for WTO members to be very quickly put in a defensive position.

9.4.2 Limits on the impact of prohibitions on discrimination on supervisory assessments

505. As already discussed with regard to the provisions on discrimination and the right to regulate, it is possible to identify limits to the impact of the provisions at the level of 'likeness' and of 'less favourable treatment'. With regard to likeness, we found that the focus on competitive relationships and thus on consumer perceptions might quickly lead to a conclusion that banks or banking services are 'like'. As WTO case

[617] Appellate Body Report, *Korea – Various Measures on Beef*, para. 144.

law stands at present, the regulatory objectives that a supervisory authority pursues in its decision are not taken into account as criteria for determining likeness.[618] Nonetheless, arguably, a panel might consider 'objective criteria' when determining 'likeness' (above, para. 485).[619] One such objective criterion may, for instance, be whether the bank is operating in a regulatory framework in which the Basel principles and standards have been implemented. Considering such objective elements may already limit somewhat the impact of the provisions on non-discrimination on the right to supervise. A supervisor may decide not to grant a licence precisely because the supervisory framework in the home country of the foreign bank deviates from the Basel standards and principles. When such objective criteria are taken into account, this may already somewhat alleviate concerns that the GATS provisions on discrimination constitute an important limit to the right to supervise. However, when determining 'likeness', a panel or the Appellate Body cannot use criteria that would require a subjective assessment of the reasons why a supervisor decided to grant a licence or not.

506. A further limit on the impact of the GATS provisions on discrimination may be situated in the second tier of the discrimination test. We discussed (above, paras. 347–349) that in order to prove a violation of Article II or XVII, a complainant will have to demonstrate convincingly that the 'less favourable treatment' is based on the origin of the group of adversely affected banks. When discussing the impact of the GATS on the right to regulate, reference was made to the statement by the Appellate Body in *EC – Asbestos*[620] and the arguments by Ehring that a measure must have an aggregate asymmetrical impact on the foreign supplier before it can be found to violate a provision that prohibits discrimination. However, in order to compare the impact on groups of banks, it is required that the individual supervisory decision affects several banks at the same time. This is not always clearly the case. For instance, a decision whereby a licence (which is not limited in numbers) is refused to an applicant does not directly affect other banks with a

[618] Appellate Body Report, *Japan – Taxes on Alcoholic Beverages II*, pp. 18–19; and Appellate Body Report, *EC – Bananas III*, para. 241.

[619] The panel in *EC – Bananas III* mentioned the nature and characteristics of the services as criteria for determining likeness. See Panel Report, *EC – Bananas III*, para. 7.322.

[620] Appellate Body Report, *EC – Asbestos*, para. 100.

licence, except when it is argued that the refusal affects these other banks by shielding them from a new competitor. The impact is more clearly seen for a decision whereby a limited number of licences are being allocated to a number of candidate banks or in the case of a decision whereby a banking supervisor or competition authority determines that among several potential acquirers only one can take over the domestic bank. In such cases, it is possible to compose groups of banks that are affected differently by the decision. Still, the group of 'less favourably treated' banks will include only the bank for which the licence is refused. The group of banks that are treated 'more favourably' constitutes all the banks that have obtained a licence. In the case of a decision relating to an acquisition, the group of 'less favourably' treated banks is composed of all banks that could not acquire the target bank and the group of the 'more favourably' treated banks includes only the bank that has acquired the target bank. In all such cases, one comes almost immediately to an asymmetrical impact, since in one group there is only one bank. Arguably, this shows that the asymmetrical impact analysis is not useful to address situations where an individual decision allegedly treats banks of a certain origin less favourably.

507. However, when determining whether a measure treats certain banks less favourably, it may be derived from the case law relating to trade in goods that it is nevertheless also important to look at the 'intent' of the supervisory authority. The Appellate Body in *Chile – Alcoholic Beverages* stated that 'the measure's purposes, objectively manifested in the design, architecture and structure of the measure, *are* intensely pertinent to the task of evaluating whether or not that measure is applied so as to afford protection to domestic production'.[621] We considered that, even if the provisions on discrimination in the GATS do not use the expression 'so as to afford protection', the underlying purpose of these provisions is to rule out discriminatory measures that protect the domestic services or suppliers from foreign competition. Therefore, in the present author's view, when an individual decision is assessed under a GATS provision that prohibits discrimination, a panel would need to be convinced by the complainant that this individual decision had protectionist intent. The complaining member will have to advance factual evidence of protectionist intent, which will only rarely be available. Alternatively, the complainant has to show that the criteria used to

[621] Appellate Body Report, *Chile – Alcoholic Beverages*, para. 71.

distinguish between the specific bank obtaining support and a foreign-owned bank that is in a very similar situation are in fact based on the origin of the bank rather than any other reason. It goes without saying that, while the analysis of the impact of a measure on *groups* of banks can still be based on factual evidence, the analysis of whether an *individual* supervisory decision is merely based on origin or on some other reason inevitably involves a subjective assessment by a panel and thus almost necessarily concerns 'second-guessing' of the decision of the WTO member's authorities. It is therefore likely that a panel or the Appellate Body will be quite deferential and only accept the claim of a violation if there is very clear evidence of protectionist intent. This is also in line with the argument of several authors, mentioned above, namely that the obligations of most-favoured-nation treatment and national treatment in international trade law should be applied differently from these obligations in international investment law. If a case of an allegedly discriminatory treatment of an individual bank were to come before the WTO (as is theoretically possible), the panel might stress the need for actual proof of protectionist intent (even if this is normally not necessary, since an actual or potential modification of conditions of competition is generally sufficient). Non-discrimination in trade law would not be about protection of individual investors, but about competitive opportunities. If a claim with regard to an allegedly discriminatory individual decision were to end up before a panel, the panel would probably only find a violation if there is clear trade protectionism at issue. In such circumstances, the competitive opportunities are affected, since the decision may discourage other foreign suppliers from seeking access to the market of the WTO member in question.

508. Nonetheless, the question must again be asked what a complainant would seek to achieve by challenging such decision 'as such' under Article II or XVII. If the panel or the Appellate Body concludes that the decision was based on protectionist grounds, it will recommend removing the measure. For instance, if a decision to refuse a bank licence was found to violate 'as such' Article XVII GATS, the measure must be brought into conformity with the GATS – that is, the measure must be removed. The applicant for a bank licence might then introduce a new application for a licence. Nonetheless, it is again not certain that the licence will now be granted. The authorities may just give better reasons supporting their decision and show that protectionism was not at issue.

9.4.3 *Conclusion on non-discrimination and supervisory assessments*

509. In sum, the provisions in the GATS that prohibit discrimination will only affect individual decisions for which a complainant can prove that there was an underlying protectionist objective. Arguably, panels will be very careful to conclude that an individual decision violates Article II or Article XVII GATS, since an assessment of such a provision under these Articles would relatively quickly involve second-guessing the reasons why the supervisory authority made such decision. Therefore it is likely that a panel will only find a violation where the protectionist objective is proven. Even if a complainant were able to prove the existence of protectionist intent, a decision by a panel or the Appellate Body in this sense does not imply that a new decision will now be favourable to the banks from the complainant.

510. It should finally be mentioned that, even if it would be rather unusual for a *single* supervisory decision to be found to violate Article XVII, it is still possible that *several* such individual measures form a general 'practice' that establishes a non-written norm with a general and prospective application and is 'as such' discriminatory (see above, para. 216)[622] or that several individual decisions taken together provide evidence that the measure 'as applied' is discriminatory.

9.5 Procedural requirements for individual supervisory assessments

9.5.1 *Introduction*

511. On the basis of the analysis in the previous two sections – sections 9.3 and 9.4 – we can conclude that the provision on market access and the provisions prohibiting discrimination in the GATS only restrict the right of WTO members to make supervisory assessments to a limited extent. A recurring question was to what extent these provisions are meant to apply to individual decisions. We found that these decisions are within the scope of these provisions and that it is possible to think of situations where such a decision would violate the respective provisions. However, the analysis indicated that their application to such individual decisions will not always be very easy, showing that the provisions

622 Appellate Body Report, *US – Zeroing (EC)*, paras. 193 and 198.

are most fit for applying to general measures. Nevertheless, there are still other provisions in the GATS that apply to individual decisions. It involves specifically a number of obligations relating to domestic regulation. These provisions affect mainly the *procedural* aspects of coming to an individual decision. However, the distinction between procedural and substantive aspects may sometimes be blurred, as can be seen for Article VI:1 GATS.

9.5.2 Reasonable, objective and impartial administration

512. The general discipline imposed by Article VI:1 GATS with regard to domestic regulations of general application is that members must ensure that they are administered in a *reasonable, objective and impartial manner.*

513. There is at present no case law in which Article VI:1 GATS was applied.[623] Several authors have referred to the fact that a similar requirement can be found in Article X:3(a) GATT and the case law on the interpretation of these concepts within the framework of the GATT may be informative on how to interpret these concepts in the GATS.[624] However, the requirements imposed by Article X:3(a) GATT are not entirely the same as those of Article VI:1 GATS. While Article X:3(a) requires '*uniform*, impartial and reasonable' (emphasis added)

[623] Art. VI:1 GATS was invoked by Antigua in the *US – Gambling* case. However, the panel found that Antigua had failed to identify the 'measures of general application', the administration of which would violate this provision. See Panel Report, *US – Gambling*, paras. 6.434 and 6.437.

[624] However, Art. X:3(a) applies to specific categories of measures, namely laws, regulations, judicial decisions and administrative rulings of general application, made effective by any contracting party, pertaining to the classification or the valuation of products for customs purposes, or to rates of duty, taxes or other charges, or to requirements, restrictions or prohibitions on imports or exports or on the transfer of payments therefor, or affecting their sale, distribution, transportation, insurance, warehousing inspection, exhibition, processing, mixing or other use. Art. X:1 GATT. Delimatsis refers to the *EC – Bananas III* case, where the Appellate Body found that Art. X:3(a) GATT is similar to Art. I:3 of the Agreement on Import Licensing Procedures. According to the Appellate Body, the two relevant phrases were 'for all practical purposes, interchangeable'. Appellate Body Report, *EC – Bananas III*, para. 203. Delimatsis argues that the same reasoning can apply to Art. X:3 GATT and Art. VI:1 GATS. Delimatsis, above n. 510, at 20 (n. 27); and see T. Sunde, 'Möglichkeiten und Grenzen innerstaatlicher Regulierung nach Art. VI GATS', in C. Tietje, G. Kraft and R. Sethe (eds.), *Beiträge zum Transnationalen Wirtschaftsrecht* (Halle-Wittenberg: Martin-Luther-Universität, July 2006), Part 59, at 22 (n. 80).

administration, Article VI:1 requires administration to be 'reasonable, *objective* and impartial' (emphasis added).

9.5.2.1 The scope of application of Article VI:1 GATS

514. The text of Article VI:1 clearly suggests that it does not apply to the content of these measures but, rather, to their administration.[625] However, it may be derived from case law relating to Article X:3(a) GATT that a complainant may in certain cases challenge not only the practical application of a measure, but also the substantive content of the measure. This is possible provided that the substantive content of the measure is of an administrative nature (i.e. it involves an indication of how certain measures should be applied).[626] However, to establish a violation it is then also necessary that the indications in the measure result in non-objective, unreasonable or partial administration.[627]

515. When a complainant relies on Article VI:1, the complainant seeks to achieve that the specific *procedural practices* that violate Article VI:1 will no longer be applied. It does not seek the removal of the measure of general application 'as such', nor that a certain interpretation of the measure is no longer applied. Article VI:1 is thus focused on the *process* of reaching a decision.

516. The case law with regard to Article X:3(a) GATT indicates that this obligation does *not* cover a situation where, in a single individual case, the administration is not uniform, impartial or reasonable. The panel in *US – Hot-Rolled Steel* stated that the actions must have a 'significant impact on the overall administration of the law, and not simply on the

[625] Panel Report, *US – Gambling*, para. 6.432.

[626] Panel Report, *Argentina – Measures Affecting the Export of Bovine Hides and Import of Finished Leather* (*Argentina – Hides and Leather*), WT/DS155/R and Corr.1, adopted 16 February 2001, paras. 11.70 and 11.71. The panel stated: 'Of course, a WTO member may challenge the substance of a measure under Art. X. The relevant question is whether the substance of such a measure is administrative in nature or, instead, involves substantive issues more properly dealt with under other provisions of the GATT 1994.'

[627] Delimatsis, above n. 510, at 23. See also Appellate Body Report, *European Communities – Selected Customs Matters* (*EC – Selected Customs Matters*), WT/DS315/AB/R, adopted 11 December 2006, paras. 200–201. The Appellate Body stated: '[W]e see no reason why a legal instrument that regulates the application or implementation of that instrument cannot be examined under Art. X:3(a)', and, further, 'If a WTO member challenges under Art. X:3(a) the substantive content of a legal instrument that regulates the administration of a legal instrument of the kind described in Art. X:1, it will have to prove that this instrument necessarily leads to a lack of uniform, impartial, or reasonable administration. It is not sufficient for the complainant merely to cite the provisions of that legal instrument.'

outcome in the single case in question'.[628] It seems that, when this case law is applied to Article VI:1 GATS, a situation where a measure of general application (e.g. the general criteria for obtaining a licence) is applied in an individual case (e.g. the decision by a banking supervisor whether to grant a banking licence to an applicant or not) does not come within the scope of the obligation.

517. Nonetheless, one may wonder whether such interpretation is correct for Article VI:1 GATS. It conflates the requirement that the measure must be of general application with the specification that Article X:3(a) GATT and Article VI:1 GATS are concerned with the administration of such a measure.[629] Moreover, the case law may be inspired by the presence in Article X:3(a) GATT of the requirement for 'uniform' administration. This requirement suggests a consideration of several instances of administration but is not mentioned in Article VI:1 GATS. In the present author's view, the scope of application of Article VI:1 is limited to measures of general application. Nonetheless, the application of this general measure in an individual case (e.g. the decision whether or not to grant a licence to a bank) can come within the scope of the obligation. What is in fact excluded is the administration of a measure with an individual reach, *independent of any general measure*, such as, for example, an individual decision that lays down the specific regulatory conditions for a specific bank, completely disconnected from a general measure. Therefore, if a complainant is able to show that the administration of a measure of general application in an individual case is

[628] Panel Report, *United States – Anti-Dumping Measures on Certain Hot-Rolled Steel Products from Japan* (*US – Hot-Rolled Steel*), WT/DS184/R, adopted 23 August 2001, as modified by Appellate Body Report, WT/DS184/AB/R, para. 7.268. It concerned the application of the US Anti-dumping Act in a single anti-dumping investigation.

[629] Sunde has argued that the combination of the phrase 'measures of general application' with the word 'administration', implies that individual measures (that apply measures of general application) are also covered by the scope of Art. VI:1 GATS. He states: 'Für die Beantwortung der Frage, ob nur abstrakt-generelle Maßnahmen von Art. VI:1 erfasst werden, ist es deshalb notwendig, das Tatsbestandsmerkmal "of general application" im Zusammenhand mit dem Tatsbestandsmerkmal "administered" zu lesen'. Sunde, above n. 624, at 13–14. In contrast, Krajewski has argued: 'This view ignores the difference between the scope of application of an obligation and its effects. While the obligation of Art. VI:1 affects the outcome of individual decisions, it nevertheless does not apply to individual decisions. Only the administration of measures of general application can be tested under Art. VI:1.' M. Krajewski, 'Article VI GATS. Domestic Regulation', in Wolfrum, Stoll and Feinäugle, above n. 156, at 170. Krajewski seems to stress that an individual measure that does not involve the administration of a general measure cannot be challenged under this provision.

'unreasonable, not objective or not impartial', this administrative act 'as such' already violates Article VI:1.

518. Nonetheless, the importance of this case law may lie in the fact that it points out that the impact of the unreasonable, subjective and partial administration needs to be *sufficiently important* to be of concern for international trade.

519. Given the fact that the procedural obligations in the relevant WTO Agreement are meant to facilitate international trade, there will only be a violation if the non-objective, unreasonable or partial administration leads to a modification of the competitive situation of the suppliers in question. The panel in *Argentina – Bovine Hides* noted that the real effect of the measure in the commercial world needs to be shown. However, no actual trade damage needs necessarily to be proven; a *potential* modification of the competitive positions would be sufficient.[630] Related to this, one can note that the panel in *EEC – Dessert Apples* (a GATT 1947 case) stated that minor administrative variations are not sufficient to find a violation of Article X:3(a) GATT.[631] Moreover, the Appellate Body in *US – Corrosion-Resistant Steel Sunset Review* stated that allegations that measures are administered in a non-uniform, unreasonable or partial way 'are serious under any circumstances' and 'should not be brought lightly'.[632] Hence such a claim should be supported by solid evidence.

520. What is more, a challenge against an 'unreasonable, non-objective or partial' administration of a general measure in a single instance will not necessarily result in a decision (i.e. the outcome of the administration of a measure) that is favourable to the bank that seeks access to the host market. For example, when a refusal for a bank licence is successfully challenged on the basis of Article VI:1 GATS, the WTO member is obliged to remove the administrative practices that were 'unreasonable, non-objective or partial'. However, a supervisory assessment that is made without these administrative practices will not

[630] Panel Report, *Argentina – Hides and Leather*, para. 11.77.

[631] GATT Panel Report, *European Economic Community – Restrictions on Imports of Dessert Apples – Complaint by Chile* (*EEC – Dessert Apples*), adopted 22 June 1989, BISD 36S/93, para. 12.30.

[632] Appellate Body Report, *United States – Sunset Review of Anti-Dumping Duties on Corrosion-Resistant Carbon Steel Flat Products from Japan* (*US – Corrosion-Resistant Steel Sunset Review*), WT/DS244/AB/R, adopted 9 January 2004, para. 217.

necessarily lead to a different final decision for the service suppliers affected by the initial decision. It only improves the chance for a more favourable decision. Therefore a WTO member may only want to bring a case against an 'unreasonable, non-objective or partial' administration of a measure of general application if such administration occurs repeatedly.

9.5.2.2 Impartial administration

521. It is useful to start the analysis of the requirement of 'impartial' administration in Article VI:1 GATS by contrasting it with the requirement in Article X:3(a) GATT. The first requirement imposed by Article X:3(a) GATT is the requirement of 'uniform' administration of measures of general application. The requirement of 'uniformity' has been defined by the panel in *Argentina – Hides and Leather*, as an obligation to treat traders 'in the same manner both over time and in different places and with respect to other persons. Uniform administration requires that Members ensure that their laws are applied consistently and predictably and is not limited, for instance, to ensuring equal treatment with respect to WTO members'. Contrary to the obligation of most-favoured-nation treatment, it involves the same treatment not only of WTO members, but also of individual traders and even of the same trader at different points in time.[633] Arguably, this may thus even concern the treatment of different traders from the same WTO member.[634] Nevertheless, the panel clearly stated that this does not involve a broad non-discrimination provision in the sense that all suppliers should be treated identically. Day-to-day administration of measures differs from case to case, so that it cannot be expected that in all specific practical cases the same treatment is given. The panel concluded, 'There are many variations in products which might require differential treatment and we do not think this provision should be read as a general invitation for a panel to make such distinctions.'[635] Clearly, uniformity must be something more than broadly equal treatment of WTO members, but is also something less than absolute similarity in the handling of the individual cases.

522. The panel in *EC – Selected Customs Matters* also noted that it is 'impossible to determine a single concept of "uniformity" that would

[633] Panel Report, *Argentina – Hides and Leather*, para. 11.83.
[634] Sunde, above n. 624, at 19.
[635] Panel Report, *Argentina – Hides and Leather*, para. 11.84.

apply across the board'.[636] The 'uniformity' requirement will vary, depending on the breadth of the challenge. If the administration of a wide range of measures and instances of administration is challenged, the requirement of uniformity will be applied more flexibly, whereas when the challenge is narrower, the requirement for uniformity will be applied more strictly.[637] The panel further stated that there is no requirement for absolute or instantaneous geographic uniformity, especially when the measure being challenged forms part of the legislation of a large WTO member such as, in that case, the European Union.[638] Moreover, the uniformity must be considered over a reasonable period of time. One cannot expect uniformity to be instantaneous, since administrations will only be able to attain it over a certain period of time. Which period of time is considered 'reasonable' depends on the form, nature and scale of the administration in question.[639] Yet in all cases the administration 'should not fall below certain minimum standards of due process, which encompass notions such as notice, transparency, fairness and equity'.[640] The panel referred to the statements of the Appellate Body in *US – Shrimp* that link Article X:3 to due process.[641]

523. Nonetheless, it is not self-evident that the interpretation of 'uniform' as developed in the case law on Article X:3(a) GATT should be applied to Article VI:1 GATS. As indicated already, Article VI:1 GATS does not mention the requirement of 'uniformity' but, besides the identical requirements 'reasonable' and 'impartial', the requirement of 'objective' administration. Krajewski also points to these differences in the criteria of Article X:3(a) GATT. He argues that, for assessing 'uniformity', it is 'usually necessary to take more than one decision into account'. In contrast, 'objectivity' 'refers to the circumstances of an individual decision'.[642] Hence it is difficult to apply the reasoning the panel developed with regard to 'uniformity' in Article X:3(a) GATT (a 'consistent and predictable application of laws to different traders, in different places and at different points of time') to the requirement 'objectivity' in Article VI:1 GATS.

[636] Panel Report, *European Communities – Selected Customs Matters* (*EC – Selected Customs Matters*), WT/DS315/R, adopted 11 December 2006, as modified by Appellate Body Report, WT/DS315/AB/R, para. 7.128.
[637] Ibid., para. 7.129. [638] Ibid., para. 7.131. [639] Ibid., para. 7.132.
[640] Ibid., para. 7.134. [641] Appellate Body Report, *US – Shrimp*, paras. 181–183.
[642] M. Krajewski, above n. 629, at 171–2.

524. Still, one can argue that the requirement of 'uniformity' is contained in a *combined* reading of the criteria 'reasonable, objective and impartial'. It has already been pointed to the fact that the Appellate Body in *US – Shrimp*[643] and the panel in *EC – Certain Customs Matters*[644] stressed that the standard of 'due process' underlies the requirements in Article X:3(a) GATT. The latter panel further clarified that

> [T]he due process theme underlying Article X of the GATT 1994 suggests that the aim of Article X:3(a) of the GATT is to ensure that traders are treated fairly and consistently when seeking to import from or export to a particular WTO member. The Panel also considers that an object and purpose of the WTO Agreement is to ensure security and predictability in the trading environment.[645]

The panel did not refer specifically to 'uniformity' here, but to all three criteria in Article X:3. Therefore, if banks were to be treated non-uniformly, in the sense that non-consistent treatment is granted over time, in different places or with regard to different persons, this treatment might also violate Article VI:1 GATS.

525. What, then, would be the specific meaning of 'impartiality' in Article VI:1 GATS? According to the *Compact Oxford English Dictionary*, the ordinary meaning of 'impartiality' is 'treating all rivals or disputants equally'.

526. Sunde and Krajewski have read into this requirement a prohibition on discrimination.[646] The problem, however, is that this obligation is already included in the GATS provisions that prohibit discrimination on the basis of origin: Article II and Article XVII. What, then, is the use of a provision that merely repeats this prohibition? To be sure, Article VI:1 only covers the 'administration' of measures of general application. Nonetheless, as indicated earlier (above, paras. 212 and 213) it is also possible to challenge a measure 'as applied' as a violation of Article II or

643 Appellate Body Report, *US – Shrimp*, paras. 182–183.

644 Panel Report, *EC – Selected Customs Matters*, para. 7.134. 645 Ibid., para. 7.431.

646 Sunde, above n. 624, at 20: 'Aus der Auslegung des Wortlauts folgt also ein Diskriminierungsverbot, in dessen Rahmen gewisse Gesichtspunkte, wie typischerweise die Nationalität eines Unternehmens oder sein Sitz, als irrelevant bei der Anwendung einer Maßnahme zu betrachten sind'. See also Krajewksi, above n. 629, at 172: 'While the requirement of impartiality contains elements of the fundamental principle of non-discrimination, it differs from the requirements of Art. II (most-favoured-nation treatment) and Art. XVII (national treatment)'.

XVII GATS. According to Krajewski, the difference between Articles II and XVII, on the one hand, and Article VI:1, on the other hand, would primarily be that

> Arts. II and XVII prohibit less favourable treatment of one service or service supplier compared to a 'like' service or service supplier irrespective of the goals and objectives pursued by the administration, which may possibly justify the different treatment. ... However, the application of a measure which treats two comparable ('like') situations differently with good reason does not necessarily violate the standards of Art. VI:1.[647]

527. In the present author's view, the main difference lies in the fact that the non-discrimination obligations in Articles II and XVII involve the treatment of different services and service suppliers based on their *origin* (MFN: the treatment of services/service suppliers of one WTO member compared with those from another WTO member; national treatment: the treatment of services/service suppliers of one WTO member compared with those with a domestic origin), requiring a comparison of different groups of affected services or suppliers and linking the adverse treatment to the origin (see above, paras. 347–349), whereas Article VI:1 does not necessarily involve a comparison of the treatment of services or suppliers based on their origin. This was also recognized by the panel in *Argentina – Hides and Leather* in its already mentioned statement (admittedly with regard to the requirement of 'uniform' administration): 'This is a requirement of uniform administration of Customs laws and procedures between individual shippers and even with respect to the same person at different times and different places.'[648] The panel in *Argentina – Hides and Leather* concluded that there was a situation of a 'partial' administration in the case at hand:

> Whenever a party with a commercial interest, but no relevant legal interest, is allowed to participate in an export transaction ... there is an inherent danger that the customs laws, regulations and rules will be applied in a partial manner so as to permit persons with adverse commercial interests to obtain confidential information to which they have no right.[649]

The panel did not refer at any point to the origin of the traders here. Article VI:1 would thus address situations where one or more service

[647] Krajewski, above n. 629, at 172. It would thus be easier to prove discrimination in case of Art. II and XVII than of Art. VI:1.

[648] Panel Report, *Argentina – Hides and Leather*, para. 11.83. [649] Ibid., para. 11.100.

suppliers are treated in a manner that is not taking into account their interests, whereas this is done for other service suppliers without there being good reason for making this distinction. This thus involves a more individualized assessment of the treatment of one or a few suppliers in comparison with other suppliers. To be sure, the panel in *Argentina – Hides and Leather* warned that there is not a broad non-discrimination provision that requires all traders to be treated *identically*, and recognized that it is not for a panel to make the difficult distinctions. Therefore a panel would only find a violation in cases of blatant 'partial' administration, for instance if it is proven that competitors are able to influence the decision by the authority that administers the measure of general application. The fact that the application of the 'impartiality' requirement can involve only a marginal test by the panel (probably leaving much leeway for authorities in the WTO member in question to advance reasons for differential treatment) may also clarify why the panel in *Argentina – Hides and Leather* made in its analysis a link between the requirement of 'reasonable' and of 'impartial' administration.[650]

528. The chair's draft text for horizontal disciplines on domestic regulation includes a paragraph (paragraph 18) that obliges each WTO member to ensure that the 'procedures used by, and the decisions of, the competent authority in the licensing process are impartial with respect to all applicants'.[651] When the disciplines are eventually adopted and if this paragraph is not modified, it will thus complement the obligation in Article VI:1 with regard to impartiality. It is very clearly stated that the *decision* should be impartial. What is more, the paragraph further specifies that the competent authority 'should be operationally independent and not accountable to any supplier of the services for which the licence is required'. This requirement seems not as firm as the impartiality requirement, since the word 'should' is used rather than 'shall'. However, even if an authority is not operationally independent, it must still work according to procedures that are impartial and take decisions that are impartial. Arguably, operational independence is an 'institutional guarantee' for impartiality, but it is neither a necessary nor a sufficient condition for it. The second sentence of paragraph 18 thus needs to be read together with and in the light of the first sentence of that paragraph.

650 Ibid., para. 11.86.

651 Paragraph 18 Working Party on Domestic Regulation, Disciplines on Domestic Regulation Pursuant to GATS Art. VI:4, Second Revision, above n. 494.

9.5.2.3 Reasonable administration

529. The second requirement in Article VI:1 GATS is that the measures are 'reasonably' administered. The panel in *Dominican Republic – Cigarettes* noted that the 'ordinary meaning' of 'reasonableness' is 'in accordance with reason', 'not irrational or absurd', 'proportionate', 'having sound judgment', 'sensible', 'not asking for too much', 'within the limits of reason, not greatly less or more than might be thought likely or appropriate', or 'articulate'.[652]

530. Given the complexities of banking regulation and its application, a panel will arguably be quite hesitant to decide that the administration of a banking regulation is unreasonable. The panel in *Argentina – Hides and Leather* found that a process that is aimed at assuring proper classification of products but which inherently contains the possibility of revealing confidential business information constitutes an 'unreasonable' administration of a measure.[653] The panel linked this 'unreasonable' 'impartial' administration in the case at hand, because 'a party with a contrary commercial interest, but no legal interest' was allowed to participate in the customs transaction at stake and thus could get hold of the confidential information that was disclosed. Sunde has made an extensive analysis of the 'reasonableness' requirement in Article VI:1 GATS, and has concluded that this in fact involves a 'proportionality test'.[654] Whether the application of the measure was 'suitable' for the objective pursued and whether the application was 'necessary' to achieve the goal (or rather less trade-restrictive alternatives were reasonably available) would need to be assessed. He notes, however, that this test cannot be as far-reaching as the test in Article VI:4 (above, paras. 406–419). Therefore the suitability test would be quite lightly assessed: it would be sufficient that the measure 'contributes' to the objective pursued.[655]

9.5.2.4 Objective administration

531. Finally, there is a third condition imposed by Article VI:1 GATS, namely that the administration of measures of general application must be 'objective'. This condition is absent in Article X:3(a) GATT, and it is thus difficult to find indications of an interpretation in the case law on

652 Panel Report, *Dominican Republic – Import and Sale of Cigarettes*, para. 7.385.
653 Panel Report, *Argentina – Hides and Leather*, para. 11.94.
654 Sunde, above n. 624, at 49.
655 Ibid., at 50. This would be similar to the 'relating to' requirement in Art. XX(g) GATT. Ibid., at 51 (n. 229).

this GATT provision. According to Krajewski, this condition would require that the process of application 'disregards irrational, emotional or personal intentions'.[656] In contrast with the obligation to apply measures in an 'impartial' manner (and 'uniform' manner in Article X:3(a) GATT), this involves not a comparison between the treatment of different service suppliers or the same supplier at different points in time, but, rather, an assessment of whether the personal intentions in an individual application have not prevailed over an objective analysis of the situation.[657]

9.5.3 Information within a reasonable period of time of the decision being made

532. A second provision of a procedural nature is Article VI:3 GATS. This provision requires that the competent authorities in the WTO members inform the applicant within a reasonable period of time after the submission of a complete application of the decision that was taken by the administration with regard to the application for authorization to supply the service. If the applicant so requests, the competent authorities must provide without undue delay information concerning the status of the application. The panel in *US – Gambling* stated that, pursuant to this provision, authorization procedures should be performed according to the principles of transparency and due process.[658]

533. Importantly, these procedural obligations (Article VI:1 and VI:3) do not apply to all possible services sectors, but only as far as specific commitments are undertaken by the WTO member in question. Nevertheless, once commitments are made, the administration of all possible measures of general application are within the scope of Article VI:1 and 3. There is no further specification with regard to the specific type of measure. Hence, measures that fall within the scope of Article XVI or Article XVII may also need to be assessed on whether they are administered in conformity with Article VI:1 or applied in conformity with Article VI:3.[659] In the *US – Gambling* case, the panel, after finding a violation of Article XVI, considered that Antigua had not made a prima

[656] Krajewski, above n. 629, at 171.

[657] Ibid., at 172: 'Objectivity, on the other hand, refers to the circumstances of an individual decision. The first application of a general measure can therefore already violate the requirement of objectivity'.

[658] Panel Report, *US – Gambling*, para. 6.432.

[659] See also Pauwelyn, above n. 325, at 152.

facie demonstration that the measures in dispute were also inconsistent with Article VI:1 or 3.[660]

9.5.4 *The possibility of reviewing administrative decisions*

534. In contrast, Article VI:2 – the third procedural obligation at stake in Article VI GATS – applies independently of whether specific commitments were made in a particular services sector. The provision requires WTO members to provide the possibility of review of administrative decisions affecting trade in services. This review can be with judicial, arbitral or administrative tribunals. It is indicated that this review should be prompt. When decisions are reviewed and anomalies found, appropriate remedies must be provided to address these anomalies. In principle, the review body should be independent[661] from the agency that made the decision. Nevertheless, Article VI:2(a) does not exclude the review being performed by the agency that has made the initial decision. However, if this is the case, WTO members are obliged to ensure that this review is objective and impartial.

535. Importantly, Article VI:2(b) indicates that national constitutions have a higher hierarchical status than this obligation to provide the possibility of review. If the establishment of such a review would violate the constitutional structure or nature of the legal system of a WTO member, the WTO member is not obliged to establish such a review.

536. Once again, the case law on Article X:3(b) GATT can provide guidance on Article VI:2. In *EC – Selected Customs Matters*, the United States argued that the European system, whereby review relating to a decision by a member state customs administration (that applies the European customs rules) is carried out by a tribunal of this member state, was violating Article X:3(b). According to the United States, there was a violation because the decision by the tribunal or other review body is

[660] Ibid., para. 6.437. According to the panel, Antigua had failed to indicate the specific measures that would violate Art. VI:1, nor did Antigua indicate which measures imposed authorization requirements in the sense of Art. VI:3 or provide examples where service suppliers were denied such authorization.

[661] In the context of Art. X:3(b) GATT, the panel in *EC – Selected Customs Matters* noted that the ordinary meaning of 'independent' is that 'the judicial, arbitral or administrative tribunals or procedures for the review and correction of administrative action relating to customs matters under Art. X:3(b) of the GATT 1994 must be free of control or influence from the administrative agencies whose decisions are the subject of review'. Panel Report, *EC – Selected Customs Matters*, para. 7.520.

only binding within the member state concerned and not across the EU. Thus, according to the United States, there should be one EU customs court in order for the EU to comply with Article X:3(b) GATS. The panel decided that this provision exists 'to ensure that a trader who has been adversely affected by a decision of an administrative agency has the ability to have that adverse decision reviewed'. The panel concluded, '[T]o require decisions issued by judicial, arbitral or administrative tribunals or procedures pursuant to Article X:3(b) of the GATT 1994 to apply and have effect throughout the territory of a Member would go beyond what is demanded by this due process objective'.[662]

9.5.5 *Procedures to grant licences and assess qualifications*

537. The chair's draft text for Horizontal Disciplines on Domestic Regulation has a specific Chapter VI with disciplines for licensing procedures. These disciplines will certainly have an impact on the way each individual decision is reached, and thus determine the procedures a banking supervisory or other competent authority should follow. The procedures to be followed for obtaining the authorization to provide banking services arguably involve procedures for obtaining a licence. Hence the disciplines on licensing procedures are most relevant here. However, since foreign banks that want to operate in a host member may want to employ foreign professionals in this host territory, qualifications will also be relevant.

9.5.5.1 Licensing procedures

538. Chapter VI of the chair's draft text for the Horizontal Disciplines sets out a number of disciplines for licensing procedures. These disciplines seek to meet the mandate in Article VI:4, namely that each WTO member's measures relating to licensing procedures are 'based on objective and transparent criteria, such as the competence and the ability to supply the services, and do not constitute disguised restrictions on trade in services'.[663]

539. The draft Horizontal Disciplines oblige WTO members to ensure that the procedures should be as simple as possible and that they do not

[662] Ibid., para. 7.538.

[663] Working Party on Domestic Regulation, Disciplines on Domestic Regulation Pursuant to GATS Art. VI:4, Second Revision, above n. 494, para. 2.

in themselves constitute a restriction on the supply of services.[664] The latter is a repetition of the requirement in Article VI:4(c) of the GATS. The expression 'as simple as possible' has been considered by some WTO members and commentators as very vague and thus potentially creating a far-going restriction on the possibility to design and maintain licensing procedures.[665]

540. It is far from clear how a panel would interpret this requirement. In theory, it can always be argued that a procedure can be made simpler, up to the point that abolishing the procedure at all is the simplest option. The expression 'as simple as possible' does figure at present in Article 1.5 and 1.6 of the Agreement on Import Licensing Procedures[666] in relation to application forms and procedures for automatic and non-automatic import licensing. Nonetheless, these articles have up to the time of writing never been interpreted by a panel. To be sure, Article 1.6 was invoked by the United States in the *Turkey – Rice* dispute.[667] The United States had argued that the 'rice importation process in Turkey is far from simple' and described how an importer had to file papers with four different agencies, had to fill out the same customs paperwork three times and had to make separate trips to the regional and central (Ankara) authorities.[668] The focus was thus mainly on the large number of authorities (something dealt with explicitly at the end of Article 1.6) and the

[664] Ibid., para. 17.

[665] See J. Stumberg, Briefing Memo to Kay Wilkie, WPDR chairman's fourth draft on domestic regulation, dated 23 January 2008, Harrison Institute for Public Law, Georgetown University Law Center, 12 February 2008 – Version 5, at 27, available at www.law.georgetown.edu/clinics/hi/documents/Stumberg-WPDRchairsdraft23-Jan-08v6copy.doc.

[666] Art. 1.5 of the Import Licensing Agreement reads: 'Application forms and, where applicable, renewal forms shall be as simple as possible. Such documents and information as are considered strictly necessary for the proper functioning of the licensing regime may be required on application'. Art. 1.6 reads: 'Application procedures and, where applicable, renewal procedures shall be as simple as possible. Applicants shall have to approach only one administrative body previously specified in the rules referred to in paragraph 4 above in connection with an application and shall be allowed a reasonable period therefor. In cases where it is strictly indispensable that more than one administrative body is to be approached in connection with an application, these shall be kept to the minimum number possible.'

[667] Panel Report, *Turkey – Measures Affecting the Importation of Rice* (*Turkey – Rice*), WT/DS334/R, adopted 22 October 2007, para. 7.277.

[668] *Turkey – Measures Affecting the Importation of Rice*, Answers of the United States of America to the Questions of the Panel and Turkey Following the Second Substantive Meeting with the Parties, 6 February 2007, at para. 21, available at www.ustr.gov/webfm_send/609.

duplication in the paperwork. Nonetheless, the panel did not address this argument for reasons of 'judicial economy'.[669]

541. In the present author's view, the requirement that licensing procedures are 'as simple as possible' requires an assessment of the procedure in the light of the objectives pursued by this procedure. Arguably, this requirement thus becomes very similar to a test whereby a panel needs to assess whether there exist a less trade-restrictive procedure that is also able to achieve the objective (a 'necessity test' *sensu stricto*). It could even be argued that the criterion against which the necessity is measured is not solely the cost to trade, but the costs of the procedure in general.

542. Furthermore, paragraph 17 of the draft Horizontal Disciplines requires that the procedures 'do not in themselves constitute a restriction on the supply of services', and thereby repeats the requirement in Article VI:4(c) GATS. At the beginning of the negotiations on disciplines on domestic regulation (at that time still within the framework of the Working Party on Professional Services), the WTO Secretariat referred in a Note of 11 September 1996 to the language in the Agreement on Import Licensing Procedures.[670] Article 3.2 of this Agreement requires that non-automatic import licensing procedures shall 'not have trade-restrictive or -distortive effects on imports additional to those caused by the imposition of the restriction'. A recent annotation of the draft disciplines by the chair of the Working Party on Domestic Regulation again takes up this reference, but rightly notes that the contexts of the disciplines and of the Agreement on Import Licensing Procedures may be different.[671] In the case of import licensing procedures, the quantitative import restriction for which licences are granted is per definition a restriction on trade. Article 3.2 of the Agreement seeks to avoid that the procedures for granting such a licence further worsen this restriction. However, in the case of the measures of domestic regulation covered by the disciplines, it is far from clear whether they are prohibited trade

669 Panel Report, *Turkey – Rice*, para. 7.281.

670 Working Party on Professional Services, The Relevance of the Disciplines of the Agreements on Technical Barriers to Trade (TBT) and on Import Licensing Procedures to Art. VI.4 of the General Agreement on Trade in Services, Note by the Secretariat, S/WPPS/W/9, 11 September 1996, at para. 36.

671 Working Party on Domestic Regulation, Disciplines on Domestic Regulation Pursuant to GATS Art. VI:4, Annotated Text, Informal Note by the Chairperson, Room Document of 14 March 2010, at para. 163.

restrictions in the first place. They concern measures that do not qualify as market access restrictions within the scope of Article XVI GATS (above, paras. 394–399).

543. It is thus far from clear what the negotiators mean by using the expression 'not in themselves constitute restrictions on the supply of services'. A possible approach is to read the expressions 'as simple as possible' and 'not in themselves constitute a restriction on the supply of services' together and consider that together they involve a test of considering whether the procedure is used for protectionist purposes rather than for a legitimate goal. The test would then involve a consideration of whether there exist less trade-restrictive alternatives for the procedure.

544. It is also specified that the procedures and decisions by the competent authorities must be impartial. The authority should be operationally independent of, and not accountable to, the supplier of the service for which the licence is required.[672] It has already been indicated (above, para. 528) that the use of 'should' indicates that this is not a firm requirement. However, operational independence may be an 'institutional guarantee' of impartiality.

545. Further, the draft text has a number of disciplines that seek to reduce the administrative burden that is imposed on applicants. Applicants must in principle not be required to approach more than one competent authority in connection with an application.[673] Arguably, this should be taken to mean that only one authority must be approached, but not that this single authority must be responsible for dealing with all aspects of an application. There is thus a 'single window' principle. Moreover, this requirement is most likely only limited to the licence that is required to become an authorized service supplier (bank) in the host member. It probably does not concern the further permits necessary to carry out activities in the territory of this member.[674] Nonetheless, it needs to be admitted that this is not a certainty and it

[672] Working Party on Domestic Regulation, Disciplines on Domestic Regulation Pursuant to GATS Art. VI:4, Second Revision, above n. 494, para. 18.

[673] Working Party on Domestic Regulation, Disciplines on Domestic Regulation Pursuant to GATS Art. VI:4, Second Revision, above n. 494, para. 19.

[674] Working Party on Domestic Regulation, Disciplines on Domestic Regulation Pursuant to GATS Art. VI:4, Annotated Text, Informal Note by the Chairperson, Room Document of 14 March 2010, at para. 183.

may be quite difficult to delineate in a concrete case what should be included in the single window. However, the use of the expression 'in principle' may mitigate the impact of this discipline in such ambiguous cases.

546. Application for submissions should be possible at any time, except where there are limited numbers of licences to grant (e.g. in public tendering). In the latter case, the applicant should be allowed a reasonable period of time for the application. It is not indicated that foreign applicants should be allowed a longer time than domestic applicants, but it seems that it can at least be read into the wording 'reasonable period' that the particular difficulties of a foreign applicant need to be taken into account. Where possible, electronic applications should be accepted under the same conditions of authenticity as paper submissions.[675] The draft Horizontal Disciplines indicate that authenticated copies should be accepted where possible instead of original documents.[676]

547. Importantly, the competent authority is obliged to notify the applicant within a reasonable period of time of the fact that an application is incomplete.[677] In an earlier draft it was suggested that the authority should notify also the fact that the application was *complete*. This was removed because it might have overburdened administrations. The applicant should be informed as to the information that is lacking and be given an opportunity to remedy deficiencies. To the extent feasible, the authority shall identify the additional information that is required to complete the application and provide an opportunity to correct deficiencies.

548. In the case of rejection of the application, the applicant must be informed in writing[678] without undue delay. When the applicant

[675] Working Party on Domestic Regulation, Disciplines on Domestic Regulation Pursuant to GATS Art. VI:4, Second Revision, above n. 494, para. 20.

[676] Ibid., para. 22. [677] Ibid., para. 21.

[678] The question may arise whether authorities may fulfil this requirement by using electronic means of communicating the rejection, or whether it is necessary to communicate the rejection on paper by sending a letter. In the light of various 'e-government' and 'administrative simplification' programmes, several states have introduced legislation enabling electronic communication between the public administration and the citizens. Many states introduced possibilities for citizens to provide information to the government in electronic form. Moreover, states have also introduced the possibility for authorities to communicate decisions to recipients in an electronic form, which is the issue at hand here. Arguably, requiring that members communicate their decisions on paper in a letter would

so requests, the reasons for the rejection must, in principle, be communicated as well as the time frame for appeal.[679] The addition 'in principle' may provide the WTO members with some leeway to argue that no reasons need be given in certain situations (e.g. for security reasons). It might be useful to add that this reply with the reasons for rejection needs to be communicated within a reasonable period of time so as to allow an applicant to resubmit an application. Indeed, it is further indicated that the applicant should be permitted to resubmit, within reasonable time limits. If the reasons for rejection are communicated late in the procedure, resubmission may no longer be of use because 'reasonable time limits' have been surpassed.

549. In any case, the entire procedure must be completed within a reasonable time frame. It is added that the members shall endeavour to establish the normal time frame in advance.[680] Once granted, the licence must enter into effect without undue delay.[681] Any licensing fees that may be charged must be reasonable in terms of the costs incurred by the competent authorities (including those for activities related to regulation and supervision of the relevant service) and cannot themselves restrict the supply of the service.[682] This requirement was perceived with concern by many WTO members, because fees are often charged to service

for some states be a step back in the light of the efforts for simplification and digitalization of public administration. On the other hand, it is clear that the applicant for a licence or for the verification and assessment of qualifications needs to be informed in a manner that allows him or her to take notice of the rejection without undue delay and such as to enable him or her to lodge an appeal or resubmit the application. In this respect, electronic communication may not always be able to achieve this objective, especially if the applicant has no access to means of electronic communication (the so-called 'digital divide'). This will, of course, be doubtful if the application was filed in an electronic format. Hence, on the one hand, electronic communication reduces administrative delays and hurdles, but, on the other hand, it may not always be the preferred form of communication for applicants. An important recurring principle in legislation is that the use of electronic communication with the government should be voluntary. While the use of e-mail is a common form of electronic communication of decisions, other electronic forms are imaginable, e.g. the posting of a decision on a website that is accessible by means of a password. However, no matter the technology that is used, it is important that the decision is accessible for subsequent reference. C. Prins, 'E-government: A Comparative Study of Multiple Dimensions of Required Regulatory Change', (2007) 11 *Electronic Journal of Comparative Law* 113, available at www.ejcl.org/113/article113-35.pdf; and Working Party on Domestic Regulation, Disciplines on Domestic Regulation Pursuant to GATS Art. VI:4, Annotated Text, Informal Note by the Chairperson, Room Document of 14 March 2010, at para. 226.

[679] See paragraph 23 Working Party on Domestic Regulation, Disciplines on Domestic Regulation Pursuant to GATS Art. VI:4, Second Revision, above n. 494.

[680] Ibid., para. 24. [681] Ibid., para. 25. [682] Ibid., para. 26.

suppliers to fund the activities of the regulatory and supervisory authorities. A previous draft included the requirement that the fees were 'commensurate' with the costs. If the fees that the disciplines refer to also cover those charged for supervision and regulation, a more lenient requirement was preferred. The paragraph was modified and replaced by a more flexible requirement that the fees had to be 'reasonable' in terms of the costs. A footnote to this paragraph in the draft Horizontal Disciplines also indicates that licensing fees 'do not include fees for the use of natural resources, payments for auction, tendering or other non-discriminatory means of awarding concessions, or mandated contributions to universal service provision'. The latter addition may allow WTO members still to use licensing fees for certain public policy goals (e.g. universal service provision).[683]

9.5.5.2 Qualification procedures

550. Similar provisions relate to qualification procedures. These procedures are relevant for the banking sector with regard to the foreign professionals whom a foreign bank wants to employ in the host country. Like licensing procedures, they must be as simple as possible and not in themselves constitute a restriction on the supply of the services.[684] In principle, to apply to more than one competent authority shall not be required,[685] and applicants should be able to submit at any time.[686] The competent authorities must inform the applicant of incomplete applications, to the extent feasible identify the required additional information and allow the opportunity to correct deficiencies.[687] Application should be accepted by means of authenticated copies rather than original documents.[688] Rejections of an application for verification and assessment of the qualification must be communicated in writing without undue delay. Reasons for rejection must, in principle, be communicated on request, and resubmission should be permitted within a reasonable

[683] With regard to para. 13 of the Accountancy Disciplines (which requires that licensing fees shall not exceed administrative costs) Krajewski has expressed the concern that governments would no longer be able to use fees or charges to 'internalise external costs or discourage certain behaviour'. Thus the 'goals a government is allowed to pursue with a certain measure' would be restricted. See Krajewski, above n. 348, at 127. The draft Horizontal Disciplines at least allow for collecting contributions for funding universal service supply.

[684] Working Party on Domestic Regulation, Disciplines on Domestic Regulation Pursuant to GATS Art. VI:4, Second Revision, above n. 494. para. 31.

[685] Ibid., para. 32. [686] Ibid., para. 33. [687] Ibid., para. 35. [688] Ibid., para. 36.

period.[689] The time frame for application, verification and assessment must be reasonable and members must endeavour to establish the normal time frame.[690] The fees should be commensurate with the cost incurred by the authorities, and not in themselves restrict the supply. Here, the requirement that the fees are 'commensurate' with the costs is maintained.

551. An important difference from licensing procedures is that qualification procedures are focused on the personal professional knowledge and experience of the applicant. This may be assessed through examinations. These must be scheduled at reasonable intervals, and a reasonable period of time shall be allowed for submitting applications.[691]

9.5.6 Conclusion on procedural requirements for individual supervisory assessments

552. In conclusion, the process of reaching supervisory decisions that apply criteria in measures of general application can be assessed under Article VI:1 GATS. Therefore Article VI:1 constitutes a relevant limit on the right of WTO members to supervise their market for banking services. Admittedly, WTO members may rather bring a claim before the WTO once several supervisory assessments point to a lack of reasonable, objective or impartial administration. Still, in principle Article VI:1 does not prevent WTO members from bringing a challenge on the basis of *one* individual supervisory assessment by the banking supervisor in another WTO member for failure to comply with Article VI:1.

553. Nevertheless, this does not mean that the finding of a violation will be reached lightly. In order to prove that the administration of this general measure in this individual decision is 'partial', 'unreasonable' or 'not objective', the complainant will have to advance solid evidence. For instance, with regard to the criterion of 'reasonable' administration, it is doubtful (and, arguably, undesirable) that a panel would make its own determination of the situation of an applicant for a banking licence or a candidate acquirer of a domestic bank, and second-guess the policy reasons considered by the bank supervisor. It is thus unlikely that a panel will decide that there is no rational reason for refusing the benefit of

[689] Ibid., para. 37. [690] Ibid., para. 38. [691] Ibid., para. 34.

government funding to a specific bank.[692] However, the individual decision may be found unreasonable if, for instance, it grants a licence, but on the condition that confidential information is disclosed by the bank in a manner that does not provide the necessary safeguards to prevent this information from being obtained by competitors.[693] The individual application of a general measure may also lack impartiality and objectivity, for instance if competitors of the candidate bank in question were able to influence the decision by the supervisory authority. Nonetheless, such claims should be based on solid evidence.

554. The disciplines are thus rather focused on the *process* of coming to a decision rather than on *outcome* of this process (the content of the decision). The panel in *EC – Selected Customs Matters* has noted that Article X:3(b) GATS sets a *general standard of due process*. Traders must be treated fairly and consistently such that the security and predictability of the trading system is ensured. It was argued that the combined reading of the conditions in Article VI:1 GATS supports the conclusion that the same standard of due process is contained in Article X:3(b) GATS.

9.6 Prudential exception

555. In the previous sections the analysis addressed the limits the GATS imposes on the right of WTO members to supervise their market for banking services. The analysis may show that the GATS does impose a potential limit on this right. Nonetheless, the practical application of the GATS obligations to individual supervisory assessments will probably only target decisions that are clearly within the scope of Article XVI, for which there is evidence of protectionist intent or for which there is solid evidence that the decisions constitute a lack of impartial, objective or reasonable administration of a general measure.

556. If a supervisory decision is proven to violate one of the obligations in the GATS, the defendant may of course have recourse to the prudential exception in paragraph 2(a) of the GATS Annex on Financial Services. As discussed, this exception is available for 'measures for prudential reasons' and there is no indication that 'measures' should

[692] Note that *several* of such individual applications may form a general 'practice' that provides proof that the general support scheme 'as applied' is discriminatory and thus violates Art. XVII.

[693] Cf. Panel Report, *Argentina – Hides and Leather*, para. 11.94.

have a meaning here that would exclude individual decisions. Therefore, if the banking supervisor in a WTO member were, for instance, to make a decision that requires a specific bank to set up a local subsidiary in the territory of the host member, and this member did not make a limitation to its market access commitments in the banking sector for such a measure, a violation of Article XVI will be found. However, the defending member may then still argue with success that this decision was meant to ensure the integrity and stability of the financial system because the establishment of the local subsidiary allows the host supervisor to perform effective supervision of the bank. To be sure, in cases where the protectionist intent of a decision was already established at the level of the obligation that is arguably violated (especially in the case of the provisions on non-discrimination), it is very unlikely that the conditions for the prudential exception will be fulfilled.

10

Conclusion to Part II

557. In Part II the international approach to liberalizing international trade in banking services has been examined. We considered how the obligations in the GATS might affect both regulatory and supervisory measures taken by WTO members in their attempt to make an appropriate trade-off between competition and stability in their markets for banking services. It was thereby also considered what possible role the principles and standards developed by the Basel Committee can play.

558. The analysis of the provisions in the GATS was complicated by the fact that only limited case law on the GATS is available. To be sure, there is more case law available on the GATT, which is useful when interpreting similar obligations. Nevertheless, as may be clear from the previous discussion, the decisions that are available have sometimes created further uncertainties, and it remains to be seen how future panels and the Appellate Body will deal with this case law. For these reasons, the analysis of the limit the international legal framework imposes on the right to regulate and supervise inevitably remains subject to criticism. Nonetheless, by trying to explicate the meaning of obligations in combination with the flexibilities and exceptions that exist in the GATS, we sought to provide a nuanced assessment of the real restriction the GATS imposes. In drawing general conclusions, such nuances may get somewhat lost.

559. With regard to the right of WTO members to *regulate* their market of banking services, three main sets of obligations in the GATS were considered: the obligation of market access, the obligation to treat banks and banking services from a different origin without discrimination and the disciplines on domestic regulation.

560. We first of all considered the limit imposed by Article XVI on the right to regulate. The *US – Gambling* decision provided an interpretation of Article XVI that made it clear that this provision constitutes a potentially very important limitation to the regulatory autonomy of members.

Even if Article XVI prohibits only six specified types of market access restriction, the fact that the panel and the Appellate Body accepted that a measure that 'amounts to' a zero quota is a measure that limits the number of service suppliers or the number of service operations in the sense of Article XVI:2(a) and (c), indicates that the scope of Article XVI is very broad. In principle, any banking regulation a (candidate) bank needs to comply with in order to provide banking services in a host member could be considered to be a measure that amounts to a zero quota. Nevertheless, one can identify limits to this scope. We concluded that a measure should only be considered to be of the type listed in Article XVI:2 if it (i) explicitly imposes quantitative maximum limitations; (ii) can *ex ante* be translated into a numerical quota; or (iii) involves an absolute restriction on an entire service sector, subsector or mode of supply. Hence requirements for obtaining and maintaining the authorization to provide banking services, such as capital requirements, are minimum requirements and thus are not of the type listed in Article XVI:2.

561. The second set of obligations considered involved the two main non-discrimination obligations in the GATS: most-favoured-nation and national treatment. The two steps for applying these provisions were analysed: the determination of 'likeness' and the establishment of 'less favourable treatment'. As discussed, when considering the existing case law on non-discrimination in the GATS and when drawing parallels with the existing GATT case law on discrimination, one may come to the conclusion that the GATS provisions that prohibit discrimination have an important impact on the right to regulate. This is due to the fact that the main focus for determining 'likeness' seems to be on *consumer perceptions* about the competitive relationship of banking services and banks of a different origin. This *market-based* approach will often lead to a conclusion that two banking services or banks of a different origin are 'like', even if there may be important policy-reasons for treating them differently. We concluded, however, that a panel could consider the regulatory and supervisory context as 'objective' characteristics of a service. Hence the fact that a bank or banking service originates in a WTO member that has not implemented the Basel principles or standards may be an 'objective characteristic' of the bank and the service it supplies. Further, we argued that it is still required for the complainant to establish that the banks of a certain origin are treated 'less favourably'. The complainant must convince a panel that the regulatory distinction is made to afford protection to banks or banking services of a certain origin. This can be done by providing actual proof of protectionist intent or by linking the regulatory distinction to the origin (by means of an asymmetrical aggregate impact analysis). The defendant must then advance factual evidence based on the regulatory structure of the measure that protectionism is not at issue. It will be for the panel to weigh these arguments.

562. The third set of obligations in the GATS for determining the extent to which the GATS limits the regulatory leeway of WTO members concerns the provisions and disciplines on domestic regulation. We concluded that, at present, the only restriction imposed on the freedom of WTO members to determine the substantive content of domestic regulation for banks is Article VI:5. It already imposes the requirements that are set forth in the mandate under Article VI:4. However, it only applies to the measures that are adopted after the point in time when the WTO member in question has made commitments. Moreover, the complainant must show nullification and impairment of commitments.

563. Even if the GATS does not entail positive integration, international standards of banking regulation, such as those developed by the Basel Committee on Banking Supervision, may play a role. Article VII GATS, which provides an exception to the most-favoured-nation obligation for recognition arrangements, may provide an important incentive for the WTO members to use international standards as a basis for recognition. Furthermore, the fact that a bank or banking service originates in a member that has implemented the Basel standards may arguably be an element to take into account when applying Article II and XVII GATS. Finally, these international standards can also be used as a source for defining the 'ordinary meaning' of certain terms in the exceptions in the GATS.

564. We also examined whether the GATS influences the right of the banking supervisors of the WTO members to make *individual supervisory assessments*. The real obstacles a bank experiences when trying to access a host market may only be revealed when considering the practical supervisory assessments that are made by banking supervisors. Such individual decisions are clearly within the scope of the GATS, but it may be disputed whether individual obligations in the GATS are suitable for being invoked in a challenge against a single supervisory assessment. Such claims may more naturally be brought in investment arbitrations. It is clear from Article VI:1 GATS and the draft text of the disciplines on domestic regulation that the GATS also includes obligations that specifically concern the rights of individual traders (banks), although only governments can bring claims to enforce these rights.

565. The provision in the GATS that seem *most suitable* to address claims with regard to individual supervisory assessments is Article VI:1. This provision states that *each WTO member must administer its measures of general application in a reasonable, objective and impartial manner.* Arguably, a panel will leave quite some margin of discretion to the authorities of the WTO members and will thus not redo the assessment the authority has performed. The provision is focused on the *process* of reaching the supervisory decision, and thus a claim on the basis of Article VI:1 seeks to ensure that the challenged administrative practices are no longer applied. The complainant must bring solid evidence of facts that show an unreasonable, non-objective and partial administration. A general 'due process' standard underlies these criteria, which implies that traders must be treated fairly, predictably and consistently.

566. When the analysis of the obligations in the GATS is combined with the analysis of the prudential exception, *one comes to the conclusion that the extent to which the international approach restricts WTO members to determine the trade-off between competition and financial stability is quite limited. As a consequence, the role of the GATS in promoting international competition in banking also seems limited.* However, in the absence of conditions for 'deeper integration' of markets in banking services (harmonized banking regulation that can quickly be amended and binding supervisory cooperation and centralization – existing to a greater extent within the EU), *the current approach of the GATS is probably the most that can be achieved.* In this sense, the current constellation of the GATS (with some restrictions on the host country competence to regulate and supervise) is an appropriate approach to intensifying international trade in banking services.

567. The analysis and the conclusions of this chapter in fact provide a 'stepping stone' to Part III, the final part of this volume. If the current approach at the international level at present can go not much further than prohibiting specific market access restrictions, prohibiting discriminatory measures and imposing due process requirements, and the conditions for 'deeper integration' are more likely realized within a regional trade integration process such as the European Union, the question arises how the international project interacts with such a regional process.

PART III

The European approach to international trade in banking services and its interaction with the GATS

11

Introduction to Part III

> There is never an 'acquis' in economics, certainly not in such a hypercompetitive environment as ours, in the world. We also need to strengthen our economic infrastructure to play a role on the world stage, to defend European interests and values. We need a strong economy for internal and external reasons. That's why we need more Europe; it is as simple as that.
>
> Herman Van Rompuy, President of the European Council, Address to the first congress of Solvay Business School, 25 October 2010

568. In this final part, we examine the extent to which the European approach to liberalizing international trade in banking restricts the member states in regulating and supervising banks that originate in WTO members that are not EU member states but seek access to the market of the EU member states. When addressing this question, we also focus on the connected question of how the WTO obligations influence the way in which the European project defines this treatment of third-country banks and banking services. The development of a European approach towards third-country banks happens against the background of an international project of liberalizing international trade in banking services. The EU, as well as its member states, is a member of the WTO.

569. As is well known, the European project has since 1957 sought to remove barriers to trade in services, including banking services. Moreover, since the White Paper on the Completion of the Internal Market of 1985, the European Commission (Commission) intensified work towards creating an internal market for banking services. In this respect, the EU project has on the basis of primary EU law (interpreted by the CJEU), as well as through regulations and directives, influenced the trade-off that member states can make between efficiency and stability in markets for banking services. The principles of mutual recognition and home country control were introduced and were supplemented by (minimum) harmonization of the authorization conditions for a credit institution or for carrying on its activities. Hence the EU seeks a balance between the goal of creating an internal market for banking services and the right of member states to determine for themselves how to regulate and supervise this market. Since the global financial crisis these efforts have been intensified. New harmonized rules on the treatment of hybrid capital instruments, large exposures and securitization were adopted,[694] as well as on the calculation of capital requirements and on remuneration policies.[695] Moreover, measures were adopted to reform the supervisory arrangements between home and host supervisors in the EU[696] and to create a single supervisory mechanism in the EU.[697]

570. However, the European legal framework also contains provisions that determine how member states must treat third-country banks that seek access to the market of the EU member states. The internal market thus also has an external dimension. To the extent the EU approach also restricts this right of its member states, it will affect the trade-off between stability and efficiency that the member states make with regard to the access of third-country banks. Until recently, the European legal framework seemed to leave quite some leeway to its member states to determine their own approach towards third-country banks and banking services. EU law did not prevent its member states from imposing stricter requirements with regard to the establishment of credit institutions by these banks than those that had been harmonized for the establishment of credit institutions by EU nationals. In areas where no internal EU harmonization had taken place, its member states did not even have to respect the 'floor' of EU harmonization. Hence the external dimension of the internal market did not consist of a fully harmonized external policy. However, since the entry into force of the Lisbon Treaty, radical steps have been taken towards a common and uniform external

[694] Directive 2009/111/EC of the European Parliament and of the Council of 16 September 2009 amending Directives 2006/48/EC, 2006/49/EC and 2007/64/EC as regards banks affiliated to central institutions, certain own funds items, large exposures, supervisory arrangements, and crisis management, OJ 2009 L 302/97.

[695] Directive 2010/76/EU of the European Parliament and of the Council of 24 November 2010 amending Directives 2006/48/EC and 2006/49/EC as regards capital requirements for the trading book and for re-securitisations, and the supervisory review of remuneration policies, OJ 2010 L 329/3.

[696] Directive 2009/111/EC, above n. 694, Arts. 42a, 49, 129, 130 and 131a.

[697] European Commission, Proposal for a Council Regulation conferring specific tasks on the European Central Bank concerning policies relating to the prudential supervision of credit institutions, COM(2012) 511 final.

EU policy with regard to the treatment of third-country banks that seek to expand their activities in the EU. What is more, with the creation of a single banking union for eurozone member states, significant centralization of supervision is created.

571. Still, this European framework does not exist independently of the international legal framework. We examine how the European legal framework interacts with the international obligations that are imposed by the GATS. The EU is a fully fledged member of the WTO, in addition to its member states. Hence the GATS influences their right to determine their own trade-off between stability and efficiency with regard to competition by third-country banks.

572. Part III consists of three chapters. First of all, we consider an overview of the sources of EU banking law that contain provisions that relate to the treatment of third-country banks (Chapter 12). The EU has, through the different stages in which this legal framework was developed, tried to use its regulation (and more specifically a 'reciprocity' requirement) to further the interests of the EU credit institutions in third countries. However, the WTO obligations imposed on the EU required the EU eventually to revise this approach. Next, we analyse those provisions in the Treaty on the Functioning of the European Union (TFEU) and the relevant EU regulations and directives that restrict the member states in determining how they regulate activities by subsidiaries of third-country banks (Chapter 13). Finally, we analyse the extent to which EU member states and the EU can supervise the activities by such subsidiaries (Chapter 14). Each time, we examine the interaction with the obligations in the GATS.

12

Sources of EU banking law relating to third-country banks

12.1 Introduction

573. In this chapter the different sources of EU law that relate to third-country banks are set out. The relevant provisions are situated in *primary EU law* (in particular the Treaty on the Functioning of the European Union), more specifically the provisions relating to free movement of services and capital and relating to the freedom of establishment. Furthermore, different directives and regulations have been adopted (*secondary EU law*), some implementing and clarifying the provisions of primary EU law, others going beyond the fundamental freedoms. The case law of the CJEU has interpreted and clarified provisions of both primary and secondary EU law. It is thus important to also take this source of EU law into account.

574. The evolution of the European rules affecting the treatment of third-country banks is closely related to the general evolution of the European efforts towards the realization of an internal market without obstacles to the free movement of goods, persons, services and capital. It is therefore useful to present the different sources of European law by reference to the historical evolution of this area of law. By means of gradual steps, the European Commission sought to create an internal market for banking services. When taking these steps, attention was also paid to the treatment of banks coming from outside the EU. Several directives have been adopted over the years and some have amended, added to or abolished provisions of previous directives. It is thus useful to clarify here what the relevant sources are, before embarking on the substantive analysis of the provisions that relate to third-country banks.

575. The historical evolution towards an internal market for banking services in the EU is divided into five stages. First, one can consider the era before the White Paper on the Completion of the Internal Market, in which the major tools for market integration were the treaty provisions on freedom of establishment, free movement of services and free movement of capital, be they combined with a number of directives that supported and clarified the functioning of these provisions, especially with regard to banking services. Second, the era *after* the Commission presented its White Paper, is characterized by active legislative work that produced results that went beyond the effect of the free movement provisions in the treaty. Third, there is the era after the Financial Services Action Plan of 1999, which gave rise to a new institutional structure for European banking regulation and to a wide range of measures that sought further integration of the European financial services market. By the deadline of the implementation of the Financial Services Action Plan in 2005, the European Commission issued a White Paper on Financial Services Policy 2005–2010. This fourth stage of the realization of an internal market for banking services focused on the further implementation and enforcement of European rules. Finally, this was abruptly distorted by the global financial crisis that broke out in 2007. A new range of regulatory measures was proposed, as well as a reform of the banking supervision in the EU.

576. In this overview of the relevant sources of EU law, we pay particular attention to the provisions relating to credit institutions from countries outside the EU that seek to provide banking services in the EU.

12.2 The period before the White Paper on the Completion of the Internal Market

577. From the establishment of the EEC by the Treaty of Rome in 1957, the provisions were in force prohibiting the member states from imposing restrictions on the free movement of services, the freedom of establishment and the free movement of capital. These fundamental freedoms were relevant for the realization of the free movement of banking services and the freedom of establishment of banks. Nevertheless, the application of some of these fundamental freedoms needed further legislative steps during a transitional period which lasted until 1 January 1970. The provisions on the freedom of establishment as well as the free movement of services were accompanied by a General Programme on the abolition of restrictions to the freedom of establishment[698] and free movement of

[698] General Programme for the abolition of restrictions on the freedom of establishment, OJ 1962 2/36 English special edition: Series II Volume IX, p. 7.

services.[699] The General Programme listed a number of restrictions that needed to be eliminated. However, to implement the General Programme, the Council of the European Communities adopted a number of directives.[700]

578. In 1977 the First Banking Directive was adopted.[701] It was the outcome of almost twelve years of negotiations.[702] Despite the Commission's ambitions, the First Banking Directive did not go much beyond the effect of the Treaty freedoms. The only provisions that prevented EC member states from taking protectionist measures were the prohibition on basing the grant of authorization on an examination of the economic needs of the market for another credit institution[703] and the obligation to impose the same authorization requirements on branches of credit institutions with the head office in another member state as on domestic institutions (in the case where an authorization was required for branches). The First Banking Directive went to a limited extent beyond a requirement of national treatment by prohibiting member states from refusing authorization to a branch 'on the sole ground that it is established in another Member State in a legal form which is not allowed in the case of a credit institution carrying out similar activities in the host country'.[704]

579. The First Banking Directive also paid attention to branches of credit institutions with their head office in a third country. It prohibited EEC member states from treating branches of such credit institutions more favourably than branches of credit institutions with their head office in the EEC.[705] The Directive also required member states to notify the Commission and the Advisory Committee of all authorizations granted to branches of credit institutions with the head office in a third

[699] General Programme for the abolition of restrictions on the freedom to provide services, OJ 1962 2/32 English special edition: Series II Volume IX, p. 3.

[700] Directive 73/183/EEC of 28 June 1973 on the abolition of restrictions on freedom of establishment and freedom to provide services in respect of self-employed activities of banks and other financial institutions, OJ 1973 L194/1.

[701] First Council Directive 77/780/EEC of 12 December 1977 on the coordination of the laws, regulations and administrative provisions relating to the taking up and pursuit of the business of credit institutions, OJ 1977 L322/30 (hereinafter First Banking Directive).

[702] An excellent overview of the negotiations is given by Clarotti: P. Clarotti, 'La coordination des legislations bancaires', (1982) *Revue du Marché Commun* 68, at 70–2. See also U. Leanza, 'An Outline of the EEC Discipline on Credit Institutions', (1987) 7 *Journal of Regional Policy* 59; and B. Sousi-Roubi, *Droit bancaire européen* (Paris: Dalloz, 1995), 62.

[703] Art. 3(3) of the First Banking Directive.

[704] This did not apply to credit institutions that did not possess separate own funds. First Banking Directive, Art. 4(2).

[705] Ibid., Art. 9(1).

country.[706] Furthermore, the Community was given the right to conclude agreements with third countries, on the basis of reciprocity, to grant such branches identical treatment throughout the territory of the Community.

12.3 The White Paper on the Completion of the Internal Market 1985

580. The second era is characterized by minimum harmonization of banking law to enable mutual recognition of banking regulations and home country control of credit institutions with a head office in an EC member state, but with activities in other member states by means of cross-border supply or the establishment of branches.

581. The Commission announced its 'new approach' towards the completion of the internal market in its White Paper of 1985.[707] Removing technical barriers to trade in the Community on the basis of wide-ranging harmonization of all kinds of technical regulations in the member states had proven unsatisfactory. Even if harmonization had produced results, the process was found to be slow (especially because of the requirement of unanimity in the Council for adopting directives that coordinated national laws, regulations and administrative actions, but also because complete harmonization of such technical issues required detailed and complicated negotiations).[708] The 'new approach' consisted of only harmonizing essential requirements and then obliging member states to recognize the equivalence of the rules and controls applied by other member states.[709] This was explicitly based on the decision by the CJEU in *Cassis de Dijon*.[710] The White Paper set 31 December 1992 as the deadline for the implementation of the programme.

582. While the *Cassis de Dijon* decision related only to free movement of goods, the Commission stated in its White Paper that '[w]hat is true for goods, is also true for services and people'.[711] A specific section on financial services indicated that the free circulation of financial products would be facilitated by means of minimal coordination of rules as the

[706] Ibid., Art. 9(2).
[707] Commission White Paper, 'Completing the Internal Market', COM (85) final, 14 June 1985.
[708] Ibid., at paras. 61 and 67–68. [709] Ibid., at para. 58.
[710] Ibid., at para. 77; CJEU Case 120/78, *Rewe-Zentral AG* v. *Bundesmonopolverwaltung für Branntwein*, [1979] ECR 649.
[711] Commission White Paper, above n. 707, at para. 58.

basis for mutual recognition.[712] The Commission announced also that the harmonization would be guided by the principle of 'home country control'. The Second Banking Directive implemented these principles. Case law that read the principle of mutual recognition into the treaty provisions relating to free movement of services and establishment, as did the CJEU in *Cassis de Dijon* for trade in goods, emerged only at the end of (for services[713]) or after (for establishment[714]) the implementation period of the White Paper.

583. In line with what was announced in the White Paper timetable for completing the internal market by 1992,[715] the European Commission presented a proposal for a Second Banking Directive in December 1987.[716] This Directive was adopted by the Council on 15 December 1989, right in time to meet the deadline set in the timetable of the White Paper.[717] Member states had to implement the Directive by 1 January 1993.

584. The Second Banking Directive provided minimum harmonization (i.e. the member states could apply higher standards to domestic banking

[712] Ibid., at para. 102. Also A. Corcoran and T. Hart, 'The Regulation of Cross-Border Financial Services in the EU Internal Market', (2002) 8 *Columbia Journal of European Law* 221, at 233–7.

[713] CJEU, Case C-76/90 *Säger* v. *Dennemeyer*, [1991] ECR I-4221.

[714] CJEU, Case C-55/94 *Gebhard* [1995] ECR I-4165.

[715] Annex to the Commission White Paper, above n. 707, at 25.

[716] Commission Proposal for a Second Council Directive on the Coordination of Laws, Regulations and Administrative Provisions Relating to the Taking-Up and Pursuit of the Business of Credit Institutions and Amending Directive 77/780/EEC, COM (87) 715 final, OJ 1988 C 84/1.

[717] Second Council Directive 89/646/EEC of 15 December 1989 on the Coordination of Laws, Regulations and Administrative Provisions Relating to the Taking-Up and Pursuit of the Business of Credit Institutions and Amending Directive 77/780/EEC, OJ 1989 L 386/1 (hereinafter Second Banking Directive). See P. Clarotti, 'Un pas décisif vers le marché commun des banques', (1989) *Revue du Marché Commun* 453; F. Dehousse and B. Dirick, 'Horizon 1992: le marché unique des services financiers', (1992) 111 *Journal des Tribunaux* 825; J. Deschanel and J. Stoufflet, 'La directive communautaire No. 89/646 du 15 décembre 1989 concernant l'accès à l'activité des établissements de crédit et son exercice. Vers un statut bancaire européen', (May–June 1991) *Banque et droit* 83; M. Gruson and W. Feuring, 'The New Banking Law of the European Economic Community', (1991) 25 *International Lawyer* 1; S. Katz, 'The Second Banking Directive', (1992) 12 *Yearbook of European Law* 249; P. Phillips, 'EC Second Banking Directive: The Practical Effect', (1993) 4 *European Business Law Review* 43; A. Steinherr, 'Stony Road to an Integrated Financial Market', (1989) 3 *European Affairs* 61; R. Strivens, 'The Liberalization of Banking Services in the Community', (1992) 29 *Common Market Law Review* 283; and G. Zavvos, 'Banking Integration and 1992: Legal Issues and Policy Implications', (1990) 31 *Harvard International Law Journal* 463.

services and branches of domestic banks) of a number of essential standards of prudential regulation. It amended, but did not abolish, the First Banking Directive. Hence both directives applied in combination.

585. In addition to harmonizing some essential regulations for authorization and exercising the business of credit institutions, the Second Banking Directive elaborated two principles that still constitute the cornerstone of the internal market for banking services in the EU: the principle of 'home country control' and that of 'mutual recognition'. With respect to the first principle, the Second Banking Directive required prudential supervision of a credit institution to be performed by the home member state, subject to some exceptions where the host country could still supervise.[718] In respect of the second principle, the Directive provided that a credit institution that is authorized and supervised by a certain member state must be allowed by other member states to carry on in their territory any of the banking services for which it was granted authorization by the home member state, as far as these services are listed in the Annex to the Directive. These services can be provided by means of cross-border service supply or by means of the establishment of a branch.

586. The Second Banking Directive also included a number of provisions relating to the authorization by authorities of the member states of subsidiaries of third-country credit institutions. It introduced an obligation for member state authorities to notify the Commission of any authorizations granted to such subsidiaries and of situations where a parent undertaking governed by the laws of a third country acquires a holding in a Community credit institution such that the latter becomes its subsidiary.[719]

587. Furthermore, the Directive focused on the treatment of the EU credit institutions in third countries. The member states had to inform the Commission of any difficulties that their credit institutions experienced when establishing themselves or carrying on their activities in third countries.[720] Moreover, the Commission had to draft a report on such treatment.[721] If concerns were to arise with regard to the treatment of EEC credit institutions in third countries, a procedure was foreseen to address these concerns. Two alternative scenarios were possible. First, when the Commission found that EEC credit institutions did not receive effective market access in a third country comparable with that granted

[718] Second Banking Directive, Art. 13(1). [719] Ibid., Art. 8 Second Banking Directive.
[720] Ibid., Art. 9(1). [721] Ibid., Art. 9(2).

by the EEC to credit institutions from that third country, it could submit a proposal to the Council to obtain a mandate for negotiation in order to obtain comparable opportunities for EEC credit institutions.[722] Second, if the Commission found that EEC credit institutions in a third country do not receive national treatment offering the same competitive opportunities as are available to domestic credit institutions in that third country and the conditions of effective market access are not fulfilled, it could initiate negotiations to remedy this situation.[723]

588. Branches of third-country credit institutions were not covered by the Second Banking Directive. Hence the provisions of the First Banking Directive still governed such branches.

589. Two further directives were adopted in 1989 and entered into force on the same date as the Second Banking Directive: the Solvency Ratio Directive and the Own Funds Directive. The Solvency Ratio Directive[724] sought to harmonize the solvency ratios with which credit institutions in the EEC had to comply.[725] Depending on what banking regulators allow to be considered as 'own funds', it will be more or less easy to meet the minimum solvency ratio. The Own Funds Directive provided a list of the number of sources that can be considered as own funds.[726]

590. In April 1991, the European Commission presented a proposal for a Directive on Large Exposures.[727] The Basel Committee had in January 1991 issued a report on measuring and controlling large credit exposures.[728] The proposal included an exposure limit of 25 per cent to one client or a connected group of clients.[729] Moreover, a large exposure would exist as soon as the level of 10 per cent of own funds would be reached.[730] These limits corresponded to what was recommended in the 1991 Report of the

[722] Ibid., Art. 9(3). [723] Ibid., Art. 9(4).

[724] Council Directive 89/647/EEC of 18 December 1989 on a solvency ratio for credit institutions, OJ 1989 L 386/14 (hereinafter Solvency Ratio Directive).

[725] Recital No. 11 to the Solvency Ratio Directive reads: 'Whereas, in a common banking market, institutions are required to enter into direct competition with one another and whereas the adoption of common solvency standards in the form of a minimum ratio will prevent distortions of competition and strengthen the Community banking system'.

[726] Council Directive 89/299/EEC of 17 April 1989 on the own funds of credit institutions, OJ 1989 L 124/16 (hereinafter Own Funds Directive), Art. 2(2).

[727] Commission Proposal for a Council Directive on monitoring and controlling large exposures of credit institutions, COM(91) 68 final, 23 April 1991, OJ 1991 C 123/18.

[728] Basel Committee on Banking Supervision, 'Measuring and Controlling Large Credit Exposures', January 1991, available at www.bis.org/publ/bcbsc121.pdf?noframes=1.

[729] Proposed Art. 4(1). [730] Proposed Art. 3(2).

Basel Committee.[731] The Large Exposures Directive was adopted on 21 December 1992.[732]

12.4 The Financial Services Action Plan 1999

591. In 1998, the European Council, meeting in Cardiff, asked the Commission to draft a framework for action on financial services. This framework had to examine the effectiveness of the implementation of the legislation that was prepared after the White Paper on the Completion of the Internal Market 1985, and identify any gaps that would require the amendment of the legislation.[733]

592. The Commission prepared such a 'framework for action' by 28 October 1998.[734] The Commission concluded that the prudential regulation of financial services markets did not need a radical overhaul, but that the Council of the European Union and the European Parliament had to consider procedures that would make it possible to amend legislation in a flexible, streamlined and fast manner when the market circumstances changed quickly. The 'framework for action' was discussed by the European Council meeting in Vienna on 11 and 12 December 1998, and the Council asked for a further report on the necessary steps to be taken.[735]

593. In cooperation with the Financial Services Policy Group (a group of representatives of economics and finance ministers of the member states and the European Central Bank), the European Commission drafted an Action Plan on Implementing the Framework for Financial Services Markets, presenting it on 11 May 1999.[736] The Financial Services Action Plan 1999 (FSAP) itself was in fact an annex to this communication, setting out three strategic objectives[737] and the mechanisms for achieving them

[731] Paras. 18 and 20 Basel Committee, above n. 728.

[732] Council Directive 92/121/EEC of 21 December 1992 on the monitoring and control of large exposures of credit institutions, OJ 1993 L 29/1 (hereinafter Large Exposures Directive).

[733] Presidency Conclusions of the Cardiff European Council of 15 and 16 June 1998, para. 17.

[734] Commission Communication of 28 October 1998, Financial Services: Building a Framework of Action, COM (98) 625 final.

[735] Presidency Conclusions of the Vienna European Council of 11 and 12 December 1998, para. 51.

[736] Commission Communication of 11 May 1999, Financial Services: Implementing the Framework for Financial Services Markets: Action Plan, COM (1999) 232 final.

[737] Strategic Objective 1: a single EU wholesale market; Strategic Objective 2: open and secure retail markets; Strategic Objective 3: state-of-the-art prudential rules and supervision.

according to a specific timescale. In fact, the FSAP set out forty-two actions that, according to the Presidency Conclusions of the Lisbon European Council, had to be adopted before 2005.[738] The FSAP thus became an essential aspect of the Lisbon Agenda that set the strategic goal of the European Union as by 2010 'becom[ing] the most competitive and dynamic knowledge-based economy in the world capable of sustainable economic growth with more and better jobs and greater social cohesion'.[739] The FSAP led to a far-reaching adaptation of the national financial regulation of the EU member states.[740]

594. The era of the FSAP was characterized not only by new European legislation in the financial sector, but also by a major overhaul of the regulatory structure for producing and implementing such European financial regulation. In the framework of the FSAP, the economic and finance ministers of the EU asked a number of prominent policymakers to report on the reasons for the lack of integration of securities markets in Europe.[741] In the Report of the Committee of Wise Men under the chairmanship of Baron Alexandre Lamfalussy, the lack of efficiency in adopting and implementing European legislation with regard to financial services liberalization was found to be the most important reason for the slow development of European securities markets.[742] The report therefore included a proposal to create a more rapid and efficient regulatory process for securities regulation ('Lamfalussy process').[743] The suggested process

[738] Presidency Conclusions of the Lisbon European Council on 23 and 24 March 2000, para. 21.

[739] Ibid., para. 5.

[740] For an evaluation see G. Walker, 'European Financial Programme: Content, Structure and Completion', (2004) 15 *European Business Law Review* 305, at 336–45.

[741] Report of the 2283rd ECOFIN Council Meeting in Brussels on 17 July 2000, at 7.

[742] Final Report of the Committee of Wise Men on the Regulation of European Securities Markets, Brussels, 15 February 2001, 13–15.

[743] D. Alford, 'The Lamfalussy Process and EU Bank Regulation: Preliminary Assessment and Future Prospects', (2006) 21 *Journal of International Banking Law and Regulation* 59; E. Avgouleas, 'The New EC Financial Markets Legislation and the Emerging Regime for Capital Markets', (2004) *Yearbook of European Law* 321, at 328–33; D. Chalmers, C. Hadjiemmanuil, G. Monti and A. Tomkins, *European Union Law. Text and Materials* (Cambridge University Press, 2006) 804–18; B. De Meester, 'Multi-level Banking Regulation: An Assessment of the Role of the EC in the Light of Coherence and Democratic Legitimacy', in A. Follesdal, R. Wessel and J. Wouters (eds.), *Multilevel Regulation and the EU. The Interplay between Global, European and National Normative Processes* (Leiden: Nijhoff, 2008) 101–43; G. Gari and R. Lastra, 'Assessing the Lamfalussy Process: Success and Failures', (July/August 2009) *Butterworths Journal of International Banking and Financial Law* 37; M. Nieto and J. Peñasola, 'The European

involved decision-making that would be organized over four different levels where specific bodies would become involved. The process introduced in 2001 for securities was extended to banking, insurance and occupational pensions in 2005.

595. An important simplification of the European legislative framework for banking was achieved in 2000, when several of above-mentioned directives were codified as one Codified Banking Directive.[744] The codification of this directive was not part of the FSAP, but was in fact the result of an initiative begun in 1987 by the Commission to make the European legislative instruments more readable.[745] Legislative instruments had to be codified as soon as ten amendments had been made to the original instrument. The initiative was endorsed by the European Council in Edinburgh in 1992.[746] This codification exercise may not involve amendments of substance.

596. With regard to banking, the Commission proposed in 1997 to codify several of the above-mentioned directives relating to banking services.[747] The directives that were codified were the early directive on the removal of restrictions on freedom of establishment and freedom to provide services in respect of activities of banks and other financial institutions (in the framework of the General Programmes, see above, para. 577), the First and Second Banking Directives, the Solvency Ratio and Own Funds Directives, the Large Exposures Directive and the Consolidated Supervision Directive.

12.5 The era after the Commission White Paper on Financial Services Policy 2005–2010 until the global financial crisis

597. In 2005, when the deadline of the FSAP passed, the European Commission produced a White Paper setting out financial services policy

Architecture of Regulation, Supervision and Financial Stability: A Central Bank Perspective', (2004) 5 *Journal of International Banking Regulation* 228; and B. Vaccari, 'Le processus Lamfalussy: une réussite pour la comitologie et un exemple de "bonne gouvernance européenne"', (2005) *Revue du Droit de l'Union Européenne* 803.

744 Directive 2000/12/EC of the European Parliament and of the Council of 20 March 2000 relating to the taking up and pursuit of the business of credit institutions, OJ 2000 L 126/1.

745 Commission Decision of 1 April 1987, COM (1987) 868 PV.

746 Conclusions of the European Council of Edinburgh of 11–12 December 1992, at 4a.

747 Commission Proposal for a European Parliament and Council Directive relating to the taking up and pursuit of the business of credit institutions (codified version), COM(97) 706 final, 15 December 1997.

until 2010.[748] The Commission did not foresee any wide-ranging legislative initiatives. In fact, Charlie McCreevy, the European Commissioner for Internal Market and Services at that time, announced a 'regulatory pause'.[749] Nonetheless, some legislative work was finalized or performed during this period. What is more, the global financial crisis suddenly required the Commission to consider a wide range of regulatory and supervisory reforms.

12.5.1 Recasting the Codified Banking and Capital Adequacy Directives

598. A first legislative development in the White Paper 2005–2010 era was the adoption of the recast Codified Banking Directive[750] in June 2006. The result was the Capital Requirements Directive (CRD). The work on the CRD had already started before the White Paper of 2005 and had already been announced in the FSAP.[751] It sought to improve the European rules on capital adequacy for credit institutions and investment firms, and work was undertaken in parallel with the work by the Basel Committee on a revised capital framework (Basel II).[752] The work of the Basel Committee was finalized in June 2004,[753] and the CRD

[748] Commission White Paper on Financial Services Policy 2005–2010, 5 December 2005.

[749] C. McCreevy, 'Recent Developments in the Internal Market for Financial Services and Financial Reporting', speech to the Association of Corporate Treasurers, Brussels 8 December 2005, available at http://europa.eu/rapid/pressReleasesAction.do?reference=SPEECH/05/778&format=HTML&aged=0&language=EN&guiLanguage=en.

[750] The 'recasting' technique involves amending an existing legislative text and at the same time codifying it into a new text. The technique is based on an inter-institutional agreement between the European Parliament, the Council of the European Union and the European Commission. Inter-institutional Agreement of 28 November 2001 on a more structured use of the recasting technique for legal acts, OJ 2002 C 77/1.

[751] Commission Communication COM (1999) 232 final, above n. 736, at 29.

[752] The first capital framework of 1988 was criticized as insufficiently taking into account the very diverse risk profiles of banks. The first framework set as a standard that the own funds should at least amount to 8 per cent of the 'risk-weighted assets' of a bank. The 'risk-weighted assets' were calculated by multiplying the outstanding credits of a bank by certain risk weights. These estimates were very crude (there were five general categories) and did not consider the sophisticated risk mitigation techniques credit institutions sometimes used. There was also a danger that credit institutions would engage in regulatory arbitrage by making use of innovative financial instruments that were not taken into account in the first framework.

[753] Basel Committee on Banking Supervision, 'International Convergence of Capital Measurement and Capital Standards. A Revised Framework', June 2004, available at www.bis.org/publ/bcbs128.pdf.

was adopted only after the deadline of the Action Plan. In July 2004, the Commission presented a proposal for recasting Directive 2000/12/EC as well as the Capital Adequacy Directive.[754] The new directives were adopted on 14 June 2006. New capital standards were included in the Capital Requirements Directive (CRD),[755] for credit risk and operational risk of credit institutions, and in a recast Directive on capital adequacy of investment firms and credit institutions[756] for market risk.

599. The CRD modified the competence of the EU Commission to intervene in the decisions of the banking supervisors of the EU member states that considered applications for authorization by third-country credit institutions. There is no longer an assessment of the 'comparable market access' and 'national treatment' of the EU credit institutions in third countries. The Commission retains the competence to conclude agreements with third countries to agree to apply to branches of credit institutions with the head office outside the EU identical treatment throughout the EU.[757] While under the Codified Banking Directive this still needed to be based on reciprocity, this requirement was now omitted from the CRD. These modifications were included with no further explanation in the Commission proposal.[758] However, it can be noted that on 1 January 1995, the GATS entered into force. The European Community had not included any exceptions to the obligation of most-favoured-nation treatment in its list of most-favoured-nation exemptions that would exempt a measure that required reciprocity as a condition for market access. Indeed, requiring reciprocity would be a violation of the most-favoured-nation obligation. It was thus necessary to delete these elements in the Directive.

[754] Proposal for Directives of the European Parliament and of the Council Recasting Directive 2000/12 of the European Parliament and of the Council of 20 March 2000 relating to the taking up and pursuit of the business of credit institutions and Council Directive 93/6/EEC of 15 March 1993 on the capital adequacy of investment firms and credit institutions, COM (2004) 486 final, 14 July 2004.

[755] Directive 2006/48/EC of the European Parliament and of the Council of 14 June 2006 relating to the taking up and pursuit of the business of credit institutions (recast), OJ 2006 L 177/1.

[756] Directive 2006/49 of the European Parliament and of the Council of 14 June 2006 on the capital adequacy of investment firms and credit institutions (recast), OJ 2006 L 177/201.

[757] Art. 38(3) Directive 2006/48/EC.

[758] Commission Proposal, COM (2004) 486 final, above n. 754, at 63.

12.5.2 *Directive on procedures and criteria for the prudential assessment of acquisitions and increase in shareholdings in the financial sector*

600. The White Paper on Financial Services Policy 2005–2010 announced a revision of the competence of the EU member state authorities to review and possibly block legal or natural persons obtaining certain holdings in credit institutions.[759] The competent authorities in the member state have the competence to satisfy themselves as to the 'suitability' of the acquiring person 'in view of the need to ensure sound and prudent management of the credit institution'.[760] There were concerns that national authorities would abuse this competence to block acquisitions of domestic credit institutions by foreign credit institutions merely on protectionist grounds.[761] In response to these findings, Article 19 of the Capital Requirements Directive was amended on 5 September 2007.[762] The new rules aimed to ensure that the competent authorities of the member states would carry out a prudential assessment of a banking merger or acquisition 'within a framework of clear assessment criteria and procedures'.[763] Article 23 of the

[759] Commission White Paper, above n. 748, at 12.

[760] Art. 19(1), second subparagraph Directive 2006/48/EC.

[761] In September 2004, European finance ministers found that cross-border mergers and acquisitions in financial services in Europe were much lower than in other sectors. In a study effectuated by the European Commission, market participants identified a number of obstacles to cross-border acquisitions in the EC. The first group of obstacles concerned elements that lower the economic value of a cross-border acquisition and thus make it less attractive. This included the fact that a large cross-border banking institution needs to comply with disparate supervisory rules and procedures. Cross-border banking mergers also appeared less attractive because the corporate rules for a pan-European institution were not adapted. Finally, different regulatory regimes for retail financial products made it difficult to sell products across borders. A second group of obstacles that was identified concerns political interference by the local authorities and legal defence mechanisms in corporate statutes when takeover bids are launched. A third group of obstacles involved the individual negative perceptions by consumers towards large cross-border institutions. Commission Staff Working Document, 'Cross-border Consolidation in the EU Financial Sector', SEC (2005) 1398, 26 October 2005, at 25–30.

[762] Directive 2007/44/EC of 5 September 2007 amending Council Directive 92/79/EEC and Directives 2002/83/EC, 2004/39/EC, 2005/68/EC and 2006/48/EC as regards procedural rules and evaluation criteria for the prudential assessment of acquisitions and increase in shareholdings in the financial sector, OJ 2007 L 247/1.

[763] Recital No. 3 of the Commission Proposal for a Directive amending Council Directive 92/79/EEC and Directives 2002/83/EC, 2004/39/EC, 2005/68/EC and 2006/48/EC as regards procedural rules and evaluation criteria for the prudential assessment of acquisitions and increase in shareholdings in the financial sector, COM(2006) 507 final of 12 September 2006.

Capital Requirements Directive now provides five criteria on the basis of which the competent national authorities can assess the suitability of the acquiring person.[764] These criteria also apply where a legal or natural person from a third country wishes to acquire a certain holding in a credit institution in the EU.

12.6 The global financial crisis

601. The global financial crisis suddenly disrupted the 'regulatory pause'. The crisis gave rise to the amendment of existing measures, but also triggered important new legislative proposals.

12.6.1 Directive 2009/111/EC of 16 September 2009 (CRD II)

602. The immediate reaction of the European Commission to the financial crisis was to propose amendments to the Capital Requirements Directive and the Capital Adequacy Directive.[765] On 1 October 2008, the European Commission issued a first proposal for an amending directive.[766] It involved four main issues: (i) criteria for the treatment of hybrid capital instruments as original own funds;[767] (ii) adjusted limits to large exposures;[768] (iii) new

[764] See below para. 644.

[765] Paulina Dejmek indicates that, even without a financial crisis, the directives would have been amended, since they left open certain areas of regulation, including the treatment of hybrid capital. P. Dejmek, 'The EU Internal Market for Financial Services – A Look at the First Regulatory Responses to the Financial Crisis and a View to the Future', (2009) 15 *Columbia Journal of European Law* 455, at 468.

[766] European Commission, Proposal for a Directive of the European Parliament and of the Council amending Directives 2006/48/EC and 2006/48/EC as regards banks affiliated to central institutions, certain own funds items, large exposures, supervisory arrangements, and crisis management, COM (2008) 602 final, 1 October 2008.

[767] Before the global financial crisis, the original Capital Requirements Directive left the decision on the treatment of 'hybrid capital instruments' to the member states. These hybrid instruments are securities that contain features of both equity and debt: they provide a higher return to investors than would a normal loan while at the same also involving more risk for the investors since, in the case of liquidation of the credit institution, they will only be redeemed after all other liabilities are met and immediately before common share capital. CRD IV and Regulation 575/2013 involve a harmonization of the criteria to determine whether such hybrid instruments are eligible as 'original own funds'.

[768] The definition of 'connected clients' is extended not only to the situation where a natural or legal person potentially experiences repayment difficulties because of the interconnection on the asset side with another natural or legal person that experiences financial difficulties, but also to the situation where a natural or legal person may be experiencing repayment difficulties because it is connected at the funding side to a vehicle that also funds another natural person that experiences financial difficulties.

rules on securitization;[769] and (iv) new supervisory arrangements. This proposal resulted in Directive 2009/111/EC (the so-called 'CRD II'), adopted on 16 September 2009.[770]

603. A major relevant innovation that specifically affects banks from third countries is linked to the establishment of colleges of supervisors. Directive 2009/111/EC introduces a legal underpinning for setting up such colleges. Their establishment and functioning must be based on written arrangements between the supervisors involved.[771] The colleges bring together the supervisors of the EU member states where the credit institution has subsidiaries, under the chairmanship of the consolidating supervisor. However, the competent authorities of the member states where a 'systemically relevant branch' of a credit institution is located may also be included in the college.[772] The competent authorities of the host member state may make a request to the consolidating supervisor (in the case of a banking group consisting of subsidiary credit institutions and branches) or to the competent authorities in the home supervisor (if no consolidating supervisor exists) to consider the branch systemically relevant.[773] Where appropriate, authorities of third countries may participate in the colleges of supervisors. However, this participation must take place under confidentiality requirements that are equivalent to those that apply within the EU.[774]

604. CRD II does not refer explicitly to the situation where an EU credit institution has *branches* in third countries that are potentially 'systemically relevant'. It only refers to competent authorities of host *member states* where

[769] The role played by collateralized debt obligations in provoking the global financial crisis also prompted the Commission to propose rules on securitization. Directive 2009/111/EC introduces an obligation for originators or sponsors of the underlying assets of the securities to maintain at least a 5 per cent interest in the assets.

[770] Directive 2009/111/EC of the European Parliament and of the Council of 16 September 2009 amending Directives 2006/48/EC, 2006/49/EC and 2007/64/EC as regards banks affiliated to central institutions, certain own funds items, large exposures, supervisory arrangements, and crisis management, OJ 2009 L 302/97.

[771] Art. 116(2) CRD IV.

[772] Art. 116(6) CRD IV. CRD IV indicates three factors to be taken into account for defining whether a branch is systemically relevant: the size of the market share of the branch, the impact of closure of operations on payment and clearing and settlement in the host member state and the size of the branch in terms of number of clients in the host member state. However, other reasons for considering the branch as systemically relevant can be given. The decision on whether a branch should be considered systemically relevant is a joint decision by the authorities involved.

[773] CRD IV, Art. 51. [774] Ibid., Art. 116(6).

systemically relevant branches are located.[775] However, it can be argued that where a 'systemically relevant' branch is located in a third country, an arrangement can be made to include in the college the competent authority of this third country. The consolidating supervisor must ensure appropriate coordination and cooperation with relevant third-country authorities.[776]

12.6.2 Directive 2010/76 of 24 November 2010 (CRD III)

605. Directive 2010/76 (the so-called 'CRD III') made further amendments to the Capital Requirements Directive and the Capital Adequacy Directive.[777] These amendments were influenced by the de Larosière report of February 2009, the declaration of the G20 at the London Meeting of 2 April 2009,[778] the report of the Financial Stability Forum (now the Financial Stability Board, FSB) on Addressing Procyclicality in the Financial System and the FSB's Principles on Sound Compensation Practices, both also of 2 April 2009.[779]

606. CRD III dealt with three main issues. First, it strengthened the capital requirements for assets that credit institutions hold in the trading-book for short term resale. Credit institutions are required to calculate potential losses on these assets in a 'worst-case scenario'.[780] Second, it established higher capital requirements and strengthened disclosure requirements for resecuritizations (i.e. repackaging securitizations into new securities).[781] Finally, the credit institutions are required to have remuneration policies that are consistent with and promote sound and effective risk management.[782]

[775] Ibid., Art. 51. [776] Ibid., Art. 116(1).

[777] Directive 2010/76/EU of the European Parliament and of the Council of 24 November 2010 amending Directives 2006/48/EC and 2006/49/EC as regards capital requirements for the trading book and for re-securitisations, and the supervisory review of remuneration policies, OJ 2010 L 329/3.

[778] G20 Leaders' Statement of London, 2 April 2009, www.londonsummit.gov.uk/en/summit-aims/summit-communique/.

[779] Report of the Financial Stability Forum on Addressing Procyclicality in the Financial System, 2 April 2009, www.financialstabilityboard.org/publications/r_0904a.pdf; and FSF Principles for Sound Compensation Practices, 2 April 2009, www.financialstabilityboard.org/publications/r_0904b.pdf.

[780] Annex II (3) to Directive 2010/76/EU.

[781] Regulation (EU) 575/2013 of the European Parliament and of the Council of 26 June 2013 on prudential requirements for credit institutions and investment firms and amending Regulation (EU) No. 648/2012, OJ 2013 L 176/1, Arts. 404–410.

[782] Art. 74(1) of Directive 2013/36/EU.

12.6.3 Rearrangement of prudential requirements and supervision in Directive 2013/36/EU and Regulation 575/2013 (CRD IV)

607. On 26 February 2010, the Commission launched public consultations on possible further amendments of the CRD, CRD II and CRD III. These consultations were focused on the question of how the financial soundness of banks and investment firms could be assured and thus on how the minimum capital requirements for credit institutions in the EU should be revised.[783] The amendments were aligned with the amendments to the Basel II framework (creating Basel III) by the Basel Committee (see above, para. 193). Eventually, the so-called 'CRD IV' (Capital Requirements Directive IV) package transposed the new global standards on bank capital into the EU legal framework; the preceding CRD directives were repealed. The package consisted of Regulation 575/2013[784] and Directive 2013/36/EU.[785] Both entered into force on 17 July 2013.

12.6.4 The reform of financial supervision

608. Finally, a number of steps created the centralization of financial supervision at the European level. The de Larosière report of 25 February 2009 proposed the creation of a European Systemic Risk Council, responsible for monitoring macro-prudential developments, as well as a European System of Financial Supervisors, responsible for improving cooperation between the EU member state authorities responsible for micro-prudential supervision. The present 'level 3' Lamfalussy committees will be reformed into 'authorities' with enhanced competences.[786] The de Larosière report set 2012 as the deadline for reforming the financial supervision architecture.[787]

[783] Commission Services Staff Working Document, Possible Further Changes to the Capital Requirements Directive (26 February 2010), available at http://ec.europa.eu/internal_market/consultations/docs/2010/crd4/consultation_paper_en.pdf.

[784] Regulation 575/2013.

[785] Directive 2013/36/EU of the European Parliament and of the Council of 26 June 2013 on access to the activity of credit institutions and the prudential supervision of credit institutions and investment firms, amending Directive 2002/87/EC and repealing Directives 2006/48/EC and 2006/49/EC, OJ 2013 L 176/338.

[786] High Level Group on Financial Supervision in the EU, Chaired by Jacques de Larosière, 'Report' (25 February 2009), Recommendations 16 and 18.

[787] Ibid., Recommendation 22.

609. The European Commission invited the European Council to endorse the proposals in the de Larosière report,[788] which the European Council did at its spring meeting in Brussels in March 2009. The European Council agreed that the report was the 'basis for action'.[789] On 27 May 2009, the Commission issued a Communication announcing the reform of financial supervision as suggested in the de Larosière report.[790] The Commission moved the deadline to 2010[791] and also proposed a steering committee to be set above the three new authorities.[792] Eventually, legislative proposals were made in September and October 2009. On 22 September 2010, the EU Parliament voted on and approved the new supervisory framework. It entered into force on 1 January 2011. Regulations created a European Systemic Risk Board[793] as well as the European System of Financial Supervisors re-forming the 'Level 3 Committee of European Banking Supervisors into the European Banking Authority'.[794] This was accompanied by a general directive for amending the relevant sectoral directives on which the reform of financial supervision would have an impact.[795]

610. The European Systemic Risk Board (ESRB) is composed of central bank governors and chaired by the president of the European Central Bank (ECB). The ESRB will be responsible for macro-prudential supervision in the EU. It will be able to issue risk warnings and recommendations, but will,

[788] European Commission, Communication for the Spring European Council. Driving European Recovery, COM (2009) 114 final, 4 March 2009, at 19.

[789] Presidency Conclusions of the Brussels European Council of 19 and 20 March 2009, para. 5.

[790] European Commission, European Financial Supervision, COM (2009) 252 final, 27 May 2009, at 3.

[791] Ibid., at 12. [792] Ibid., at 7.

[793] Regulation No. 1092/2010 of the European Parliament and of the Council of 24 November 2010 on European Union macro-prudential oversight of the financial system and establishing a European Systemic Risk Board, OJ 2010 L 331/1.

[794] Regulation 1093/2010 of the European Parliament and of the Council of 24 November 2010 establishing a European Supervisory Authority (European Banking Authority), amending Decision No. 716/2009/EC and repealing Commission Decision 2009/78/EC, OJ 2010 L 331/12.

[795] Directive 2010/78/EU of the European Parliament and of the Council of 24 November 2010 amending Directives 98/26/EC, 2002/87/EC, 2003/6/EC, 2003/41/EC, 2003/71/EC, 2004/39/EC, 2004/109/EC, 2005/60/EC, 2006/48/EC, 2006/49/EC and 2009/65/EC in respect of the powers of the European Supervisory Authority (European Banking Authority), the European Supervisory Authority (European Insurance and Occupational Pensions Authority) and the European Supervisory Authority (European Securities and Markets Authority) Text with EEA relevance, OJ 2010 L 331/120.

nevertheless, have no binding powers. EU member states will have to act in response to the recommendations or explain why they do not do so ('act or explain'). The recommendations will not be made public unless a two-thirds majority of the ESRB members agree to make them public.

611. The establishment of the European System of Financial Supervisors (ESFS) led to limited centralization of supervision in the EU. However, the day-to-day supervision of financial markets and financial institutions remained at the national level. The ESFS is a network of financial supervisors, consisting of the European Banking Authority (EBA), the European Securities and Markets Authority (ESMA) and the European Insurance and Occupational Pensions Authority (EIOPA). These are in fact the three former Lamfalussy 'level 3' committees with enhanced competences.[796]

612. Given the fact that the financial crisis was global and started outside the EU, the role of the EBA also focuses on the cooperation of the European supervisory authorities with authorities in third countries.[797] The EBA may establish contacts with supervisory authorities from third countries and enter into administrative arrangements with the administrations of third countries.[798] Furthermore, the EBA will assist in preparing decisions that establish the equivalence of supervisory regimes

[796] In addition to the old competences of the 'level 3' committees, the three 'Authorities' have a number of new competences. This includes the development of technical standards in order to address differences in national transposition of EU law in order to ensure a 'single EU rule book'. Next, they focus on the consistent application of harmonized rules. A fast procedure via the Authorities is introduced to tackle inconsistent application by the member states of harmonized rules, which complements the existing system whereby the Commission can start infringement procedures before the CJEU against member states. The Authorities can take certain supervisory measures and register certain institutions that have EU-wide actions, especially credit rating agencies. Further, the Authorities can settle disagreements between national supervisory authorities (especially in colleges of supervisors). The Authorities may assist in reaching a settlement, take a decision to settle the matter and can take measures addressed at the financial institution in case of non-compliance. Finally, the Authorities coordinate actions of national authorities when a crisis threatens. For a discussion see A. Coibion and E. Dessy, 'La réforme des services financiers en Europe un an après le début de la crise', (2009) 17 *Journal de droit européen* 194, at 196–7; and D. Masciandaro, 'Regulating the Regulators: The Changing Face of Financial Supervision Architectures before and after the Crisis', (2009) 6 *European Company Law* 187, at 191–2.

[797] European Commission, European Financial Supervision, COM (2009) 252 final, 27 May 2009, at 11.

[798] Article 33 of Regulation 1093/2010 of the European Parliament and of the Council of 24 November 2010 establishing a European Supervisory Authority (European Banking Authority), amending Decision No. 716/2009/EC and repealing Commission Decision 2009/78/EC, OJ 2010 L 331/12.

in third countries. These decisions play an important role when a credit institution or financial holding company with a head office outside the EU sets up or acquires a credit institution in a member state (below, paras. 720–723).[799] The EBA may also issue and publish an opinion on the prudential aspects of mergers and acquisitions.[800]

613. In September 2012, the Commission adopted two proposals for the establishment of a single supervisory mechanism (SSM) in the EU. The Commission proposed that this single supervision be performed by the ECB in the euro area.[801] On 19 March 2013, the European Parliament and the Council reached agreement on entrusting the ECB with this supervisory task.

12.7 Conclusion on the sources of EU banking law relevant to third-country banks

614. This overview shows that the EU legal framework contains an elaborate set of rules and principles on banking regulation and supervision. The global financial crisis has led to a further expansion of this body of law. The internal market for banking services is thus characterized by general principles that prohibit the creation of obstacles to trade in banking services between the EU member states but also by re-regulation at the European level.

615. The harmonized regulatory requirements of CRD IV also constitute the minimum requirements that member states must impose on natural and legal persons from outside the EU that seek to establish a credit institution in the form of a subsidiary in the EU. However, CRD IV also contains a number of provisions that specifically address regulatory and supervisory aspects involving credit institutions that are owned by a natural or legal person outside the EU. We examine these rules in the following chapters. Two elements will be considered that were also present in the analysis of the international legal framework: first, the regulation of the establishment or deployment of activities in the EU and, second, the supervision of the activities and entities.

[799] Ibid., Art. 33(2).

[800] Ibid., Art. 34(2). This can only be done on application of the competent authorities.

[801] Proposal for a Council Regulation conferring specific tasks on the European Central Bank concerning policies relating to the prudential supervision of credit institutions, COM(2012) 511 final, 12 September 2012.

13

Regulation of credit institutions that are subsidiaries of third-country banks

13.1 Introduction

616. In the case where a bank wants to carry out long-term activities in a host market and thus to create a lasting presence to serve clients there, it will decide to create a local establishment in the host country. When a bank prefers a lasting presence, the decision whether to create such a presence through the establishment of a branch or a subsidiary depends on the business strategy the bank adopts, but also on the local requirements in the law of the host country. While the creation of a branch may for some banks be desirable because it allows a single corporate structure where all decisions are made at the central level, the use of subsidiaries may be desirable for performing stand-alone operations (especially in the case of retail banking). In the EU, the creation of a subsidiary by a third-country person certainly has the advantage that the credit institution that is set up in the EU will benefit from the achievements of the EU internal market. Indeed, once a credit institution is set up in the EU, it not only benefits from the free movement of services and freedom of establishment, granted in Articles 56 and 49 TFEU, but also from the rights granted in CRD IV with regard to setting up branches in other EU member states or providing services in these member states.[802]

617. The essential question is under what conditions a natural or legal person from outside the EU can set up a credit institution in the EU. These conditions are harmonized in CRD IV. The question arises to what extent the competent authorities in the member states can impose stricter or additional requirements on persons from third countries that seek to set up a credit institution in the EU. While the major part of the

[802] See the twenty-third recital of CRD IV (*in fine*), stating that 'branches of credit institutions authorized in third countries should not enjoy the freedom to provide services under the second paragraph of Art. 49 of the Treaty or the freedom of establishment in Member States other than those in which they are established'.

CRD was originally based on minimum harmonization, this principle has been departed from since the adoption of CRD IV and the accompanying regulation. We examine what leeway EU member states still have. Furthermore, CRD IV also determines how the competent authorities in the member states must make supervisory assessments when a person from outside the EU wants to set up a credit institution in the EU. In Chapter 14 we examine what leeway EU member states still have.

13.2 Freedom of establishment in Article 49 TFEU

618. The conditions the EU member states can impose upon third-country persons that seek to establish a credit institution in the EU are to a large extent determined by EU law. Member states are thus not free to determine the trade-off between efficiency and stability in their market for banking services. This applies not only to EU persons that wish to establish a subsidiary and to obtain an authorization as a credit institution, but also to persons from outside the EU that want to do so. In this section we examine the limits imposed by EU law and the GATS on member states to regulate the direct establishment of credit institutions that are subsidiaries of third-country banks. We demonstrate that EU law significantly limits the leeway EU member states have. Moreover, since the EU is also a WTO member, the EU must also respect WTO law where it wants to treat such establishment by a third-country bank more strictly than establishment by an EU credit institution.

13.2.1 Freedom of establishment and third-country nationals

619. EU law grants to natural and legal persons that originate in a member state of the EU the right to establish themselves in the territory of other member states. Article 49 of the TFEU (*ex* Article 42 EC Treaty) prohibits member states from restricting the right of establishment. This right includes the right to set up a primary establishment by a national of a member state in another member state[803] or to set up a secondary establishment (possibly in the form of an agency, branch or subsidiary)

[803] Member States are prohibited from restricting the creation of a primary establishment in their territory merely because of the fact that the person setting up this establishment is a national of another member state. CJEU, Case 2–74 *Reyners* v. *Belgian State* [1974] ECR 631, paras. 15–16. Specifically for corporate establishment, the CJEU has recognized that individuals can freely choose the member state of primary establishment (depending on the most favourable conditions available) and then deploy activities in

in another member state by a natural or legal person that is already established in a member state.[804]

620. The CJEU found in *Gebhard* and in later cases that Article 49 TFEU prohibits not only discriminatory restrictions, but also measures that are indistinctly applicable but are 'liable to hinder or make less attractive the exercise of fundamental freedoms guaranteed by the Treaty'.[805] Hence a very broad range of measures might constitute a restriction on the freedom of establishment. However, a member state may justify such measures on the basis of imperative requirements in the general interest.[806]

other member states. Hence member states must not restrict this choice of primary establishment. CJEU, Case 79/85 *Segers* [1986] ECR 2375, para. 14; CJEU, Case C-212/97 *Centros* [1999] ECR I-1458, paras. 26–27; CJEU, Case C-208/00 *Überseering* [2002] ECR I-9919, paras. 78–82; and CJEU Case C-167/01 *Inspire Art* [2003] ECR I-10155, paras. 96–98, 105. This right of primary establishment (not involving the *move* of the primary establishment) can only be invoked by a natural person, since legal persons exist only by virtue of the law. Legal persons can thus only set up a secondary establishment or move their primary establishment. See inter alia C. Panayi, 'Corporate Mobility in Private International Law and European Community Law: Debunking Some Myths', (2009) 28 *Yearbook of European Law* 123.

[804] See inter alia CJEU, Case 79/85 *Segers* [1986] ECR 2375, para. 13; CJEU, Case 270/83 *Commission* v. *France* [1986] ECR 273, para. 18; CJEU, Case C-330/91 *Commerzbank* [1993] ECR I-4017, para. 13; CJEU, Case C-264/96 *ICI* [1998] ECR I-4695, para. 20. It is important to note that the Court of Justice in *CaixaBank France* accepted that the restriction of the right to set up a secondary establishment may also be situated in regulatory requirements that do not determine the conditions for setting up a secondary establishment (in the case of a subsidiary), but in requirements that reinforce barriers to access or prevent a subsidiary from competing effectively with the companies in the host market. CJEU, Case C-442/02 *Caixabank France* [2004] ECR I-8961, paras. 13–14. The *CaixaBank France* decision included another important element with regard to the right to secondary establishment for credit institutions. In this case, the Court of Justice stressed that the Capital Requirements Directive does not grant a right to a credit institution authorized in one member state to set up a subsidiary credit institution in another member state. Ibid., para. 7.

[805] CJEU, Case C-55/94 *Gebhard* [1995] ECR I-4165, para. 37. See also CJEU, Case C-255/97 *Pfeiffer Großhandel* [1997] ECR I-2835, para. 20. It goes without saying that this case law ignited an intense academic discussion on the limits of Art. 49 TFEU. The question indeed arises whether Art. 49 prohibits any national measures that somehow restrict the freedom to deploy economic activity in a member state, unless they are justified or whether the obligation is only meant to prohibit certain measures that restrict access to the market. The discussion is similar to the one that emerged after the panel and Appellate Body reports in the *US – Gambling* case were delivered (above, para. 253).

[806] In Part II the suggestion by several authors that, in the case of freedom of establishment, a member state must have more regulatory leeway to regulate the relatively permanent establishment of a service supplier in its territory than in case of free movement of services, where the service provision constitutes only a temporary presence in the territory, has already been referred to (above n. 380).

621. Since Article 49 TFEU applies to such a broad range of measures, it is an important tool for intensifying competition in the market for banking services within the EU. However, it is of no use to non-EU legal or natural persons that seek to establish a credit institution in a member state. It does not apply for natural or legal persons that have a third-country nationality and seek to create a *primary establishment* in the EU. In other words, a person from outside the EU cannot rely on Article 49 TFEU to secure access to the EU market.

622. Article 49 TFEU applies only to persons that are 'nationals of any Member State', meaning that they are formed 'in accordance with the law of a Member State and having their registered office, central administration or principal place of business within the Union'.[807] On the other hand, a member state cannot deny the benefit of Article 49 to a national (natural person) of a member state merely because this person *also* has the nationality of a third country.[808] Hence a natural or legal person from outside the EU cannot rely on the freedom of establishment in Article 49, unless it is already established in one member state and has its principal place of business in the EU. For nationals of third countries, the right granted under Article 49 is thus limited to the creation of a *secondary establishment* in the EU.

623. The 1961 General Programme on the abolition of restrictions on the freedom of establishment indicated that a bank that does not have its principal place of business within the EU, but only its place of incorporation, should at least have a 'real and continuous link' with the economy of an EU member state. It is not necessary that the members of the company, the shareholders, or the persons with managerial or supervisory posts have the nationality of a member state.[809]

624. In conclusion, in order to benefit from the freedom to establish a subsidiary in the EU by virtue of Article 49 TFEU, a third-country credit

[807] Art. 54 TFEU.

[808] CJEU, Case C-369/90 *Micheletti and others* [1992] ECR I-4239, para. 15.

[809] General Programme for the abolition of restrictions on the freedom of establishment within the European Economic Community, OJ 1962 2/36 English special edition: Series II Volume IX, p. 7 (Title I: Beneficiaries). Note that the real and continuous link can also be with the economy of an 'overseas country or territory'. It involves non-European countries and territories which have special relations with Denmark, France, Netherlands and United Kingdom (Art. 198 TFEU). These countries and territories are listed in Annex II to the TFEU.

institution will need to establish a legal person in the EU first. The right of the member states to regulate the conditions for establishing such a legal person in the EU is not affected by Article 49 TFEU, but only by the harmonized criteria in CRD IV and the accompanying regulation. Nationals from third countries have no right to create a primary establishment in the EU on the basis of Article 49 TFEU. Moreover, in order to claim the benefit of Article 49 TFEU, the principal place of business of the legal person that was set up by a third-country national in the EU must also be within the Union. If the place of incorporation were in the EU, but the principal place of business were outside the EU, the third-country national must show a 'real and continuous link' with the economy of a member state. Nonetheless, this situation will never occur when the primary establishment of the third-country national in the EU is a credit institution. Indeed, CRD IV requires that credit institutions have their head office in the same member state as their registered office.[810]

625. It is impossible for a third-country company to establish a branch in a member state and then claim the benefit of Article 49 to establish a subsidiary in another member state. The branch does not have a legal personality and thus cannot create a subsidiary. It is also not a national of a member state precisely because it does not have a legal personality: a branch is not incorporated in a member state. For the parent company outside the EU, the creation of a subsidiary in the EU is considered the primary establishment in the EU.

13.2.2 Article 49 TFEU in the light of the GATS

626. Because only nationals of member states can benefit from Article 49 TFEU, the operation of Article 49 involves discrimination on the basis of origin. This constitutes a measure that violates the obligation of most-favoured-nation treatment in Article II GATS: a benefit (a right to challenge restrictions on establishment) is available to banks from countries that are EU member states, but not to banks from other WTO members.

627. However, Article V:1 GATS provides that the GATS 'shall not prevent any of [the WTO members] from being a party to or entering into an agreement liberalizing trade in services between or among the parties to such agreement'. Hence Article V provides an exception to the obligation of

[810] Art. 13(2)(a) CRD IV.

most-favoured-nation treatment and makes such preferential trade arrangements possible.[811] In order for this exception to apply, a number of conditions must be met. First, the preferential agreement must have 'substantial sectoral coverage' and must provide for 'the absence or elimination of substantially all discrimination in the sense of Article XVII, between or among the parties in the sectors covered ....'[812] Second, the agreement must be 'designed to facilitate trade between the parties to the agreement and shall not in respect of any Member outside the agreement raise the overall level of barriers to trade in services within the respective sector or subsectors compared to the level applicable prior to such agreement'.[813]

628. Even if Article V:1 provides an exception to Article II, Article V:6 seeks to mitigate the discriminatory effect of a preferential arrangement. Fink considers that Article V:6 establishes a 'liberal rule of origin'.[814] It requires that a juridical person constituted under the laws of a party to the preferential arrangement and that engages in substantive business operations in the territory of the parties to such arrangement must also benefit from the preferential treatment under the arrangement. Hence the GATS requires that, as soon as a third-country national establishes a juridical person under the laws of an EU member state and the person engages in substantive business operations in the territory of the EU, it must benefit from the rights granted to nationals of member states under

[811] Panel Report, *Canada – Autos*, para. 10.271, which reads in relevant part: 'Moreover, it is worth recalling that Art. V provides legal coverage for measures taken pursuant to economic integration agreements, which would otherwise be inconsistent with the MFN obligation in Art. II.' (The Appellate Body did not have to address this statement by the panel, since it had already concluded that the panel had failed to examine the relevant facts of the case and whether Art. II was actually violated. It thus reversed the panel's findings. Appellate Body Report, *Canada – Autos*, paras. 168–184. Nevertheless, with regard to the corresponding provision in the GATT (Art. XXIV:5 GATT), the Appellate Body in *Turkey – Textiles* interpreted the language in the introductory paragraph (which reads: 'the provisions of this Agreement [i.e. GATT] shall not prevent ...') and stated: 'Thus, the chapeau makes it clear that Art. XXIV may, under certain conditions, justify the adoption of a measure which is inconsistent with certain other GATT provisions, and may be invoked as a possible "defence" to a finding of inconsistency.' Appellate Body Report, *Turkey – Textiles*, para. 45.

[812] GATS, Art. V:1(a)–(b). [813] Ibid., Art. V:4.

[814] C. Fink, 'PTAs in Services: Friends or Foes of the Multilateral Trading System?', in J. Marchetti and M. Roy (eds.) *Opening Markets for Trade in Services. Countries and Sectors in Bilateral and WTO Negotiations* (Cambridge University Press, 2008) 126; and T. Cottier and M. Molinuevo, 'Art. V GATS', in Wolfrum, Stoll and Feinäugle, above n.156, 125–51, at 146. See also A. Emch, 'Services Regionalism in the WTO: China's Trade Agreements with Hong Kong and Macao in the Light of Article V(6) GATS', (2006) 33 *Legal Issues of Economic Integration* 351, at 359.

EU law. This includes the right to set up a secondary establishment (e.g. a subsidiary that is a credit institution) or to move its primary establishment to another member state, granted by virtue of primary EU law (Article 49 TFEU).

629. The degree to which third-country banks can rely on Article V:6 of the GATS to secure the benefit of Article 49 TFEU depends on two elements. First of all, it depends on the conditions EU member states impose on third-country persons to establish a credit institution in the EU. These conditions have been harmonized to an important degree in EU law and are contained in CRD IV. We discuss the content of these provisions and the possibility for member states to deviate from these requirements in the next section.

630. The second element in Article V:6 GATS involves the requirement that the legal person 'engages in substantive business operations' in the territory of one of the parties to the preferential agreement. Arguably, this requirement corresponds to the need for a 'real and continuous link' with the economy of a member state, as required by the 1961 General Programme. Persons originating outside the EU that set up a legal person in a member state, without actually having their principal place of business in that member state can only benefit from Article 49 TFEU if they engage in substantive business operations and thus have a real and continuous link with the economy of a member state. Nonetheless, persons from outside the EU may seek to establish a legal person in the member state with the lowest requirements for establishment without actually developing substantive activities there, and then try to benefit from Article 49 to expand to another member state. Article V:6 does not explicitly specify that the substantive business operations must be in the territory of the party where the juridical person is established.[815] Moreover, the 1961 General Programme only specifies that the activities of the company show a 'real and continuous link with the economy of *a* Member State' (emphasis added). Still, when the primary establishment of the third-country person is a credit institution, the credit institution must have its head office in the same member state as its registered office (above, para. 624). The credit institution that is owned by a third-country person will thus always have a real and continuous link with the member state where it is established.

631. Hence, if a third-country bank wants to expand into the EU by creating subsidiaries and wants to rely on Article 49 TFEU to challenge

[815] See also Cottier and Molinuevo, above n. 814, at 148.

any possible restrictions it experiences, it must first establish a legal person in a member state that carries out substantive business operations in the EU. Depending on the requirements the member states impose on third-country persons that seek to establish a legal person in their territory, the third-country person will find it more or less difficult to gain the benefit of Article 49. Most preferential trade integration projects do not set a common standard for the treatment of the establishment of third-country persons and thus leave it to the individual member states to determine the conditions for initial establishment.[816] However, in the case of the EU, the EU legal framework defines such conditions. Therefore EU law significantly limits the leeway member states have in determining their approach towards third-country persons.

632. The conditions for establishing a legal person in a host member state depend first of all on the company law of this state. The European Commission has taken a number of initiatives to work towards harmonization of company law in Europe, and a number of directives have been adopted on specific topics in this field (e.g. accounting rules, cross-border mergers, takeover bids, the creation of the European Company Statute).[817] It would take too much space to discuss all these elements in the light of the GATS. Still, when the establishment takes the form of a credit institution, the person must comply with the specific harmonized

[816] A parallel can be drawn with free trade areas for trade in goods, where the parties can independently determine the external customs tariff for imports of third-country goods. This stands in contrast with a customs union. UNCTAD, *The REIO Exception in MFN Treatment Clauses* (New York and Geneva: UNCTAD, 2004) 12.

[817] For a discussion, see inter alia M. Andenas and F. Wooldridge (eds.) *European Comparative Company Law* (Cambridge University Press, 2009); A. Dorresteijn, T. Monteiro, C. Teichmann and E. Werlauff (eds.), *European Corporate Law* (Alphen aan de Rijn: Kluwer, 2009); K. Geens and K. Hopt (eds.), *The European Company Law Action Plan Revisited. Reassessment of the 2003 Priorities of the European Commission* (Leuven University Press, 2010); M. Habersack, *Europäisches Gesellschaftsrecht. Einführung für Studium und Praxis* (Munich: Beck, 2003); K. Hopt, E. Wymeersch and A. Schaub, 'Company Law and Corporate Governance in Europe: Interim Report and Reflections on the Ongoing Reforms in the European Union and in Selected Member States', (2005) *Rabels Zeitschrift für ausländisches und internationales Privatrecht* 611; M. Kroeze and H. Vletter-Van Dort, 'History and Future of Uniform Company Law in Europe', (2008) 5 *European Company Law* 114; M. Menjucq, *Droit international et européen des sociétés* (Paris: Montchrestien, 2008); P. Pellé, 'Companies Crossing Borders within Europe', (2008) 5 *European Company Law* 284; M. Siems, 'Convergence, Competition, "Centros" and Conflicts of Law: European Company Law in the 21st Century', (2002) 27 *European Law Review* 47; and J. Wouters, 'European Company Law: Quo Vadis?', (2000) 37 *Common Market Law Review* 257.

criteria in CRD IV and accompanying regulation. In the next section we discuss these criteria and the possibility for the member states to deviate from these.

13.3 Harmonized criteria for taking up and pursuing the business of credit institutions

633. When a natural or legal person, no matter whether this person has the nationality of an EU member state or not, wants to establish a credit institution in the EU, it will face the requirements imposed by the member state of establishment. Through gradual steps, these requirements were harmonized at the EU level. When a person establishes a credit institution that is authorized according to the harmonized criteria in CRD IV, it will benefit from the 'single passport'. As a consequence, it is allowed to provide banking services (specified in Annex I of CRD IV and as far as is covered by the authorization by the member state of establishment) in other member states by means of cross-border supply or by means of branches. On the basis of Article 33 of CRD IV, each EU member state is obliged to recognize the equivalence of the authorization granted and the supervision performed by competent authorities of other member states. In addition, when the foreign person has established a credit institution in a member state, it can also rely on Article 49 TFEU to challenge restrictions imposed by member states relating to the establishment of subsidiaries in other member states.[818]

634. The fact that a number of authorization conditions for establishing a credit institution were harmonized in CRD IV suggests that the EU member states are significantly limited when determining the trade-off between competition and stability in their market for banking services. This trade-off is determined at the European level. Because the harmonized requirements apply also to third-country persons, this affects also the trade-off made by member states with regard to competition from banks from outside the EU. In the following subsections, the harmonized requirements for obtaining an authorization as a credit institution in the

[818] It is not necessary for the legal person established in a member state to be authorized as a credit institution in order to benefit under Art. 49 TFEU. As explained in the previous section, it is sufficient to establish a legal person in a member state and to have a real and continuous link with the economy of a member state. However, these requirements are necessarily fulfilled for a credit institution that is established and authorized in a member state.

EU are discussed. Next, we address the possibility of member states deviating from these harmonized requirements when regulating the establishment of third-country banks. Finally, we examine how such deviations would be assessed under the GATS.

13.3.1 Requirements for taking up and pursuing the business of credit institutions

635. The First Banking Directive required member states to oblige credit institutions to obtain an authorization on the basis of fulfilling certain conditions, but did not specify the content of these conditions. The Second Banking Directive specified the content of the requirements to obtain access to the business of credit institutions. These criteria remain in CRD IV. What is more, the directive and the accompanying regulation also provide harmonized rules in respect of the exercise of the business of credit institutions, and thereby incorporate not only the provisions in the First and Second Banking Directives, but also the requirements from the Own Funds, Solvency Ratio and Large Exposures Directives. The global financial crisis led to significant modifications in this legal framework. Directive 2013/36/EU (CRD IV)[819] contains the harmonized requirements for access to the activity of credit institutions, and Regulation 575/2013 (accompanying regulation)[820] contains the harmonized prudential requirements.

13.3.1.1 Requirements for obtaining an authorization as credit institution

636. Title III of CRD IV harmonizes a number of requirements member states can impose upon entities that want to take up the business of credit institutions. It requires first of all that these entities obtain *authorization* before commencing their activities.[821] In principle, member states are free to determine the requirements for obtaining an authorization, except for a number of specific requirements that have been harmonized. In any event, any requirement for authorization must be notified to the

[819] Directive 2013/36/EU of the European Parliament and of the Council of 26 June 2013 on access to the activity of credit institutions and the prudential supervision of credit institutions and investment firms, amending Directive 2002/87/EC and repealing Directives 2006/48/EC and 2006/49/EC, OJ 2013 L 176/338.

[820] Regulation (EU) 575/2013 of the European Parliament and of the Council of 26 June 2013 on prudential requirements for credit institutions and investment firms and amending Regulation (EU) No. 648/2012, OJ 2013 L 176/1.

[821] CRD IV, Art. 8.

Commission.[822] The Directive also prohibits member states from examining the request for authorization in the light of the economic needs of the market.[823]

637. The Directive harmonizes a number of essential requirements for authorization. First, it obliges the member states to require an application for authorization to be accompanied by a *programme of operations*, 'setting out, inter alia, the types of business envisaged and the structural organization of the credit institution'.[824]

638. Second, the Directive requires that each credit institution has *separate own funds* (i.e. funds separate from the personal funds of the owners) and *initial capital of at least €5 million.*[825]

639. Third, the competent authorities of the member states may only grant the authorization if the business of the credit institution is effectively *directed by at least two persons of sufficiently good repute and with sufficient expertise* to perform such duties.[826] This involves a degree of evaluation by the competent authorities in the member state. While there existed no guidance before, CRD IV now provides further criteria for determining whether there exists 'sufficiently good repute' or 'sufficient expertise', including whether 'sufficient time' is committed to performing the functions;[827] a limit on the number of directorships held;[828] the requirement of adequate collective knowledge, skills and experience to be able to understand the institution's activities, including the main risks;[829] the requirement to act with honesty, integrity and independence of mind;[830] the requirement for credit institutions to devote adequate human and financial resources to the induction and training of members of the management;[831] the requirement to take into account diversity when appointing members.[832] The EBA is tasked with developing further guidelines to clarify these criteria.[833]

640. Fourth, the competent authorities of the member state must consider the *characteristics of the important shareholders* of the credit

[822] It should be noted that the Directive does not specify sanctions in case of failure to notify.
[823] CRD IV, Art. 11. [824] Ibid., Art. 10. [825] Ibid., Art. 12(1).
[826] Ibid., Art. 13(1), referring to Art. 91(1). [827] Ibid., Art. 91(2).
[828] Members of the management body shall not hold at the same time more than one of the following combinations of directorships: (a) one executive directorship with two non-executive directorships and (b) four non-executive directorships. Ibid., Art. 91(3).
[829] Ibid., Art. 91(7). [830] Ibid., Art. 91(8). [831] Ibid., Art. 91(9).
[832] Ibid., Art. 91(11). [833] Ibid., Art. 91(12).

institution before granting authorization. The authorities must be informed of the identities of the shareholders that have 'qualifying holdings' in the credit institutions as well as of the amounts of those holdings.[834] A 'qualifying holding' is a 'direct or indirect holding in an undertaking which represents 10% or more of the capital or of the voting rights or which makes it possible to exercise a significant influence over the management of that undertaking'.[835] If the competent authorities are not satisfied with regard to the suitability of the shareholders in the light of 'the need to ensure the sound and prudent management of a credit institution', they should refuse to grant authorization.[836] This again allows the competent authorities a degree of evaluation.

641. Finally, the credit institution must have *robust governance arrangements* in place (involving a clear organizational structure with well-defined, transparent and consistent lines of responsibility), *effective risk management processes and adequate internal control mechanisms*, and *a remuneration policy that is consistent with and promote sound and effective risk management*.[837] When assessing such arrangements, processes and mechanisms, the competent authorities should take into account the 'nature, scale and complexity of the credit institution's activities'.[838] While it is not explicitly stated that this involves a requirement for obtaining the authorization to operate as credit institution, it is possible that competent authorities will assess these aspects before granting authorization. CRD IV specifies a number of technical criteria concerning the organization and treatment of risks.[839]

642. The experience of the global financial crisis revealed the effects of short-term bonus schemes of certain staff on risk-taking of the credit institutions they were part of. To avoid remuneration schemes being detrimental to the sound and effective risk management of the credit institutions, the EU adopted a directive to introduce obligatory supervisory review of

[834] Ibid., Art. 14(1). [835] Regulation 575/2013, Art. 4(1), point (36).

[836] CRD IV, Art. 14(2). [837] Ibid., Art. 74(1). [838] Ibid., Art. 74(2).

[839] The management body of credit institutions must approve and periodically review the strategies and policies for taking up, managing, monitoring and mitigating risks (ibid., Art. 76(1)). The management body must devote 'sufficient time' to the consideration of such risks (ibid., Art. 76(2)). Credit institutions must set up a 'risk committee' that advises the management body on risks (ibid., Art. 76(3)). Credit institutions must also have a 'risk management function' that is independent from the operational and management functions and with sufficient authority, stature, resources and access to the management body (ibid., Art. 76(5)).

remuneration policies.[840] The directive does not explicitly require that the institution submits its remuneration policies when applying for an authorization. However, it is likely that this will also be considered when a credit institution seeks an authorization. In the fourth recital to the proposed amendment, it is noted that 'each credit institution or investment firm should establish the general principles to be applied, and the policies should be subject to at least annual independent review'. Article 74(1) of CRD IV specifies that the credit institution must have 'remuneration policies and practices that are consistent with and promote sound and effective risk management'.[841] The CRD IV sets out a number of criteria for remuneration policies.[842] The criteria concern remuneration for staff whose professional activities have a material impact on the risk profile of credit institutions. Stricter principles apply in case of institutions that benefit from government intervention.[843] Article 94 lays down requirements for the variable elements of remuneration. Credit institutions that are significant in terms of size, internal organization and the nature, scope and complexity of their activities must establish a 'remuneration committee' to judge remuneration policies and practices.[844]

643. If the establishment of the credit institution in an EU member state by a natural or legal person from abroad takes the form of the *acquisition of control in an existing credit institution* in this member state, the competent authorities in this member state must make a prudential evaluation of this acquisition. According to Article 22 CRD IV, national authorities in the member states may assess and even oppose a plan by any natural or legal person to obtain a 'qualifying holding' in a credit institution. Such a 'qualifying holding' is a 'direct or indirect holding in an undertaking which represents 10% or more of the capital or of the voting rights or which makes it possible to exercise a significant influence over the management of that undertaking'.[845] The evaluation equally takes place where the person wants to increase his 'qualifying holding'

[840] Directive 2010/76/EU of the European Parliament and of the Council of 24 November 2010 amending Directives 2006/48/EC and 2006/49/EC as regards capital requirements for the trading book and for re-securitisations, and the supervisory review of remuneration policies, OJ 2010 L 329/3.

[841] See also Art. 1(3)(a) of Directive 2010/76/EU of the European Parliament and of the Council of 24 November 2010 amending Directives 2006/48/EC and 2006/49/EC as regards capital requirements for the trading book and for re-securitisations, and the supervisory review of remuneration policies, OJ 2010 L 329/3.

[842] CRD IV, Art. 92. [843] Ibid., Art. 93. [844] Ibid., Art. 95.

[845] Regulation 575/2013, Art. 4(1), point (36).

so that his proportion in the voting rights or capital of the credit institution reaches or exceeds 20 per cent, 30 per cent or 50 per cent or such that the credit institution would become a subsidiary of the person. Hence this provision clearly covers the situation where a natural or legal person from outside the EU acquires control in an existing credit institution in the EU.[846]

644. Competent authorities must assess the suitability of the acquirer and the financial soundness of the acquisition on the basis of five criteria: (a) the reputation of the acquirer; (b) the reputation and experience of any person who will direct the business of the credit institution as a result of the acquisition; (c) the financial soundness of the acquirer, in particular in relation to the type of business pursued in the credit institution; (d) whether the credit institution will be able to meet and continue to comply with the prudential conditions under CRD IV and Regulation 575/2013 as well as other EU law, in particular Directives 2002/87/EC (on the supplementary supervision of financial conglomerates) and 2009/110/EC (on electronic money institutions), including whether the group of which it will become a part has a structure that makes it possible to exercise effective supervision, effectively exchange information among the competent authorities and determine the allocation of responsibilities among the competent authorities; and (e) whether there are reasonable grounds for fearing money laundering or terrorist financing in connection with the acquisition.[847]

645. Attention is paid to the specific situation of acquirers from third countries. The assessment period for acquisitions originating in third countries is longer, to give due account to the fact that the supervisory systems and market structures in third countries may be different from those in the EU.[848] Supervisory authorities may need more time to evaluate the

[846] According to the definitions in the GATS, a bank from one WTO member can provide banking services by means of establishing a 'commercial presence' (Mode 3) by acquiring a juridical person within the territory of another WTO member. Art. XXVIII(d)(i) GATS.

[847] CRD IV, Art. 23(1).

[848] The competent authorities normally have sixty working days from the written acknowledgement of the receipt of the notification to examine the proposed acquisition. The Commission may request further information during the assessment period, but no later than on the fiftieth working day (ibid., Art. 22(2)–(3)). The assessment period is interrupted from the date of request for information until the receipt of the response, be it that the interruption may not exceed twenty days. What is more, if the acquirer is regulated outside the Community or is a natural or legal person not subject to supervision under one of the financial services directives, the interruption of the assessment period may be up to thirty working days.

information that would be provided and the acquiring person would need more time to prepare the specific requested information.

13.3.1.2 Rules affecting the exercise of the business of credit institutions

646. Besides the requirements for obtaining an authorization as credit institution, CRD IV also harmonizes a number of requirements that are imposed on credit institutions *while pursuing their activities.* These requirements also play a role in the decision of foreign banks whether to establish themselves in a host territory. It is not easy to make a distinction between pre-establishment and post-establishment measures when one delineates the measures that affect market access.[849]

647. A number of requirements are linked to the *initial requirements for obtaining an authorization.* During all operations, the credit institution must ensure compliance with these requirements. The competent authorities of the member state where the credit institution was authorized must ensure that the initial capital of the credit institution does not fall below the level of €5 million. If not, the authorization may be withdrawn.[850] The competent authorities may also withdraw the authorization if the institution 'no longer fulfils the conditions under which authorization was granted'.[851] Hence the credit institution must remain effectively directed by at least two persons of sufficiently good repute and with sufficient experience.[852] Furthermore, if supervisory authorities consider that the credit institution no longer has robust governance arrangements, risk management processes or internal control mechanisms, the competent supervisory authorities may consider that the institution no longer fulfils the conditions of the authorization and thus the authorization may be withdrawn. The same will arguably apply to remuneration policies where these policies endanger the sound and effective risk management of the institution, if this is considered one of the conditions for authorization. However, for these arrangements, processes, mechanisms and remuneration policies, such will be the *ultimum remedium*, and the authorities will most likely first take measures that require the credit institution to rectify the situation.[853] A number of principles with regard to administrative

[849] This is clear in WTO law from the *US – Gambling* decision, but also in EU law from the *CaixaBank France* decision.

[850] CRD IV, Art. 18(c). [851] Ibid., Art. 18(c). [852] Ibid., Art. 13(1).

[853] Ibid., Art. 102(1).

sanctions are contained in CRD IV.[854] Moreover, the competent authorities must require that the credit institutions that do not have such arrangements, processes, mechanisms and remuneration policies in place, maintain own funds in excess of the regulatory minimum level (below, para. 650). The competent authorities must also assess whether to require such higher level of own funds when they consider this necessary in the light of the risks the credit institution is taking. They should then take into account the internal assessment processes the credit institution has in place for capital adequacy as well as the mentioned arrangements, processes, mechanisms and remuneration policies.[855]

648. Along the same lines, the competent authorities must monitor changes in the qualifying holdings in the credit institution. To this end, *changes* in such holdings must be *notified in writing* to the competent authorities before they take place. It concerns situations where the holding increases so that it would 'reach or exceed 20%, 30% or 50% or so that the credit institution would become [a] subsidiary'.[856] Notification is also required in situations where a natural or legal person proposes to dispose of a qualifying holding, the holding decreases below the mentioned levels or as a consequence of disposal of a holding the credit institution ceases to be a subsidiary.[857] There exists no further assessment procedure in this case.[858]

649. In contrast to the initial conditions for authorization that also need to be complied during the operations, other requirements are only imposed once the credit institution is carrying on its activities.

650. A first requirement imposed on credit institutions during their operations is the obligation to comply with *capital adequacy requirements.* As explained (above, para. 74), the regulatory requirement that banks maintain

[854] Ibid., Art. 65(1), provides that the sanctions must be 'effective, proportionate and dissuasive'. Further specifications are made for administrative sanctions imposed for violations of authorization requirements and requirements for acquisitions of qualifying holdings (ibid., Art. 66). Pecuniary sanctions must be sufficiently high to offset the benefits that can be expected and to be dissuasive even for larger institutions and their managers. CRD IV specifies an arsenal of sanctions that member states must at least have in place. In the case of a legal person, this includes administrative sanctions of up to 10 per cent of the total annual turnover of the legal person in the preceding business year (ibid., Art. 67(2)(e)). In the case of a natural person, this includes an administrative pecuniary sanction of up to €5,000,000. Sanctions must be published, unless this would seriously jeopardize the stability of financial markets (ibid., Art. 68).

[855] Ibid., Art. 104(1)–(2). [856] Ibid., Art. 22(1). [857] Ibid., Art. 25.

[858] See Sousi-Roubi, above n. 702, at 133, discussing the Second Banking Directive. However, this is still the case under CRD IV.

minimum capital and guard their capital ratios is meant to provide incentives to banks to take less risk and to create a buffer to absorb losses that a bank suffers when there are unexpected economic shocks. Before, and certainly during, the global financial crisis, several authors questioned the ability of capital adequacy requirements to provide the necessary incentives to banks to engage in prudent behaviour. Capital adequacy requirements would in fact give incentives to bank managers to take more risk to offset the costs of maintaining high levels of capital, would be set at levels that are too low given the risks banks are incurring and would be procyclical. Moreover, harmonized capital requirements would lead to homogenization of behaviour of banks, leading to loss of liquidity in markets when a crisis occurs. The amendments of the Capital Requirements Directive in response to the global financial crisis addressed uncertainties with regard to the composition of a credit institution's own funds and led to higher levels of required capital.[859] The capital adequacy requirements in EU law implement the (non-binding) capital adequacy framework developed at the international level by the Basel Committee on Banking Supervision.

651. Regulation 575/2013 that accompanied CRD IV implemented the latest revision of the international capital framework: Basel III (see above, para. 193). Since this legislative instrument takes the form of a regulation, it is directly applicable in the member states and involves maximum harmonization, except in very limited circumstances. The Commission thus seeks to create a 'truly single rule book'.

652. The second set of harmonized requirements imposed on credit institutions during their operations is the limit on certain *large exposures* credit institutions may incur. Banks becoming excessively exposed to a single client should be avoided. Therefore Regulation 575/2013 provides a general prohibition for credit institutions to incur an exposure to one client or a group of connected clients[860] the value of which amounts to

[859] Directive 2010/76/EU of the European Parliament and of the Council of 24 November 2010 amending Directives 2006/48/EC and 2006/49/EC as regards capital requirements for the trading book and for re-securitisations, and the supervisory review of remuneration policies, OJ 2010 L 329/3 and the Arts. 404–410 of Regulation 575/2013.

[860] Directive 2009/111/EC has extended the definition of 'connected clients' not only to the situation where a natural or legal person potentially experiences repayment difficulties because of the interconnection on the asset side with another natural or legal person that experiences financial difficulties, but also to the situation where a natural or legal person may be experiencing repayment difficulties because it is connected on the funding side to a vehicle that also funds another natural person experiencing financial difficulties (Regulation 575/2013, Art. 4, point 39(b)).

more than 25 per cent of its own funds.[861] An exposure is considered a 'large exposure' (and thus taken into account for calculating the limits) where 'its value is equal to or exceeds 10%' of the own funds of the credit institution.[862]

653. The amendments to the Capital Requirements Directive by Directive 2009/111/EC modified these provisions to an important extent. The goal was to simplify the provisions and to limit national discretions.[863] The latter is especially clear from the fact that the explicit possibility for member states to impose stricter exposure limits than the level laid down in the Directive was removed.[864] CRD IV, using maximum harmonization, is a further manifestation of the creation of a 'single rule book' without national deviations.

654. A third requirement imposed on credit institutions when they develop their activities concerns a *restriction of the possibility of credit institutions to obtain participation in undertakings outside the financial sector.*[865] This dates back to the discussions relating to the Second Banking Directive, when member states disagreed on whether 'universal banks' (banks that take participations in non-bank institutions) should be allowed.[866] Regulation 575/2013 obliges member states to prohibit credit institutions to take a 'qualifying holding' that exceeds 15 per cent of its own funds in an undertaking outside the financial sector.[867] Moreover, the sum of all such qualifying holdings in undertakings outside the financial sector may not exceed 60 per cent of the own funds of the credit institution.[868] Hence, universal banking is allowed, but only up to certain limits.

655. The legislative work in response to the global financial crisis gave rise to a fourth harmonized requirement imposed on credit institutions while pursuing their activities. The role played by collateralized debt obligations (CDOs) in provoking the global financial crisis also prompted the Commission to propose rules on securitization. As explained

[861] Regulation 575/2013, Art. 395(1). The prohibition on having a total of large exposures in excess of 800 per cent of the own funds has been deleted.

[862] Ibid., Art. 392.

[863] European Commission, Proposal for a Directive of the European Parliament and of the Council amending Directives 2006/48/EC and 2006/48/EC as regards banks affiliated to central institutions, certain own funds items, large exposures, supervisory arrangements, and crisis management, COM (2008) 602 final, 1 October 2008, at 8.

[864] See old Art. 113(1) of Directive 2006/48.

[865] Regulation 575/2013, Art. 89–91.

[866] Sousi-Roubi, above n. 702, at 114.

[867] Regulation 575/2013, Art. 89.

[868] Ibid., Art. 89(2).

(above, paras. 40–49), the *securitization* of mortgage loans and repackaging of these securities into CDOs that are sold on the financial market has led to the transfer of credit risk to market players that did not know at all what the quality of the underlying assets was. It also removed incentives for originators of loans to monitor the quality of the borrower. Regulation 575/2013 now specifies that credit institutions are only allowed to invest in securitizations if a number of conditions are fulfilled. The originators or sponsors of the underlying assets must 'retain, on an ongoing basis, a material net economic interest which, in any event, shall be not less than 5%'.[869] Regulation 575/2013 specifies in a limitative manner the four situations that qualify as meeting the 'retention requirement'.[870] This should reinstate incentives of originators of loans to monitor the quality of the loans.[871] The credit institution must demonstrate to the competent authorities that it understands risks in the securitization and has procedures in place for analysing all aspects of these transactions.[872] The originators or sponsors must also disclose the level of their commitment to maintain a net economic interest and must make available all materially relevant data on the underlying assets.[873]

[869] Ibid., Art. 405(1).

[870] The regulation specifies what 'retention of net economic interest' means in Art. 405(1), second subparagraph, (a)–(e). It involves either (a) retention of no less than 5 per cent of the nominal value of each of the tranches sold or transferred; or (b) in the case of securitizations of revolving exposures, retention of the originator's interest of no less than 5 per cent of the nominal value of the securitized exposures; or (c) retention of randomly selected exposures, equivalent to no less than 5 per cent of the nominal amount of the securitized exposures, where such exposures would otherwise have been securitized in the securitization, provided that the number of potentially securitized exposures is no less than 100 at origination; or (d) retention of the first loss tranche and, if necessary, other tranches having the same or more severe risk profile than those transferred or sold to investors and not maturing any earlier than those transferred or sold to investors, so that the retention equals in total no less than 5 per cent of the nominal value of the securitized exposures; or (e) retention of a first loss exposure not less than 5 per cent of every securitized exposure in the securitization. Art. 405(3) defines situations where the 5 per cent obligation does not apply.

[871] Molostova has criticized this rule. She has argued that this requirement 'will make the cost of capital in Europe higher than elsewhere', 'will create a perverse incentive to use structures under which assets are originated by non-regulated entities which are not subject to the regulatory capital rules' and 'in the absence of international agreement will put European originators at a significant competitive disadvantage, thus potentially driving securitisation activity offshore'. I. Molostova, 'Revision of the European Regulatory Capital Regime', (January 2009) *Butterworths Journal of International Banking and Financial Law* 20, at 22.

[872] Regulation 575/2013, Art. 406. [873] Ibid., Art. 406.

656. Directive 2010/76/EU established higher capital requirements and strengthened disclosure requirements for resecuritizations (i.e. repackaging securitizations into new securities). This requirement is now contained in Regulation 575/2013. If the credit institution is not able to demonstrate to the supervisory authorities that it understands the risks linked to such financial instruments and has the necessary processes in place for analysing and monitoring these risks, the competent authorities can require the credit institution to apply an additional risk weight of no less than 250 per cent and with a maximum of 1250 per cent to these instruments.[874] This obviously would require the credit institution to have a much higher level of own funds.

13.3.2 The possibility for member states to deviate from the harmonized requirements

657. The requirements for taking up and pursuing the business of credit institutions, described in the previous section (13.3.1), were harmonized at the European level in order to allow the functioning of mutual recognition of the authorization and supervision of competent authorities of the EU member states. Governments will not likely agree to mutual recognition without being assured that there is at least a common minimum level of regulation to address externalities. The credit institutions authorized in member states would not be allowed to operate under the 'single passport' to set up branches or provide services in other member states (see Article 33 CRD IV) if there were no harmonization of the conditions for authorization and rules for pursuing activities. In principle, persons from outside the EU that seek to set up a credit institution in a member state of the EU will also face these harmonized requirements. We examine here to what extent EU law prohibits member states from deviating from these harmonized requirements when a person from outside the EU requests authorization as a credit institution.

658. The leeway for the authorities of the EU member states to determine themselves the approach they take to competition from third-country banks may manifest itself in three forms. First, member states may want to impose authorization requirements or regulations affecting aspects of bank structures or banking activities that are not addressed in

[874] Ibid., Art. 407.

the harmonized rules at the EU level. Second, member states may want to impose stricter requirements and rules than those harmonized (e.g. higher initial capital requirements). Finally, it is possible that the authorities in the member states are stricter for third-country banks than for European banks in the practical application of the general authorization requirements or other rules. We address this last possibility in Chapter 14, on supervision.

13.3.2.1 Requirements in addition to the harmonized requirements

659. A member state may impose authorization requirements on third-country persons in addition to the requirements defined in CRD IV and the accompanying regulation.[875] An important preliminary question is whether the measure a member state adopts falls within the scope of the directive or regulation or not.[876] If the subject matter of the measure at issue falls within the scope of the directive or regulation, the member states are 'pre-empted' from still acting in this area, except when the directive or regulation explicitly provides for this possibility. If the subject matter of the measures is outside the scope, the member states are not restricted.[877]

660. However, they must still respect the obligations in primary EU law. This holds, for instance, if an EU member state were to prohibit credit institutions from providing remuneration on current accounts, as was the case in *CaixaBank France*.[878] When it concerns nationals from a member state, such additional requirements must conform to Article 49 TFEU. However, when a person from outside the EU has not yet established a legal person in a member state, it is not a 'national of a member state' and thus cannot rely on Article 49 to challenge such measures. A member state is thus not bound by Article 49 in that situation. Yet such measures must still comply with the obligations in the GATS.

[875] Thirteenth recital to Regulation 575/2013.

[876] V. Mak, 'Review of the Consumer Acquis: Towards Maximum Harmonization?', (2009) 17 *European Review of Private Law* 55, at 59.

[877] See also the sole article of Protocol 25 on the Exercise of Shared Competences (2010) OJ C 83/207: 'With reference to Article 2(2) of the Treaty on the Functioning of the European Union on shared competence, when the Union has taken action in a certain area, the scope of this exercise of competence only covers those elements governed by the Union act in question and therefore does not cover the whole area.'

[878] CJEU, Case C-442/02 *Caixabank France* [2004] ECR I-8961.

13.3.2.2 Requirements that are stricter than the harmonized requirements

661. An EU member state may also want to impose authorization requirements or conditions for pursuing business that are stricter than the ones harmonized in CRD IV and its accompanying regulation. In this case, the requirements the member state wants to adopt are within the scope of the directive or the regulation. A member state is not permitted to apply requirements that would be less stringent than those laid down in the Directive or Regulation or to fail to apply the harmonized requirements at all. If it were to do either of these things, this member state fails to comply with its obligations under EU law. It is thus not possible for member states to apply requirements to third-country persons that are less stringent than those harmonized, except when the directive provided exceptions. Such weaker requirements would undermine the level of consumer protection and financial stability sought in CRD IV and its accompanying regulation and would create competitive distortions across the EU.

662. Because member states often find it very difficult to give up their own level of protection when harmonized criteria are negotiated, EU directives frequently reserve the possibility for the member states to adopt or maintain stricter requirements ('minimum harmonization'). The same can be said about protection against financial instability: member states that are concerned about the impact of competition in the bank sector on financial stability may want to reserve the possibility to be more prudent than other states.

663. In the aftermath of the global financial crisis, the areas where minimum harmonization was present were significantly reduced. The European Commission eventually proposed a regulation on prudential requirements. Regulation 575/2013 harmonizes the prudential requirements institutions need to respect, such as capital adequacy requirements and exposure limits. The fact that the prudential requirements are contained in a regulation implies that they constitute directly applicable obligations. Members are not allowed to impose any stricter requirements than those laid down in the regulation ('maximum harmonization'). The rules concerning the access to deposit-taking activities are contained in a directive (CRD IV). CRD IV also contains very few possibilities for member states to impose stricter requirements, as it involves mainly maximum harmonization.

664. Minimum harmonization has clear shortcomings for realizing an internal market. Even though such harmonization might be an efficient way of reaching agreement on harmonized rules and is sensitive to the right of member states to pursue valuable objectives such as financial stability, it cannot avoid fragmentation of the internal market by stricter rules imposed by member states (the so-called 'gold plating').[879] When member states are permitted to impose stricter requirements, producers or service suppliers will face regulatory diversity and thus may be discouraged from providing services in other member states.[880]

665. In the field of financial services, several suggestions were made about moving to a type of harmonization that prevents member states from maintaining or introducing stricter requirements. The Lamfalussy report had already noted that the EU regulatory framework was insufficient for achieving a real single market for financial services. It found that a 'large majority of interested participants share the feeling that transposition and implementation of EU directives is unsatisfactory, inhibiting the development of cross-border securities business'.[881] In its final report, the Inter-Institutional Monitoring Group on the Lamfalussy Process concluded that the implementation of EU directives was still

[879] W. Devroe, 'Limits of Differentiation in European Economic Law: *Ne Bis In Idem* and Minimum versus Maximum Harmonisation', (2009) 16 *Maastricht Journal of European and Comparative Law* 141, at 146. See also Weatherill, who notes that this 'gold-plating' can take the form of stricter rules than those laid down in a directive, rules that extend beyond the directive's personal or material reach, national enforcement in a manner more vigorous than is required by EU law or in other member states. S. Weatherill, 'Harmonisation: How Much, How Little?', (2005) 16 *European Law Review* 533, at 539.

[880] Weatherill has asked the question, referring to the much-cited decision by the Court of Justice in *Germany* v. *European Parliament and Council (Tobacco Advertising)*, whether a legal instrument by which the EU provides *minimum* harmonization may genuinely have as its object the improvement of the conditions for the establishment and functioning of the internal market, as is required when such measures are taken on the basis of Art. 114 TFEU (ex Art. 95 EC Treaty) (which forms the legal basis for measures for the approximation of the laws of member states which have as their object the establishment and functioning of the internal market). S. Weatherill, 'Measures of Consumer Protection as Impediments to Exports of Goods', (2009) 5 *European Review of Contract Law* 149, at 15, referring to CJEU, Case C-376/98 *Germany* v. *European Parliament and Council* [2000] ECR I-8419, para. 84.

[881] Final Report of the Committee of Wise Men on the Regulation of European Securities Markets, Brussels, 15 February 2001, 84. The report pointed to the inadequate functioning of the institutional framework as a cause (and made suggestions to improve this), but also referred to differences in legal systems and the patchwork of applicable legislation (ibid., at 88–89). The monitoring by the Commission of the implementation of European legislation by the member states constituted 'Level 4' of the Lamfalussy Process.

insufficient and referred to 'the threat that potential "gold-plating" of EU Directives represents for the success of the Single Market'.[882]

666. The de Larosière report also pointed to this problem. It stressed that Europe suffers from 'the lack of a consistent set of rules'.[883] The cause of this lack of consistency would be the many options provided in the directives for national implementation and enforcement.[884] The report recommended remedying this problem at the European level by relying on regulations rather than directives and using maximum harmonization of core issues when directives are used.[885] A double justification underpins such maximum harmonization. Lack of consistent rules not only creates competitive distortions in the single market; it may also threaten financial stability: differences between EU member states compound problems of crisis prevention and management. Spillovers of financial problems from one country to another point to the need for common approaches.[886] The drafters of the report nevertheless added that, under certain circumstances, it may be appropriate that member states adopt safeguards or requirements that are stricter than the common framework. Yet this 'should of course be done while respecting the principles of the internal market'.[887]

667. In the case of 'maximum harmonization', there is no possibility for member states to adopt stricter measures in the area within the scope of

[882] Inter-institutional Monitoring Group, Final Report Monitoring the Lamfalussy Process (15 October 2007), available at http://ec.europa.eu/internal_market/finances/docs/committees/071015_final_report_en.pdf, para. 23. The group recommended that legislative measures clearly spell out the level of harmonization to be achieved – that is, whether the measure is a maximum or minimum harmonization measure. Furthermore, it would need to be required that member states 'to report on any regulatory add-ons they intend to adopt' (ibid., para. 24).

[883] High Level Group on Financial Supervision in the EU, Chaired by Jacques de Larosière, 'Report' (25 February 2009), para. 99.

[884] Ibid., paras. 102–103.

[885] The report notes: 'When directives are used, the co-legislator should strive to achieve maximum harmonisation of the core issues. Furthermore, a process should be launched to remove key differences stemming from the derogations, exceptions and vague provisions currently contained in some directives' (ibid., para. 109).

[886] Ibid., para. 104. See also Mavromati, discussing how the Payment Services Directive (Directive 2007/64/EC) tries to 'find the necessary balance and flexibility' between facilitating the freedom of establishment and a high protection of consumers. This would be reflected in the use of Art. 47 EC Treaty (now Art. 53 TFEU) in combination with Art. 95 EC Treaty (now Art. 114 TFEU). D. Mavromati, *The Law of Payment Services in the EU. The EC Directive on Payment Services in the Internal Market* (Alphen aan de Rijn: Kluwer Law International, 2008) 96.

[887] Larosière report, above n. 883, para. 108.

the directive. If a directive is 'exhaustive in nature', in the sense that the subject matter covered by the measure a member state plans to take is covered by the directive, the member states are 'pre-empted' from acting in this field.[888]

668. The amendments to the Capital Requirements Directive as a response to the global financial crisis reduced the number of options and uncertainties.[889] CRD IV and its accompanying regulation reduce to a minimum the circumstances in which member states can adopt stricter requirements. 'Maximum harmonization' thus became the default rule in EU banking regulation.

669. In contrast to the previous directives, the Preamble of CRD IV no longer contains paragraphs specifying what provisions involve 'minimum harmonization'.[890] The second recital merely specifies that the new legislation should consist of two different legal instruments. On the one hand is a directive containing the provisions governing the authorization of credit institutions and investment firms, the acquisition of qualifying holdings, the exercise of the freedom of establishment and of the freedom to provide services, the powers of supervisory authorities and the provisions governing

[888] CJEU, Case 5/77 *Tedeschi* [1977] ECR 1555, para. 35; CJEU, Case 148/78 *Ratti* [1979] ECR 1629, para. 36; CJEU, Case 60/86 *Commission* v. *United Kingdom (Dim-Dip)* [1988] ECR 3921, paras. 11–12; and, more recently, CJEU, Joined Cases C-281/03 and C-282/03 *Cindu Chemicals BV and Others* [2005] ECR I-8069, para. 44 and CJEU, Case C-478/07 *Budějovický Budvar* v. *Rudolf Ammersin GmbH* [2009] ECR I-7721, para. 106. See M. Dougan, 'Minimum Harmonization and the Internal Market', (2000) 37 *Common Market Law Review* 853, at 866; P. Slot, 'Harmonisation', (1996) 21 *European Law Review* 378, at 388–9; and S. Weatherill, 'Supply of and Demand for Internal Market Regulation: Strategies, Preferences and Interpretation', in N. Shuibne (ed.), *Regulating the Internal Market* (Cheltenham: Edward Elgar, 2006) 29–60, at 42.

[889] See, e.g., the new provisions on 'hybrid capital' (above n. 767), the deletion of certain exemptions for large exposures as well as the deletion of Art. 133(1) that allowed member states to impose stricter large exposure limits. Note that also the amendment to Art. 19 on the prudential assessment of mergers and acquisitions explicitly provides that member states cannot impose stricter requirements.

[890] Recital No. 15 in the Preamble of Directive 2006/48 reads: 'The Member States may also establish stricter rules than those laid down in Art. 9(1), first subparagraph, Art. 9(2) [minimum level of initial capital] and Arts. 12 [assessment of the suitability of persons having a qualifying holding], 19 to 21 [acquisition and disposal of qualifying holdings in credit institutions], 44 to 52 [exchange of information and professional secrecy], 75 [minimum level of own funds] and 120 to 122 [qualifying holdings outside the financial sector] for credit institutions authorized by their competent authorities . . .' Recital No. 28 reads: 'This Directive specifies that for certain own funds items qualifying criteria should be specified, without prejudice to the possibility of Member States to apply stricter provisions.'

the initial capital and supervisory review. On the other hand, it involves a regulation establishing 'uniform and directly applicable' prudential requirements for credit institutions and investment firms.

670. CRD IV nevertheless provides a few exceptions permitting member states to apply stricter rules for minimum capital. First, CRD IV specifies that each member state is competent to set the level of the counter-cyclical capital buffer. This buffer is indeed determined based on a member state's own economic situation, credit cycle and risks due to excess credit growth in that state.[891] Second, member states may impose an additional systemic risk buffer that would further increase the minimum capital required. This buffer is meant to prevent and mitigate long-term, non-cyclical systemic or macroprudential risks.[892] Third, Article 12(1) of CDR IV specifies that competent authorities may not grant authorization 'where initial capital is less than EUR 5 million'. Arguably, the use of the words 'less than' implies that member states can impose higher initial capital requirements.

671. Given its nature as a 'uniform and directly applicable' legal instrument, Regulation 575/2013 involves maximum harmonization.[893] Yet the regulation also contains a number of exceptions, where competent authorities in the member states have the possibility of addressing specific concerns at the national level and thus to impose higher minimum capital requirements. It involves, first, situations where credit institutions engage in real-estate lending. Since the emergence of real-estate bubbles is specific to the national context, the competent authorities in a member state can set higher capital requirements.[894] Second, the authorities in the member state may increase requirements on capital, liquidity, large exposures and risk weights to address specific national macroeconomic or systemic risks.[895]

672. EU banking law thus evolved towards 'maximum harmonization' with only limited possibilities for member states to impose stricter requirements. Such is only possible in areas not covered by European harmonization and in the specific situations where CRD IV and the accompanying regulation provide for such a possibility.

673. Two questions arise. First, are member states allowed to apply requirements to persons from third countries that seek to establish a credit

[891] CRD IV, Art. 136. [892] Ibid., Arts. 133–134.
[893] Ninth recital to Regulation 575/2013. [894] Regulation 575/2013, Art. 124(2).
[895] Ibid., Art. 458. The member states have to notify these measures to the Commission, the EBA and the ESRB, and justify their adoption.

institution in the EU that are stricter than those imposed on EU nationals? Second, can the EU develop harmonized rules that are weaker for EU nationals compared with nationals from other WTO members?

13.3.2.3 Restrictions imposed when measures fall within the common commercial policy

674. The EU common commercial policy is an exclusive competence of the EU.[896] It covers conventional measures (trade and investment agreements) as well as autonomous measures.[897] The question is whether autonomous measures that lay down specific conditions for the establishment of credit institutions by third-country banks are within the scope of the common commercial policy of the EU. As far as this is the case, this involves an exclusive competence of the EU and, as a consequence, the member states are excluded from acting, unless they are empowered by the EU to do so.[898]

675. In Opinion 1/94, the CJEU confirmed that trade in services in the GATS falls within the scope of this competence as far as the cross-border provision of services is at stake without any movement of natural or legal persons (Mode 1), since this was similar to cross-border trade in goods, which definitely fell within the scope of the common commercial policy in Article 133 EC Treaty (now Article 207 TFEU). The other modes of supply did not fall within the scope of the common commercial policy.[899] However, the CJEU concluded that the EC had an implicit external competence with regard to these modes of supply when it adopted internal acts that include

[896] CJEU, Opinion 1/75, *Understanding on a Local Cost Standard* [1975] ECR 1355, at B.2. This is now confirmed in Art. 3(1)(e) TFEU.

[897] P. Eeckhout, *External Relations of the European Union. Legal and Constitutional Foundations* (Oxford University Press, 2004) 355–6. The fact that both types of measure can be adopted within the framework of the common commercial policy can also be derived from the fact that Art. 207(2) TFEU indicates that the 'European Parliament and the Council, acting by means of *regulations* in accordance with the ordinary legislative procedure, shall adopt the *measures* defining the framework for implementing the common commercial policy' (emphasis added). In contrast, Art. 207(3) talks specifically about situations '[w]here *agreements* with one or more third countries or international organisations need to be negotiated and concluded' (emphasis added). See C. Herrmann, 'Die Zukunft der mitgliedstaatlichen Investitionspolitik nach dem Vertrag vom Lissabon', (2010) 21 *Europäische Zeitschrift für Wirtschaftsrecht* 207, at 209. Moreover, the reference to the 'ordinary legislative procedure' points to the fact that autonomous measures can be also adopted within the framework of the common commercial policy.

[898] Art. 2(1) TFEU.

[899] CJEU, Opinion 1/94, *Competence of the Community to conclude international agreements concerning services and the protection of intellectual property (WTO)*, [1994] ECR I-5267, paras. 44–45.

provisions dealing with the treatment of nationals of third countries, or as far as the EC had adopted internal acts providing for complete harmonization of the rules governing access to a self-employed activity.[900] Since this was not the case for all services sectors, the competence to conclude the GATS was shared between the EU and its members. The Treaty of Nice amended Article 133 EC Treaty explicitly to include trade in services by means of modes of supply other than Mode 1.[901] Therefore it could be argued that measures directly affecting service provision through Mode 3 – as is the case here: the establishment of a credit institution by a third-country bank – would fall within the scope of the common commercial policy. This argument is further strengthened since the adoption and entry into force of the Treaty of Lisbon. The description of the common commercial policy in Articles 206 and 207(1) now explicitly mentions trade in services and foreign direct investment.[902] The treaty also makes it clear that this competence is exclusive.[903] Therefore any measure whereby an EU member state decides to apply stricter requirements to banks from third countries that seek to establish a subsidiary in this member state constitutes an act that falls within the common commercial policy of the EU.

[900] Ibid., paras. 95–96. The latter situation is an application of the ERTA judgment. CJEU, Case 22/70 *Commission* v. *Council (ERTA)*, [1971] ECR, 263, at 274, paras. 12–19. The CJEU referred to the 'reciprocity' provisions in the Second Banking Directive as an example of an internal act that included provisions that dealt with the treatment of nationals of non-members. These provisions are now removed from CRD IV.

[901] Art. 133(5) EC Treaty. See also CJEU, Opinion 1/08, *Conclusion of agreements on the grant of compensation for modification and withdrawal of certain GATS commitments following the accession of new Member States to the EU*, [2009] ECR I-11129, para. 122.

[902] After Nice, one could still argue that 'trade in services' does not include service supply by means of Mode 3 in the GATS, because this involves 'establishment' (Art. 49 EC Treaty) under EU law rather than 'trade in services' (Art. 49 EC Treaty). See A. Hable, 'The European Constitution: Changes in the Reform of Competences with a Particular Focus on the External Dimension', Europainstitut Wirtschaftsuniversität Wien Working Paper No. 67, March 2005, 37. *Contra*, stating that after Nice the common commercial policy already includes Mode 3 service supply, Eeckhout, above n. 897, at 55. Note that the CJEU has confirmed in *Daiichi* that, since the amendment of Art. 207(1) by the Lisbon Treaty, the *entire* TRIPS Agreement falls within the scope of the Common Commercial Policy, which is an exclusive EU competence. CJEU, Case C-414/11, *Daiichi and Sanofi-Aventis/DEMO*, not yet reported, paras. 46–55. The same arguably applies to the *entire* GATS.

[903] Art. 3(1)(c) TFEU. The only exception is arguably the area of transport. Art. 207(5) indicates that the negotiation and conclusion of international agreements in the field of transport are governed by Title VI of Part Three and Art. 218 TFEU rather than Art. 207. It is thus not covered by the common commercial policy. Moreover, Art. 4(2)(g) TFEU explicitly mentions transport as a shared competence between the EU and its member states.

676. Several authors have defended the position that, since the Lisbon Treaty, the common commercial policy covers autonomous measures to liberalize *and regulate* foreign direct investment.[904] Krajewski has defended a more limited interpretation of the competence. He argues (with regard to the corresponding provision in the Treaty on a Constitution for Europe), 'It seems more appropriate to understand Article III-315(1) in such a way that only investment negotiations which have a clear trade component are part of the common commercial policy', and, further, that 'foreign direct investment is only part of the common commercial policy as far as restrictions to foreign direct investment are concerned, but not investment protection against expropriation, which is traditionally an element of investment agreements'.[905] This limited focus on removal of restrictions to investment (hence on liberalization) seems nevertheless contradicted by Opinion 1/78. In this opinion, the Court of Justice clarified that even if the first subparagraph of Article 131 EC Treaty (now Article 206 TFEU) indicated that the objective of the common commercial policy is 'the progressive abolition of restrictions on international trade and the lowering of customs barriers' and thus only refers to trade *liberalization*, the common commercial policy also includes the competence to *regulate* trade.[906]

[904] J. Ceyssens, 'Towards a Common Foreign Investment Policy? – Foreign Investment in the European Constitution', (2005) 32 *Legal Issues of Economic Integration* 259, at 282; and Herrmann, above n. 897, at 209, 211.

[905] M. Krajewski, 'External Trade Law and the Constitutional Treaty: Towards a Federal and More Democratic Common Commercial Policy?', (2005) 42 *Common Market Law Review* 91, at 114.

[906] The Court of Justice stated in this respect: 'It is therefore not possible to lay down, for Article 113 of the EEC Treaty [now Art. 206 TFEU], an interpretation the effect of which would be to restrict the common commercial policy to the use of instruments intended to have an effect only on the traditional aspects of external trade to the exclusion of more highly developed mechanisms such as appear in the agreement envisaged. A "commercial policy" understood in that sense would be destined to become nugatory in the course of time. Although it may be thought that at the time when the Treaty was drafted liberalization of trade was the dominant idea, the Treaty nevertheless does not form a barrier to the possibility of the Community's developing a commercial policy aiming at a regulation of the world market of certain products rather than at a mere liberalization of trade.' CJEU, Opinion 1/78, *International Agreement on Natural Rubber* [1979] ECR 2871, paras. 44–45. Ceyssens has argued (with regard to the almost identical provision on common commercial policy in the defunct Treaty establishing a Constitution for Europe): 'International instruments that deal with a comprehensive regulation of foreign investors for human rights, social and other public purposes, like the OECD Guidelines for Multinational Enterprises are probably at the edge of the new investment competence. If it is assumed that liberalization and regulation of foreign investment are closely linked, it appears sensible to conclude

Consequently, EU member states are not permitted to adopt laws and regulations that specifically target the establishment and operation of subsidiaries of third-country banks.[907]

677. Therefore the extent to which EU law limits the leeway of the member states to adopt requirements for the establishment and pursuit of the business of credit institutions that are subsidiaries of third-country banks is as follows: the member states may not apply requirements that fall within the scope of CRD IV and its accompanying regulation and that are *less stringent* than the harmonized requirements. The answer is more complex when member states want to adopt requirements that are *stricter*. When the measures the member state wants to adopt fall within the scope of CRD IV or its accompanying regulation, whether the specific measure is subject to minimum or maximum harmonization needs to be considered.

678. First, if a measure is subject to maximum harmonization, the member state is not permitted to apply stricter requirements. This is the case for the majority of the requirements harmonized in CRD IV and the accompanying regulation.

679. Second, if a measure is subject to minimum harmonization, member states are in principle allowed to adopt stricter requirements.

680. Third, with regard to requirements not currently covered by EU law, member states are allowed to adopt their own requirements.

681. In the second and third situations, if a member state wanted to target specifically and solely subsidiaries of third-country banks this would arguably constitute a measure that is part of the common commercial policy of

that even such instruments fall within the scope of the new CCP, provided that their focal point is the regulation of foreign investment rather than a single public policy.' Ceyssens, above n. 904, at 282. Hence, even if measures that specifically seek to impose stricter requirements for the establishment of credit institutions by third-country banks have a financial stability rationale, they are specifically focused on regulation of foreign investment, since they only apply to the investment of third-country banks.

[907] In a footnote to its Communication on a 'Comprehensive European international investment policy', the Commission has stated that 'under Article 207(2) TFEU, the Union has exclusive competence to autonomously legislate on FDI, as in the other areas of the common commercial policy, such as the import and export regulation'. Communication from the Commission to the Council, the European Parliament, the European Economic and Social Committee and the Committee of the Regions, Towards a comprehensive European international investment policy, COM(2010) 343 final, 7 July 2010, 5 (n. 14).

the EU. It concerns a measure that regulates trade in services and foreign direct investment by third-country nationals in the EU. Since this competence is exclusive to the EU, member states are no longer allowed to act in this field. Nonetheless, were a member state to adopt the same requirements for domestic and third-country banks, these actions should arguably not be considered to fall within the common commercial policy and thus still be within member states' competence.

13.3.3 Requirements for credit institutions owned by third-country persons in the light of the GATS

682. The leeway member states have in determining the balance between efficiency and stability in their market for banking services when it concerns competition by subsidiaries of third-country banks is thus significantly limited by EU law. However, in situations where member states still have the competence to adopt such measures, they must respect the obligations in the GATS. The same applies to the EU, when it would adopt measures that fall within the common commercial policy.

13.3.3.1 Requirements adopted by member states

683. An EU member state may still adopt requirements that are outside the scope of CRD IV and the accompanying regulation, or that are stricter than requirements subject to minimum harmonization in CRD IV or the regulation. When such requirements are part of the general requirements imposed by national law on both domestically owned credit institutions and credit institutions that are owned by third-country banks, they would arguably not fall within the common commercial policy of the EU. Such measures are nevertheless subject to the GATS.

13.3.3.1.1 Market access 684. When a member state would adopt legislation that requires banks to have an initial capital of €6 million (stricter than what is harmonized in CRD IV), one might wonder whether this is a violation of the obligation of market access (Article XVI GATS). As explained (above, paras. 268–271), the *US – Gambling* decision made it clear that Article XVI covers measures that are indistinctly applicable. Therefore, at first sight, all banking regulation would fall within the scope of Article XVI. However, the relevant types of market access limitations listed in Article XVI:2 only constitute measures that explicitly impose quantitative maximum restrictions, measures that *ex ante* can be translated into numerical quotas and measures that involve an absolute prohibition of trade in the entire scheduled sector or mode of supply (above, para. 261). Arguably, the mentioned measure (initial capital of €6 million) is not of this type. It does not involve a maximum restriction, but is rather a minimum requirement, as is explicitly indicated in the Scheduling Guidelines.[908]

685. On the other hand, if a member state would adopt (indistinctly applicable) measures that are not covered by CRD IV or the accompanying regulation, such as, for example, a general prohibition on offering remuneration on sight accounts or to advertise loans, one could argue that such a measure amounts to a zero quota, since it restricts the access to an entire sector (the offer of remuneration on sight accounts or to make publicity for the new product might be an indispensable means of competing in the host market[909]). Yet the WTO member will face a difficult task in proving that such a prohibition implies that banks have no access to the host market at all. It is therefore not likely that indistinctly applicable measures that affect trade in banking services will be assessed under Article XVI.

13.3.3.1.2 Prohibition of discrimination **686.** As argued, measures that specifically address the establishment of credit institutions by third-country banks arguably fall within the common commercial policy, which is an exclusive EU competence. Therefore member states cannot adopt measures that *only* apply to subsidiaries of third-country banks. If a member state still wants to adopt stricter requirements, such requirements must also be applied to its own credit institutions. Such measures thus necessarily provide national treatment to third-country banks, in line with Article XVII GATS.

13.3.3.1.3 Domestic regulation **687.** Still, one can scrutinize measures adopted by a member state under Article VI:5 GATS (as long as the Disciplines on Domestic Regulation are not finalized and adopted). A WTO member may claim that an initial capital requirement of, for example, €6 million is 'more burdensome than necessary' to ensure the quality of the banking service. One can make a similar claim against a measure that prohibits the advertisement for loans or to provide remuneration on sight accounts. We recall that, in order to invoke Article VI:5

[908] Guidelines for the Scheduling of Specific Commitments under the General Agreement on Trade in Services (GATS), S/L/92 (28 March 2001), para. 11.

[909] Cf. the *CaixaBank France* decision by the Court of Justice (above n. 804).

against a member's measure, the WTO member in question must have made specific commitments in banking services. Further, it is necessary that the measure leads to 'nullification and impairment' of the specific commitment. Finally, one can invoke Article VI:5 only for measures taken by member states *after* their accession to the WTO.

688. Yet, in all these cases, the member state in question may invoke the prudential exception to justify such measures. As argued (above, para. 440), when interpreting the prudential exception, a panel may consider existing international standards for their 'informative character'. This implies that when a member state adopts requirements that go beyond the levels laid down in, for example, the Basel standards, it will have to convince a panel that the Basel standards are inappropriate for the national context at hand.

13.3.3.2 Requirements adopted by the EU

689. Arguably, only the EU can adopt measures that specifically address the establishment of credit institutions that are subsidiaries of third-country banks, since they fall within the common commercial policy. Such measures must comply with the obligations imposed by the GATS. Because the EU might adopt stricter requirements (e.g. minimum initial capital requirement) that apply *solely* to the establishment of credit institutions that are subsidiaries of third-country banks, it is important to consider the obligation of national treatment in Article XVII GATS. The question is to what extent this obligation limits the possibility of the EU applying stricter requirements to the direct establishment of credit institutions that are subsidiaries of third-country banks as compared with credit institutions that are established by EU nationals.

13.3.3.2.1 National treatment **690.** The obligation of national treatment means that credit institutions that are owned by foreign banks cannot be treated less favourably than credit institutions that are owned by nationals of the WTO member adopting the measures (in this case the EU). The national treatment obligation in the GATS applies to 'all measures affecting the supply of services'. Therefore it also applies to measures that lay down the conditions for or influence the possibility of providing services in the EU by means of directly establishing a credit institution in the EU.

691. We should first consider whether the EU has made a commitment with regard to national treatment in the banking sector and whether it has made a relevant limitation to this commitment. According to its schedule of commitments the EU has made a national treatment commitment for banking services by means of Mode 3. What is more, it has not made a limitation for measures affecting the treatment of the direct establishment of credit institutions in the EU by third-country banks.

692. Yet footnote 52 to the general heading in the schedule of commitments on the financial services sector specifies that the restrictions member states have inscribed in the schedule can be applied

> only with regard to the direct establishment from a third-country of a commercial presence or to the provision of cross-border services from a third-country; consequently, a Member State may not apply these restrictions, including those concerning establishment, to third-country subsidiaries established in other Member States of the Community, unless these restrictions can also be applied to companies or nationals of other Member States in conformity with Community law.[910]

Hence all the market access restrictions a member state would have inscribed in the schedule for the provision of banking services by means of Mode 3 can only be applied to the direct establishment of third-country banks in the EU, and not to the establishment of a subsidiary by an EU credit institution. However, the question we address here is to what extent *the EU* can impose stricter requirements for establishment of a credit institution by a third-country bank when compared with those laid down internally by CRD IV and the accompanying regulation, or other harmonization measures. Arguably, footnote 52, which focuses on restrictions by EU member states, does not provide a relevant exception to the EU's national treatment obligation.

693. The next step in the assessment under Article XVII is considering whether foreign-owned and domestically owned banks are 'like' and whether the measure at issue provides 'less favourable treatment' to the 'like' foreign-owned banks. The first requirement is particularly controversial. Can one consider a third-country bank that seeks to establish a credit institution in the EU to be 'like' a bank from an EU member state that establishes a subsidiary in another member state? We considered

[910] Communication of the European Communities and its Member States, Draft Consolidated GATS Schedule, 14 and 29 September 2006, S/C/W/273 (9 October 2006), p. 177. Note that the expression 'direct establishment from a third country of a commercial presence' means either the direct establishment of a branch or a subsidiary.

(above, paras. 314–318 and 324) that the principal criterion for determining 'likeness' is whether consumers perceive the services provided by these banks as interchangeable. Such an analysis will quite often lead to a conclusion that the banks from both inside and outside the EU are 'like'. Therefore panels might arguably also take into account 'objective characteristics' of the services at stake. The fact that a banking service originates in a country that does not adhere to the Basel principles may be such an 'objective characteristic'. Still, this reasoning would arguably not apply to an EU measure that treats the establishment by *all* third-country banks more strictly. While some third countries may fail to implement any Basel standards, this is not a general rule. Hence a general measure that applies stricter requirements to the direct establishment of all third-country banks in the EU raises a national treatment problem.

13.3.3.2.2 Measures for prudential reasons and exception for preferential trade agreements **694.** When the EU applies stricter requirements to the establishment of credit institutions by third-country banks, the EU may claim that it does so for prudential reasons. For instance, there may be a concern that a credit institution's relation with persons from third countries will endanger the 'sound and prudent' activities of the credit institution and that, therefore, stricter requirements (e.g. a higher initial capital requirement) are a necessity. Even though the alleged objective of such a measure is arguably prudential (risky activities of the parent bank in a third country may affect the activities of the subsidiary bank in the EU or the supervision of the bank owner may be complicated by applicable laws in the home country), it is not obvious that such a discriminatory measure would be justified under the prudential exception in the GATS.

695. The final sentence of paragraph 2(a) of the GATS Annex on Financial Services notes that a measure that is taken for prudential reasons but does not comply with a provision in the GATS 'shall not be used as a means of avoiding the Member's commitments or obligations under the Agreement'. We argued (above, paras. 464–465) that this sentence has the same rationale as the chapeau of Article XX GATT or Article XIV GATS: it seeks to prevent WTO members from abusing their rights under the exception. It is not obvious that, from a prudential perspective, the situation where a credit institution in an EU member state is controlled by a third-country bank is so much different from the situation where this credit institution is controlled by a bank from another member state. To be sure, the harmonization of a number of prudential rules at the EU level may support an argument that the situation of EU-controlled credit institutions is different from third-country-controlled institutions.

696. Nonetheless, this cannot be a general rule. For instance, because the own-funds requirements in CRD IV are based on the Basel capital standards, banks from third countries may in fact also operate within a regulatory framework based on these standards. Arguably, distinctions should be made case by case[911] rather than as a general rule.

697. Nonetheless, could the EU still rely on Article V GATS to justify a refusal to provide national treatment to banks from third countries that seek to establish a subsidiary credit institution in the EU? Does the exception for preferential trade agreements permit the EU to apply stricter conditions to the direct establishment (investment) by third-country persons and thereby restrict the possibility of third-country banks to benefit from the achievements of the internal market?

698. Article V provides not only an exception to the obligation of most-favoured-nation treatment in the GATS, but also to the obligation of national treatment. The text of Article V:1 points to this fact. It indicates: '*This Agreement* shall not prevent any of its Members from being a party to or entering into an agreement liberalizing trade in services between or among the parties to such an agreement . . . ' (emphasis added). Reference is thus made not only to the obligation of most-favoured-nation treatment, but to the GATS in general (including the national treatment obligation).[912] A similar question (but relating to trade in goods) was at stake in *Turkey – Textiles*, where India challenged quantitative restrictions Turkey had introduced when creating a customs union with the European Community. While the panel had concluded that Article XXIV GATT only provides an exception to the most-favoured-nation obligation in Article I GATT and not to other provisions, including Article XI GATT (prohibiting quantitative restrictions),[913] the Appellate Body found that the 'chapeau [of paragraph 5 of Article XXIV GATT] makes it clear that Article XXIV may, under certain conditions, justify the adoption of a measure which is

911 As explained (below, paras. 725–744), the GATS is much more deferential to such individual assessments.

912 See also UNCTAD, above n. 816, at 51.

913 Panel Report, *Turkey – Restrictions on Imports of Textile and Clothing Products* (*Turkey – Textiles*), WT/DS34/R, adopted 19 November 1999, as modified by Appellate Body Report, WT/DS34/AB/R, paras. 9.188–9.192.

inconsistent with certain other GATT provisions, and may be invoked as a possible "defence" to a finding of inconsistency'.[914] Given the fact that Article V:1 GATS applies the same language as the chapeau of Article XXIV:5 GATT, it is highly likely that a panel or the Appellate Body will adopt the same interpretation.

699. The decision of the Appellate Body in *Brazil – Retreaded Tyres* nevertheless shows that it is problematic to invoke the exception for preferential trade arrangements to justify the non-application of a restriction to trade in services (justified on the basis of a general exception provision) to the parties to a preferential agreement. When a trade restriction would be justified on the basis of an exception, the fact that the WTO member in question does not apply this measure to the WTO members with whom it has a preferential trade agreement may in fact undermine the achievement of the objective pursued by the trade restriction.[915] On the basis of the *Brazil – Retreaded Tyres* decision, it appears that only when the distinction between goods, services or service suppliers from inside the preferential agreement, on the one hand, and those

[914] Appellate Body Report, *Turkey – Textiles*, para. 45.

[915] The panel in *Brazil – Retreaded Tyres* accepted that a number of measures that Brazil had taken and that restricted the import of retreaded tyres were justified on the basis of Art. XX(b) GATT. The panel concluded that the non-application of the import ban to retreaded tyres from MERCOSUR countries did not constitute 'arbitrary or unjustifiable discrimination' (a requirement imposed by the chapeau of Art. XX) since it was based on a ruling of the MERCOSUR arbitral tribunal (and therefore not arbitrary) and because it did not give rise to imports from these countries in such amounts as significantly to undermine the objective of the measure (and therefore not unjustifiable). Panel Report, *Brazil – Measures Affecting Imports of Retreaded Tyres*, WT/DS332/R, adopted 17 December 2007, as modified by Appellate Body Report WT/DS332/AB/R, paras. 7.281 and 7.287–288. In contrast, the Appellate Body found that the non-application of the import ban to MERCOSUR countries did constitute 'arbitrary or unjustifiable discrimination'. According to the Appellate Body, the analysis whether the application of a measure that is justified under Art. XX(b) nevertheless constitutes 'arbitrary or unjustifiable discrimination' needs to be made in the light of 'cause or rationale of the discrimination'. The discrimination is arbitrary or unjustifiable 'when a measure provisionally justified under a paragraph of Art. XX is applied in a discriminatory manner "between countries where the same conditions prevail", and when the reasons given for this discrimination bear no rational connection to the objective falling within the purview of a paragraph of Art. XX, or would go against that objective'. Appellate Body Report, *Brazil – Measures Affecting Imports of Retreaded Tyres*, WT/DS332/AB/R, adopted 17 December 2007, paras. 225 and 227. On this basis, the Appellate Body concluded that the MERCOSUR exception 'bears no relationship to the legitimate objective pursued by the Import Ban that falls within the purview of Art. XX(b), and even goes against this objective, to however small a degree' (ibid., para. 228).

from outside the preferential agreement, on the other hand, can be linked to the regulatory objective pursued, rather than protectionism, is the non-application of the restriction to the parties to the preferential agreement acceptable.[916] If not, the measure is used to circumvent the obligations under the agreements. It seems that the prudential concerns with regard to the establishment of a credit institution by EU banks and third-country banks are the same, or at least that no general rule that one should always consider the establishment by third-country banks more dangerous to financial stability can apply. Hence the application of such a measure would not be justified under the prudential exception, even when considered in combination with Article V GATS.

700. Still, could the EU invoke Article V GATS *on its own* as a justification of this measure?[917] In other words, could the EU argue that the maintenance of stricter requirements, even if the measures are not taken

[916] The Appellate Body thus makes an assessment of the non-application of the measure in the light of the regulatory objectives that can be invoked under WTO law and thereby shows no deference to the assessment that may have been made within the preferential trade arrangement (e.g. by an arbitral tribunal or other adjudicating body). Even if it had been concluded *within the preferential arrangement* that the control of credit institutions by banks from member states raises fewer prudential concerns than the control by banks from third countries, the Appellate Body made it clear that this analysis would also be made at the level of the WTO, possibly with a different result. See also the critical assessment in J. Qin, 'Managing Conflicts between Rulings of WTO and RTA Tribunals: Reflections on the Brazil – Tyres Case', Wayne State University Law School Research Paper no. 09-24, 16 October 2009, at 19–22, arguing that the panels and the Appellate Body must explore alternative interpretations that avoid conflict between the WTO legal order and the regional trade agreements. Mathis has concluded that the Appellate Body in *Brazil – Retreaded Tyres* 'effectively concluded that the GATT Art. XX chapeau establishes a hierarchy between this non-discrimination GATT obligation and whatever inconsistent provisions or rulings may occur under a regional system'. J. Mathis, 'The WTO *Brazil – Tyres* Case and GATT Article XXIV: One More Step to a Legal Regime?', in N. Lavranos (ed.), 'Multilevel Judicial Governance between Global and Regional Economic Integration Systems: Institutional and Substantive Aspects', EUI Working Papers 2009/41 23–32, at 30.

[917] Gray has noted that panels will prefer to examine the discriminatory application of measures as a result of the existence of a preferential trade arrangement in the light of the chapeau of Art. XX GATT rather than in the light of Art. XXIV GATT. He argues that dealing with the intersection between Arts. XX and XXIV 'could have potentially profound consequences for the institutional health and strength of the multilateral trading system'. However, he also admits that the parties to a preferential arrangement 'may strategically construct their legal arguments [in order to see certain questions answered]'. K. Gray, 'Case Comment – WTO Appellate Body: Brazil – Tyres Dispute', (2008) 102 *American Journal of International Law* 616, at 615–16.

for prudential reasons or any objective listed in Article XIV GATS, is nevertheless required for creating a preferential trade agreement?

701. Such a defence is arguably problematic. It is necessary for the EU to prove that the conditions laid down in Article V for the creation of a preferential trade agreement in services are fulfilled.[918] First of all, Article V:1 GATS sets out a number of requirements for the level of liberalization that must take place among the parties to a preferential arrangement. It is required that (i) the agreement has substantial sectoral coverage;[919] and (ii) there must be an absence or elimination of substantially all discrimination in the sense of Article XVII GATS between or among the parties to the agreement.[920] The EU can arguably show compliance with these elements. The EU legal framework does not foresee a general exclusion of a service sector. Moreover it covers all modes of supply in the sense of the GATS. Finally, Articles 49 and 56 TFEU prohibit discrimination and have been interpreted as even going beyond a prohibition of discriminatory measures.

702. Second, Article V:4 imposes a requirement that relates to the external impact on WTO members that are not parties to the preferential agreement. The provision requires that the preferential agreement 'shall be designed to facilitate trade between the parties to the agreement and shall not in respect of any Member outside the agreement raise the overall level of barriers to trade in services within the respective sectors or subsectors compared to the level applicable prior to such an agreement'. One must read this requirement together with the third requirement in Article V: if the EU wants to rely on Article V, it must show that the measure in question is 'necessary' for the creation of the preferential trade agreement.[921] The Appellate Body in

[918] It is far from clear exactly what the conditions mean. See S. Stephenson, 'GATS and Regional Integration', in P. Sauvé and R. Stern (eds.), *GATS 2000. New Directions in Services Trade Liberalization* (Washington, DC: Brookings Institution, 2000) 509–27, at 509–10.

[919] A footnote to Art. V:1(a) clarifies that this condition must be examined in the light of the number of sectors, volume of trade affected and modes of supply, and that the agreement must not provide for any a priori exclusion of any mode of supply.

[920] Art. V:1(b) specifies further the means for substantially eliminating all discrimination: there must be an elimination of discrimination and/or a prohibition of new or more discriminatory measures. On these means see Cottier and Molinuevo, above n. 814, at 137; see also F. Ortino and A. Sheppard, 'International Agreements Covering Foreign Investment in Services: Patterns and Linkages', in L. Bartels and F. Ortino (eds.), *Regional Trade Agreements and the WTO Legal System* (Oxford University Press, 2006) 201–14, at 213–14.

[921] One may wonder whether the exception in Art. V GATS and the necessity test also apply to measures taken *after* the formation of the preferential agreement. This is arguably the case. Brink has argued (with regard to Art. XXIV GATT): 'PTAs do evolve.

Turkey – Textiles derived this from the chapeau of Article XXIV:5 GATT, which is similar to the first sentence of Article V:1 GATS.[922]

703. Hence not *all* types of measure are covered by the exception for preferential trade agreements in the GATS. The EU will have to prove that failing to apply stricter requirements to the direct establishment of a credit institution in the EU by a bank from a third country would prevent the formation or maintenance of the EU preferential trade agreement. The EU arguably cannot claim that its preferential agreement would be prevented without stricter general requirements for banks from third countries. The adoption of such measures goes exactly against the rationale of Article V:4 GATS: avoiding the use of preferential trade agreements for trade diversion and thus erecting barriers for banks from other WTO members. At most, such a justification may lie in the different prudential situation prevailing in the WTO members that are EU member states when compared with other WTO members. However, as argued (above, para. 699), such a *general* rule is not justified.

704. In conclusion, because it is not possible for the EU to claim that measures that are stricter for direct establishment by third-country banks in the EU are *necessary* for the preferential trade agreement, a defence based on Article V on its own will also fail.

13.4 Conclusion on regulation of credit institutions that are subsidiaries of third-country banks

705. This chapter discussed the extent to which EU and WTO law restrict the EU and its member states in regulating the establishment of credit institutions in the EU that are subsidiaries of banks in third countries.

706. With regard to the regulation of the establishment of credit institutions by nationals from other states, the EU member states are clearly

For example, some PTAs provide a framework for further integration and harmonization, whether in the field of tariff reductions or technical standards. Presumably, in such cases, PTAs would have to continue to comply with WTO disciplines, including with Art. XXIV to the extent it was relied upon as an exception.' T. Brink, 'Which WTO Rules Can a PTA Lawfully Breach? Completing the Analysis in *Brazil – Tyres*', (2010) 44 *Journal of World Trade* 813, at 835.

[922] Appellate Body Report, *Turkey –Textiles*, para. 58; and see above para. 83.

restricted in determining the balance between efficiency and stability in their market for banking services. With regard to the establishment of credit institutions by nationals of other member states, this restriction is first of all determined by primary EU law: Article 49 TFEU. Furthermore, to a large extent the requirements for taking up and pursuing the business of credit institutions are harmonized in CRD IV and the accompanying regulation. In the limited instances where these requirements are subject to minimum harmonization (e.g. the initial capital requirement), the member states can, in principle, impose stricter requirements than those harmonized.

707. EU law nevertheless imposes an important limit on the possibility of member states regulating the direct establishment of credit institutions by banks that are nationals from third countries. Since the Treaty of Lisbon, it has been clearly indicated that the common commercial policy covers trade in services as well as foreign direct investment and that both fall within exclusive EU competence. Therefore measures that specifically regulate the direct establishment in the EU of credit institutions by third-country banks are within the common commercial policy of the EU, and the member states are excluded from adopting such measures. It was submitted, however, that measures that are stricter than the requirements that are subject to minimum harmonization in the EU or not subject to EU harmonization can still be adopted by the member states as long as they apply without distinction to both domestic and third-country banks. While such measures may have the effect of also applying such stringent requirements to the direct establishment of credit institutions by third-country banks, they are not within the common commercial policy of the EU. Still, in that case EU member states must respect the obligations in the GATS. Such stricter requirements (e.g. an initial capital requirement of €6 million) may need to be scrutinized under Article VI:5 GATS.

708. If the member states felt that it is appropriate to adopt requirements that specifically address the direct establishment of credit institutions in the EU by third-country banks and that are stricter than the requirements that apply with regard to intra-EU establishments, it will be for the EU to adopt such measures. In doing so, the EU has to respect its GATS obligations. When considering the possibility of the EU treating the direct establishment of credit institutions by third-country banks more strictly (and thus to restrict third-country banks in benefiting from the achievements of the internal market) the obligation of national treatment is essential. It was argued that the schedules of commitments of the EU do not contain a relevant limitation to the national treatment commitment for the provision of banking services by means of Mode 3. To be sure, a footnote indicated the possibility for member states to apply restrictions that were inscribed as limitations to the commitments in the schedules *solely* to the direct establishment of credit institutions by third-country banks. However, since the EU is now exclusively competent to adopt measures with regard to direct establishments of third-country banks and thus the member states can no longer adopt such measures, it would be required that the EU inscribes a limitation to the national treatment commitment in its schedules if it wants to adopt general measures that make a distinction between intra-EU establishment and direct establishment by third-country banks. If not, it is difficult to avoid a violation of the obligation of national treatment. Such a violation would arguably not be justified under the prudential exception or under the exception for preferential trade agreements. The EU thus clearly has a 'liberal rule of origin': third-country banks can in principle benefit from the achievements of the internal market by setting up a credit institution in the EU in the same way as EU nationals.

709. Nonetheless, this does not mean that it is never possible to treat the direct establishment of third-country banks in the EU more strictly than the establishment of EU nationals and thus that it is impossible to take into account the specific prudential concerns such direct establishments may entail. As will be explained in Chapter 14, such differentiations can be made on a case-by-case basis.

14

The supervision of credit institutions that are subsidiaries owned by a person in a third country

14.1 Introduction

710. In the previous section we concluded that the interaction of EU law and the GATS implies that a 'liberal rule of origin'[923] applies in the EU. Third-country banks that establish a credit institution as a subsidiary in the EU will benefit from the achievements from the internal market. As the law currently stands, it appears that the general conditions for setting up such a credit institution must be the same as those that apply to the establishment of a credit institution by a national of an EU member state.

711. Nonetheless, even if a number of requirements for taking up and pursuing the business of credit institutions are harmonized at the EU level, there is an important margin of appreciation for the competent authorities when applying these requirements (i.e. supervising compliance with them).[924] This allows for differentiation in the treatment of the establishment of credit institutions by third-country banks, depending on the specific prudential concerns that arise. Furthermore, CRD IV has a number of provisions that specifically address the prudential assessment of such an establishment. These provisions focus on the ability of the authorities in the EU member states to supervise the activities of credit institutions that are owned by persons outside the EU and on the quality of supervision of the banking group that is created.

712. As explained earlier, in Part II, the GATS contains obligations that also affect the right of WTO members to make prudential assessments. In this chapter we examine how the GATS affects the right of competent

[923] Fink, above n. 814, at 126; and Cottier and Molinuevo, above n. 814, at 146. See also A. Emch, above n. 814, at 359.

[924] See also Strivens, above n. 717, at 302.

authorities to make such prudential assessments with regard to subsidiaries of third-country banks. The GATS mainly seeks to ensure transparency and objectivity in making such assessments and will rarely affect the content of a decision that is the outcome of the assessment process.

14.2 Supervisory assessments by authorities of member states and centralized EU supervision

14.2.1 Centralization of supervision of EU credit institutions

713. While the *regulation* of banking services has clearly moved to the EU level, it proved more challenging to achieve such centralization of the *supervision* of banking activity in the EU.[925] The global financial crisis made policymakers once again[926] aware of the problematic asymmetry between the development of international banking activities and national supervision.[927]

714. The Lamfalussy report of 2001 did not specifically address the supervisory architecture in the EU, but rather focused on creating an institutional framework that enabled efficient and high-quality rule-making at the EU level to address the fragmentation of the financial sector in the EU.[928] The de Larosière report of 2009 did address the fragmentation of supervision in the EU, but proposed to create a European System of Financial Supervisors as a 'decentralized network'.[929] The authorities of the individual member

[925] E. Wymeersch, 'The Future of Financial Regulation and Supervision in Europe', (2005) 42 *Common Market Law Review* 987, at 994.

[926] Note that the Basel principles and standards on banking supervision as well as their subsequent amendments and revisions were most often a response to banking crises that had occurred (above, para. 179).

[927] M. Lamandini, 'When More Is Needed: The European Financial Supervisory Reform and Its Legal Basis', (2009) 6 *European Company Law* 197, at 197; and see M. Andenas and L. Panourgias, 'Applied Monetary Policy and Bank Supervision by the ECB', in J. Norton and M. Andenas (eds.), *International Monetary and Financial Law upon Entering the New Millennium. A Tribute to Sir Joseph and Ruth Gold* (London: BIICL, 2002) 119–170, especially at 133–5; and Coibion and Dessy, above n. 796, at 195.

[928] Gari and Lastra, above n. 743, at 382.

[929] High Level Group on Financial Supervision in the EU, Chaired by Jacques de Larosière, 'Report' (25 February 2009), Recommendation 18. The High Level Group stated that the 'unification of all supervisory activities for cross-border institutions at the pan-EU level ... could only be considered if there were irrefutable arguments in favour of such a proposal'. The group had doubts whether the complexities, costs and political implications could be dealt with at the time. It concluded: 'This scenario could become more viable, of course, should the EU decide to move towards greater political integration' (ibid., para. 218).

states will perform the day-to-day supervision of credit institutions. Coordination and cooperation among the supervisors of a group of credit institutions was enhanced by the creation of colleges of supervisors, for which Directive 2009/111/EC has introduced a legal basis.[930] The European Banking Authority has the task of improving consistent application of the harmonized rules by the national supervisors in the colleges of supervisors[931] and assists in settling disagreements between supervisory authorities.[932]

715. Nonetheless, efforts to further centralize supervision continued. In September 2012, the European Commission adopted two proposals for the establishment of a single supervisory mechanism (SSM) in the EU. The Commission proposed that this single supervision be performed by the European Central Bank (ECB) in the euro area.[933] On 19 March 2013, the European Parliament and the Council of the European Union reached agreement on entrusting the ECB with this supervisory task. The SSM applies only to member states in the euro area.[934] The ECB will directly supervise banks having assets more than €30 billion, that constitute at least 20 per cent of their home country's gross domestic product (GDP) (unless the total value of the bank's assets is below €5 billion) or that have requested or received direct public financial assistance from the European Financial Stability Facility or the European Stability Mechanism. The ECB will perform key supervisory tasks, including licensing and authorization of credit institutions, assessing qualifying holdings and assessing compliance with capital requirements.[935] The ECB will perform the role of the national supervisors of participating SSM states in the colleges of supervisors. For less significant banks, the ECB monitors the supervision by national supervisors. The ECB also performs the role of home and host supervisor for credit

[930] Art. 116 CRD IV.

[931] Art. 8(1)(b) Regulation 1093/2010 of the European Parliament and of the Council of 24 November 2010 establishing a European Supervisory Authority (European Banking Authority), amending Decision No. 716/2009/EC and repealing Commission Decision 2009/78/EC, OJ 2010 L 331/12. The EBA will thus play an active role in building a 'common supervisory culture' in the EU.

[932] Regulation 1093/2010, Art. 19.

[933] Council Regulation 1024/2013 of 15 October 2013 conferring specific tasks on the European Central Bank concerning policies relating to the prudential supervision of credit institutions, OJ 2013 L 287/63, and Regulation 1022/2013 of the European Parliament and of the Council of 22 October 2013 amending Regulation 1093/2010 establishing a European Supervisory Authority (European Banking Authority) as regards the conferral of specific tasks on the European Central Bank pursuant to Council Regulation 1024/2013, OJ 2013 L 287/5.

[934] Other member states can join the SSM by establishing close cooperation between their authorities and the ECB.

[935] For a full list see Art. 4 of Council Regulation 1024/2013, above n. 933.

institutions providing banking services by means of branches or cross-border supply in other EU member states that participate in the SSM.

716. National supervisors remain competent to perform all supervisory tasks not entrusted to the ECB, including supervising third-country credit institutions that set up branches or provide cross-border services within a member state, consumer protection, combating money laundering and supervising payment services. Further, although the ECB has become exclusively competent to exercise supervision, in practice there is still an important role for the national supervisors. The day-to-day supervision of credit institutions is still performed by the national supervisor, and the national supervisor can assess the authorization conditions when receiving an application or when considering withdrawing an authorization. It is indeed possible that specific additional authorization conditions can exist in a certain member state. The national supervisor can then propose a decision to the ECB.

14.2.2 Prudential assessment of the establishment and operation of credit institutions by third-country banks

14.2.2.1 Assessments made by competent authorities of member states or by the ECB

717. The centralization of supervision that has taken place at the EU level implies that for certain large and systemically important third-country banks, the ECB will be competent to authorize their establishment of a credit institution in the EU and to exercise prudential supervision. For smaller third-country banks, the national supervisors will still perform this task. It is in exercising these supervisory tasks that distinctions can be made between banks originating in different third countries and between credit institutions owned by third-country banks and other EU credit institutions.

718. The competent authority has to apply the general requirements for authorization that are applicable to any establishment of a credit institution, be that owned by a third-country bank or not. Yet CRD IV also contains some requirements that are specifically focused on third-country banks.

14.2.2.2 Specific requirements for EU subsidiaries of third-country banks

719. First, supervisors pay specific attention to 'close links'[936] with natural or legal persons in third countries. If the laws, regulations or administrative

[936] The notion of 'close links' is used to cover situations that go beyond the situations where consolidated supervision is required. Hence it does not only involve

provisions in a third country governing these natural or legal persons, or difficulties relating to the enforcement of these norms, prevent the effective exercise of supervisory functions, the authorization of the credit institution must be refused.[937] On this basis, the competent authority can thus block the establishment of a credit institution by a third-country bank.

720. Second, the competent authority that considers an application for authorization by a third-country bank must also assess the quality of the *consolidated supervision* that will be performed by the authorities of the third country where the head office of the parent of the credit institution is situated. The consolidated supervision of the group to which such a credit institution belongs is not directly regulated by CRD IV, since the European authorities have no jurisdiction over the parent in a third-country. Therefore Article 48 CRD IV indicates that the European Commission may 'submit proposals to the Council, either at the request of a Member State or on its own initiative, for the negotiation of agreements with one or more third countries regarding the means of exercising supervision of a consolidated basis'.[938]

721. If such agreements do not exist, the credit institution that is a subsidiary of a parent in the third country is not subject to consolidated supervision as provided for in CRD IV and the regulation.[939] In such cases the competent authorities must verify whether the consolidated supervision exercised by the authority in the third country is 'equivalent' to that normally exercised under CRD IV and the regulation.[940]

relationships between parent undertakings and subsidiaries, as defined in Art. 1(1) and (2) of Directive 83/349/EEC or a similar relationship and situations of 'participation', defined as 'ownership, direct or by way of control, of 20 per cent or more of the voting rights or capital of an undertaking'. 'Close links' also covers situations 'in which two or more natural or legal persons are permanently linked to one and the same person by a control relationship' (Regulation 575/2013, Art. 4(1), point 37).

[937] Art. 14(3), second subparagraph CRD IV.

[938] The agreements may not only cover situations where a credit institution in the EU has its parent undertaking in a third country, but also situations where credit institutions are situated in third countries but have as parent undertaking a credit institution or financial holding company with head offices in the EU. They seek to ensure information exchange between the competent authorities for the purpose of consolidated supervision (Art. 48(2) CRD IV). There exists only a statement of cooperation with the United States: Statement of Co-operation on the Exchange of Information for the Purposes of Consolidated Supervision of 17 September 1999, available at http://ec.europa.eu/internal_market/bank/docs/third countries/coop1_en.pdf.

[939] M. Gruson, 'Supervision of Financial Conglomerates in the European Union', (2004) 19 *Journal of International Banking Law and Regulation* 363, at 364.

[940] Art. 127(1) CRD IV.

722. When assessing the equivalence of the consolidated supervision by the authorities in the third countries, the competent authority must take into account the guidance by the European Banking Committee, if such guidance is available. There exists such general guidance on the equivalence of supervision in the United States[941] and Switzerland.[942] However, up to the time of writing, no such guidance has come into existence for other countries. In any case, the authority must consult the European Banking Committee before taking a decision.[943] The European Banking Authority assists the Commission and the European Banking Committee in performing this task.[944]

723. Where the competent authority decides that the supervision is not equivalent, it must apply the provisions of CRD IV and the regulation by analogy or apply appropriate supervisory techniques that would achieve the objectives of supervision on a consolidated basis.[945] The provisions can be applied 'by analogy' – that is, by applying them as if the supervised entities belonged to an EU group.[946] The competent authority will then need to provide the supplementary supervision. For the member states that are part of the SSM, this will be the ECB if the banks are sufficiently large. In other cases, the competent authority is that of the member states. If the credit institution that is acquired operates only in one member state, the authority of this state will have to perform the supervision. If the credit institution that is acquired operates in several member states, the consolidated supervision will need to be performed

[941] The first guidance dates from 2004. The Commission and the European Banking Committee called in 2007 for technical advice from the Committee of European Banking Supervisors in order to update their guidance. This advice was published in February 2008: IWCFC and CEBS advice to the EU Commission on whether the supervisory arrangements of relevant US supervisors are likely to achieve the objectives of consolidated and supplementary supervision as set out in Directives 2002/87/EC, 2006/48/EC and 2002/49/EC, February 2008, available at www.c-ebs.org/Advice/documents/USAdviceonEquivalence.pdf.

[942] As with the United States, the first guidance for Switzerland dates from 2004. New advice was published in February 2008: IWCFC and CEBS advice to the EU Commission on whether the supervisory arrangements of relevant Swiss supervisors are likely to achieve the objectives of consolidated and supplementary supervision as set out in Directives 2002/87/EC, 2006/48/EC and 2002/49/EC, February 2008, available at www.c-ebs.org/Advice/documents/SwissAdviceonEquivalence.pdf.

[943] CRD IV, Art. 127(2). [944] Ibid., Art. 127(2) *in fine*.

[945] Ibid., Art. 127(3), first subparagraph.

[946] Commission Proposal for a Directive of the European Parliament and of the Council on the Supplementary Supervision of Credit Institutions, Insurance Undertakings and Investment Firms in a Financial Conglomerate, COM (2001) 213 final, 24 April 2001, p. 7.

on the basis of an arrangement between the states. As an alternative, CRD IV suggests as an 'appropriate supervisory technique' the requirement for the third-country parent to establish a financial holding company with its head office in the EU.[947] This will arguably be the case when the third-country bank has already a subsidiary in a member state and now seeks to establish another subsidiary in another member state.

724. When making an assessment of the consolidated supervision by the third-country supervisor, the competent supervisor cannot block the establishment of the credit institution. It can only impose an additional supervisory burden (supplementary consolidated supervision of the EU group) or a requirement to set up a financial holding company in the EU.[948] This stands in contrast with the task of the supervisor to assess whether the close links with the third-country bank (and the laws, regulations and administrative practices in this third country) do not prevent the effective exercise of supervision. In the latter situation, the authority can refuse authorization and thus block the establishment.

14.2.3 Prudential assessments in the light of the GATS

725. When the competent authority in the EU makes prudential assessments of the establishment of credit institutions by third-country banks, it needs to comply with the applicable provisions in the GATS. We concluded (above, paras. 476–481) that individual supervisory assessments are measures within the general scope of the GATS. However, whether a WTO member will be able to challenge such assessments under the GATS depends much on the specific GATS provision at stake. While it is not entirely unthinkable that a prudential assessment made by a supervisory authority is challenged under a GATS provision, it is quite unlikely that a panel would conclude that a supervisory decision violates the GATS because

[947] CRD IV, Art. 127(3), third subparagraph.

[948] Scott and Viñuales consider that the requirement of 'equivalent' consolidated supervision has put important pressure on regulators in third countries to develop consolidated supervision systems based on the European model. Regulatory developments in the United States and Switzerland, in particular with regard to group-wide supervision, can be traced back to these requirements. H. Scott, 'International Finance: Rule Choices for Global Financial Markets', in A. Sykes and A. Guzman (eds.), *Research Handbook in International Economic Law* (Cheltenham: Edward Elgar, 2007) 361–417, at 384–5; and J. Viñuales, 'The International Regulation of Financial Conglomerates: A Case Study of Equivalence as an Approach to Financial Integration', (2006) 37 *California Western International Law Journal* 1, at 24–41.

of the content of the decision (or outcome of the assessment process), unless a specific market access restriction is imposed or blatant protectionism is shown. The interaction with the disciplines that exist and are developed at the level of the WTO will mainly contribute to more predictable and transparent prudential assessment *processes*.

14.2.3.1 Prudential assessments and market access

726. In Part II we explained that when supervisory assessments are challenged on the basis of Article XVI, the question is whether the general *criteria* that are applied in this assessment are market access restrictions in the sense of Article XVI:2. The supervisory decision as such to refuse a bank licence or to refuse the acquisition of a controlling stake does not constitute such market access restriction. A complainant would thus challenge the *regulation* rather than the supervisory assessment made, since it seeks the removal of the general measure that constitutes a market access restriction. The only exception would be a situation where a supervisory decision imposes an ad hoc requirement to set up a specific legal person.

727. For most of the present criteria in CRD IV and the accompanying regulation on the basis of which prudential assessments are made by the competent authorities, it is obvious that they are not of the type listed in Article XVI:2. They involve qualitative criteria (bank directors must have 'sufficient expertise'; authorization is only granted after an assessment of the 'suitability' of the shareholders and members with qualifying holdings in a credit institution in the light of 'sound and prudent management'; 'close links' between the credit institution and persons (possibly in third countries) must not prevent 'effective exercise of supervisory functions') rather than criteria of a 'quantitative nature'.

728. Nonetheless, one can argue that a decision whereby the competent authority requires a third-country bank to set up a 'financial holding company' in the EU constitutes a measure of the type listed in Article XVI:2(e). Such decisions constitute restrictions or requirements regarding the type of legal entity or joint venture through which a service supplier may supply a service. However, the authority will not always require the establishment of a holding company. This is only the case when the authority concludes that the consolidated supervision by the third-country supervisor is not 'equivalent' to that governed by the principles in CRD IV and its regulation.[949] The decision to require a specific legal entity is a market

[949] CRD IV, Art. 127(3), first subparagraph.

access restriction, because it is an application of a general measure that qualifies as a market access restriction in the sense of Article XVI:2(e). Hence the WTO member in question must make a limitation for such decision if it wants to maintain the possibility to take such decisions.

729. One could argue that the EU has inscribed a relevant limitation to its commitments in its schedules of commitments for financial services in this regard. In note 6 of the horizontal section under the general heading on the financial services sector in the Schedules of the EU, the EU has indicated: 'As a general rule and in a non-discriminatory manner, financial institutions incorporated in a Member State of the Community must adopt a specific legal form'.[950] The limitation does not specify further what 'a specific legal form' entails. It may suggest that the EU considered that requiring a specific legal form in order to supply banking services constitutes a market access restriction. This may cover also the requirement to set up a holding company first.

730. In any event, the decision requiring the setting up of a financial holding company is likely justified under the prudential exception. The Revised Basel Concordat of 1983 indicates that the host supervisor must consider the quality of the supervision that will be exercised by the home supervisor of a cross-border banking group before allowing expansion in the host territory (above, paras. 181–182). If this is not the case, the host supervisor should refuse the expansion, or allow it after imposing necessary conditions or restrictions.[951] Requiring the establishment of a holding company to facilitate the supervision is thus clearly in line with international principles on prudential supervision.

14.2.3.2 Prudential assessments and non-discrimination

731. The GATS also contains provisions that prohibit discrimination: Article II GATS (most-favoured-nation treatment) and Article XVII (national treatment). However, as argued in Part II, it is difficult to apply these provisions to individual decisions, since these provisions are more focused on 'equality of competitive opportunities' rather than on the

[950] Communication of the European Communities and its Member States, Draft Consolidated GATS Schedule, 14 and 29 September 2006, S/C/W/273 (9 October 2006), p. 177. See also Note 12 by Slovenia in the horizontal section of the general heading for the Financial Services Sector (second part) (ibid., at p. 203).

[951] Basel Committee on Banking Supervision, Principles for the Supervision of Bank's Foreign Establishments, Bank for International Settlements, May 1983, available at www.bis.org/publ/bcbsc312.pdf, especially Section III.

possibility of an individual service supplier trading. Therefore a panel might only accept that such an individual decision (which is the outcome of the application of a general measure in an assessment process, for instance the assessment whether 'close links' with persons in third countries impedes effective supervision) violates Article II or Article XVII, if the complainant can show that protectionist intent underlies the decision.

732. The amendment of the Capital Requirements Directive by Directive 2007/44/EC of 5 September 2007 addressed the possibility of discriminatory supervisory assessments. In order to avoid discrimination between the possible candidates to acquire qualifying holdings in a credit institution, Article 23(5) CRD IV explicitly indicates that the different applications must be treated in a non-discriminatory way.

733. A specific aspect of supervisory assessments in the EU is the consideration of whether the consolidated supervision over the bank group that is created is 'equivalent' to the consolidated supervision exercised under CRD IV and the accompanying regulation. If the supervision is not equivalent, the competent authority will need to perform supplementary supervision or may first require the third-country bank to set up a financial holding company in the EU. This imposes an additional burden on the bank from, for example, third-country A that seeks to provide services in the EU, which is not imposed on banks from third-country B for which an agreement was concluded between the EU and third-country authorities with regard to consolidated supervision *or* for which it was concluded that the consolidated supervision was 'equivalent'. Could one argue that the third-country bank from country A is treated less favourably than third-country banks from country B and thus a violation of the obligation of most-favoured-nation (Article II) is at issue? It is difficult to challenge successfully the individual supervisory decision that the consolidated supervision is not equivalent on the basis of Article II unless evidence of protectionist intent is available. The determination by the supervisory authority will be based on several prudential considerations (e.g. cooperation with the third-country authorities, quality of the group supervision and implementation of international standards) and, therefore, the panel will be hesitant to reassess these considerations.

14.2.3.3 Prudential assessments and Article VI

734. The obligations of market access and non-discrimination in the GATS have only a limited impact on the right to make supervisory assessments. As long as the competent authority in the EU does not apply market access restrictions for which there exists no limitation in the schedules and as long as there is no evidence that a supervisory decision is based on protectionist grounds, it is free to make a trade-off between efficiency and stability for each individual application for authorization as a credit institution. It is possible to make distinctions among different applicants that seek to establish a credit institution in the EU, based on the supervisory assessment they make. Nevertheless, the procedure through which such decisions are reached is still subject to a number of requirements in the GATS.

14.2.3.3.1 Due process and consistency **735.** Article VI:1 GATS affects the *process* for reaching a supervisory decision. Article VI:1 GATS requires that measures of general application are administered in a 'reasonable, objective and impartial manner'. The panel in *EC – Selected Customs Matters* has noted that Article X:3(b) GATT sets a general standard of due process.[952] Traders must be treated fairly and consistently such that the security and predictability of the trading system is ensured. This principle also applies to Article VI:1 GATS (above, para. 524).

736. A question that may arise with regard to the EU framework for regulation and supervision of the market for banking services is whether the fact that supervision of credit institutions – even if based on harmonized requirements and criteria in CRD IV and the accompanying regulation – is still decentralized in certain cases, and thus in the hands of the member states, could lead to a lack of due process. Might the possibility of inconsistent application of the harmonized requirements by national authorities in individual supervisory assessments lead to a violation of Article VI:1? The authorities in the member states may apply these requirements in a different manner depending on whether they want to attract more foreign banks to their territory or whether they are more concerned about the financial stability implications of the presence of foreign banks. The application by the same member state may also differ over time. From the perspective of the banks, a lack of consistent application by the member states may have a negative impact on the benefits third-country banks seek to achieve in establishing themselves in the EU.[953] The legal uncertainty that arises

[952] Panel Report, *EC – Selected Customs Matters*, para. 7.134.

[953] See also B. Hoekman and P. Mavroidis, 'Nothing Dramatic (. . .Regarding Administration of Customs Laws). A Comment on the WTO Appellate Body Report *EC – Selected Customs Matters*', (2009) 8 *World Trade Review* 31, at 39.

from inconsistent application may lead banks to decide to delay or even refrain from the establishment of subsidiaries in the EU.

737. Nevertheless, the panel in *Argentina – Hides and Leather* stressed that the day-to-day administration of measures differs from case to case, so that it cannot be expected that in all specific practical cases the same treatment is given.[954] Hence the practical application of general measures will necessarily differ somewhat, because the individual situations differ from case to case. Furthermore, the Appellate Body in *EC – Selected Customs Matters* argued that

> in order to substantiate a claim of violation based on an administrative process, it is not sufficient that the complainant merely recites the features of the administrative processes; it will also have to show how and why those features *necessarily* lead to a lack of uniform, impartial, or reasonable administration of a legal instrument of the kind described in Article X:1.[955]

Some (potential) divergence in the application of a measure of general application is thus not sufficient. It must also be linked to the results and outcomes of this application. It is thus far from easy to bring a challenge on the basis of Article X:3 GATT. Recall that the Appellate Body in *US – Corrosion-Resistant Steel Sunset Review* stated that allegations that measures are administered in a non-uniform, unreasonable or partial way 'are serious under any circumstances' and 'should not be brought lightly'.[956] Hence such a claim should be supported by solid evidence. The same reasoning applies to Article VI:1 GATS.

738. Such a challenge may in fact be pre-empted by the EU. The reform of financial supervision has entrusted the EBA with the task of creating a 'common supervisory culture' in the EU. Such a common supervisory culture is sought, inter alia, by promoting best practices but also by contributing to developing high-quality and uniform supervisory standards, reviewing the application of technical standards and creating training programmes and personnel exchanges among supervisors in the member states.[957] The role of the EBA may also contribute to

[954] Panel Report, *Argentina – Hides and Leather*, para. 11.84.
[955] Appellate Body Report, *EC – Selected Customs Matters*, para. 226.
[956] Appellate Body Report, *US – Corrosion-Resistant Steel Sunset Review*, para. 217.
[957] Regulation (EU) No. 1093/2010 of the European Parliament and of the Council of 24 November 2010 establishing a European Supervisory Authority (European Banking Authority), amending Decision No. 716/2009/EC and repealing Commission Decision 2009/78/EC, OJ 2010 L 331/12, Art. 29.

consistency in the assessment of third-country cases because it will assist in preparing equivalence decisions pertaining to supervisory regimes in third countries[958] and may publish advice with regard to prudential assessments of cross-border mergers and acquisitions.[959]

14.2.3.3.2 Reasonableness **739.** Is it possible that a complainant argues that certain prudential assessments by a banking supervisor in an EU member state are not 'reasonable'? A panel will likely be very hesitant to strike down individual decisions on such a basis and would wish to avoid redoing the analysis already carried out by the banking supervisor.

14.2.3.3.3 Due process and clarity of prudential assessments **740.** On the basis of the case law relating to Article X:3(a) GATT, one can argue that the due process standard in Article VI:1 and VI:3 GATS involves also the requirement of fairness and transparency.[960] Arguably, this implies that prudential assessments based on a vague reasoning must be avoided. Articles VI:4 and VI:5 GATS further contribute to this by requiring that the criteria for prudential assessments are objective and transparent.

741. A good example of how the EU addressed this concern is the general requirement that bank directors must be 'of sufficiently good repute' and with 'sufficient experience'. It could be argued that these criteria were not sufficiently transparent and unambiguous to meet the requirements in Articles VI:4 and VI:5. CRD IV now provides criteria for determining whether these conditions are met,[961] and the EBA has the task of developing further guidelines to clarify these criteria.[962]

14.3 Conclusion on supervision by the EU and member states on the establishment of subsidiaries by third-country banks

742. While the supervision of the access of third-country banks by establishing a subsidiary credit institution in the EU was until recently

[958] Ibid., Art. 33(2). [959] Ibid., Art. 34(2).

[960] Appellate Body Report, *US – Shrimp*, para. 183; and Panel Report, *EC – Selected Customs Matters*, para. 7.134. Note, moreover, that the panel in *US – Gambling* stated that pursuant to Art. VI:3 GATS (the obligation to provide information without undue delay), authorization procedures should be performed according to the principles of transparency and due process. Panel Report, *US – Gambling*, para. 6.432.

[961] CRD IV, Art. 91. [962] Ibid., Art. 91(12).

firmly in the hands of the national authorities of the member states, this has significantly changed since the creation of the ESFS and the SSM for the eurozone. To a large extent, EU law thus also limits the possibility of individual member states striking their own balance between competition and financial stability when making supervisory assessments. In many cases, it will now be the ECB that strikes such a balance, be it in close cooperation with the national authorities of the individual member states.

743. When exercising their supervisory function, the competent authorities are also subject to the requirements in the GATS. However, the impact of the GATS on the right to supervise is relatively limited. In general, WTO members might only exceptionally challenge an individual supervisory decision by an EU member state because a panel or the Appellate Body cannot recommend the national authorities of the WTO member to make a favourable decision with regard to the authorization of an individual credit institution.

744. The major interaction between the GATS and the EU supervisory architecture that leaves supervision in the hands of the EU member states will manifest itself with regard to the due process requirements imposed by Article VI:1 GATS. The due process standard in this provision seeks to avoid supervisory assessments (the *administration* of the harmonized requirements) threatening the stability and predictability of the trading system. The fact that supervision in the EU is in certain cases still left in the hands of the member states may be considered problematic in the light of the standard set in Articles VI:1. Nonetheless, the case law relating to Article X:3 GATT indicates that it is far from easy to bring a challenge before the WTO and claim that due process standards are not met. It is unavoidable that applications of general measures in individual cases will differ somewhat. Yet a claim based on Article VI:1 must be based on solid evidence that there is 'unreasonable, partial or non-objective' administration. The legal impact of the requirements of Article VI:1 must thus not be overestimated.

745. The relatively lenient approach of the GATS towards supervisory assessments is understandable and defensible from the perspective of financial stability: as long as there exists no centralized entity that is responsible for supervising and assessing the establishment and operation of large, cross-border banking groups, the WTO members must retain the competence to determine the balance between stability and efficiency when evaluating applications for access to the market. This is also confirmed in the Basel Minimum Standards for the Supervision on International Banking Groups that firmly stress the responsibility of the host country authorities to be careful when allowing a foreign bank to expand in the territory. However, from the perspective of international competition (and thus efficiency) in the banking sector, this lenient approach can be problematic. The discretionary power left to the national supervisory authorities may easily be abused for protectionist purposes. The EU experience with regard to intra-EU bank mergers and acquisitions may provide an example and serve as a warning.

15

Conclusion to Part III

746. Part III has examined the interaction between EU law and the GATS with regard to the right of the EU member states to regulate and supervise the establishment of credit institutions in the EU that are subsidiaries of third-country banks. The more EU law and the GATS restrict this right, the less the EU member states are able to determine the balance between efficiency and stability they consider to be appropriate in their market for banking services.

747. It was explained in Part I that it is important that governments can determine for themselves the trade-off between efficiency and stability in their market for banking services. One can only achieve higher efficiency through increased international competition without compromising financial stability if the competent authorities are satisfied that third-country banks are regulated and supervised according to rules and principles that achieve the same objectives. However, this requires trust with regard to the quality of each other's supervision and often harmonization of a number of regulatory requirements. This trust requires a regulatory system at the supra-national level that allows a swift amendment of requirements in the light of changing situations. Moreover, the operation of large cross-border banking groups requires centralized supervision to ensure that financial stability is not threatened. As long as such a supra-national framework is unavailable, the legal rules on trade liberalization can only address the most blatant forms of protectionism.

748. The EU and international levels were examined together because EU member states must comply with both EU law and the GATS. If EU law were to leave some leeway with regard to the treatment of the establishment of subsidiaries (either in regulating or in making specific supervisory assessments), this leeway might still be restricted by the GATS. Moreover, the EU is itself a WTO member. Hence any EU policies that determine whether and how third-country banks may establish credit institutions in the EU must be consistent with the obligations in the GATS.

749. The ability of each EU member state to decide to what extent it designs its own policy towards financial stability is significantly restricted. EU law definitely restricts the member states' right to regulate to a very important extent. Also the GATS imposes a number of limits with regard to the distinctions the EU can make between third-country banks and EU banks. For areas where the EU has harmonized the requirements to set up a credit institution in the EU, its member states cannot apply less stringent requirements. They can be stricter as far as the harmonization constitutes *minimum* harmonization and provided that these requirements apply to both domestic and foreign credit institutions. CRD IV and the accompanying regulation have significantly reduced the number of instances of minimum harmonization. Furthermore, since the entry into force of the Lisbon Treaty, it is clear that the EU is exclusively competent to adopt requirements specifically and solely targeting the establishment of subsidiary credit institutions by third-country banks. Such measures still need to comply with the obligation of national treatment in the GATS. Hence no less favourable treatment can be granted to the direct establishment of subsidiaries by third-country banks.

750. EU law also significantly restricts the right of member states to make their own supervisory assessments of the applications of third-country banks to set up a credit institution in their territory. Through the creation of the EBA, tasked with creating a common supervisory culture in the EU, supervisory assessments by national authorities will become much more aligned. What is more, for the eurozone the ECB has become the single supervisor for the most important banks, also when these are owned by third-country persons. To a large extent EU law thus also limits the possibility of individual member states striking their own balance between competition and financial stability when making supervisory assessments. In many cases, it will now be the ECB that strikes such a balance, be it in close cooperation with the national authorities of the individual member states.

751. In respect of the objective of increasing efficiency through international competition, the interaction between EU law and the GATS arguably achieves an appropriate outcome. The GATS deals in a sensible manner with the EU preferential trade arrangement. It does not prevent EU market integration but at the same time avoids this preferential arrangement threatening the benefits of the multilateral process. The interaction of the EU system with the national treatment obligation in the GATS leads to a 'liberal rule of origin': third-country banks can benefit from the achievements of the internal market by setting up a credit institution in the EU on the same conditions as EU persons. EU law also reduces to a significant extent the margin of appreciation of national authorities when they make specific supervisory assessments, by clarifying conditions, creating a common supervisory culture through the EBA and through the creation of the SSM for the eurozone.

16

General conclusion

752. It is essential for governments to make a trade-off between efficiency and stability in the market for banking services. As was found in Part I, increased competition in the banking sector will improve the efficiency of channelling of funds from savers to investors and eventually contribute to economic growth. Increased competition is realized by removing regulatory barriers not only with regard to banking activities within a territory (deregulation), but also with regard to activities originating outside the territory (internationalization). However, competition also affects financial stability. Regulation of the banking sector is necessary to correct market failures that arise (e.g. the difficulty of monitoring risky activities in response to competition by foreign banks). Hence governments must seek a balance between liberalization and regulation.

753. The projects undertaken at the level of the EU and at the international level (the WTO) have as their objective increased trade in banking services. By enabling competition between banks from different countries, they can improve efficiency according to an above-national scale. The law of trade integration seeks to develop legal techniques to remove barriers to trade. They essentially define to what extent a state can still exercise its competence to regulate and supervise activities of foreign banks in its market. Different legal 'proxies' were developed to identify protectionist measures. EU law has gone quite far in developing and applying such legal techniques with regard to intra-EU trade in banking services. The legislative principle of mutual recognition and home-country control in CRD IV supplemented principles of non-discrimination and market access. These principles suppose trust between states that each other's regulation and supervision is able to achieve the same objectives they pursue in their own territory. In the EU, building such trust involved harmonization of a number of conditions for the taking up and pursuit of the business of credit institutions and the centralization of supervision.

754. At the international level, the GATS imposes a number of obligations in respect of market access, non-discrimination and domestic regulation, the impact of which seems at first sight significant. Nonetheless, we considered in Part II that these obligations sometimes apply only as far as WTO members have accepted this factor of inapplicability (market access and national treatment depend on specific commitments) and provide panels and the Appellate Body with sufficient flexibility to deal wisely with claims that a banking regulation would be in violation of WTO law. Moreover, when we also take into account the prudential exception, we can conclude that the GATS restricts WTO members in taking regulatory measures only to a limited extent. On the basis of these provisions, it is possible to identify measures that are clearly protectionist. In contrast, for measures where no such intent is clear, but that still impede trade, it is not likely that they will be removed through the GATS. The most relevant provision affecting supervisory assessments by banking supervisors is Article VI:1 GATS, which imposes a due process requirement. Nonetheless, bringing a successful claim on this basis requires solid evidence of a lack of reasonable, objective and impartial administration of a measure of general application. Even if there are situations where a strict application of the obligations in the GATS would lead to the conclusion that a certain banking regulation, or supervisory assessment, violates the GATS, it is likely that the WTO member in question would rely on the prudential exception. In sum, WTO members have significant leeway in regulating and supervising their market for banking services, but at the same time many obstacles to international trade in banking services will remain unaffected by the GATS.

755. The EU first of all focuses on fostering intra-EU trade in banking services. However, we saw in Part III that some elements in primary and secondary EU law also affect the right of member states to determine their own approach towards third-country banks. At the same time, the EU member states as well as the EU itself must respect the obligations they have undertaken within the framework of the WTO. The analysis in Part III was double. First, we considered the leeway EU law and the GATS leave to the member states and the EU itself to regulate and supervise the market for banking services. Second, we examined whether the EU project threatens the benefits of multilateral liberalization. This depends on the degree to which third-country banks are excluded from benefiting from the achievements of the EU integration project.

756. The entry into force of the Lisbon Treaty constitutes an important step towards a common external policy of the EU with regard to activities by third-country banks in the EU. We concluded that member states cannot take regulatory measures that specifically and solely apply to third-country banks that seek to carry out activities in the EU by means of subsidiaries. Such measures fall within the common commercial policy, which is an exclusive EU competence. To be sure, existing measures by member states remain in place as long as the EU has not taken any measures. Moreover, we considered that regulatory measures by member states that apply without distinction to domestic and third-country banks do not fall within the common commercial policy of the EU.

757. Because the EU is itself a WTO member, it has to comply with the obligations in the GATS when adopting new measures that lay down the common EU treatment of third-country banks. The analysis in Part II showed that the impact of the GATS on the right to regulate the market for banking services must not be overestimated. The obligations of market access and national treatment only apply as far as specific commitments have been taken for the banking sector and limitations to these commitments exist. Moreover, there exists a prudential exception.

758. Nonetheless, as shown in Part III, the obligation of national treatment in the GATS requires the EU to provide to third-country banks treatment that is not less favourable than that provided to EU credit institutions. This does not mean that the third-country banks must benefit from the achievements of the single market (free movement provisions and the 'single passport') *without* establishing a legal person in the EU first, which is justified on the basis of the exception for preferential trade agreements. However, it means that the regulatory requirements harmonized at the EU level for the establishment of credit institutions must also be applied to third-country banks. The obligation of national treatment prevents the EU from applying stricter requirements to third-country banks than those applied to EU credit institutions. We argued that the prudential exception does not permit the non-application of specific banking regulations (e.g. higher capital requirements) to EU credit institutions which are nevertheless applied to the third-country banks. Such a general distinction between EU banks and third-country banks is not justified on the basis of the prudential exception. There cannot be a general principle that all EU banks must necessarily be considered less dangerous for financial stability than all third-country banks. Such would constitute an abuse of the prudential exception for protectionist reasons. We also argued that the GATS exception for the creation of preferential trade agreements would not justify such general distinctions either.

759. Nonetheless, the fact that the national treatment obligation prevents the adoption of general measures that make such a general distinction between EU credit institutions and third-country banks does not mean that no distinctions between EU and third-country banks can be made at all. We found that such distinctions can be made on a case-by-case basis in individual supervisory decisions. The GATS does not prevent the EU supervisor or the competent supervisors of the member states from making such assessments, except when an ad hoc market access restriction would be imposed or clear protectionist intent can be shown, or when there is solid evidence of a lack of due process.

760. The interaction between EU law and the GATS leads to a conclusion that the EU does not constitute a threat to the benefits of multilateral liberalization. To be sure, third-country banks cannot benefit from the principles of freedom of establishment and free movement of services in primary EU law or the legislative principles of mutual recognition and home country control in CRD IV, unless they establish a legal person in the EU. Article V of the GATS ensures the legality of this situation. However, the operation of the national treatment obligation ensures that the conditions for the initial establishment of a credit institution that is a subsidiary of a third-country bank are not less favourable than those conditions imposed on EU credit institutions. Therefore the EU has a 'liberal rule of origin': once these conditions are met, the third-country banks can benefit from the achievements of the internal market.

BIBLIOGRAPHY

Abu-Akeel, A., 'The MFN as It Applies to Service Trade. New Problems for an Old Concept', (1999) 33 *Journal of World Trade* 103.

Adlung, R., 'Negotiations on Safeguards and Subsidies in Services: A Never-Ending Story?', (2007) 10 *Journal of International Economic Law* 235.

'Services Negotiations in the Doha Round: Lost in Flexibility', (2006) 9 *Journal of International Economic Law* 865.

Adlung, R. and M. Molinuevo, 'Bilateralism in Services Trade: Is There Fire behind the (BIT-) Smoke?', (2008) 11 *Journal of International Economic Law* 365.

Adlung, R., P. Morrison, M. Roy and W. Zhang, 'Fog in GATS Commitments – Boon or Bane?', WTO Staff Working Paper ERSD-2011-04, 31 March 2011.

Akerlof, G. and R. Kranton, *Identity Economics. How Our Identities Shape Our Work, Wages, and Well-Being* (Princeton University Press, 2010).

Akoth Osiro, D., 'GATT/WTO Necessity Analysis: Evolutionary Interpretation and its Impact on the Autonomy of Domestic Regulation', (2002) 29 *Legal Issues of Economic Integration* 123.

Alexander, K., R. Dhumale and J. Eatwell, *Global Governance of Financial Systems* (Oxford University Press, 2006).

Alexander, K., J. Eatwell, A. Persaud and R. Reoch, 'Financial Supervision and Crisis Management in the EU', Study for the Policy Department on Economic and Scientific Policy of the European Parliament, IP/A/ECON/IC/2007-069, December 2007, available at www.europarl.europa.eu/activities/committees/studies/download.do?file=19191#search=%20Financial%20supervision%20.

Alford, D., 'Core Principles for Effective Banking Supervision: An Enforceable International Financial Standard?', (2005) 28 *Boston College International and Comparative Law Review* 237.

'The Lamfalussy Process and EU Banking Regulation: Preliminary Assessment and Future Prospects', (2006) 21 *Journal of International Banking Law and Regulation* 59.

Allen, F. and D. Gale, 'Financial Markets, Intermediaries and Intertemporal Smoothing', (1997) 105 *Journal of Political Economy* 523.

'Competition and Financial Stability', 36 *Journal of Money, Credit and Banking* 453 (2004).

Allen, F. and A. Santomero, 'What do financial intermediaries do?', (2001) 25 *Journal of Banking and Finance* 271.

Andenas, M. and L. Panourgias, 'Applied Monetary Policy and Bank Supervision by the ECB', in J. Norton and M. Andenas (eds.), *International Monetary and Financial Law upon Entering the New Millennium. A Tribute to Sir Joseph and Ruth Gold* (London: BIICL, 2002) 119–70.

Andenas, M. and S. Zleptnig, 'Proportionality: WTO Law in Comparative Perspective', (2007) 42 *Texas International Law Journal* 371.

Andenas, M. and F. Wooldridge (eds.), *European Comparative Company Law* (Cambridge University Press, 2009) 648.

Avgouleas, E., 'The New EC Financial Markets Legislation and the Emerging Regime for Capital Markets', (2004) *Yearbook of European Law* 321.

Ayadi, R. and F. Musch, 'Basel II Implementation in the Midst of Turbulence', CEPS Task Force Reports, 2008.

Barnard, C., *The Substantive Law of the EU*, 2nd edn (Oxford University Press, 2007).

Barth, J., G. Caprio and R. Levine, *Rethinking Bank Regulation. Till Angels Govern* (Cambridge University Press, 2006).

Barth, J., J. Marchetti, D. Nolle and W. Sawangngnoenyuang, 'Foreign Banking: Do Countries' WTO Commitments Match Actual Practices?', WTO Staff Working Paper ERSD-2006-11, October 2006.

Basel Committee on Banking Supervision, 'About the Basel Committee', available at www.bis.org/bcbs/index.htm.

Bast, J., 'Annex on Movement of Natural Persons' in R. Wolfrum, P. Stoll and C. Feinäugle (eds.), *WTO – Trade in Services* (Leiden: Martinus Nijhoff, 2008) 573–95.

Beck, T., A. Demirgüç-Kunt and R. Levine, 'Law and Finance: Why Does Legal Origin Matter?', (2003) 31 *Journal of Comparative Economics* 653.

Bednarski, P., and G. Bielicki, 'Home and Host Supervisors' Relations from a Host Supervisor's Perspective', in G. Caprio, D. Evanoff and G. Kaufman (eds.) *Cross-Border Banking. Regulatory Challenges* (New Jersey: World Scientific, 2006) 211–29.

Benston, G., *Regulating Financial Markets: A Critique and some Proposals* (London: Institute of Economic Affairs, 1998).

Bernanke, B. and M. Gertler, 'Inside the Black Box: The Credit Channel of Monetary Policy Transmission', (1995) 9 *Journal of Economic Perspectives* 27.

Bernanke, B., M. Gertler and S. Gilchrist, 'The Financial Accelerator in a Quantitative Business Cycle Framework', in J. Taylor and M. Woodford (eds.), *Handbook of Macroeconomics* (Amsterdam: Elsevier, 1999), Vol. 15, 1341–93.

Besanko, D. and A. Thakor, 'Banking Deregulation: Allocational Consequences of Relaxing Entry Barriers', (1992) 16 *Journal of Banking and Finance* 909.

Bhagwati, J., 'Economic Perspectives on Trade in Professional Services', (1986) 2 *University of Chicago Legal Forum* 45.

Bigos, J., 'Contemplating GATS Article XVIII on Additional Commitments', (2008) 42 *Journal of World Trade* 723.

Bismuth, R., 'Financial Sector Regulation and Financial Services Liberalization at the Crossroads: The Relevance of International Financial Standards in WTO Law', (2010) 44 *Journal of World Trade* 489.

Bloom, N., 'The Impact of Uncertainty Shocks', (2009) 77 *Econometrica* 623.

Blot, C., S. Le Bayon, M. Lemoine and S. Levasseur, 'De la crise financière à la crise économique: une analyse comparative France–Etats-Unis', (2009) *Revue de l'OFCE* 255.

Blum, J. and M. Hellwig, 'The Macroeconomic Implications of the Capital Adequacy Requirements for Banks', (1995) 39 *European Economic Review* 739.

Boot, A. and A. Thakor, 'Can Relationship Banking Survive Competition?', (2000) 55 *Journal of Finance* 679.

Bowd, K., 'The Case for Financial Laissez-Faire', (1996) 106 *Economic Journal* 679.

Brink, T., 'Which WTO Rules Can a PTA Lawfully Breach? Completing the Analysis in *Brazil – Tyres*', (2010) 44 *Journal of World Trade* 813.

Bronkers, M. and N. McNelis, 'Rethinking the "Like Product" Definition in GATT 1994: Anti-Dumping and Environmental Protection', in M. Bronkers (ed.), *A Cross-Section of WTO Law* (London: Cameron May, 2000) 15–56.

Byttebier, K. and S. Fares, 'The EU Liberalisation of Financial Services: The EC Obligations in Comparison to the GATS Commitments', in K. Byttebier and K. Van der Borght (eds.), *WTO Obligations and Opportunities: Challenges of Implementation* (London: Cameron May, 2007) 85–119.

Calomiris, C. and C. Kahn, 'The Role of Demandable Debt in Structuring Optimal Banking Arrangements', (1991) 81 *American Economic Review* 497.

Carletti, E., *Background Note to OECD, Competition and Financial Markets* (Paris: OECD, 2009).

Ceyssens, J., 'Towards a Common Foreign Investment Policy? – Foreign Investment in the European Constitution', (2005) 32 *Legal Issues of Economic Integration* 259.

Chalmers, D., C. Hadjiemmanuil, G. Monti and A. Tomkins, *European Union Law. Text and Materials* (Cambridge University Press, 2006).

Charnovitz, S., 'The Law of Environmental "PPMs" in the WTO: Debunking the Myth of Illegality', (2002) 27 *Yale Journal of International Law* 59.

Choi, W. M., *'Like Products' in International Trade Law: Towards a Consistent GATT/WTO Jurisprudence* (Oxford University Press, 2003).

Claessens, S., 'Access to Financial Services: A Review of the Issues and Public Policy Objectives', World Bank Policy Research Working Paper No. 3589, May 2005.

'Competitive Implications of Cross-Border Banking', World Bank Policy Research Working Paper No. 3854, February 2006.

Claessens, S. and L. Laeven, 'Financial Dependence, Bank Sector Competition, and Economic Growth', (2005) 3 *Journal of the European Economic Association* 179.

Claessens, S., A. Demirgüç-Kunt and H. Huizinga, 'How Does Foreign Entry Affect Domestic Banking Markets?', (2001) 25 *Journal of Banking and Finance* 891.

Clarke, G., R. Cull and M. Martínez Pería, 'Foreign Bank Participation and Access to Credit across Firms in Developing Countries', (2006) 34 *Journal of Comparative Economics* 774.

Clarotti, P., 'La coordination des legislations bancaires', (1982) *Revue du Marché Commun* 68.

'Un pas décisif vers le marché commun des banques', (1989) *Revue du Marché Commun* 453.

Coibion, A. and E. Dessy, 'La réforme des services financiers en Europe un an après le début de la crise', (2009) 17 *Journal de droit européen* 194.

Committee on the Global Financial System, 'Foreign Direct Investment in the Financial Sector. Experiences in Asia, Central and Eastern Europe and Latin America', Bank for International Settlements, June 2005.

Cooter, R. and T. Ulen, *Law & Economics*, 5th edn (Boston: Addison-Wesley, 2008).

Corcoran, A. and T. Hart, 'The Regulation of Cross-Border Financial Services in the EU Internal Market', (2002) 8 *Columbia Journal of European Law* 221.

Cossy, M., 'Determining "Likeness" under the GATS: Squaring the Circle?', WTO Staff Working Paper ERSD-2006-08, September 2006, available at www.wto.org/english/res_e/reser_e/ersd200608_e.pdf.

Cottier, T. and M. Molinuevo, 'Article V GATS', in R. Wolfrum, P. Stoll and C. Feinäugle (eds.), *WTO – Trade in Services* (Leiden: Martinus Nijhoff, 2008) 125–51.

CPB Netherlands Bureau for Economic Policy Analysis, 'Competition and Stability in Banking', December 2001, available at www.cpb.nl/eng/pub/cpbreeksen/document/15/.

Cranston, R., *Principles of Banking Law* (Oxford University Press, 2002).

Cremona, M., 'The External Dimension of the Single Market: Building (on) the Foundations', in C. Barnard and J. Scott (eds.), *The Law of the Single EU Market. Unpacking the Premises* (Oxford University Press, 2002) 351–93.

Crosby, D., 'Banking on China's WTO Commitments: "Same Bed, Different Dreams" in China's Financial Services Sector', (2008) 11 *Journal of International Economic Law* 75.

Dalhuisen, J., *Dalhuisen on Transnational and Comparative Commercial, Financial and Trade Law* (Oxford: Hart, 2007).

Daniele, L., 'Non-discriminatory Restrictions to the Free Movement of Persons', (1997) 22 *European Law Review* 191.

Das, S. and A. Nanda, 'A Theory of Banking Structure', (1999) 23 *Journal of Banking and Finance* 863.

Davey, W. and J. Pauwelyn, 'MFN Unconditionality: A Legal Analysis of the Concept in View of Its Evolution in the GATT/WTO Jurisprudence with Particular

Reference to the Issue of "Like Product"', in T. Cottier, P. Mavroidis and P. Blatter (eds.), *Regulatory Barriers and the Principle of Non-Discrimination in World Trade Law* (Ann Arbor: University of Michigan Press, 2000) 13–50.

Davies, G., *Nationality Discrimination in the European Internal Market* (The Hague: Kluwer, 2003).

De Búrca, G., 'Unpacking the Concept of Discrimination in EC and International Trade Law', in C. Barnard and J. Scott (eds.), *The Law of the Single European Market. Unpacking the Premises* (Oxford: Hart, 2002) 181–95.

Degryse, H. and S. Ongena, 'The Impact of Competition on Bank Orientation', (2007) 16 *Journal of Financial Intermediation* 399.

De Haas, R. and I. Naaborg, 'Foreign Banks in Transition Countries: To Whom Do They Lend and How Are They Financed?', (2006) 15 *Financial Markets, Institutions and Instruments* 159.

Dehousse, F. and B. Dirick, 'Horizon 1992: le marché unique des services financiers', (1992) 111 *Journal des Tribunaux* 825.

Dejmek, P., 'The EU Internal Market for Financial Services – A Look at the First Regulatory Responses to the Financial Crisis and a View to the Future', (2009) 15 *Columbia Journal of European Law* 455.

Delimatsis, P., 'Don't Gamble with GATS – The Interaction between Articles VI, XVI, XVII and XVIII GATS in the Light of the US – Gambling Case', (2006) 40 *Journal of World Trade* 1059.

'Due Process and "Good" Regulation Embedded in the GATS – Disciplining Regulatory Behaviour in Services through Article VI of the GATS', (2007) 10 *Journal of International Economic Law* 13.

International Trade in Services and Domestic Regulation (Oxford University Press, 2007).

Delimatsis, P. and M. Molinuevo, 'Article XVI GATS', in R. Wolfrum, P. Stoll and C. Feinäugle (eds.), *WTO – Trade in Services* (Leiden: Martinus Nijhoff, 2008) 367–95.

De Meester, B., 'The Global Financial Crisis and Government Support for Banks: What Role for the GATS?', (2010) 13 *Journal of International Economic Law* 27.

'Multi-level Banking Regulation: An Assessment of the Role of the EC in the Light of Coherence and Democratic Legitimacy', in A. Follesdal, R. Wessel and J. Wouters (eds.), *Multilevel Regulation and the EU. The Interplay between Global, European and National Normative Processes* (Leiden: Martinus Nijhoff, 2008) 101–43.

Demirgüç-Kunt, A. and E. Detragiache, 'Financial Liberalization and Financial Fragility', World Bank Policy Research Working Paper No. 1917, May 1998.

Demirgüç-Kunt, A., R. Levine and H. Min, 'Opening to Foreign Banks: Issues of Stability, Efficiency, and Growth', in S. Lee (ed.), *The Implications of Globalization of World Financial Markets* (Seoul: Bank of Korea, 1998) 83–105.

Dermine, J., 'European Banking Integration and the Societas Europaea: From Host-Country to Home-Country Control', in G. Caprio, D. Evanoff and G. Kaufman (eds.), *Cross-Border Banking. Regulatory Challenges* (New Jersey: World Scientific, 2006) 49–63.

Deschanel, J. and J. Stoufflet, 'La directive communautaire No. 89/646 du 15 décembre 1989 concernant l'accès à l'activité des établissements de crédit et son exercice. Vers un statut bancaire européen', (May–June 1991) *Banque et droit* 83.

Desmedt, A., 'Proportionality in WTO Law', (2001) 4 *Journal of International Economic Law* 441.

Detragiache, E., T. Tressel and P. Gupta, 'Foreign Banks in Poor Countries: Theory and Evidence', (2008) 63 *Journal of Finance* 2123.

Devroe, W., 'Limits of Differentiation in European Economic Law: Ne Bis In Idem and Minimum Versus Maximum Harmonisation', (2009) 16 *Maastricht Journal of European and Comparative Law* 141.

Dewatripont, M. and J. Tirole, *The Prudential Regulation of Banks* (Cambridge, MA: MIT Press, 1994).

Diamond, D., 'Financial Intermediation and Delegated Monitoring', (1984) 51 *Review of Economic Studies* 393.

Diamond, D. and P. Dybvig, 'Bank Runs, Deposit Insurance, and Liquidity', (1983) 91 *Journal of Political Economy* 401.

DiMascio, N. and J. Pauwelyn, 'Non-discrimination in Trade and Investment Treaties: Worlds Apart or Two Sides of the Same Coin?', (2008) 102 *American Journal of International Law* 48.

Djordevic, M., 'Domestic Regulation and Free Trade in Services – A Balancing Act', (2002) 29 *Legal Issues of Economic Integration* 305.

Dorresteijn, A., T. Monteiro, C. Teichmann and E. Werlauff (eds.), *European Corporate Law* (Alphen aan de Rijn: Kluwer, 2009).

Dougan, M., 'Minimum Harmonization and the Internal Market', (2000) 37 *Common Market Law Review* 853.

Dowd, K., 'Moral Hazard and the Financial Crisis', (2009) 29 *Cato Journal* 141.

Eeckhout, P., 'Constitutional Concepts for Free Trade in Services', in J. Scott and G. De Búrca (eds.), *The EU and the WTO: Legal and Constitutional Issues* (Oxford: Hart, 2001) 211–235.

The European Internal Market and International Trade: A Legal Analysis (Oxford: Clarendon Press, 1994).

External Relations of the European Union. Legal and Constitutional Foundations (Oxford University Press, 2004).

Ehlerman, C.-D. and L. Ehring, 'WTO Dispute Settlement and Competition Law: Views from the Perspective of the Appellate Body's Experience', (2003) 26 *Fordham International Law Journal* 1505.

Ehring, L., '*De Facto* Discrimination in World Trade Law. National and Most-Favoured-Nation Treatment – or Equal Treatment?', (2002) 36 *Journal of World Trade* 921.

Emch, A., 'Services Regionalism in the WTO: China's Trade Agreements with Hong Kong and Macao in the Light of Article V GATS', (2006) 33 *Legal Issues of Economic Integration* 351.

European Central Bank, 'The New Basel Capital Framework and Its Implementation in the European Union', ECB Occasional Paper Series No. 42, December 2005.

Farber, D. and R. Hudec, 'GATT Legal Restraints on Domestic Environmental Regulations', in J. Bhagwati and R. Hudec (eds.), *Fair Trade and Harmonization: Prerequisites for Free Trade?, Vol. 2 Legal Analysis* (Cambridge, MA: MIT Press, 1996) 59–94.

Fink, C., 'PTAs in Services: Friends or Foes of the Multilateral Trading System?', in J. Marchetti and M. Roy (eds.), *Opening Markets for Trade in Services. Countries and Sectors in Bilateral and WTO Negotiations* (Cambridge University Press, 2008) 113–48.

Freixas, X. and J. Rochet, *Microeconomics of Banking* (Cambridge, MA: MIT Press, 1997).

Fuller, G. and F. Ranero, 'Collateralised Debt Obligations', (2005) 20 *Butterworths Journal of International Banking and Financial Law* 343.

Gari, G. and R. Lastra, 'Assessing the Lamfalussy Process: Success and Failures', (July/August 2009) *Butterworths Journal of International Banking and Financial Law* 37.

Geens, K. and K. Hopt (eds.), *The European Company Law Action Plan Revisited. Reassessment of the 2003 Priorities of the European Commission* (Leuven University Press, 2010).

Ghosh, S., 'Evolving International Supervisory Architecture: Design, Rationale and Policy Reform', (2005) 6 *Journal of Banking Regulation* 246.

Giovanoli, M., 'Architecture for the Global Financial Market: Legal Aspects of International Standard Setting', in M. Giovanoli (ed.), *International Monetary Law. Issues for the New Millennium* (Oxford University Press, 2000) 3–59.

Gkoutzinis, A., 'International Trade in Banking Services and the Role of the WTO: Discussing the Legal Framework and Policy Objectives of the General Agreement on Trade in Services and the Current State of Play in the Doha Round of Trade Negotiations', (2005) 39 *International Lawyer* 877.

'The Prudential Supervision of Internet Banking in the United Kingdom – Is the "Basel Approach" Finding Its Way through National Regulations?', (2002) 17 *Journal of International Banking Law* 249.

Goh, G. and A. Ziegler, 'Retrospective Remedies in the WTO after Automotive Leather', (2003) 6 *Journal of International Economic Law* 545.

Goldberg, L., 'Financial Sector FDI and Host Countries: New and Old Lessons', (March 2007) *Federal Reserve Bank of New York Economic Policy Review* 1.

Goldberg, L., R. Sweeney and C. Wihlborg, 'From Subsidiary to Branch Organization of International Banks: New Challenges and Opportunities for Regulators', LEFIC Working Paper, 14 November 2005, available at http://research.cbs.

dk/research/from_subsidiary_to_branch_organization_of_international_banks(12824)/.

Goldsmith, R., *Financial Structure and Development* (New Haven: Yale University Press, 1969).

Goodhart, C., 'The Regulatory Response to the Financial Crisis', CESifo Working Paper No. 2257, March 2008.

Goodhart, C., P. Hartmann, D. Llewellyn, L. Rojas-Suárez and S. Weisbrod, *Financial Regulation. Why, How and Where Now?* (London: Routledge, 1998).

Gordy, M. and B. Howells, 'Procyclicality in Basel II: Can We Treat the Disease without Killing the Patient?', (2006) 15 *Journal of Financial Intermediation* 395.

Gorton, G. and A. Winton, 'Financial Intermediation', Wharton Financial Institutions Center Working Paper 02–28, March 2002, 10, also published in G. Constantinides (ed.), *Handbook on the Economics of Finance* (Amsterdam: Elsevier, 2003) 431–530.

Grane, P., 'Remedies under WTO Law', (2001) 4 *Journal of International Economic Law* 755.

Gray, K., 'Case Comment – WTO Appellate Body: Brazil – Tyres Dispute', (2008) 102 *American Journal of International Law* 616.

Gruson, M., 'Supervision of Financial Conglomerates in the European Union', (2004) 19 *Journal of International Banking Law and Regulation* 363.

'Supervision of Financial Holding Companies in Europe: The EU Directive on Supplementary Supervision of Financial Conglomerates', (2002) 36 *International Lawyer* 1229.

Gruson, M. and W. Feuring, 'The New Banking Law of the European Economic Community', (1991) 25 *International Lawyer* 1.

Gruson, M. and W. Nikowitz, 'The Second Banking Directive of the European Economic Community and Its Importance for Non-EEC Banks', (1988) 12 *Fordham International Law Journal* 205.

Gurley, J. and E. Shaw, 'Financial Aspects of Economic Development', (1955) 45 *American Economic Review* 515.

Guzman, A., 'Bank Structure, Capital Accumulation, and Growth: A Simple Macroeconomic Model', (2000) 16 *Economic Theory* 421.

Habersack, M., *Europäisches Gesellschaftsrecht. Einführung für Studium und Praxis* (Munich: Beck, 2003).

Hable, A., 'The European Constitution: Changes in the Reform of Competences with a Particular Focus on the External Dimension', Europainstitut Wirtschaftsuniversität Wien Working Paper No. 67, March 2005.

Hatzopoulos, V., 'Recent Developments of the Case Law of the ECJ in the Field of Services', (2000) 37 *Common Market Law Review* 43.

Hauswald, R. and R. Marquez, 'Relationship Banking, Loan Specialization and Competition', Wharton Paper, February 2000, available at http://fic.wharton.upenn.edu/fic/papers/00/0013.pdf.

Hellman, T., K. Murdock and J. Stiglitz, 'Liberalization, Moral Hazard in Banking and Prudential Regulation: Are Capital Requirements Enough?', (2000) 90 *American Economic Review* 147.

Hellwig, M., 'Systemic Risk in the Financial Sector: An Analysis of the Subprime-Mortgage Financial Crisis', *Preprints of the Max Planck Institute for Research on Collective Goods*, Bonn 2008/43, November 2008.

Heremans, D., 'Financial Regulation and Supervision of Banks. The Basel II Capital Framework', in D. Heremans et al. (eds.), *Current Developments in European Integration: Financial Services, Transport Policy: Legal and Economic Contributions to the Fortis Bank Chair 2001–2003* (Leuven: Universitaire Pers Leuven, 2004) 115–33.

'Regulation of Banking and Financial Markets', in B. Bouckaert and G. De Geest (eds.), *Encyclopedia of Law and Economics. Volume III. The Regulation of Contracts* (Cheltenham: Edward Elgar, 2000) 950–86.

Herrmann, C., 'Die Zukunft der mitgliedstaatlichen Investitionspolitik nach dem Vertrag vom Lissabon', (2010) 21 *Europäische Zeitschrift für Wirtschaftsrecht* 207.

Hilf, M. and S. Oeter, *WTO-Recht. Rechtsordnung des Welthandels* (Baden-Baden: Nomos Verlag, 2005).

Hilf, M. and S. Puth, 'The Principle of Proportionality on Its Way into WTO/GATT Law', in A. Von Bogdandy, P. Mavroidis and Y. Meny (eds.), *European Integration and International Coordination. Studies in Transnational Economic Law in Honour of Claus-Dieter Ehlermann* (The Hague: Kluwer, 2002) 199–218.

Hill, T., 'On Goods and Services', (1977) 23 *Review of Income & Wealth* 315.

Hoekman, B. and P. Mavroidis, 'Nothing Dramatic (. . .Regarding Administration of Customs Laws). A Comment on the WTO Appellate Body Report *EC – Selected Customs Matters*', (2009) 8 *World Trade Review* 31.

The World Trade Organization. Law, Economics, and Politics (London: Routledge, 2007).

Hopt, K., E. Wymeersch and A. Schaub, 'Company Law and Corporate Governance in Europe: Interim Report and Reflections on the Ongoing Reforms in the European Union and in Selected Member States', (2005) *Rabels Zeitschrift für ausländisches und internationales Privatrecht* 611.

Horn, H. and P. Mavroidis, 'Still Hazy after All These Years: The Interpretation of National Treatment in the GATT/WTO Case-Law on Discrimination', (2004) 15 *European Journal of International Law* 39.

Howse, R. and E. Chalamish, 'The Use and Abuse of WTO Law in Investor–State Arbitration: A Reply to Jürgen Kurtz', (2009) 20 *European Journal of International Law* 1087.

Howse, R. and D. Regan, 'The Product/Process Distinction – An Illusory Basis for Disciplining "Unilateralism" in Trade Policy', (2000) 11 *European Journal of International Law* 249.

Howse, R. and E. Türk, 'The WTO Impact on Internal Regulations – A Case Study of the Canada – EC Asbestos Dispute', in J. Scott and G. De Búrca (eds.), *The EU and the WTO: Legal and Constitutional Issues* (Oxford: Hart, 2001) 283–328.

Hudec, R., 'GATT/WTO Constraints on National Regulation: Requiem for an "Aim and Effects" Test', (1998) 32 *International Lawyer* 619.

Hughes, J., L. Mester and C. Moon, 'Are Scale Economies in Banking Elusive or Illusive? Evidence Obtained by Incorporating Capital Structure and Risk-Taking into Models of Bank Production', (2001) 25 *Journal of Banking and Finance* 2169.

IMF, *Balance of Payments Manual*, 5th edn (Washington, DC: IMF, 1993).

IMF and World Bank, 'The Financial Sector Assessment Program After Ten Years: Experience and Reforms for the Next Decade', 28 August 2009, available at www.imf.org/external/np/pp/eng/2009/082809B.pdf.

Irwin, D. and J. Weiler, 'Measures Affecting Cross-Border Supply of Gambling and Betting Services (DS 285)', (2008) 7 *World Trade Review* 71.

Israel, M., 'Services as Experience Goods: An Empirical Examination of Consumer Learning in Automobile Insurance', (2005) 95 *American Economic Review* 1444.

Jackson, J., 'Comments on Shrimp/Turtle and the Product/Process Distinction', (2000) 11 *European Journal of International Law* 303.

Jarreau, S., 'Interpreting the General Agreement on Trade in Services and the WTO Agreements Relevant to the International Trade of Financial Services: The Lawyer's Perspective', (1999) 25 *North Carolina Journal of International Law and Commercial Regulation* 1.

Kane, E., 'Confronting Divergent Interests in Cross-Country Regulatory Arrangements', in G. Caprio, D. Evanoff and G. Kaufman (eds.), *Cross-Border Banking. Regulatory Challenges* (New Jersey: World Scientific, 2006) 265–85.

Katz, S., 'The Second Banking Directive', (1992) 12 *Yearbook of European Law* 249.

Kaufman, G., 'Bank Contagion: A Review of the Theory and Evidence', (1994) 8 *Journal of Financial Services Research* 123.

Keeley, M., 'Deposit Insurance, Risk, and Market Power in Banking', (1990) 80 *American Economic Review* 1183.

Kern, A., R. Dhumale and J. Eatwell, *Global Governance of Financial Systems. The International Framework of Systemic Risk* (Oxford University Press, 2006).

Key, S., *The Doha Round and Financial Services Negotiations* (Washington, DC: AEI Press, 2003).

'Financial Services', in P. Macrory, A. Appleton and M. Plummer (eds.), *The World Trade Organization. Legal, Economic and Political Analysis* (New York: Springer, 2005), Vol. 1, 955–88.

Keynes, J., *The General Theory of Employment, Interest and Money, repr.* (London: Macmillan, 1957).

Kono, M. and M. Yokoi-Arai, 'Dissecting Regional Integration in Financial Services from the Competition Policy and Trade Policy Perspectives', BIS Paper No. 42, October 2008, www.bis.org/publ/bppdf/bispap42c.pdf.

Korobkin, R. and T. Ulen, 'Law and Behavioral Science: Removing the Rationality Assumption from Law and Economics', (2000) 88 *California Law Review* 1051.

Krajewski, M., 'Article VI GATS. Domestic Regulation', in R. Wolfrum, P. Stoll and C. Feinäugle (eds.), *WTO – Trade in Services* (Leiden: Martinus Nijhoff, 2008) 165–96.

'External Trade Law and the Constitutional Treaty: Towards a Federal and More Democratic Common Commercial Policy?' (2005) 42 *Common Market Law Review* 91.

National Regulation and Trade Liberalization in Services: The Legal Impact of the General Agreement on Trade in Services (GATS) on National Regulatory Autonomy (The Hague: Kluwer, 2003).

'Playing by the Rules of the Game? Specific Commitments after US – Gambling and Betting and the Current GATS Negotiations', (2005) 32 *Legal Issues of Economic Integration* 417.

Kroeze, M. and H. Vletter-Van Dort, 'History and Future of Uniform Company Law in Europe', (2008) 5 *European Company Law* 114.

Kroszner, R. and P. Strahan, 'Obstacles to Optimal Policy: The Interplay of Politics and Economics in Shaping Bank Supervision and Regulation Reforms', in F. Mishkin (ed.), *Prudential Supervision: What Works and What Doesn't?* (University of Chicago Press, 2001) 233–71.

Kysar, D., 'Preferences for Processes: the Process/Product Distinction and the Regulation of Consumer Choice', (2004) 118 *Harvard Law Review* 525.

Lamandini, M., 'When More Is Needed: The European Financial Supervisory Reform and Its Legal Basis', (2009) 6 *European Company Law* 197.

La Porta, R., F. Lopez-de-Silanes and A. Schleifer, 'Government Ownership of Banks', (2002) 57 *Journal of Finance* 265.

Lastra, R., *Legal Foundations of International Monetary Stability* (Oxford University Press, 2006).

Leanza, U., 'An Outline of the EEC Discipline on Credit Institutions', (1987) 7 *Journal of Regional Policy* 59.

Lee, L., 'The Basle Accords as Soft Law: Strengthening International Banking Supervision', (1998) 39 *Virginia Journal of International Law* 1.

Lehner, M. and M. Schnitzer, 'Entry of Foreign Banks and Their Impact on Host Countries', (2008) 36 *Journal of Comparative Economics* 430.

Leigh Case, K., 'The Daiwa Wake-Up Call: The Need for International Standards for Banking Supervision', (1996) 26 *Georgia Journal for International and Comparative Law* 215.

Leroux, E., 'Eleven Years of GATS Case Law: What Have We Learned?', (2007) 10 *Journal of International Economic Law* 749.

'Trade in Financial Services under the World Trade Organization', (2002) 36 *Journal of World Trade* 413.

'What is a "Service supplied in the exercise of governmental authority" under art. I:3(b) and of the General Agreement on Trade in Services?', (2006) 40 *Journal of World Trade* 345.

Lescrauwaet, P., 'Links between institutional investors and banks', Background paper prepared for the Working Group on institutional investors, global savings and asset location, December 2006, available at www.bis.org/publ/wgpapers/cgfs27lescrauwaet.pdf.

Levine, R., 'Finance and Growth: Theory, Evidence and Mechanisms', in P. Aghion and S. Durlauf (eds.), *Handbook of Economic Growth* (Amsterdam: Elsevier, 2005) 865–934.

'Foreign Banks, Financial Development, and Economic Growth', in C. Barfield (ed.), *International Financial Markets: Harmonization versus Competition* (Washington, DC: AEI Press, 1996) 224–55.

Levine, R. and S. Zervos, 'Stock Markets, Banks, and Economic Growth', (1998) 88 *American Economic Review* 537.

Levine, R., N. Loayza and T. Beck, 'Financial Intermediation and Growth: Causality and Causes', (2000) 46 *Journal of Monetary Economics* 31.

Llewellyn, D., 'The Economic Rationale for Financial Regulation', FSA Occasional Paper Series No. 1, April 1999, available at www.fsa.gov.uk/pubs/occpapers/OP01.pdf.

Mak, V., 'Review of the Consumer Acquis: Towards Maximum Harmonization?', (2009) 17 *European Review of Private Law* 55.

Malloy, M., 'Emerging International Regime of Financial Services Regulation', (2005) 18 *Transnational Lawyer* 329.

Manning, M., 'Finance Causes Growth: Can We Be So Sure?', (2003) 3 *Contributions to Macroeconomics* Article 12.

Marchetti, J. and P. Mavroidis, 'I Now Recognize You (and Only You) as Equal. An Anatomy of (Mutual) Recognition Agreements in the GATS', in I. Lianos and O. Odudu (eds.), *Regulating Trade in Services in the EU and the WTO: Trust, Distrust and Economic Integration* (Cambridge University Press, 2012) 415–43.

'Walking the Tightrope between Domestic Policy and Globalization: Market Access, Discrimination and Regulatory Intervention under the GATS', mimeo, 2006.

Marchetti, J. and M. Roy, 'Services Liberalization in the WTO and in PTAs', in J. Marchetti and M. Roy (eds.), *Opening Markets for Trade in Services. Countries and Sectors in Bilateral and WTO Negotiations* (Cambridge University Press, 2008) 61–112.

Masciandaro, D., 'Regulating the Regulators: The Changing Face of Financial Supervision Architectures before and after the Crisis', (2009) 6 *European Company Law* 187.

Mason, E., 'Price and Production Policies in Large-Scale Enterprises', (1939) 29 *American Economic Review* 61.

Mathis, J., 'Mutual Recognition Agreements: Transatlantic Parties and the Limits to Non-tariff Barrier Regionalism in the WTO', (1998) 32 *Journal of World Trade* 5.

'The WTO *Brazil – Tyres* Case and GATT Article XXIV: One More Step To a Legal Regime?', in N. Lavranos (ed.), *Multilevel Judicial Governance between Global and Regional Economic Integration Systems: Institutional and Substantive Aspects*, EUI Working Papers 2009/41, 23–32.

Matsushita, M., T. Schoenbaum and P. Mavroidis, *The World Trade Organization. Law Practice and Policy* (Oxford University Press, 2006).

Mattoo, A., 'MFN and the GATS', in T. Cottier, P. Mavroidis and P. Blatter (eds.), *Regulatory Barriers and the Principle of Non-discrimination in World Trade Law* (Ann Arbor: University of Michigan Press, 2000) 51–99.

'National Treatment in the GATS. Corner-Stone or Pandora's Box?', (1997) 31 *Journal of World Trade* 107.

Mattoo, A. and P. Sauvé, 'Domestic Regulation and Trade in Services: Key Issues', in A. Mattoo and P. Sauvé (eds.), *Domestic Regulation and Service Trade Liberalization* (Washington, DC: World Bank, 2003) 1–6.

Mattoo, A. and A. Subramanian, 'Currency Undervaluation and Sovereign Wealth Funds: A New Role for the World Trade Organization', World Bank Policy Research Working Paper No. 4668, July 2008.

'Regulatory Autonomy and Multilateral Disciplines. The Dilemma and a Possible Resolution', (1998) 1 *Journal of International Economic Law* 303.

Mavroidis, P., 'Highway XVI Revisited: The Road from Non-discrimination to Market Access in GATS', (2007) 6 *World Trade Review* 1.

'Transatlantic Regulatory Cooperation: Exclusive Club or "Open Regionalism"?', in G. Bermann, M. Herdegan and P. Lindseth (eds.), *Transatlantic Regulatory Cooperation: Legal Problems and Political Prospects* (Oxford University Press, 2001) 263–70.

Mavromati, D., *The Law of Payment Services in the EU. The EC Directive on Payment Services in the Internal Market* (Alphen aan de Rijn: Kluwer Law International, 2008).

Mayes, D. and P. Granlund, 'Polar Approaches to Regulating Cross-Border Banking: Nordic and Antipodean Routes to Financial Stability', (2008) 9 *European Business Organization Law Review* 63.

Mayes, D. and Y. Vesala, 'On the Problems of Home Country Control', Bank of Finland Discussion Papers 20/98, 23 September 1998.

Menjucq, M., *Droit international et européen des sociétés* (Paris: Montchrestien, 2008).

Mishkin, F., 'Prudential Supervision: Why is it Important and What Are the Issues?', in F. Mishkin (ed.), *Prudential Supervision: What Works and What Doesn't?* (University of Chicago Press, 2001) 1–29.

Molostova, I., 'Revision of the European Regulatory Capital Regime', (January 2009) *Butterworths Journal of International Banking and Financial Law* 20.

Nelson, P., 'Information and Consumer Behavior', (1970) 78 *Journal of Political Economy* 311.

Neumann, J. and E. Türk, 'Necessity Revisited: Proportionality in World Trade Organization Law after Korea – Beef, EC – Asbestos and EC – Sardines', (2003) 37 *Journal of World Trade* 199.

Nicolaïdis, K., 'Non-discriminatory Mutual Recognition: An Oxymoron in the New WTO Lexicon?', in T. Cottier, P. Mavroidis and P. Blatter (eds.), *Regulatory Barriers and the Principle of Non-discrimination in World Trade Law* (Ann Arbor: University of Michigan Press, 2000) 267–301.

Nicolaïdis, K. and J. Trachtman, 'From Policed Regulation to Managed Recognition: Mapping the Boundary of GATS', in J. Trachtman (ed.), *The International Economic Law Revolution and the Right to Regulate* (London: Cameron May, 2006) 281–321.

Nielson, J., 'Trade Agreements and Recognition', in OECD, *Quality and Recognition in Higher Education* (Paris: OECD Publishing, 2004) 155–203.

Nieto, M. and J. Peñasola, 'The European Architecture of Regulation, Supervision and Financial Stability: A Central Bank Perspective', (2004) 5 *Journal of International Banking Regulation* 228.

Northcott, C., 'Competition in Banking: A Review of the Literature', Bank of Canada Working Paper 2004-24, June 2004, available at www.bankofcanada.ca/en/res/wp/2004/wp04-24.pdf.

Ortino, F., *Basic Legal Instruments for the Liberalization of Trade: A Comparative Analysis of EC and WTO Law* (Oxford: Hart, 2004).

'The Principle of Non-discrimination and Its Exceptions in GATS: Selected Legal Issues', Working Paper presented at 'Conflict and Crises? – The WTO after Hong Kong', Vienna, 24–25 April 2006, available at http://ssrn.com/abstract=979481.

'Treaty Interpretation and the WTO Appellate Body Report in *US – Gambling*: A Critique', (2006) 9 *Journal of International Economic Law* 117.

Ortino, F. and A. Sheppard, 'International Agreements Covering Foreign Investment in Services: Patterns and Linkages', in L. Bartels and F. Ortino (eds.), *Regional Trade Agreements and the WTO Legal System* (Oxford University Press, 2006) 201–14.

Pallemaerts, M., *EU and WTO Law: How Tight is the Legal Straitjacket for Environmental Product Regulation?* (Brussels: VUB Press, 2006).

Panayi, C., 'Corporate Mobility in Private International Law and European Community Law: Debunking Some Myths', (2009) 28 *Yearbook of European Law* 123.

Panourgias, L., *Banking Regulation and World Trade Law* (Oxford: Hart, 2006).

Pauwelyn, J., '*Rien ne Va Plus?* Distinguishing Domestic Regulation from Market Access in GATT and GATS', (2005) 4 *World Trade Review* 131.

'The Unbearable Lightness of Likeness', in M. Panizzon, N. Pohl and P. Sauvé (eds.), *GATS and the Regulation of International Trade in Services* (Cambridge University Press, 2008) 358–69.

Peek, J. and E. Rosengren, 'The Capital Crunch: Neither a Borrower nor a Lender Be', (1995) 27 *The Journal of Money, Credit and Banking* 625.

Pellé, P., 'Companies Crossing Borders within Europe', (2008) 5 *European Company Law* 284.

Persaud, A., 'Sending the Herd off the Cliff Edge: The Disturbing Interaction between Herding and Market-Sensitive Risk Management Practices', ERisk, December 2000, available at www.erisk.com/ResourceCenter/ERM/persaud.pdf, 2.

Petersen, M. and R. Rajan, 'The Effect of Credit Market Competition on Lending Relationships', (1995) 110 *Quarterly Journal of Economics* 407.

Phillips, P., 'EC Second Banking Directive: The Practical Effect', (1993) 4 *European Business Law Review* 43.

Pigou, A., *The Economics of Welfare*, repr. (London: Macmillan, 1950).

Porges, A. and J. Trachtman, 'Robert Hudec and Domestic Regulation: The Resurrection of Aim and Effects', (2003) 37 *Journal of World Trade* 783.

Posner, R., 'Theories of Economic Regulation', (1974) 5 *The Bell Journal of Economics and Management Science* 335.

Prins, C., 'E-government: A Comparative Study of Multiple Dimensions of Required Regulatory Change', (2007) 11 *Electronic Journal of Comparative Law*, available at www.ejcl.org/113/article113-35.pdf.

Qin, J., 'Managing Conflicts between Rulings of WTO and RTA Tribunals: Reflections on the Brazil – Tyres Case', Wayne State University Law School Research Paper no. 09-24, 16 October 2009.

Rajan, R. and L. Zingales, 'Financial Dependence and Growth', (1998) 88 *American Economic Review* 559.

Ram, R., 'Financial Development and Economic Growth: Additional Evidence', (1999) 35 *Journal of Development Studies* 164

Regan, D., 'The Meaning of "Necessary" in GATT Article XX and GATS Article XIV: the Myth of Cost-Benefit Balancing', (2007) 6 *World Trade Review* 347.

Robinson, J., *The Rate of Interest and Other Essays* (London: Macmillan, 1952).

Rousseau, P. and P. Wachtel, 'Equity Markets and Growth: Cross-Country Evidence on Timing and Outcomes 1980–95', (2000) 24 *Journal of Banking and Finance* 1933.

Rybczynski, T., 'Industrial Financial System in Europe, US and Japan', (1984) 5 *Journal of Economic Behavior & Organization* 275.

Saez, L. and X. Shi, 'Liquidity Pools, Risk Sharing and Financial Contagion', (2004) 25 *Journal of Financial Services Research* 5.

Sauvé, P., *Trade Rules behind Borders: Essays on Services, Investments and the New Trade Agenda* (London: Cameron May, 2003).

Sauvé, P. and A. Mattoo, 'Domestic Regulation and the GATS: Untangling the Issues', in P. Sauvé (ed.), *Essays on Services, Investment and the New Trade Agenda* (London: Cameron May, 2003) 113–30.

Sauvé, P. and C. Wilkie, 'Investment Liberalization in GATS', in P. Sauvé and R. Stern (eds.), *GATS 2000. New Directions in Services Trade Liberalization* (Washington, DC: Brookings Institution Press, 2000) 331–63.

Schmidt, R., A. Hackethal and M. Tyrell, 'Disintermediation and the Role of Banks in Europe: An International Comparison', (1999) 8 *Journal of Financial Intermediation* 36.

Scholtens, B. and D. van Wensveen, 'A Critique on the Theory of Financial Intermediation', (2000) 24 *Journal of Banking and Finance* 1243.

'The Theory of Financial Intermediation: An Essay on What it Does (Not) Explain', SUERF Studies, 2003/1, available at www.suerf.org/download/studies/study20031.pdf.

Schüler, M., 'Incentive Problems in Banking Supervision – The European Case', Zentrum für Europäische Wirtschaftsforschung Discussion Paper No. 03-62, November 2003, available at http://opus.zbw-kiel.de/volltexte/2004/1492/pdf/dp0362.pdf.

Schumpeter, J., *The Theory of Economic Development* (Cambridge, MA: Harvard University Press, 1968 [1934; first published in German 1911]).

Schwartz, F., 'Risk Distribution in the Capital Markets: Credit Default Swaps, Insurance and a Theory of Demarcation', (2007) 12 *Fordham Journal of Corporate and Financial Law* 167.

Scott, H., *International Finance: Law and Regulation* (London: Sweet and Maxwell, 2008).

'International Finance: Rule Choices for Global Financial Markets', in A. Sykes and A. Guzman (eds.), *Research Handbook in International Economic Law* (Cheltenham: Edward Elgar, 2007) 361–417.

Shaffer, S., 'The Winner's Curse in Banking', (1998) 7 *Journal of Financial Intermediation* 359.

Siems, M., 'Convergence, Competition, "Centros" and Conflicts of Law: European Company Law in the 21st Century', (2002) 27 *European Law Review* 47.

Simser, J., 'GATS and Financial Services: Redefining Borders', (1996) 3 *Buffalo Journal of International Law* 34.

Slot, P., 'Harmonisation', (1996) 21 *European Law Review* 378.

Smith, F. and L. Woods, 'A Distinction without a Difference: Exploring the Boundary between Goods and Services in the World Trade Organization and the European Union', (2005) 12 *Columbia Journal of European Law* 1.

Sousi-Roubi, B., *Droit bancaire européen* (Paris: Dalloz, 1995).

Spaventa, E., 'From Gebhard to Carpenter: Towards a (Non-)Economic European Constitution', (2004) 41 *Common Market Law Review* 743.

Steinherr, A., 'Stony Road to an Integrated Financial Market', (1989) 3 *European Affairs* 61.

Stephenson, S., 'GATS and Regional Integration', in P. Sauvé and R. Stern (eds.), *GATS 2000. New Directions in Services Trade Liberalization* (Washington, DC: Brookings Institution Press, 2000) 509–27.

Stigler, R., 'The Theory of Economic Regulation', (1971) 2 *Bell Journal of Economics and Management Science* 3.

Strivens, R., 'The Liberalization of Banking Services in the Community', (1992) 29 *Common Market Law Review* 283.

Stumberg, J., Briefing Memo to Kay Wilkie, WPDR chairman's fourth draft on domestic regulation, dated 23 January 2008, Harrison Institute for Public Law, Georgetown University Law Center, 12 February 2008, Version 5, available at www.law.georgetown.edu/clinics/hi/documents/Stumberg-WPDR chairsdraft23-Jan-08v6copy.doc, 27.

Sunde, T., 'Möglichkeiten und Grenzen innerstaatlicher Regulierung nach Art. VI GATS', in C. Tietje, G. Kraft and R. Sethe (eds.), *Beiträge zum Transnationalen Wirtschaftsrecht* (Halle-Wittenberg: Martin-Luther-Universität, 2006), Part 59.

Sweeney Samuelson, E. and S. Ebere, 'Could a Foreign Investor Use GATS Disciplines in a BIT Claim?', discussion draft of 12 March 2010, Harrison Institute for Public Law, Georgetown Law, available at www.boell.org/web/146–558.html.

Sykes, A., 'Regulatory Protectionism and the Law of International Trade', (1999) 66 *University of Chicago Law Review* 1.

Tison, M., 'Unravelling the General Good Exception: The Case for Financial Services', in M. Andenas and W. Roth (eds.), *Services and Free Movement in EU Law* (Oxford University Press, 2002) 321–81.

Trachtman, J., 'Accounting Standards and Trade Disciplines. Irreconcilable Differences?', (1997) 31 *Journal of World Trade* 63.

'FDI and the Right to Regulate: Lessons from Trade Law', in UNCTAD, *The Development Dimensions of FDI and Rule-Making Perspectives*, 189 UN Doc. UNCTAD/ITE/IIA/2003/4 (2003).

'Lessons for GATS Article VI from the SPS, TBT and GATT Treatment of Domestic Regulation', 29 January 2002, available at http://ssrn.com/abstract=298760.

'Negotiations on Domestic Regulation and Trade in Services (GATS Article VI): A Legal Analysis of Selected Current Issues', in E.-U. Petersmann (ed.), *Reforming the World Trading System. Legitimacy, Efficiency and Democratic Governance* (Oxford University Press, 2005) 205–19.

'Trade in Financial Services under GATS, NAFTA and the EC: A Regulatory Jurisdiction Analysis', (1996) 34 *Columbia Journal of Transnational Law* 40.

'Trade and ... Problems, Cost-Benefit Analysis and Subsidiarity', (1998) 9 *European Journal of International Law* 32.

'Transatlantic Regulatory Cooperation from a Trade Perspective: A Case Study in Accounting Standards', in G. Bermann (ed.), *Transatlantic Regulatory Cooperation: Legal Problems and Political Prospects* (Oxford University Press, 2000) 223–42.

'United States – Measures Affecting the Cross-Border Supply of Gambling and Betting Services', 99 *American Journal of International Law* 861 (2005).

Trebilcock, M. and R. Howse, *The Regulation of International Trade*, 2nd edn (London: Routledge, 1999).

The Regulation of International Trade, 3rd edn (London: Routledge, 2005).

Tversky, A. and D. Kahneman, 'Rational Choice and the Framing of Decisions', (1986) 59 *Journal of Business* 251.

Ulen, T., 'Rational Choice Theory in Law and Economics', in B. Bouckaert and G. De Geest (eds.), *Encyclopedia of Law and Economics. Volume 0. General Works, History and Methodology* (Cheltenham: Edward Elgar, 2000) 790–818.

UNCTAD, *The REIO Exception in MFN Treatment Clauses* (New York and Geneva, UNCTAD, 2004).

Vaccari, B., 'Le processus Lamfalussy: une réussite pour la comitologie et un exemple de "bonne gouvernance européenne"', (2005) *Revue du Droit de l'Union Européenne* 803.

Van Calster, G., *International and EU Trade Law: The Environmental Challenge* (London: Cameron May, 2000).

VanDuzer, J., 'Health, Education and Social Services in Canada: The Impact of the GATS', in J. Curtis and D. Ciuriak (eds.), *Trade Policy Research 2004* (Ottawa: Trade Policy Canada, 2004) 303–505.

Verhoosel, G., *National Treatment and WTO Dispute Settlement. Adjudicating the Boundaries of Regulatory Autonomy* (Oxford: Hart, 2002).

Viñuales, J., 'The International Regulation of Financial Conglomerates: A Case-Study of Equivalence as an Approach to Financial Integration', (2006) 37 *California Western International Law Journal* 1.

Von Bogdandy, A. and J. Windsor, 'Annex on Financial Services', in R. Wolfrum, P. Stoll and C. Feinäugle (eds.), *WTO – Trade in Services* (Leiden: Martinus Nijhoff, 2008) 618–39.

'Understanding on Commitments in Financial Services', in R. Wolfrum, P. Stoll and C. Feinäugle (eds.), *WTO – Trade in Services* (Leiden: Martinus Nijhoff, 2008) 647–66.

Von Bogdandy, A., P. Mavroidis and Y. Mény (eds.), *European Integration and International Co-ordination. Studies in Transnational Economic Law in Honour of Claus-Dieter Ehlermann* (The Hague: Kluwer Law International, 2002).

Vranes, E., 'The WTO and Regulatory Freedom: WTO Disciplines on Market Access, Non-Discrimination and Domestic Regulation Relating to Trade in Goods and Services', (2009) 12 *Journal of International Economic Law* 953.

Waincymer, J., 'Reformulated Gasoline under the Reformed WTO Dispute Settlement Procedures: Pulling Pandora out of a Chapeau?', (1996) 18 *Michigan Journal of International Law* 141.

Walker, G., 'European Financial Programme: Content, Structure and Completion', (2004) 15 *European Business Law Review* 305.

Wang, Y., 'Most-Favoured-Nation Treatment under the General Agreement on Trade in Services – and Its Application in Financial Services', (1996) 30 *Journal of World Trade* 91.

Weatherill, S., 'Harmonisation: How Much, How Little?', (2005) 16 *European Law Review* 533.

'Measures of Consumer Protection as Impediments to Exports of Goods', (2009) 5 *European Review of Contract Law* 149.

'Supply of and Demand for Internal Market Regulation: Strategies, Preferences and Interpretation', in N. Shuibne (ed.) *Regulating the Internal Market* (Cheltenham: Edward Elgar, 2006) 29–60.

Weiler, J. (ed.), *The EU, the WTO and the NAFTA: Towards a Common Law of International Trade?* (Oxford University Press, 2001).

Weiler, T., 'NAFTA Article 1105 and the Principles of International Economic Law', (2003) 42 *Columbia Journal of Transnational Law* 35.

Wiers, J., *Trade and Environment in the EC and the WTO: A Legal Analysis* (Groningen: Europa Law Publishing, 2002).

Wood, P., *The Law and Practice of International Finance Series*, Volume 5: *Project Finance, Securitisations, Subordinated Debt* (London: Sweet & Maxwell, 2007).

Wouters, J., 'European Company Law: Quo Vadis?', (2000) 37 *Common Market Law Review* 257.

'Freedom of Establishment, Freedom to Provide Services and Aspects of Conflict of Laws Concerning Financial Services', in D. Heremans et al. (eds.), *Current Developments in European Integration* (Leuven University Press, 2004) 15–91.

Wouters, J., D. Coppens and B. De Meester, 'The European Union's External Relations after the Lisbon Treaty', in S. Griller and J. Ziller (eds.), *The Lisbon Treaty. EU Constitutionalism without a Constitutional Treaty* (Vienna: Springer, 2008), 143–203.

WTO, *A Handbook on the WTO Dispute Settlement System* (Cambridge University Press, 2004).

'Opening Markets in Financial Services and the Role of the GATS', WTO Special Studies, 1997.

The Results of the Uruguay Round of Multilateral Trade Negotiations. The Legal Texts (Cambridge University Press, 1999).

WTO, OECD and UNCTAD, 'Report on G20 Trade and Investment Measures', 14 September 2009, available at www.wto.org/english/news_e/news09_e/trdev_dg_report_14sep09_e.doc.

Wu, E., 'Basel II: A Revised Framework', (2005) 24 *Annual Review of Banking and Financial Law* 150.

Wymeersch, E., 'The Future of Financial Regulation and Supervision in Europe', (2005) 42 *Common Market Law Review* 987.

Wyplosz, C., 'International Financial Instability', in I. Kaul, I. Grunberg and M. A. Stern (eds.), *Global Public Goods. International Cooperation in the 21st Century* (Oxford University Press, 1999) 152–89.

Yanovich, A. and T. Voon, 'What is the Measure at Issue?', in A. Mitchell (ed.), *Challenges and Prospects for the WTO* (London: Cameron May, 2005) 115–63.

Yasseen, M. K., 'L'interprétation des traités d'après la Convention de Vienne sur le droit des traités', (1976) 149 *Receuil des Cours*.

Zampetti, A., 'Market Access through Mutual Recognition: The Promise and Limits of GATS Article VII', in P. Sauvé and R. Stern (eds.), *GATS 2000. New Directions in Services Trade Liberalization* (Washington, DC: Brookings Institution Press, 2000) 283–306.

Zaring, D., 'International Law by Other Means: The Twilight Existence of International Financial Regulatory Organizations', (1998) 33 *Texas International Law Journal* 281.

Zdouc, W., 'WTO Dispute Settlement Practice Relating to the General Agreement on Trade in Services', in F. Ortino and E.-U. Petersmann (eds.), *The WTO Dispute Settlement System 1995–2003* (Antwerp: Kluwer, 2004) 381–420.

Zleptnig, S., 'The GATS and Internet-Based Services: Between Market Access and Domestic Regulation', (2007) 20 *Cambridge Review of International Affairs* 133.

INDEX